# Practical Object-Oriented Development in C++ and Java™

## CAY S. HORSTMANN

WILEY COMPUTER PUBLISHING

John Wiley & Sons, Inc.
New York • Chichester • Weinheim • Brisbane • Singapore • Toronto

Executive Publisher: Katherine Schowalter
Editor: Marjorie Spencer
Managing Editor: Erin Singletary
Electronic Products, Associate Editor: Mike Green
Text Design & Composition: North Market Street Graphics

Designations used by companies to distinguish their products are often claimed as trademarks. In all instances where John Wiley & Sons, Inc., is aware of a claim, the product names appear in initial capital or ALL CAPITAL LETTERS. Readers, however, should contact the appropriate companies for more complete information regarding trademarks and registration.

This text is printed on acid-free paper.

This publication is designed to provide accurate and authoritative information in regard to the subject matter covered. It is sold with the understanding that the publisher is not engaged in rendering legal, accounting, or other professional service. If legal advice or other expert assistance is required, the services of a competent professional person should be sought.

*Library of Congress Cataloging-in-Publication Data:*
Horstmann, Cay S., 1959–
    Practical object-oriented development in C++ and Java / Cay S.
Horstmann.
        p.    cm.
    Includes index.
    ISBN 0-471-14767-2 (pbk. : alk. paper)
    1. Object-oriented programming (Computer science)   2. C++
(Computer program language)   3. Java (Computer program language)
I. Title.
QA76.64.H675      1997
005.13—dc21                                              97-1736
                                                             CIP

Printed in the United States of America
10 9 8 7 6 5 4 3

# C O N T E N T S

# P R E F A C E

This book is a revision of a successful college book, combined with information from articles that I wrote over a period of several years for *C++ Report*, and numerous presentations that I gave at conferences such as Software Development, the Borland Developers Conference, and a number of C++ and Java conferences organized by Sigs Publications.

Of course, your local bookseller stocks hundreds of C++ and Java books. Why publish yet another one? Frankly, the majority of books try to teach you *syntax*. I try to give you *insights* instead.

I assume that you know how to program and have some experience with the basic syntax that is common to C, C++ and Java, such as { } to delimit blocks, for loops and function definitions. I also assume that you prefer a guided tour that shows the highlights and pitfalls, not an encyclopedic listing of all features.

Here are seven specific reasons for using this book.

1. C++ has become so large and complex that a complete description of its features is not useful except for compiler specialists. I explain which features of the language and its libraries are actually useful in real-life programming situations, and which ones you can safely ignore in most circumstances.

2. There is a big difference between explaining the syntax of a language feature and actually showing how to put the feature to work. This book contains many tips on how to use the C++ and Java language features effectively, and how to stay away from the pitfalls. Some tips may be controversial—I purposefully made them as memorable and simple as possible (but no simpler). Even if you find yourself in disagreement, such a tip can make you rethink your code and whether or not the tip could improve it.

3. Today, many programmers need to know both C++ and Java. C++ and Java are similar in many ways, but they also have differences. These differences can trip up programmers who move back and forth between the languages so I give you early warnings of these problems. Also, by looking at both the C++ and Java implementations of a concept in object-oriented programming, you get a better understanding of the underlying concept.

4. Both C++ and Java are excellent languages overall, but both have features that were written in a hurry or adopted with good but misguided intentions. Nevertheless, most books describe all language features as being equally perfect. I find it much more tolerable to use a mediocre or lousy feature if I know that it is flawed. In this book, I point out the good, the bad and the ugly, so that you can appreciate the good, avoid the ugly and learn to live with the bad.

5. Object-oriented design techniques, such as class diagrams and CRC cards, are really useful for the practitioner. Unfortunately, most OO design books cultivate a priesthood mentality of turgidly written methodologies that are too complex to be actually useful. In this book, I present a "mini-methodology" that uses CRC cards and "UML Lite", a small but useful subset of the "Unified Method Language" notation. (That notation is a combination of the notations of Booch, Rumbaugh and Jacobson and is far too complex to be used by mere mortals in its entirety.)

6. This book contains up to date information, discussing the newest versions of C++, Java and MFC. For example, I use the ANSI string and vector classes throughout, and I think you will be delighted to see how their systematic use frees you from much pointer drudgery. The book's web site will update the information whenever the ANSI C++ committee, the Java designers or Microsoft change their minds on any features that are discussed in the book.

7. Of course, every book has its share of educational toy programs, and this book is no exception. But in addition, you will find genuinely useful code namely:

   ■ a smart reference counted pointer class that is easy to use and actually works
   ■ a set of classes that make the C++ Standard Template Library (STL) safe to use
   ■ classes for formatted output in C++ (where they replace the Byzantine format state manipulators) and Java (where formatted output is not supported at all)

■ a nifty utility that automatically extracts header files from source files, cutting in half the number of files you need to maintain

I hope you enjoy reading this book, and that you gain some useful insights from it.

Suggestions for improvement and bug reports are much appreciated— please check my web page `http://www.horstmann.com/Practicaloo.html` for a current bug list and a submission form.

# A C K N O W L E D G M E N T S

I would like to thank Jiaoyang Zhou for her careful reading of the book draft and for reimplementing much of the code—she found a large number of errors and inconsistencies, and her dedicated work truly made this a better book.

Tina Hu helped with the conversion of the college book chapters.

I am grateful to Diane Cerra, for believing in this project and offering me a contract, and to Marjorie Spencer for her constant encouragement and gentle pressure to see the book to completion

Thanks to Erin Singletary and her production team at John Wiley & Sons for making the book look terrific!

As always, my love and gratitude go to my wife Hui-Chen and my children Tommy and Nina for helping me struggle through yet another book project.

Finally, thanks to my students at San Jose State University for suffering through impossible project assignments at the bleeding edge of C++ and Java, and to my *C++ Report* readers and conference audiences who gave me so much interesting feedback that helped shape my thinking on many challenging and fascinating issues.

C  H  A  P  T  E  R

# 1

# Objects and Classes

In this chapter, you will learn about the main topics of this book—objects and classes. You will see how to find the main relationships among classes, using basic rules for discovering classes, operations of classes, and relationships between classes. Finally, this chapter contrasts object-oriented design with traditional design methods.

## *What Are Objects and Classes?*

### What Are Objects?

The central notion of object-oriented programming is, not surprisingly, the *object*. From the object-oriented point of view, a program is populated by objects, which communicate with each other to solve a programming task cooperatively. By delegating specific and narrow responsibilities to each object, the programmer can break down the programming problem into chunks and thus manage its complexity more easily.

Because of their generality, objects are necessarily hard to define. Consider the example of an electronic mail system. You may think of a number of distinct entities, such as mailboxes, messages, passwords, and menus. What makes them objects?

Objects are commonly characterized by the following three properties:

■ State
■ Operations
■ Identity

Let us examine these characteristic properties.

An object can store information that is the result of prior operations. That information may determine how the object carries out operations in the future. The collection of all information held by an object is the object's state. An object's state may change over time, but not spontaneously. State change must be the consequence of operations performed on the object.

Consider the mail system example. A mailbox may be in an empty state (as immediately after its creation) or full (as after receiving a large number of mail messages). This state affects the behavior of the mailbox object: A full mailbox may reject new mail messages, whereas an empty mailbox may give a special response ("no messages waiting") when asked to list all new messages.

Objects permit certain operations and do not support others. For example, a mailbox can add a mail message to its collection or list its stored messages, but it cannot carry out other tasks; for example, it cannot do either of these tasks—"translate this mail message into Lithuanian" or "solve this system of linear equations".

Object-oriented programs contain statements, in which objects are asked to carry out certain operations. Because not all operations are suitable for all objects, there must be a mechanism for rejecting improper requests. Object-oriented programming systems differ in this regard. Some systems attempt to weed out unsupported operations at compile time; others generate run-time errors. In either case, the collection of admissible operations is an important attribute of an object.

The momentary state and the collection of admissible operations, however, do not fully characterize an object. It is possible for two or more objects to support the same operations and to have the same state, yet to be different from each other. Each object has its own identity. For example, two different mailboxes may, by chance, have the same contents, yet the execution environment can tell them apart, and as the result of further operations their states may again differ.

Some researchers define objects as entities that have state, behavior, and identity. This definition is somewhat unsatisfactory—what, after all, is an "entity"? The definition is also quite broad. As one computer scientist has pointed out, it then follows that his cat is an object: It has a rich internal state (hungry, purring, sleeping); it reacts to certain operations (eat, catch a mouse) while not supporting others (solve this system of linear equations); and it has an identity that differentiates it from its twin brother.

Of course, in computer programming we consider objects that have an existence in the computation system and that are, by necessity, models of real or abstract entities. While we would not consider the physical cat as an object, a software product (perhaps the software controlling a vacuum-cleaning robot) may well contain objects that simulate certain relevant aspects of real cats. Let us not attempt to give a rigorous definition of an object and instead rely on intuition and experience in recognizing them.

Of course, the narrower question, "What is an object in programming language X?", can be answered with precision. We will see in Chapter 3 what objects are in the context of C++ and in Chapter 9 what objects are in the context of Java.

## What Are Classes?

A *class* describes a collection of related objects. Although there are exceptions, most object-oriented programming systems support the grouping of similar objects into classes. Objects of the same class support the same collection of operations and have a common set of possible states. A class description must therefore list the following:

- The operations that are allowed on the objects of the class
- The possible states for objects of the class

Consider, for example, a class `Mailbox` that describes those aspects common to all mailboxes. All mailboxes support the same operations (add a mail message, list all stored messages, delete a message, and so forth).

The state of an individual mailbox is not arbitrary but fulfills certain constraints. For example, the mailbox may keep the messages sorted by their arrival time. The set of all legal states is a property of the `Mailbox` class.

Objects that conform to a class description are called *instances* of that class. For example, my mailbox in the company mail system is an instance of the Mailbox class. The message that my boss sent me yesterday is an instance of class Message.

Each object is constrained by the properties of its class. It supports only those operations that the class lists as admissible, and its legal states must stay within the range that the class permits.

## Inheritance

An important aspect of object-oriented design is to exploit similarities between classes. It often happens that one class is a specialized version of another class, with most operations identical or similar, but with a few differences.

For example, consider a system administrator in an electronic mail system. Administrators receive messages and manage their message collections in their mailboxes in the same way that all other users do. In addition, administrators have special privileges, namely, they are able to create new accounts and delete old ones. The set of all administrators is a subset of the set of all users.

Some voice mail systems support special broadcast messages that are sent by a privileged user, such as the company president, to all users. In most regards, these messages are identical to regular messages. They can be stored in mailboxes and played. However, they cannot be deleted until they are listened to at least once. (The voice mail system at my workplace actually has such a feature—as you can imagine, it is not a big hit with the employees.) The set of all privileged messages is a subset of the set of all messages.

Object-oriented programming languages support a direct modeling of this subset relationship, called *inheritance*. A class, called the subclass or derived class, inherits from a class, the so-called superclass (or parent or base class) if its objects form a subset of the base class objects. The objects in the subclass must support all operations that are supported by the superclass, but they may carry out these operations in a special way. They may also support additional operations.

For example, in C++ or Java, we can derive a class `Administrator` from `User` or `PrivilegedMessage` from `Message`.

A subclass object must be legally usable in all situations in which a superclass object is expected. For example, a privileged message object can be played, just like any other message. But a greeting in a voice mail system, even though it is in many respects similar to a message, is not usable in the same contexts as messages are. Users cannot forward their greeting to another user. We conclude that `PrivilegedMessage` may inherit from `Message` but that `Greeting` may not.

## From Problem to Code

This book discusses the design and implementation of computer programs from the object-oriented point of view. We focus on small and medium-sized problems. Although much of what we say remains valid for very large projects, there are added complexities that we will not address.

Programming tasks originate from the desire to solve a particular problem. The task at hand may be simple, such as writing a program that generates and formats a report, or complicated, such as writing a word processor. The end product is a working program. Toward this end, it is traditional to break up the development process into three phases:

- Analysis
- Design
- Implementation

This section briefly discusses the goals and methods of these phases. Of course, it is simplistic to assume that development is a simple linear progression through these three phases, as is suggested by the traditional *waterfall model*. Successful software products evolve over time. Implementation experiences may suggest an improved design. New requirements are added, forcing another iteration through analysis and design. Experience suggests that object-oriented design leads to software that withstands the evolution phase better than software developed with traditional procedural design because the objects that underlie a problem domain tend to be more fundamental and stable than the procedural requirements.

## The Analysis Phase

In the analysis phase, a usually vague problem understanding is transformed into a precise description of the tasks to be solved. The result of the analysis phase is a detailed textual description that has the following characteristics:

- Completely defines the tasks to be solved
- Is free from internal contradictions
- Is readable both by experts in the problem domain and by software developers
- Is reviewable by diverse interested parties
- Can be tested against reality

Consider, for example, the task of writing a word processing program. The analysis phase must define terms, such as fonts, footnotes, multiple columns, and document sections, and the interaction of those features, such as how footnotes in multiple-column text ought to look on the screen and the printed page. The user interface must be documented, explaining, for example, how the user is to enter and move a footnote or specify the font for footnote numbers. You can think of an analysis document as a combination of a user manual and a reference manual, both very precisely worded to remove as much ambiguity as possible.

The analysis phase concerns itself with the description of what needs to be done, not how it should be done. The selection of specific algorithms,

## The Object-Oriented Design Process

Clearly, a structured approach to find classes and their features will be help-ful. This book follows the method developed by Grady Booch, which identi-fies the following goals within the design phase:

- Identify the classes.
- Identify the functionality of these classes.
- Identify the relationships among these classes.

These are goals, not steps. It is usually not possible to find all classes first, then give a complete description of their functionality, then elaborate on their relationships. The discovery process is iterative—the identification of one aspect of a class may force changes in or lead to the discovery of others.

Recall that a class is simply a data type. It is implemented as a struc-ture (or record) type in a programming language. Operations correspond to functions and procedures that operate on these types.

The end result of the design process is a list of class descriptions and an overview of the class relationships. For each class we explain its purpose, list its operations, and describe how it is composed of other classes. These class descriptions can be recorded on paper, in a text file, or in a special database tool. The class relationships are customarily expressed in a graph-ical notation. See Chapter 5 for examples of class descriptions and class relationship diagrams.

The information gathered in this phase becomes the foundation for the implementation of the system in an actual programming language. Typ-ically, the design phase is more time-consuming than the the actual pro-gramming, or—to put a positive spin on it—a good design greatly reduces the time required for implementation and testing.

## Finding Classes

A simple rule of thumb for identifying classes is to look for nouns in the problem analysis. Here are some candidates:

Mailbox

Message

User

Passcode

Extension

Administrator

MailSystem

Menu

Many, but not necessarily all of them, are good choices for classes. Other classes will become necessary, even though they are not explicit in the problem description. For example, consider the storage of messages in a mailbox.

Messages are inserted and retrieved in a FIFO (first in, first out) fashion. A `MessageQueue` class can store the messages and support the FIFO retrieval. (However, the exact implementation of the queue, as a linked list or a circular array, is of no interest in the design phase.)

## Finding Operations

Just as classes correspond to nouns in the problem description, operations correspond to verbs. Messages are recorded, played, and deleted; users connect to a mailbox; the administrator adds a mailbox.

A central role of object-oriented design is to group each operation with one class. Each operation must have *exactly one class* that is *responsible* for carrying it out.

For some classes finding operations is quite easy because we are familiar with the territory. For example, any textbook on data structures will tell us the operations of the `MessageQueue` class:

- Initialize to an empty queue
- Add a message to the tail of the queue
- Remove a message from the head of the queue
- Return the message from the head without removing it
- Test whether the queue is empty

With other classes, finding the right operations is more difficult. Consider, for example, the `Message` class. We found one operation: Play it.

Playing a message (listing the message text on the screen) is an obvious operation. But what other operations should be defined? Here is a bad idea: Add it to a mailbox. (no!)

What is wrong with this operation? Let us think through how a message could perform it. To add itself to a mailbox, the message would have to know to what mailbox it should be added. That is not a problem; operations can have arguments, and the add operation may receive a mailbox object as an argument. The message could indeed add itself to a mailbox if it knew the internal structure of the mailbox. If the mailbox contained an array of messages and an integer index denoting the last received message, the add operation could copy the message text into the array and update the index. If the mailbox contained a linked list of messages, a different manipulation would be required. Therefore, this approach is not recommended. We will always assume that an object has no insight into the internal structure of another object. All activities on objects other than itself must be achieved by performing an operation, not by direct manipulation of internal data.

In our situation, the responsibility of adding a message to a mailbox lies with the mailbox, not with the message—the mailbox has sufficient understanding of its structure to perform the operation. When discovering operations, programmers commonly make wrong guesses and assign the responsibility to an inappropriate class. For that reason, it is helpful to have more than one person involved in the design phase. If one person assigns an operation to a particular class, another can ask the hard question, "How can an object of this class possibly carry out this operation?" The question is hard because we are not yet supposed to get to the nitty-gritty of implementation details. But it is appropriate to consider a "reasonable" implementation, or, better, two different possibilities, and make it plausible that the operation can be carried out.

Following this process makes us realize that "add a message to a mailbox" is an operation of the `Mailbox` class.

## Finding Class Relationships

Three relationships are common among classes:

- Association or use
- Aggregation or containment
- Inheritance or specialization

A class *uses* another class if it manipulates objects of the other class in any way. For example, the class `User` in a voice mail system uses the `Message` class because `User` objects create `Message` objects.

It is almost easier to understand when a class *doesn't* use another. If a class can carry out all of its tasks without being aware that the other class even exists, then it doesn't use that class. For example, the `Message` class does not need to use the `Mailbox` class at all. Messages need not be aware that they are stored inside mailboxes. However, the `Mailbox` class uses the `Message` class. `Mailbox` operations receive and return messages, and mailboxes store messages. This shows that association is an asymmetric relationship.

One important design goal is to minimize the number of using relationships; that is, to minimize the *coupling* between classes. If one class is unaware of the existence of another, it is also unconcerned about any changes in that other class. A low degree of coupling not only reduces the possibility of errors in the implementation but, more importantly, eases future modifications.

The *aggregation* relationship is very concrete. If objects of one class contain objects of another, then the first class aggregates the second. For example, Mailbox objects contain `Message` objects, and we therefore say that the `Mailbox` class has an aggregation relationship with the `Message` class.

Actually, the aggregating class need not hold actual copies of objects of the second class. It could hold pointers or some other mechanisms, such as keys, indexes, or handles, that lead to the objects.

Aggregation is often informally described as the "has-a" relationship. A `Mailbox` "has-a" `Message`. Actually, a mailbox has several messages. With aggregation relationships, it is useful to keep track of these *cardinalities*. There may be a 1:1 or 1:*n* relationship. For example, each mailbox has exactly one greeting (1:1), but each mailbox may contain many messages (1:*n*).

Aggregation is a special case of association. Of course, if a class contains objects of another class, then it is acutely aware of the existence of that class.

When classes are implemented as structures in a programming language, containment maps easily into the layout of the structured type: The structure A contains one or more fields of type B (or pointer to B).

Inheritance, or specialization, is a less familiar relationship because traditional programming languages do not permit a direct way of expressing it. A derived class D inherits from a base class B if all objects of class D are special cases of objects of class B. In particular, all B operations must be valid for D objects, although the implementation of these operations may differ. We say these operations are inherited from B. However, the D objects support additional operations or enhance the inherited operations in some way. We will learn later how the "correct" operations for a specific object are selected.

Inheritance is often called the "is-a" relationship. This intuitive notion makes it easy to distinguish inheritance from aggregation. For example, a system administrator *is* a user (inheritance) and *has* a password (aggregation).

As we will see, exploiting inheritance relationships can lead to very powerful and extensible designs. However, we must point out that inheritance is much less common than the association and containment relationships. Many designs can best be modeled by employing inheritance in a few selected places only.

# Contrast with Traditional Design Techniques

## Procedural Decomposition

One of the first problem-solving skills that a software programmer acquires is the identification, combination, and decomposition of tasks. Tasks are modeled as procedures or functions in a programming language. There are two fundamental ways of finding solutions to complex tasks. You can first write procedures to solve simple tasks and compose them into more sophisticated procedures until the desired functionality is implemented. This is the bottom-up approach. Or you can decompose the task to be performed into subtasks and recursively decompose those subtasks, until the subtasks are simple enough to be implemented directly. This is the top-down approach. Of course, we usually use a mixture of the top-down and bottom-up strategies to solve a programming problem.

A rule of thumb for discovering procedures is to look for verbs or actions in the problem description. In this regard, procedures are quite similar to the operations we discussed previously. However, operations have an important difference: Each operation is associated with a class, which is responsible for carrying out the operation. The operation is invoked by an object of that class.

For small problems, the decomposition into procedures works very well, but for larger problems, classes and operations have two advantages. The classes provide a convenient clustering mechanism. A simple word processor may require 2,000 functions for its implementation, or it may require 100 classes with an average of 20 operations per class. The latter structure is much easier for a programmer to grasp. Classes also hide their data representations from all code except their own operations. If a program bug messes up a data item, it is easier to search for the culprit among the 20 operations that had access to that data item than among 2,000 procedures.

In this sense, classes are more powerful than procedures. You can always transform a procedural program into an object-oriented program: Make a single class called `Application` whose state is all global data, and make each procedure into an operation of `Application`. Naturally, this is rarely a good idea. It just shows that object-oriented programs are at least as powerful as procedural programs.

In summary, procedural decomposition has two drawbacks. Procedures are small, and a great many of them are needed to solve a nontrivial task. Furthermore, procedures do not regulate the access to data fields. In contrast, classes are larger entities, and their data is protected from modification by other procedures.

## Module Decomposition

An important organizing device for programs is the decomposition into separate units. Traditionally, programming tasks are broken up into *modules*, which communicate with each other through procedure calls only, not by sharing data. There are two advantages. Users of the module need not understand how the module achieves its tasks, and users cannot accidentally damage the data local to the module.

The traditional definition of a module has, however, one great limitation. Consider a typical module implementing a queue. There is a private circular array, with an index into the head and the tail. Functions such as `add`, `remove`, `isfull`, or `isempty` are exported and can be called by other modules. Look in [Horowitz], p. 71, for a typical example.

The limitation is this: There is only one queue. A program that requires two queues cannot simply link in the module twice. (You may think that few programs ever need more than one queue, but consider the mail message program. Each mailbox has a separate message queue. In fact, each mailbox has two queues: one for the unread messages and one for the saved messages.)

Classes do not have this limitation. Once a class has been defined, any number of objects can be constructed. Classes can be thought of as factories for objects, each of which acts like a module. In this sense, classes are more powerful than modules. You can always translate a traditional module into a class, translate its functions into operations of that class, construct a single object, and export it to the client code.

## Opaque Types

An *opaque type* is a data type whose nature is hidden from the user, together with a collection of functions. Opaque types are usually represented as handles or pointers to structures with unknown layout. A creation function returns a new handle, and other functions take that handle as an argument. Of course, the implementation of these functions is hidden inside a module.

The typical example is the file interface in C. To open a file, the programmer calls `fopen` and receives a "magic cookie" value that must be passed to subsequent calls to `fscanf`, `fgetc`, or `fread`. The value is of type `FILE*` (pointer to a structure of type `FILE`), but most mortals have no idea what is inside the `FILE` structure.

An opaque type is very similar to a class. Any number of instances can be provided simultaneously. The functions that know what to do with an argument of the opaque type correspond to operations of a class. If you always organize your program into a collection of modules, each of which is responsible for managing one opaque type, you have practiced object-oriented programming, perhaps without knowing it. Well, almost. One feature of object-oriented programming is quite difficult to imitate in a traditional programming language, namely, inheritance.

## *Design Hints*

### Classes Model Sets of Objects

The keyword here is *set*. You should not use a class to describe a single object. This sounds simple, but even experienced designers sometimes have trouble with it.

Here is an example from [Wiener and Pinson], p. 176, slightly modified for a more natural string set. A finite-state machine reads an input string to test whether it satisfies a certain property. As characters are read, the machine state changes according to the transition rules of the machine. A transition rule has the form: "If the current state is *s*, and the current input character is *c*, move to state *t*." Some states are marked as accepting states. If the machine ends up in an accepting state when all input characters are read, the input string is accepted. Figure 1.1 shows a finite-state machine to test whether a string is a legal C floating-point number. For example, +.5E-3 is accepted, but -3E+.5 is not. State 1 is the start state. Final states are marked in bold.

Pinson and Wiener discover a class State and an operation transition, which reads the next input character and returns the next state. They then derive eight classes, State1 . . . State8, from State. Each implements its own transition operation. For example, the transition operation of State1 returns an object of class State4 when it reads a character 0 . . . 9.

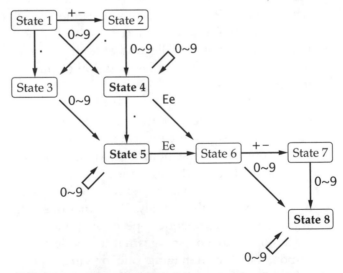

**FIGURE 1.1**   A finite-state machine accepting floating-point numbers.

There is no question that `State` is a legitimate class to describe the set of states in finite-state machines. The class `State1`, however, is problematic. What objects does it describe?

Only one: the first state of the particular finite-state machine depicted in Figure 1.1. It is generally not useful to write a class to describe a behavior of a single object. Classes should collect objects with similar behavior.

Of course, it is easy to come up with a better design for finite-state machines. Let us assume that an object of class `State` carries with it a table of the correspondence between input characters and successor states. The transition operation simply performs a lookup in this table. One additional operation is required: to set the entries in the table.

Now we have designed a much more useful abstraction. This `State` class can be used for *any* finite-state machine, not just a particular one.

## Classes Need Meaningful Operations

Classes should be large enough to describe a significant set of objects, but they should not be too large, either. It is tempting to design classes of glorious generality, but that is not usually helpful.

Consider the mailbox example. How does a message get into a mailbox? The boring answer is that class `Mailbox` has an operation `append`, which takes an object of type `Message` as an argument. Here is a much more exciting alternative. Suppose that `Mailbox` is derived from a class `Component`, that components are connected to one another with objects from a class `Connection`, that connections can carry objects of type `Data`, and that the class `Message` is inherited from class `Data`.

This architecture was seriously proposed by a senior designer on a voice mail project. And, after all, why not? Perhaps the system would need to carry fax and computer data in addition to voice. And how about color graphics and full-motion video? Integration with other equipment, such as photocopy machines and mail-sorting equipment, is also covered by the design.

The problem with the design became apparent when it turned out to be very difficult to be specific about the operations of the discovered classes. It was not at all clear what operations made sense for `Component` or `Data`.

If the task at hand is very broad, to develop a general system for transporting arbitrary information to devices ranging from supercomputers to toaster ovens, the design may well be appropriate. If the problem to be solved is simply the linkage of existing telephones with a message delivery system, then the generality is completely inappropriate and of little help in developing the software.

# 2

# A Crash Course
# in Basic C++

This chapter contains a very rapid introduction of basic C++ language features. You should be familiar with a procedural language such as C, Pascal/Delphi, or Basic. We will not discuss all language constructs of C++. Instead, we cover only those features that are indispensable for writing programs. The emphasis is on simplicity, clarity, and safety, not speed. In particular, you will see how programming is greatly simplified by using the ANSI standard vector template and string class. This allows us to bypass inconvenient and error-prone built-in arrays and strings.

Look into the standard C and C++ reference books ([Kernighan and Ritchie], [Stroustrup]) for greater detail. The delightful book [Koenig] is particularly recommended for help with the pitfalls of C programming, and much of it applies to C++ as well.

This chapter covers the following topics:

- Header files
- Comments
- Output
- Types and variables

- Operators
- Arrays and vectors
- Strings
- Blocks
- Control flow
- Functions
- Input
- Assertions

Because C++ is essentially a superset of C, most of this material will be familiar to a C programmer. The sections on function arguments, arrays, strings, and stream I/O contain new information.

## Header Files

Virtually every C++ program file needs to include one or more header files to inform the compiler about predefined constants, data types, and procedures. The #include preprocessor directive is used for this purpose.

```
#include <vector>
#include <sys/socket.h>
#include "setup.h"
```

These directives cause the compiler to read in the vector standard library facilities, the system header file sys/socket.h and the local header file setup.h. System header files are delimited by < . . . > and located in the "standard places" for such header files. If the header name does not end in an extension (such as #include <vector>), then the compiler is free to store the information in a more efficient form than a traditional header file. This is a very recent change to the C++ language, and it is not yet implemented in all compilers.

**PITFALL**

The command

```
#include <string>
```

includes the header that defines ANSI C++ strings. This is completely different from the ANSI C string header. To include the ANSI C header, you use

```
#include <cstring>
```

or, for compatibility with older programs,

```
#include <string.h>.
```

■

**WEB**

Because not all compilers support all ANSI features, the code that accompanies this book contains a file setup.h that includes the most common libraries—namely, strings, vectors, and streams—using the appropriate commands for a number of popular compilers. If you #include "setup.h" and add the \Practical00 directory to the search path for header files, you automatically have access to these common features. ■

Local files are delimited by " . . . ", and the compiler first looks into the current directory before searching the standard places. Once a header file has been included, the features that it advertises can be used in a program.

**TIP**

It is useful to know what your compiler considers the "standard places." For example, Microsoft Visual C++ sets an environment variable INCLUDE to point to the appropriate directories, such as \MSDEV\INCLUDE. You can also add your own directories in the Tools|Options dialog box (see Figure 2.1). ■

**TIP**

Once in a while it is useful or necessary to look inside header files. Try it out: locate and read the standard header file math.h. ■

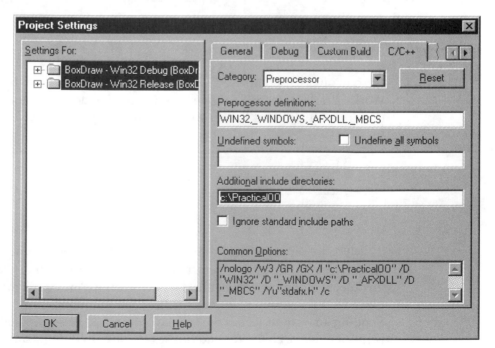

**FIGURE 2.1** Dialog to add header file directories.

## Comments

There are two styles of comments. Any text from `//` to the end of the current line

```
// like this
```

is ignored. This comment style is useful only if you are sure that the comment will never grow beyond one line. It is painful to modify `//`-style comments that extend over multiple lines. Use `/*...*/` for multiline comments

```
/* like
   this
*/
```

Unfortunately, the `/*...*/` comments do not nest. If you need to comment out a large block of code that itself contains comments, surround it with the `#if...#endif` preprocessor directives.

```
#if 0
code to be masked out
#endif
```

## Output

Here is our first complete C++ program, which prints the message "Hello, World" on the screen. The code is contained inside a function `main`, the customary starting point in many programming environments.

```
#include <iostream>
int main()
{  cout << "Hello, World" << endl;
   // return 0 to indicate normal completion
   return 0;
}
```

The `iostream` header file must be included in all source code using stream input and output operations. This header file defines, among others, an object cout representing the standard output. Any data sent to cout is displayed on the terminal or sent to a file if standard output is redirected. Sending an output stream the special object `endl` (also defined in `iostream`) prints a newline character and flushes the stream buffer, causing the display of the buffered characters on the output device.

The << operator is used to send data to a stream. Integers, floating-point numbers, characters, and strings can be printed.

```
cout << "The value of pi is approx. ";
cout << 3.14159;
cout << endl;
```

Output operations to the same stream can be chained:

```
cout << "The value of pi is approx. " << 3.14159 << endl;
```

Data can be sent to a file instead of standard output:

```
include <fstream>
ofstream os("output.dat");
os << "The value of pi is approx. " << 3.14159 << endl;
```

## Types and Variables

C++ has the following numeric types:

```
int
short int (or short)
long int (or long)
unsigned int (or unsigned)
unsigned long int (or unsigned long)
unsigned short int (or unsigned)
char
signed char
unsigned char
float
double
long double
```

The sizes of these types depends on the platform. Integers are typically 32-bit values, but on a PC under MS-DOS they are only 16-bit values.

There is also a Boolean type `bool` with exactly two values, `false` and `true`. This is a recent change to C++.

New types can be constructed as enumerated types:

```
enum Color { BLACK, BLUE, GREEN, CYAN, RED,
   PURPLE, YELLOW, WHITE };
```

The `typedef` construct introduces a type synonym, a new name for an existing type. For example, the standard header file `stddef.h` defines `size_t` to be a type suitable to describe the size of memory blocks, typically

```
typedef unsigned int size_t;
```

More importantly, we will see in Chapter 3 how to define class types.

Variables are declared by listing the type, then the variable name and an optional initializer. Constants are prefixed by `const`.

```
unsigned int n = 1;
char ch = 'A';
string s = "Hello";
Color c = PURPLE;
size_t s = 1000;
Employee joe;
bool done = false;
const double pi = 3.14159265358979323846;
```

Character constants are enclosed in single quotes. The constant `'\n'` denotes the newline character, which separates lines in a text file. String constants are enclosed in double quotes.

There is no true character type. `char` is simply a subrange of `int`, and characters are represented by their codes in some encoding scheme, usually ASCII. International users will find that eight-bit extended character codes greater than 127 are no end of trouble because some implementations treat `char` as a signed quantity, others as an unsigned quantity. This makes a difference when `char` values are promoted to `int`.

# Operators

## Arithmetic Operators

The usual arithmetic operators +, -, *, / are used in C. The / operator denotes integer division if both arguments are integers and floating-point division otherwise. Integer remainder is denoted by %. For example, `11 / 4` is 2, `11 % 4` is 3, and `11.0 / 4` is 2.75. There is no operator for raising a quantity to a power; use the `pow` function in `math.h`.

The increment and decrement operators ++ and -- add or subtract 1 to a variable. For example, the code

```
int n = 5;
n++;
```

changes n to 6. Because these operators change the value of a variable, they cannot be applied to constants. For example, `4++` is not legal. There are actually two forms of these operators, a prefix and a postfix form. Both have the same side effect of changing a variable by 1. Their difference becomes apparent only if they are used inside expressions. The prefix form evaluates to the new value after the increment or decrement operator, whereas the postfix form evaluates to the old value of the variable.

```
int m = 5;
int n = 5;
int a = 2 * ++m; // now a is 12, m is 6
int b = 2 * n++; // now b is 10, n is 6
```

We recommend against using ++ inside other expressions. Of course, it is the ++ operator that gives the C++ language its name. (Perhaps ++C would have been a more appropriate choice—after all, we want to use the language after it has been improved.)

## Relational and Boolean Operators

Values can be compared with == (equality; note that this is not the same as =), != (inequality), and the usual <, >, <=, and >= operators.

Conditions can be combined with the operators and, or, and not. Many people use the more traditional forms &&, ||, and ! for these operators. For example,

```
1 <= x and x <= 10
```

tests if x is between 1 and 10, as does

```
1 <= x && x <= 10
```

**WEB**

The and, or, and not operators are not yet supported by many compilers. Include the header file setup.h from the companion website in your program to define them if your compiler doesn't. ■

The and/&& and or/|| operators are evaluated in "short-circuit" fashion: Once the truth value of an expression has been established, further subexpressions are left unevaluated. For example,

```
if (x != 0 and f(1 / x) > 0) // ...
```

does not evaluate 1 / x if x is zero.

There are bitwise operators & ("and"), | ("or"), ^ ("xor"), ~ ("not") that work on the bit patterns of their arguments. The >> and << operators shift a bit pattern to the right or left. These operators are intended for bit fiddling. They are occasionally useful for setting and clearing single-bit flags. The >> and << are also used for stream input and output.

## Assignment

Assignment is denoted by a single =. Assignment has a value—namely, the value that has been assigned. That means that assignment expressions can be nested inside other expressions. A typical example is

```
while ((y = f(x)) > 0)
{  // do something with y
   x++;
}
```

This is advantageous because it avoids coding the function call twice:

```
y = f(x);
while (y > 0)
{  // do something with y
   x++;
   y = f(x);
}
```

Assignment associates right to left. In the expression

```
z = y = f(x);
```

the assignment y = f(x) is executed first, and its value (namely the new value of y) is assigned to z. In other words, both y and z are set to f(x).

Binary arithmetic operators can be combined with assignment. For example,

```
x += 4;
```

is equivalent to

```
x = x + 4;
```

## *Arrays and Vectors*

C++ uses the same array construct as the C language, and it is not particularly powerful or convenient. Fortunately, there is an alternative. The ANSI C++ standard includes a much more convenient alternative, the vector template. Writing the code to implement templates is not easy; we will cover the details in Chapter 14. Using templates, however, is straightforward and requires no knowledge of the implementation details.

The declaration

```
vector<X> a(n);
```

specifies a "smart" array of any type X, with space for n elements. You access the ith element as

```
a[i]
```

The index i ranges from 0 to n − 1. This is usually inconvenient, but it keeps compatibility with C arrays. If you access a[i] where i is less than 0 or ≥ n, then the behavior of the program is undefined. In most implementations of the standard library, you will corrupt other data in your program in some way.

**WEB**

If you use the safe STL library on the companion website, then index access is *safe*. When you access an invalid index, a run-time error is generated. That is a great convenience during debugging. ■

For example,

```
vector<double> a;
```

defines an array of 10 floating-point numbers, a[0] ... a[9].

If you do not specify a size,

```
vector<X> a;
```

then the vector is initially empty and must be grown to make space for elements. There are two ways to grow a vector: adding elements and resizing the vector.

You can add elements at the end:

```
a.push_back(1.3);
a.push_back(2.15);
```

The dot notation a.push_back(1.3) is very common in C++, as we will see shortly. It is the syntax for applying an operation (push_back) to an object (the vector a).

Instead of growing the vector one element at a time, you can resize it. For example, the following command grows a to hold 10 elements.

```
a.resize(10);
```

The size of a vector can be determined with the size operation.

```
for (int i = 0; i < a.size(); i++)
   // do something with a[i]
```

You can shrink a vector in two ways. You can call `resize` with a smaller size. And the operation

```
a.pop_back();
```

reduces the size of the vector by 1.

**PITFALL**

The `pop_back` operation doesn't quite work like the pop operation of a stack data structure. It removes the last element of the vector, but it does not return it. If you want to know the last element before removing it, you must first fetch it.

```
double last = a[a.size() - 1];
a.pop_back();
```

■

Vectors of the same type can be copied with the = operator.

```
vector<double> b;
b = a;
```

Any existing elements in b are discarded, and all elements of a are copied into the corresponding slots in b. Afterwards, b is the same size as a.

Very occasionally, we will use the arrays that are built into C. A built-in array a of n elements of type X is defined as

```
X a[n];
```

Here n is a compile-time constant. As with vectors, the index range is from 0 to n − 1. These arrays are of limited utility because they cannot be resized, and you must program a loop each time you want to make a copy. However, they are more efficient than vector templates, and they are easier to initialize. For example,

```
int days_per_month[12] =
   { 31, 28, 31, 30, 31, 30, 31, 31, 30, 31, 30, 31 };
```

# Strings

Traditionally, the support for strings in C and C++ was weak, but this has all changed with ANSI C++. Now C++ programmers have access to a safe, convenient, and standardized string class.

Strings can be initialized with quoted strings or left uninitialized, in which case they are constructed as empty strings.

```
string s = "Hello";
string t;
```

Strings can be copied with the = operator. The + operator concatenates strings.

```
string u = s + ", World";
```

The relational operators == != < <= > >= represent lexicographic comparison.

```
if (s <= t) // ...
```

The [] operator provides access to individual characters in a string. The starting character of a string has index 0. (Again, this is inconvenient, but it keeps compatibility with C strings.) The length operation returns the length of the string. The substr operation extracts a substring with given starting index and length.

```
String s = "Hello, World";
int n = s.length(); // n is 12.
char ch = s[0]; // the starting character 'H'
   // s[11] is 'd', and s[13] is illegal.
t = s.substr(0, 4); // substring s[0]...s[3], "Hell"
```

Sometimes string objects must be passed to library functions that require C-style character arrays. This happens commonly with file names. Apply the c_str operation to a string object whenever a C string is expected.

```
String filename = basename + ".dat";
ifstream is(filename.c_str());
```

# Blocks

In C++, statement blocks are delimited by {...}.

When a numeric or pointer variable is declared local to a block without an initializer, its value is random. Explicit initialization on declaration is therefore highly recommended. Fortunately, you can declare variables anywhere within a block, and you can usually defer their declaration until the initializer value is computed. Consider this example.

```
double x1 = x0 - xc;
double y1 = y0 - yc;
// some computations
x1 = x1*x1 / a;
y1 = y1*y1 / b;
// now we are ready to compute r
double r = x1 + y1;
```

## Control Flow

The conditional statement has the form

```
if (condition) block_1 else block_2
```

The else part is optional. An `else` groups with the closest `if`. That is,

```
if (C_1) B_1 else if (C_2) B_2 else B_3
```

is the same as

```
if (C_1) B_1 else { if (C_2) B_2 else B_3 }
```

There are two similar forms of repeating loops:

```
while (condition)
   block
```

and

```
do
   block
while (condition);
```

These execute a block while a condition remains true. The `do/while` loop executes the block at least once. The `while` loop may never execute if the condition is false at the outset.

C++ has a very general construct to support iteration. Typical examples are as follows:

```
for (int i = 1; i <= 10; i++) a[i] = 0;
for (i = 0; i < 10; i += 2) a[i] = 2 * i;
```

Note that it is possible to define a variable in the first slot of the for statement!

**PITFALL**

The rules for the scope of a variable defined in the header of a for loop have recently changed. The ANSI standard specifies that the variable is defined only inside the for loop.

```
int main()
{   for (int i = 1; i <= 10; i++)
    { // i defined here
        a[i] = 0;
    }
    // ANSI: i no longer defined here
    . . .
}
```

Previously, the variable had been defined until the end of the *enclosing* block.

```
int main()
{   for (int i = 1; i <= 10; i++)
    { // i defined here
        a[i] = 0;
    }
    . . .
    // before ANSI: i defined until here
}
```

This causes no end of grief if you write a function with two loops using the same variable.
The code

```
for (int i = 1; i <= 10; i++) a[i] = 0;
for (int i = 1; i <= 10; i++) b[i] = 0;
```

is legal in ANSI C++ and illegal in earlier versions of C++. The code

```
for (int i = 1; i <= 10; i++) a[i] = 0;
for (i = 1; i <= 10; i++) b[i] = 0;
```

is illegal in ANSI C++ and legal in earlier versions of C++. Remedy: Don't define a variable inside the header of the for loop. The code

```
int i;
for (i = 1; i <= 10; i++) a[i] = 0;
for (i = 1; i <= 10; i++) b[i] = 0;
```

compiles in all versions of C++.                                              ■

It is an unwritten rule of good taste that the three slots of a for statement should only initialize, test, and update a variable. You can write very
obscure loops by disregarding this rule. For example,

```
for (p = head; p != 0; p = p->next) // ...
```

is acceptable, but

```
for (i = a[0] = 0; i < 8; a[i] = 2 * i) i += 2; // DON'T
```

is not.

The multiple selection statement offered by C++ is somewhat cumbersome. Execution starts at the case label matching the value of the
expression in the switch and continues until the next break or return or
the end of the switch. Here is an example that shows a number of typical
situations:

```
switch (s[i])
{   case '0':
    case '1':
    case '2':
    case '3':
    case '4':
    case '5':
    case '6':
    case '7':
    case '8':
    case '9':
        v = 10 * v + s[i] - '0';
        i++;
        break;
    case '-':
        sign = -1;
        // FALL THROUGH
    case '+':
        i++; break;
    case '0': case ": case ' ':
        return sign * v; default:
        verr = TRUE; break;
}
```

The default clause is optional. A range of constants can be specified only by listing all elements of the range explicitly. If the `break` or `return` at the end of a case is omitted, execution "falls through" past any `case` labels to the next statement group. This is a very common cause of programming errors. In the extremely rare situation in which this behavior is desired, it ought to be commented clearly.

# *Functions*

## Function Definitions

A function definition lists the type of the returned value, the name of the function, and the types and names of its arguments, followed by the implementation code. Here is a typical example, a function that computes the binomial coefficient, which is

$$\binom{n}{k} = \frac{n!}{k!(n-k)!}$$

```
long int binom(int n, int k)
{   if (2 * k > n) k = n - k;
    if (k < 0) return 0;
    long r = 1;
    for (int i = 1; i <=k; i++)
    {   r = r * n / i;
        n-;
    }
    return r;
}
```

When a function is called, local variables for all function arguments are allocated on the run-time stack and initialized with the values of the call expressions. In the example, local variables n and k are initialized with the call values and modified during execution of the function. This modification has no effect on the values supplied in the function call.

Function arguments can be of any type. In particular, class and array template arguments are permitted. These are copied field by field from the caller into the local argument variables. (Naturally, for large class objects and arrays, that copy can be inefficient. We will later learn how to minimize the associated cost.) For example, here is a function that computes the average of an array of floating-point numbers:

```
double average(vector<double> a)
{   double sum = 0;
    int n = a.size();
    if (n == 0) return 0;
    for (int i = 0; i < n; i++)
        sum += a[i];
    return sum / n;
}
```

Functions with no arguments are declared and called with an empty argument list.

```
int rand() { /*...*/ }
. . .
x = rand();
```

This is different from C. In C, functions with no arguments have an argument list (void). Most C++ compilers tolerate this style, but your fellow programmers will hold you in low esteem if you use it.

C++ does not distinguish between functions and procedures. Procedures are simply functions with the special return type void.

```
void print(vector<double> a)
{   for (int i = 0; i < a.size; i++)
    cout << a[i] << endl;
}
```

## Reference Arguments

Consider the task of writing a function swap that is to swap two integers. The following code does not work:

```
void swap(int x, int y) // NO
{   int temp = x;
    x = y;
    y = temp;
}

int a = 1;
int b = 2;
swap(a, b);
// a is still 1, b is still 2
```

When the swap function is called, its argument variables x and y are initialized with the values 1 and 2, and their contents are interchanged.

When the `swap` function terminates, the local variables x and y are abandoned. At no time are a and b affected.

A mechanism is required that communicates to the `swap` function the location, not merely the value, of the arguments. This is usually referred to as "call by reference." In C++, an argument is passed by reference by declaring it as a reference type:

```
void swap(int& x, int& y)
{   int temp = x;
    x = y;
    y = temp;
}


int a = 1;
int b = 2;
swap(a, b);
// now a is 2, b is 1
```

Pascal programmers can consider reference arguments the equivalent of var parameters. C programmers should think of references as pointers with "syntactic sugar". Recall the swap procedure in C:

```
void cswap(int* x, int* y)
{   int temp = *x;
    *x = *y;
    *y = temp;
}


int a = 1;
int b = 2;
cswap(&a, &b);
// now a is 2, b is 1
```

When using references, the compiler automatically supplies all those * and &.

A function that changes an argument of array template or string type must use call by reference as well. Examples are as follows:

```
void sort(vector<double>& a);
void reverse(string& s);
```

Call by reference is the most common and straightforward application of reference types in C++, but a number of other important uses exist, which will be discussed later. By the way, `int&` is usually pronounced as "int ref."

## Return Values

C++ functions can return a result of any type except built-in arrays. In particular, class objects and array templates can be returned as function values. Examples are as follows:

```
Employee find(vector<Employee> staff, string name);
vector<Employee> find_all(vector<Employee> staff, string regex);
```

The return statement causes an immediate exit from the function.

```
long int binom(int n, int k)
{  if (2 * k > n) k = n - k;
   if (k < 0) return 0; // exits immediately
   long r = 1;
   for (int i = 1; i <= k; i++)
   {  r = r * n / i;
      n-;
   }
   return r;
}
```

The expression following the `return` keyword is the function result.

Return values are copied from the scope of the function to a temporary location in the scope of the caller. For large objects and vectors, this copy can be somewhat expensive. We will discuss possible remedies later.

## Function Declarations

Before a function can be called, the C++ compiler must know its argument and return types. This is necessary because the compiler may need to generate code to convert between types. Moreover, it allows the compiler to generate error messages if the argument types of the function do not match the arguments used in the call.

For many short programs this requirement can be easily fulfilled by placing the code of any function before its first usage. In particular, main comes last if you follow this simple rule. However, this arrangement breaks down for mutually recursive calls and for calls to functions defined in another source file.

For that reason, you can declare a function by supplying only its *prototype*. A function declaration or prototype is the first line of the function definition, listing the return type, name, argument types, and a semicolon. Argument names are optional but recommended for clarity. The function code is omitted.

Examples are as follows:

```
int find(String s, char ch);
void sort(vector<double> );
```

The declaration of a function is merely an advertisement of its existence somewhere—in the same module, another module, or a library. The actual code is supplied in the function definition. A function can be declared multiple times in a program but must have one and only one definition.

## Name Overloading

In C++, the same name can be used for different functions as long as the function argument types are different. For example, find can name both a function to find a character in a string and a function to find an employee in an array. This phenomenon is called *function overloading*.

```
int find(string s, char ch);
Employee find(vector<Employee> staff, String name);
```

Of course, the code for each function is completely unrelated. In any specific call to find,

```
r = find(a, x);
```

the compiler checks the types of the arguments and selects the correct function. In the example, if a is of type string and x of type char, the first function is called. If no matching function exists, an error is reported. The function return type is not used for matching.

If no exact match for an overloaded function can be found, some type conversions are attempted. This might result in a match or an ambiguous situation, which is reported as an error. The exact rules are somewhat arcane (see [Ellis and Stroustrup], Chapter 13). It is best to stay away from situations that depend on the intricacies of these rules. If the compiler has a hard time figuring out which function to call, programmers will have an even harder time understanding and maintaining the code.

## The main Function

In traditional command-line environments, C++ program execution begins in the function called main. This function must process the command-line arguments, call other functions as necessary, and eventually terminate the program. The prototype for main is

```
int main(int argc, char* argv[]);
```

This means that main receives two arguments: an integer argc, reporting the number of command-line arguments, and an array of character pointers argv, one for each command-line argument. It is customary that command-line arguments starting with a dash (-) are options.

**TIP**

Command-line parameters are one of the few places where you still need to use C strings in C++. But there is an easy way to turn them into C++ strings.

```
string(argv[i])
```

is the ith command line argument as a C++ string.                                    ■

If you have no interest in processing command-line arguments, you can declare main as

```
int main();
```

The main function returns a value that may be processed by the calling environment, usually the operating system shell. It is traditional to return 0 for success and a nonzero value to report an error condition.

Nontraditional operating environments may use a different function to start a program. For example, Windows programs start with WinMain and receive arguments that make sense only in a Windows program, such as handles to the current and previous instance of the program task.

## Input

The iostream header defines an istream class and an object cin to read from standard input (either the keyboard or a redirected file). The >> operator is used for reading data.

```
double x;
string s;
cin >> s >> x;
```

In reading any object with the >> operator, any leading white space is skipped. To read a single character without skipping the preceding white space (that is, to read the white space itself, if present), use the `get` operation:

```
char ch = cin.get();
```

To read an entire line, use

```
string line;
getline(cin, line);
```

You can peek at the next character of an input stream without actually reading it. This is useful for making decisions on the upcoming input. For example:

```
double x;
string s;
char ch = cin.peek();
if (isdigit(ch) or ch == '+' or ch == '-')
   cin >> x;
else
   cin >> s;
```

Input operations can fail for two reasons. If the characters in the input do not match the data type, the stream state is set to "fail" and all subsequent operations fail. This happens most frequently in trying to read a number in when the stream does not contain a sequence of digits. You can detect and reset the stream state, but it is easiest not to get into this situation in the first place. You can read all input as strings and convert the string contents into numbers at your leisure. Or you can peek at the next character before you read.

More importantly, input fails at the end of the file. It is best to test that the stream is still in a good state after each input operation.

```
cin >> s;
if (cin.fail()) return FALSE;
```

If the stream has reached the end of file, or an operation has failed, all subsequent input operations will fail as well. When an input operation fails, it never changes the value of the item to be read.

Note that `fail()` is never a predictor of future success; it is just an indicator of past failure. You must first try to read and then check whether the input succeeded.

Here is a loop that reads in numbers from standard input and computes their average. The loop may terminate either at the end of file or at an input string that is not a number.

```
double t = 0;
int n = 0;
while (not cin.fail())
{  double x;
   cin >> x;
   if (not cin.fail()) { t += x; n++; }
}
if (n > 0) cout << "average: " << t / n << endl;
```

Instead of reading from standard input, you can read from any file.

```
include <fstream>
ifstream is ("input.dat");
is >> s >> x;
if (is.fail()) return FALSE;
```

C programmers may wonder why we are not using the `scanf`/`printf` functions for input and output. The stream library has two advantages over the `stdio` routines with which C programmers are familiar: It is type-safe, and it is extensible. There can be no mismatch between formatting instructions and data values, and the formatted input/output capabilities can be extended for any user-defined types. We will discuss this library in detail in Chapter 12. In this chapter we covered just the basics that suffice for simple programming tasks.

## Assertions

The `assert` macro, defined in `assert.h`, tests a condition and generates a run-time error reporting the condition, the file, and the line number if it fails. Assertions are used to check against conditions that "cannot" happen and cause program failure if, due to a programming error, they do occur.

```
#include <assert.h> // or #include <cassert>
// ...
y = f(x);
assert(y >= 0);
z = sqrt(y);
```

In this case we know that the function f is never supposed to compute negative numbers. If the unthinkable happens and f does return a negative number, the program is terminated. Then it either displays an on-screen message

```
File woozle.cpp Line 197 Assertion failed: y >= 0
```

or it shows a dialog box (see Figure 2.2).

Assertions are very useful during debugging, but less so in a shipping program. Most customers do not enjoy it if their application terminates with an "assertion failed" message without first saving their work. We will see in Chapter 16 how to use exceptions for more robust error handling.

To turn assertions off once debugging is complete, you need to define the NDEBUG preprocessor variable and recompile. On a command-line compiler, this is typically done by using the compiler's -D switch and invoking the compiler as:

```
cc -DNDEBUG sourcefile
```

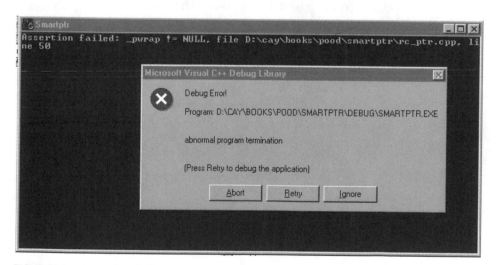

**FIGURE 2.2** Assertion failure.

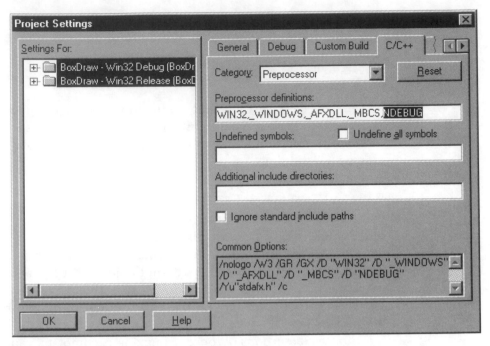

**FIGURE 2.3**   Defining a preprocessor variable.

Integrated development environments have some other way to specify definitions in a special dialog (see Figure 2.3).

You can also simply place the line

```
#define NDEBUG
```

into the source code or a common header file.

# 3

# Implementing Classes

This chapter presents the mechanics of implementing classes and operations in C++. We cover the mechanics of the public and private interface, accessor and mutator operations, and construction. This is a language chapter. If you prefer to learn about the why before the how, read the section "Classes in C++" and then Chapters 5 and 4 first before returning here. Chapters 3–5 are written in such a way that their order can be reversed.

## *Classes in C++*

Three steps are necessary to implement a class in C++:

- Declare operations in the public section of the class definition.
- Define data fields in the private section of the class definition.
- Define the implementation of the operations following the class definition.

It sounds simple, and it actually is. (Well, actually C++ lets you make more complicated arrangements, but this one is by far the most useful.)

## Declaring Operations

Here is a partial definition of a C++ class implementing a mailbox:

```
class Mailbox
{
public:
   void add(Message);
   Message get_current();
   void delete_current();
   // ...
};
```

The operations are declared public because they can be applied to mailbox objects anywhere in a program.

In C++, objects are simply variables whose type is their class. An object of class Mailbox can be defined like this:

```
Mailbox mbox;
```

This code gets the current message from a mailbox and plays it:

```
Message msg;
msg = mbox.get_current();
msg.play();
```

Operations can have arguments; for example:

```
mbox.add(msg);
```

As you can see, an operation is applied to an object using the dot (.) notation:

```
object.operation(arguments);
```

We will soon see how to specify the implementation of the operations.

## Declaring Fields to Represent Object State

In C++, the state of an object is described by the values of one or more data fields. For example, here is an (incomplete) description of objects representing calendar dates:

```
class Date
{
```

```
public:
   // ...
private:
   int _day;
   int _month;
   int _year;
};
```

The data fields are declared `private` to ensure that they can be accessed only by the operations of the `Date` class. They are hidden from all other program code. We will see the significance of the underscore (_) prefix later in this chapter.

The state of a `Date` object is characterized by three values: the settings for the day, month, and year. Actually, the set of legal states is only a subset of the set described by the class definition. There are additional restrictions on the data fields. For example, it is expected that $\_day \le 31$. In this case, the C++ class definition gives an incomplete description of the set of legal states. We will see later how class invariants can be utilized to sharpen the definition.

The `Date` class, as described here, is similar to a C structure (or Pascal record):

```
struct date
{  int day;
   int month;
   int year;
};
```

But C structures provide no privacy. The data fields of the structure can be inspected and modified freely anywhere:

```
struct date birthday = { 31, 3, 1961 };
// ...
birthday.day = birthday.day + 1;
```

The corresponding code in C will not compile.

```
Date birthday;
birthday._day = birthday._day + 1; // ERROR
```

Only operations of a class can inspect and modify its private data.

## Defining Operations

A worthwhile operation on a date is to advance it by a certain number of days. For example, after the call

```
b.advance(30);
```

the date stored in b is 30 days after the original date. To implement this operation, two steps are required. First, the operation must be declared in the definition of the Date class:

```
class Date
{
public:
    void advance(int nday);
    // ...
};
```

Next, the function itself must be defined. Of course, date arithmetic is somewhat tedious because the number of days in a month varies. Rather than fussing with months that are 28, 29, 30, or 31 days long, we will use Julian day numbers for date arithmetic. The Julian day number is the number of days from Jan. 1, 4713 B.C. For example, the calendar date May 23, 1968, beginning at noon Greenwich time, corresponds to the Julian day 2,440,000. Standard functions can compute the Julian day number from a calendar date and a calendar date from the Julian day number.

**WEB**

On the website, you will find the implementations of two conversion functions between Julian day numbers and calendar dates:

```
long dat2jul(int, int, int)
void jul2dat(long, int&, int&, int&)
```

The functions are taken from [Press].                                          ■

Here is the implementation of the advance operation:

```
void Date::advance(int nday)
{   // convert to Julian day
    long j = dat2jul(_day, _month, _year);
    // add n days
    j += nday;
    // convert back from Julian day
    jul2dat(j, _day, _month, _year);
}
```

Note the scope resolution Date:: in the definition of the function. Other classes may also have an advance operation. Because operations in C++ are defined outside the class definition, it is necessary to specify both the class and the operation name.

The details of the computation are not important now. Just observe that the operation reads and modifies the _day, _month, and _year values. But which _day, _month, and _year values? There may be many Date objects, and each of them has _day, _month, and _year values. The operation modifies the values belonging to that object that invoked the operation. For example, if the call is

```
b.advance(30);
```

then the data fields b._day, _b._month, b._year are modified, and after the call the object b has a different state.

But isn't access to these fields restricted? Indeed, it is—to operations of the class. Because advance (or, more precisely, Date::advance) is an operation of the Date class, it does have the privilege to access and modify the data fields.

In C++, an operation of a class is very similar to a regular function. However, an operation is always applied to an object, the so-called implicit argument of the operation. In addition, the operation may have no, one, or more explicit arguments, which are listed inside parentheses in the usual way. For example, the call

```
b.advance(30);
```

has two arguments: the implicit argument b and the explicit argument 30.

C++ programmers often refer to operations of a class as *member functions* because they are declared inside classes just as data fields (which they call data members) are.

If two names for the same concept are good, surely three are even better. Programmers using the Smalltalk language ([Goldberg and Robson]) call operations methods, and they refer to member function calls as messages ("send the advance(30) message to the object b"). In Java, the term "method" is also commonly used, but Java programmers don't usually talk about sending messages.

Table 3.1 presents a dictionary for the savvy object traveler.

**TABLE 3.1** The Vernacular of C++, Smalltalk, and Other Object-Oriented Languages

| *C++* | *Smalltalk* | *Other common terms* |
|---|---|---|
| Member function | Method | Operation |
| Call a member function | Send a message | Apply an operation |
| Data member | Instance variable | Field, attribute |

# *The Implementation of Operations*

## Constant Operations

In C++ it is important to make a distinction between mutator operations, which change an object, and accessor operations, which merely read its data fields. The latter need to be declared as `const` operations.

Consider the declarations of two operations `advance` and `print` in the `Date` class.

```
class Date
{
public:
   void advance(int);
   void print() const;
   // ...
};
```

The keyword `const` at the very end of the declaration indicates that the `print` operation leaves the calling object unchanged.

The absence of `const` in the advance operation indicates that it may modify its implicit argument.

The `const` keyword is replicated in the definition of the operation:

```
void Date::print() const
{ //...
}
```

If `advance` and `print` were regular functions, they would have best been declared as

```
void Date_advance(Date&, int);
void Date_print(const Date&);
```

The implicit argument of an operation is, unlike all other function arguments, always passed by reference. The `const` attribute is necessary to specify whether an operation takes advantage of the chance to modify its implicit argument.

If code in a `const` operation modifies a data field of the implicit argument, the compiler reports an error. This is an excellent feature. For example, date arithmetic (date ± integer) could be implemented in a non-destructive manner by returning the result as a value:

```
Date Date::add_days(int n) const;
Date b = a.add_days(30);
   // b is a + 30 days, a not changed
```

Suppose you are implementing this operation. If you misunderstand the intended semantics and change the implicit argument, the compiler will catch the mistake.

The `const` attribute is important because it lets the compiler check the preservation of a design property.

Conversely, what happens if you omit the `const` in a nondestructive operation like `print`? At first, nothing. The compiler will not check that the `const` is missing, even though you never modified any data field. However, as we will explain shortly, omitting the `const` attribute makes your code unusable to those programmers who use and believe in `const`.

Suppose `Date::print` is not declared as `const`. A programmer implementing an `Employee` class will then find that the following code does not compile.

```
void Employee::print() const
{   cout << _name << " " << _id << endl;
    _hiredate.print();
    // ERROR-attempt to modify a const object
}
```

The compiler does not understand your `Date::print` and assumes that it will modify its implicit argument because it is not declared `const`. That leaves the programmer using your `Date` class three options:

- Drop the `const` from `Employee::print()`.
- Play tricks with casts to "cast away constness."
- Find another `Date` class.

None of this will bring you glory or admiration.

Like [Coplien], p. 38, we recommend a canonical form for class declarations in which the mutator operations (non-const) are listed before the accessor functions (const). The rationale is that you want to know first what you can do to an object, then how you can find out what you did.

## Field Accessors and Mutators

Consider a `Date` class with fields for the day, month, and year. As always, we implement the fields as private data.

Given a date, a programmer may well need to access the month entry. But the private data field is not accessible except through class operations. It therefore makes sense to supply an operation to compute the month:

```
class Date
{
```

```
public:
    int month() const;
    // ...
private:
    int _day;
    int _month;
    int _year;
};


int Date::month() const
{   return _month;
}
```

The operation is trivial—it simply reports the value of the month field. The month operation is declared constant because the call d.month() does not change the object d.

Many classes have operations that simply report on the value of a private field. Such functions are called field accessors. For the class implementor it is more trouble to write both a private field and a public accessor function than simply a public data field. But programmers using the class are not greatly inconvenienced—they simply write d.month() instead of d._month. Now the value has become "read-only" to the outside world. Only operations of the class can modify it. In particular, should the value ever be wrong, only the class operations need to be debugged.

Now we can explain why we named the month field _month. C++ requires that the name of the field be distinct from the name of the operation month(). Because this situation commonly arises, many programmers use a standard convention to cope with it mechanically. Prefixes or suffixes for all data fields (_month, xmonth, m_month, month_) are a popular device. An alternative is to call all field accessors get...(), such as get_month() (see [Plum and Saks], pp. 22–23). That convention requires iron discipline. For example, you may design a Date class with a weekday() operation that computes the day of the week (Monday, Tuesday, . . .) of a date. Later you decide to add a weekday data field to cache the weekday and improve the performance of the operation. Oops, you should have called the function get_weekday(). But once a class is out in the field, it is too late to rename public features.

Are you prepared to prefix all const operations with get_? Some class libraries do just that. We prefer to give the operation the most convenient and succinct name and disfigure the private field data instead. Naturally, all this is a matter of taste. Find a scheme you like and stick to it.

Now suppose a programmer needs to change the month of a given date, say increment it by 1. Of course, d.advance(30) will do the trick. Well, not quite—if d is January 1 or July 31, it won't work correctly. We can provide an operation `set_month` to set the private field. Its implementation is trivial in the day/month/year representation:

```
void Date::set_month(int m)
{   if (1 <= m && m <= 12)
        _month = m;
}
```

The `set_month` operation is not declared as `const` because it modifies its implicit argument. A function like `set_month`, whose purpose is to modify a field, is called a field mutator.

Of course, most private data fields of most classes are of a technical nature and of no interest to anyone but the implementor of the operations. But small classes especially, such as our `Date` example, contain fields in which class users have a legitimate interest.

In this case, class implementors find it quite tedious to implement three items:

■ A private data field `_property`
■ A public const accessor `property()`
■ A public modifier `set_property(...)`

In C you would only need a single public data field. The tedium is undeniable, but there are considerable benefits.

The internal implementation can be changed without affecting any code other than the operations of the class. Of course, the accessor and mutator functions may need to do real work—translating between the old and the new representations rather than simply reading and writing a single field. In a large program, the code for the operations of a single class is relatively short and well localized, making such a change feasible, whereas updating the usage pattern of a public data field is usually extremely difficult.

The mutator functions can perform error checking; assignment to a field does not. For example, `b.set_month(13)` can be trapped by error-checking code in the mutator, but `b._month = 13` would have to be unearthed by a program trace. Read-only data values can be implemented by not supplying a mutator at all.

Actually, the `Date` class is a good example of a class that should not have mutators for each field. Consider the code

```
d.set_day(31);
d.set_month(3);
d.set_year(1961);
```

If d was previously February 1, then the set_day operation sets it to the invalid date February 31. In this case, of course, the situation is remedied in the set_month operation, but having three separate mutators makes error checking much more difficult than it should be. It is better to supply a single set_date function instead.

```
d.set_date(31, 3, 1961);
```

## Inline Functions

Those readers who count processor cycles will have been horrified by the suggestion of replacing a simple data access with a function call. Calling a function is much more expensive than accessing data. A return address must be pushed and popped, and the branching to the function code slows down the prefetch queue in the instruction-decoding mechanism of the processor.

Fortunately, C++ has a convenient answer to these concerns: inline functions. Consider this simple function that squares an integer.

```
int square(int x) { return x * x; }
```

Calling square(a) is certainly less efficient than evaluating a * a, but calling

```
square(x[i] - y[i])
```

may be better than evaluating

```
(x[i] - y[i]) * (x[i] - y[i])
```

depending on the compiler's ability to recognize common subexpressions. The function call certainly is easier to read.

C++ allows the programmer to declare the function as inline.

```
inline int square(int x) { return x * x; }
```

This instructs the compiler to translate

```
square(expression)
```

into

```
expression * expression
```

provided the expression is simple and has no side effects. Otherwise, the expression is stored in a temporary location `temp`, and `temp * temp` is evaluated.

**NOTE**

C programmers often use the preprocessor to implement inline functions

```
#define square(x) (x)*(x)
```

This is error-prone—consider

```
square(x[i++])
```

These preprocessor macros should be completely avoided in C++. ■

The inline feature is particularly useful for very simple class operations:

```
inline int Date::month() const { return _month; }
```

A call `d.month()` is compiled as a direct field access `d._month`, not as a function call. The compiler can generate an access to the private field, even though the programmer cannot!

Inline functions give the protection and legibility of regular functions yet avoid the performance overhead of function calls. Of course, inline functions should be used only for very short functions. Program code size increases dramatically if longer functions are inline-replaced.

The inline attribute is only a recommendation to the compiler. Compilers will refuse to treat overly complex code as inline.

An alternate method of defining inline functions includes their code inside the class definition.

```
class Date
{
public:
    int day() const { return _day; }
    // ...
private:
    int _day;
    // ...
};
```

This method saves keystrokes but is not recommended for several reasons: It clutters up the public interface with the implementation of some operations. It reveals implementation details to the reader of the public interface. It is more difficult to revoke the inline attribute for debugging or profiling purposes.

It is seductively easy to add a one-line accessor function to a data field right into the class definition—even one that perhaps should not be accessible to the public. However, this is not a good idea. Writing an operation represents a commitment for the lifetime of the class. Making the commitment is the big step; typing the complete function definition outside the class is not. We will define inline functions inside the class definition, except for trivial constructors and destructors.

## Private Operations

When implementing a class, we made all data fields private and all operations public. Public data is not useful, and thus all data fields should be private. On the other hand, although most operations are public, private functions can be useful. These functions can be called only from other operations of the same class.

To implement operations, you may wish to break up the code or to factor common code into separate functions. These functions are typically not useful to the public. They may be very close to the implementation or require a special protocol or calling order. Such functions are best implemented as private operations.

Consider, for example, a Date class that, as a part of its date arithmetic implementation, requires a function to test whether a year is a leap year.

```
class Date
{
public:
   // ...
private:
   bool is_leap_year() const;
   int _day;
   // ...
};
```

By making the function private, we are under no obligation to keep it available if we change to another implementation, such as the Julian day representation discussed in Chapter 4. The function may well be harder to implement, or unnecessary if the data representation changes. As long as the operation is private, we can be assured that it was never used outside the other class operations, and we can simply drop it. Had the function been public, we would be forced to reimplement it on change of representation because other code might have relied on it.

**TIP**

Choose private operations for those functions that are of no concern to the class user and for those functions that could not easily be supported if the class implementation changes. ■

## Class-Based Access Privileges

In C++, class operations have the privilege of accessing private data and functions of *any object of their class*, not just the implicit argument. In other object-oriented languages, such as Smalltalk, access is more restricted. Operations can access the private features of only the object on which they operate. See [Budd], p. 225, for a comparison.

Consider, for example, an operation that compares two dates for sorting purposes. The call d1.compare(d2) returns a negative number if d1 comes before d2, zero if they are the same, and a positive number otherwise.

```
int Date::compare(Date b) const
{   int d = _year - b._year;
    if (d != 0) return d;
    d = _month - b._month;
    if (d != 0) return d;
    return _day - b._day;
}
```

The function is declared const because the object invoking compare is not changed by the computation.

The compare function is permitted to access both the fields of its implicit argument (_year) and the fields of its explicit argument (b._year).

Some programmers consider this perfectly natural; others find it surprising. [Ellis and Stroustrup], p. 257, discusses the design rationale.

## *Object Construction*

### Constructors

Because all data fields of an object are private, special functions are required to initialize the data whenever an object is allocated. For example, the following code will not compile:

```
Date d;
d._day = 31; d._month = 3; d._year = 1961; // ERROR
```

In Chapter 2 we discussed a `set_date` operation that can be used to set the `Date` fields:

```
Date d;
d.set_date(31, 3, 1961);
```

This is a good way of doing it, but in C++ you can do better by placing the `set_date` functionality inside a *constructor*. A constructor is a special operation that is automatically invoked whenever an object is created.

Constructors have the same name as the class name. A `Date` constructor can be declared like this:

```
class Date
{
public:
   Date(int d, int m, int y);
   // ...
};
```

In the definition of the constructor the name `Date` occurs twice, first to denote the class name, then as the name of the constructor:

```
Date::Date(int d, int m, int y)
:  _day(d),
   _month(m),
   _year(y)
{}
```

The constructor initializes the data fields of the object. The curious notation `_day(d)` indicates that the `_day` field is constructed using `d`. In this case, it is equivalent to an assignment `_day = d`. Similarly, the `month` and `year` fields are constructed by initializing them with the values `m` and `y`. There is nothing else to be done to initialize a `Date` object; hence, the function body of the constructor is empty. Although it looks strange at first, this is the simplest and most common case. Some constructors require additional work beyond construction of their data fields, or their data field initialization is too complex to fit in the initializer list. In that case, additional code is placed inside the constructor body.

Note that the `Date::Date` constructor, like all constructors, has no return value. Constructors are special functions whose task is not to compute a value but to initialize an object.

This constructor is invoked automatically when a date object is declared in the following fashion:

```
Date d(31, 3, 1961);
```

The notation is perhaps unfortunate. Although, in fact, d is an object of type Date, it looks as if d were a function, to be called with arguments 31, 3, and 1961. In fact, a function is called with those arguments—namely, the constructor. It initializes the object d.

There is an important difference between constructors and operations. A constructor is invoked exactly once on an object, at the time of creation. It cannot be called again to "reinitialize" the object. For example, the call

```
d.Date(17, 8, 1959); // ERROR
```

is illegal. You cannot invoke a constructor on an existing object. In fact, you cannot explicitly call a constructor. You merely cause it to be invoked by supplying its arguments in an object definition.

## Argument Overloading and Default Arguments

A great advantage of constructors is the elimination of uninitialized variables—or, more accurately, variables that are initialized with random leftover bytes. Once a constructor has been declared for a class, it is no longer possible to define objects that avoid construction. For example, after adding a constructor Date(int, int, int) to the Date class, attempting to define a Date object without supplying construction values is an error:

```
Date d; // ERROR
```

This is actually a good feature. If we don't know the values of the fields of d, are we really happy to leave them to completely random bit patterns? On the other hand, if we do know the field values, there is nothing wrong with using them in the constructor. Because in C++ variables can be defined anywhere in a function, the definition of an object can be deferred until the values required for construction are computed.

Classes can have more than one constructor. For example, a constructor Date(string) could translate a string into a date:

```
Date d("March 31, 1961");
```

A constructor with no arguments can be used to initialize an object when no construction information is supplied. If a constructor Date() with no arguments is included in the Date class, it is invoked when a variable is defined as

```
Date d;
```

Such a constructor is called a *default constructor*. Most classes have a default constructor as well as one or more constructors with arguments. In fact, if a class does not have a default constructor, then you cannot define C arrays of objects of that class, and you must supply a "filler" object every time you create or grow a vector. On the other hand, if a class has a default constructor, it is invoked on each array or vector element.

Actually, you can argue that constructing a date without values for the day, month, and year makes little sense. For numbers, zero is a good choice for a default value, but there is no good default for dates. Should the default constructor initialize a date to today's date or the beginning of time (1/1/1980 or 1/1/4713 B.C.?), or maybe to an invalid date like 1/1/0? (In the Julian/Gregorian calendar, there is no year 0—the year 1 B.C. is immediately followed by 1 A.D.) In the latter case, all date functions must be able to recognize that invalid date and act appropriately. Nevertheless, classes without a default constructor are rare. Class users dislike classes without default constructors because it is impossible to allocate arrays and cumbersome to allocate vectors of objects of such classes.

If a class has more than one constructor, the compiler must be able to choose the correct one whenever an object is allocated. The compiler checks the types of the arguments in the constructor call. For example, suppose `Date` has three constructors:

```
class Date
{
public:
   Date();
   Date(int d, int m, int y);
   Date(string);
   // ...
};
```

Then the compiler can easily decide which constructor to invoke in any object definition:

```
Date d(31, 3, 1961); // Date(int, int, int)
Date e; // Date();
Date f("March 31, 1961"); // Date(string)
Date g(31, "March", 1961);
   // ERROR-no Date(int, String, int)
vector<Date> h(10); // invokes Date() ten times
```

This facility of the C compiler is called overloading. Overloading occurs if several functions have the same name (in our case `Date`) but different argument types. The compiler has to engage in overloading resolution and pick the correct function by matching the argument types of the various functions with the types of the values supplied in the call. A compile-time error occurs if no match can be found or if more than one constructor matches. In addition to constructors, C++ permits overloading of operations, regular functions, and operators.

The number of overloaded constructors can often be minimized by another C++ device: default function arguments. Consider, for example, a constructor

```
class Date
{
public:
   Date(int d, int m, int y = 0);
   // ...
};

Date::Date(int d, int m, int y)
:_day(d),
  _month(m),
  _year(y)
{ if (_year == 0) _year = current year;
}
```

If the constructor is called with only two integer arguments, the compiler automatically supplies the default value as the third one:

```
Date d(31, 1);
```

is equivalent to

```
Date d(31, 1, 0);
```

and the latter is implemented to set the year to the current year. Note that the default arguments are provided only in the constructor declaration inside the class definition. They are not replicated in the constructor definition.

More than one default can be provided:

```
class Date
{
public:
   Date(int d = 1, int m = 1, int y = 0);
   // ...
};
```

In this example,

```
Date d(31);
```

```
Date e;
```

is equivalent to

```
Date d(31, 1, 0);
Date e (1, 1, 0);
```

Default arguments are used only for those slots that are not supplied in the call. Default arguments are always filled in from the back. It is not possible to obtain defaults in the middle of a call, such as

```
Date(31, ,1961); // ERROR
```

All C++ functions, not just constructors, may supply default arguments. They are a useful feature to reduce the number of overloaded functions.

## Anonymous Objects

One characteristic of built-in types is the fact that constants are readily available without having to store them in a variable. For example,

```
int y = x + 10;
```

can be used instead of the long-winded

```
int temp = 10;
int y = x + temp;
```

Constructors can be used in a similar fashion to generate objects that are used in a computation and then go away.

```
Date d = Date(31, 3, 1961).advance(n);
```

This is more concise and less cluttered than the equivalent

```
Date temp(31, 3, 1961);
Date d = temp.advance(n);
```

Just as we think of 10 as the integer constant ten, we can think of Date(31, 3, 1961) as the date constant March 31, 1961. We leave it to the compiler to allocate an anonymous temporary object.

Anonymous objects are particularly convenient for constructing function results:

```
Date quarter_end(int q, int y)
/* PURPOSE: returns the end of a calendar quarter
   RECEIVES: q = 1, 2, 3, 4 - the quarter
             y - the year
*/
{  if (q == 1 or q == 4)
      return Date(31, 3 * q, y);
   else
      return Date(30, 3 * q, y);
}
```

There is no need to give a name to the object that the function returns—we simply instruct the function to construct an object with certain properties and to return it as the function result.

## Construction of Subobjects

All objects of a class must be constructed, including those that are contained inside other objects. An important role of a constructor is to direct the construction of its subobjects. Here is a constructor for the `Employee` class that invokes constructors for subobjects.

```
Employee::Employee(String n, int hd, int hm, int hy)
: _name(n),
  _hiredate(hd, hm, hy)
{}
```

This constructor passes arguments on to the constructors of the various subobjects. Those fields that are not explicitly listed in the initialization list (such as `_address`) are initialized with the default constructor of their class. Their contents may be changed later in the body of the constructor or through another operation, such as `set_address`. Fields that belong to a class without a default constructor must be initialized explicitly, or the compiler will report as an error that it is unable to construct the subobject. However, fields of numeric or pointer type that are missing from the initializer list are quietly left uninitialized.

The syntax for constructing subobjects in a constructor is somewhat peculiar. The colon (`:`) syntax is valid only in constructors, not in any other operation (in class declarations the `:` signifies inheritance). The constructor invocation `fieldname( arguments)` makes fieldname look like the name of a function. The syntax is fundamentally the same as that used to construct a variable, such as

```
Date hiredate(31, 3, 1961);
```

The type name is omitted because it can be inferred from the class definition. Fields of numeric or pointer type can be initialized with the same syntax:

```
Date::Date(int d, int m, int y)
:  _day(d),
   _month(m),
   _year(y)
{}
```

In this case, no constructor calls are involved: Numeric and pointer types are not classes and have no constructors. The values are simply copied into the fields. The constructor

```
Date::Date(int d, int m, int y)
// undesirable style-no initializer list
{  _day = d
   _month = m;
   _year = y;
}
```

has the same effect. However, it is considered undesirable to defer initialization until the body of the constructor. On the contrary, constructors that simply build up their fields in the initializer list and have an empty body are considered ideal.

# Design Hints

## Always Keep Data Private

It is technically legal in C++ to place a data field in the public section of a class. In practice, you should never use public data. Always keep data private and use operations to read and change it. Chapter 4 discusses the rationale for data hiding. In a nutshell, experience has shown that the data representation used in the class implementation tends to change over time as the class evolves. When data is private, it can be changed without affecting the class users.

You may sometimes be tempted to code public data fields just to get on with the task at hand, promising to make the data private later. Don't do it. Making data private after the fact usually leads to awkward code.

Coding a set of field accessors and mutators can be a bother, but if you look at the big picture, it is a minor issue. In a nontrivial program, the vast majority of operations do real work, and even if you could somehow skip all accessors and mutators, it would not make much of a difference.

## Class Types Are the Norm; Challenge Basic Types

Ultimately, all classes are composed of numbers and strings. But only low-level classes are directly composed from these types. The majority of classes have fields that are themselves of class type.

You should challenge class fields that are merely of int or string types. Consider this example of a poorly designed class in which all data fields have basic types:

```
class Employee
{
public:
    // ...
private:
    string _lname;
    string _fname;
    char _middle_initial;
    string _street;
    string _city;
    string _state;
    long _zip;
    // ...
};
```

It is much better to group the fields that describe an address into a single object of type Address. That way, you can easily cope with changes to addresses in countries with nonnumeric postal codes for cities, addresses with additional fields for organizations and departments, or separate home and work addresses. Additionally, the software package is likely to contain other addresses, such as the addresses of customers or vendors. Code that is common to all address handling, such as formatting or sorting by postal code, can be shared rather than replicated. The same idea holds for the employee name. An improved data organization looks like this:

```
class Name
{
public:
    // ...
private:
    string _lname;
    string _fname;
    char _middle_initial;
    // ...
};

class Address
{
```

```
public:
   // ...
private:
   string _street;
   string _city;
   string _state;
   long _zip;
   // ...
};

class Employee
{
public:
   // ...
private:
   Name _name;
   Address _address;
   Date _hiredate;
   // ...
};
```

## Not All Fields Need Individual Field Accessors and Mutators

You should not supply accessors and mutators to individual fields unless they are really necessary. Low-level classes, such as Date or Point, need to reveal the settings of all fields. Higher-level classes typically do not. Consider a User class of a mail system. Each user has a mailbox, a collection of messages.

```
class User
{
public:
   void add_message(Message);
   void remove_message(int);
   void list_messages() const;
   void print_message(int) const;
   // ...
private:
   vector<Message> _mailbox;
   // ...
};
```

There is no need for the User class to reveal the _mailbox field with mailbox() and set_mailbox() operations. All mailbox access and modification takes place through the public operations.

## Declare Accessor Operations as `const`

Always use the `const` attribute with accessor operations that just read from the data fields without modifying them. If you don't, you limit the utility of your operation and, ultimately, of your class.

Suppose you supply a class `Address` but don't declare `Address::print` to be `const`. If another programmer uses your class to implement `Employee`, `Employee::print` won't compile.

```
void Employee::print() const
{  // ...
   _address.print(); // ERROR-attempt to modify a const object
}
```

This will not endear you to your customer, the author of `Employee`, who may well search for a more competent supplier.

The `const` attribute is useful for finding errors.

```
int Employee::compare(Employee b) const
{  _name.to_upper(); // ERROR-attempt to modify a const object
   b._name.to_upper();
   // ...
}
```

This `compare` operation first forces the name to uppercase, thereby modifying it. Yet the operation promises, as it should, that comparing an object with another does not change it. The compiler catches this contradiction.

## Use a Canonical Form for Class Definitions

Use a standard order for presenting the features of a class.

First list the public section, then the private section. The readers of your class (including yourself) are more interested in the public interface than the details of the private implementation.

In the public section, first list the constructors, then the mutators, then the accessors. This tells the class readers the answers to the three questions they are likely to have: How do I make an object of this class? Once I have an object, what can I do with it? Once I did it, how can I find out the result?

In the private section, list the private operations (mutators, then accessors), and then the fields.

Here is an example:

```
class Date
{
public:
   Date();
   Date(int d, int m, int y); // construct from day, month, year
   void advance(long n); // advance this date by n days
   int day() const;
   int month() const;
   int year() const;
   Weekday weekday() const;
   Date add_days(long n) const; // computes n days from this date
   long days_between(Date b) const;
   // number of days between this date and b
private:
   int _day;
   int _month;
   int _year;
};
```

As we will see later, classes can have more features than just operations and fields. In particular, classes can define local types. These should be listed before the operations.

## Supply a Default Constructor

Most classes should have a default constructor. To declare an array of class objects, the class must have a default constructor.

It is usually easy enough to supply a default constructor: Initialize all numeric and pointer fields to zero and use the default constructor on all fields of class type.

Sometimes it appears desirable to compute a better default object. For example, a Date default constructor may want to set the date to today's date. That is not necessarily a good idea. Computing today's date has some cost. If a large array of dates is allocated, does it really make sense to expend computational effort to initialize each array element with today's date?

It is best if an object created by the default constructor is a valid object. For example, an Employee object whose name and address are blank is not likely to do any harm.

This does not always work. If you initialize the _day, _month, and _year fields of a Date object with zero, the resulting object is not a valid date. Such objects should not be used until they are set to a valid state as the result of some other operation. Managing this situation is always awkward.

If no valid default object can be found, and if the cost of monitoring to ensure that no invalid object enters a computation is considered too high,

then you need not supply a default constructor. Of course, you then lose the
ability to declare arrays.

## Construct All Subobjects Before the Constructor Body

A constructor consists of two parts: the initializer list and the constructor
body. By the time the constructor body is entered, all fields that are not
explicitly constructed in the initializer list are constructed with their default
constructor.

```
Employee::Employee(string n, int hd, int hm, int hy)
{   // _name, _hiredate already constructed
    // with default constructor
    _name = n;
    _hiredate = Date(hd, hm, hy);
}
```

There is no point in first running the default constructors and then
overwriting the fields with the intended value. Use the initializer list to construct the fields the way *you* want them.

```
Employee::Employee(string n, int hd, int hm, int hy)
: _name(n),
  _hiredate(hd, hm, hy)
{}
```

# 4

# Interfaces

## *Encapsulation*

### Impact of Private Data on the Programmer

In the previous chapter we studied the mechanics of making all data fields of a class private, thereby hiding the implementation details from public scrutiny. This process is called encapsulation. We will now discuss the rationale behind it.

In C++, the programmer actually has the choice of placing data fields into the private or public section. However, it is always a bad idea to make data public. Style guides and programming rule books usually prohibit public data outright. You should program as if the private section were the only legal place for data fields.

On the face of it, this appears to be a minor inconvenience to the programmer. After all, if the value of a data field is required in a computation, you can always add an operation to the class that performs the computation. Or, if private data of an object needs to be modified, you can write an operation that effects this modification.

This is indeed true, but it nevertheless comes as a surprise to most programmers just how often they are tempted to access data fields of objects casually as they code.

Furthermore, it is not a good idea to wait until the implementation phase to determine what operations to add to a class. Adding operations as the need arises typically leads to a cluttered collection of operations that is overly large, not intuitive to use, and difficult to maintain as the class functionality evolves over time. It is particularly important to design a complete and usable set of operations before starting to code.

Of course, nobody has perfect foresight, and design flaws may well surface in the implementation phase. When you find that you cannot carry out a task because you lack access to private data, you should first realize that this indicates a failure of the class design. You then have the following choices:

- Revisit the design. (OK.)
- Add the problem task as an operation. (Maybe.)
- Add an accessor or mutator operation for a data item. (Maybe.)
- Make the data public. (Don't!)

Public data and cluttered interfaces must be avoided. You have no good choice but to stop coding your immediate task and to reexamine the overall class design. You may then discover new operations or a rearrangement of responsibilities. Before you implement the changes, you should take the time to write clear documentation for the new or changed features. If you cannot explain the altered interface in words that you would not be embarrassed to read six months later, more design work appears to be required.

## Why Private Data?

We have seen that private data is actually inconvenient for the programmer during coding, so why do programmers consider it such an essential feature? Writing code is only one of the tasks of software production, and it is not the most time-consuming one. Debugging and testing must be considered as well. Most importantly, successful software products evolve over time. New user requirements must be implemented, and obsolete features are sometimes retired. The existing code must be modifiable. Rewriting all code for every product release would be too slow and expensive. (Novice programmers initially find it hard to envision this—in college, the lifetime of a program is typically between a week and a semester; indeed, then the coding phase dominates all other aspects.)

Successful software products, by the very nature of their success, are long-lived and require a great deal of modification during their lifetime. Data hiding is one strategy that can make program modification technically feasible.

Suppose a programmer changes the implementation of a data structure in a working program to speed up an algorithm or to support added functionality. What other changes are necessary to make the program compile and run again? If no protection mechanisms are in place, the programmer might have to inspect each line of the program to see whether it is affected by the change. More likely, the programmer will update all known references to the changed data but be surprised by some unexpected interactions during debugging. In a large program this approach is simply not feasible.

Data encapsulation provides a mechanism for restricting the range of the program that is affected by a change to a small subset. Once that subset has been updated to track a change, the programmer can state with confidence that no other portion of the program needs attention in this regard.

Let us consider a very simple example of how problems can arise with unencapsulated data. Suppose we defined a data type `Date` with fields `day`, `month`, `year`. If our program performs a lot of date arithmetic (date + integer = date, date_date = integer), it would benefit from a different data representation: the Julian date, which is simply a (long) integer counting the number of days from some fixed date.

**NOTE**

There is no connection between the Julian day number and the Julian calendar enacted by Julius Caesar. The sixteenth-century historian Joseph Scaliger used a combination of recurring astronomical events and the 15-year Roman tax cycle to find a synchronization point, January 1, 4713 B.C., to use as a zero for mapping every event in written history reliably to a positive day number. Scaliger named this day number after his father Julius. ■

Clearly, date arithmetic is trivial in the Julian representation, but other operations (printing a date as month/day/year) are not. Let us suppose that the trade-off is beneficial in our case. What changes need to be made? We change `Date`; remove the `day`, `month`, and `year` fields; and add a field `long julian` instead. Of course, if we used public data, now our program will no longer compile. That is good—at least we know where we must fix the code. We must supply functions to compute the day, month, and year values from the Julian date and call them whenever the field values were used previously. For example,

```
d = b.day;
```

would be replaced with

```
d = b.day(); // now computes day from Julian date
```

But what if the fields are modified? We could replace

```
b.month = 1;
b.year++;
```

with

```
b = Date(b.day(), 1, b.year() + 1);
```

This gets complex and extremely inefficient. Instead, it is necessary to revisit the way in which the dates are used in each instance. What should be a simple change of representation turns into a major effort.

In this scenario, we were lucky that the compiler located all expressions that needed to be changed. Consider a slightly more complex situation in which we keep the day, month, and year fields and then add a julian field and a flag to indicate which of the two representations is the more current. Now the compiler will accept code containing b.day, but the code may be wrong because the day field may not be currently active. It is easy to make mistakes, obtain corrupted data, and require time-consuming debugging sessions.

# Public Interfaces and Private Implementations

## The Roles of Class User and Class Designer

The design and implementation of classes must be approached from two points of view simultaneously. Programmers design and implement classes, to be used in code by other programmers, who are often referred to as class users. Class users are different from the end users of the final software application who, of course, wish to know nothing about the application code. The customer of the class designer is another programmer, the class user. As in any relationship between service providers and customers, the service provider must consider the needs of the customer.

The class designer has certain objectives, such as efficient algorithms and convenient coding. Programmers who use the classes in their code have different priorities. They want to be able to understand and use the operations without having to comprehend the internal data representations. They want a set of operations that is large enough to solve their programming tasks yet small enough to be comprehensible.

Beginning programmers in an object-oriented language often find it difficult to separate these two aspects because in their first programming projects they are both the class designer and the class user. Getting together with a colleague for a project is very helpful. Each programmer designs the necessary classes, then you switch roles and complete the assignment with the other programmer's classes. Of course, no substantial changes to the classes should be made after the switch. This gives you a feel for the difficulty both of anticipating the needs of another programmer and of working with classes that were produced with less-than-perfect anticipation of these needs. An excellent way of continuing this exercise is to switch roles once again and to have the original class designer change the internal implementation—for example, using linked lists instead of arrays or a binary instead of a linear search. The class user code should not be affected by these changes. Of course, in a project where group work is not possible, you must play Dr. Jekyll and Mr. Hyde and envision both roles yourself.

## The Class User Perspective

The class users see the public interface of a class. Even though they may peek at the private data, they often do not. The data may not be straightforward to understand, especially in complex or highly optimized representations. At any rate, it is subject to change at any time. The public interface must contain sufficient operations to enable the class user to comprehend the class and to use it effectively. For example, here is a complete interface of a Date class:

```
class Date
{
public:
   Date(int d, int m, int y);
   void advance(int);
   Date add_days(int n) const;
   long days_between(Date b) const;
   int day() const;
   int month() const;
   int year() const;
   Weekday weekday() const;
private:
   // ...
};
```

This interface is complete—anything that you may wish to do with dates can be done—but it is perhaps not convenient. For example, printing a date requires getting the day, month, and year, perhaps translating the month into a string, then printing the data in some order. Should this functionality be included in a Date class? It is highly locale-dependent. Even without the complexity of month names in various languages, the order of printout differs from country to country. Americans use month/day/year, whereas Germans use day.month.year.

Of course, these are the very issues that class users don't want to think about. It might be a good idea to delegate them to a class, either the Date class or another class whose specific focus is locale-dependent formatting.

The interface of the Date class is small. It is not uncommon for a class to have twice as many operations, but classes with 50 or more operations are rare.

## *Designing an Interface*

This section contains a checklist of criteria to determine the quality of a class interface. Note that some of the goals are in conflict with others.

### Cohesion

A class describes a single abstraction. All class operations must logically fit together to support a single, coherent purpose.

Consider this mailbox class:

```
class Mailbox
{
public:
void add_message(Message);
void remove_message(int);
   string get_command();
   void print_message(int) const;
   void list_messages() const;
   int count() const;
private:
   // ...
};
```

The get_command operation sticks out as being different from all other operations. The other operations deal with a single abstraction: a mailbox that holds messages. The get_command operation adds another wrinkle to it, the ability to get commands. From where? In what language? It would be better to have a different class deal with commands and leave the mailbox to do what it does best: store messages.

## Primitive Operations

Operations of a class should be primitive, not decomposable into smaller operations. For example, consider an operation `bool List::advance(int& x)` in a linked-list class, taken from a real class library. Its purpose is to advance a list cursor (a pointer to one element of the list) to the next element. It also reports whether the cursor was able to advance or whether it was already at the end of the list and, if the cursor did move, sets x to the element under the new cursor position.

That the explanation of this operation is so complex should make you pause. Three primitive operations make up this operation:

- Get the list element under the cursor.
- Test whether the cursor is already at the end of the list.
- Advance the cursor to the next list element.

Each of these should become a separate operation.

Of course, ultimately each operation is implemented by decomposing it into sequences of statements, but these statements act on the implementation of the class and are not defined on the interface level.

When primitive operations are supplied, programmers using the class can mix and match them in the order that is relevant to their problem.

## Completeness

A class interface must be complete. All operations that make sense on the abstraction that the class represents must be supported.

Consider this class that represents a list of integers (taken from [Stroustrup], p. 269, with operations renamed). It is incomplete.

```
class List
{
public:
    List(); // makes an empty list
    void insert(int x); // insert at head
    void append(int x); // insert at tail
    void remove(int x); // remove from head
    void set_current(int x); // set element under cursor
    void advance(); // advance list cursor
    int current() const; // report element under cursor
```

```
    bool at_end() const; // is cursor at tail of list?
private:
    // ...
};
```

At first glance it looks like a perfectly good list class, but look again! There is no way to insert and remove elements in the middle of the list. For example, there is no way to change the list (1 4 9 16 25 36) to (1 9 25).

## Convenience

An interface that is complete and consists of primitive operations is always serviceable, but it may not be convenient. As a secondary goal, you should look at typical usage patterns and supply additional operations for the convenience of programmers.

Consider the ifstream class to read data from a file. An operation seekg lets you move the file pointer to a particular location in the file. For example,

```
ifstream fs("employee.dat");
fs.seekg(100);
```

This is obviously convenient, but it is not a primitive operation. There are other ways to solve this task. Instead of executing fs.seekg(n), you could close the file, reopen the file (which positions the file pointer at the beginning), then read and discard n characters.

This is an unattractive alternative, so supplying a specialized operation for this task, a common one, makes sense.

It is important not to overdo this. A class with a great number of convenience operations is itself inconvenient to use because the programmer must first find the appropriate operation.

A good strategy is to start out with no convenience operations, watch the patterns in which other programmers use the class, solicit feedback, and then add only those convenience operations that the class customers demand.

## Consistency

The operations in a class should be consistent with each other with respect to names, arguments and return values, and behavior.

The objective is to avoid programmer surprises and misunderstandings. Confused programmers write buggy code.

Inconsistencies in operation names are irritating to class users. They are surprisingly common even though they can be easily avoided. Stick to a common pattern for capitalization: Don't call one function `set_speed` and another one `setWeight`. Use uniform prefixes: Don't mix `set_speed` and `put_weight`. Be consistent with concepts: If you have an accessor `speed`, don't call the mutator `set_velocity`.

The C++ `iostream` library supports three ways of formatting integers: decimal, octal, and hexadecimal. To pick which one you want, you turn on decimal, octal, or hexadecimal mode. The library also supports three formats for floating-point numbers: fixed, scientific, and general. If you want fixed or scientific, you turn them on. If you want general format, you can't simply turn general format on; instead, you must turn both fixed and scientific *off*. This is a confusing inconsistency in behavior.

Consider the functions operating on `FILE*` in `stdio.h`. They have a number of confusing inconsistencies that have maddened C programmers for many years. Each of these functions takes a `FILE*` parameter. For `fopen`, `fscanf`, and `fprintf`, this is the *first* parameter. For `fgets` and `fread` it is the *last* parameter.

`fputs` returns `EOF` (−1) on error. `fgets` returns 0 on error. `fgetpos` returns a nonzero value on error.

# Categories of Operations

In this section we present the most common categories of operations found in classes. This is not meant to be an exhaustive list. Many classes have operations that do not fall into any of these categories, nor does every class need operations from all the categories.

## Constructors

The purpose of constructors is to initialize every data field in an object. Every class should have at least one constructor, and most classes should have a default constructor. More than one constructor can be provided.

## Destructors

A destructor releases any resources (such as heap memory, open files, or fonts) that the object has acquired when it was constructed or as the result of an operation. If the class manages no external resources, no destructor is necessary. We will discuss destructors in Chapter 13.

## Accessors

Accessors compute a value from an object without modifying it. The simplest form is the field accessor, which simply reports the value of a data field.

Other accessors carry out a computation of some complexity to arrive at a result. Sometimes accessors cache the result of a computation, simply returning the previously computed value if the accessor is called twice with no intervening change of the object. Some accessors take no arguments, using only the information stored in the object to compute the result. Others take arguments, which enter into the computation.

## Comparison Operators

Comparison operators compare an object with another object of the same type to determine whether the objects are identical or whether one is less than the other, according to some ordering relation.

Here is an operation for ordering employees by their ID numbers. As is common with comparison operators, this one returns a negative integer if the first object comes before the second, zero if the objects have identical contents, and a positive integer otherwise.

```
int Employee::compare(Employee b) const
{   return _id - b._id;
}


Employee e, f;
// ...
if (e.compare(f) < 0) // e comes before f
```

Comparison operations look awkward because of the asymmetric syntax for invoking an operation on an object. We must arbitrarily choose one of the two objects to be compared as the active agent that carries out the computation.

Comparison operations are a special case of accessors because comparing an object with another does not change the object that carries out the comparison.

## Mutators

A mutator is any operation that modifies the object in some way. Field mutators just change the value of a single field. Other mutators carry out more general computations that can change one or more fields. Very occasionally, a class has no mutators; the values of its objects are completely set at construction time and only can be inspected, never changed.

## Iterators

Some classes manage a collection of items. Depending on the nature of the data structure, access to these items can be either through a key or through an iteration protocol. In the latter case, the state includes the notion of a current item, and operations look at the current item and move on to the next.

Here is an example of a class that returns the names of files in a directory, using an iteration protocol.

```
class Directory
{
public:
    Directory(String path);
    void reset(); // restart iteration
    void next(); // move to next file
    string current() const; // return current filename
    bool at_end() const; // at end of iteration?
    // ...
private:
    // ...
};

Directory dir(".");
dir.reset();
while (not dir.at_end())
{   cout << dir.current() << endl;
    dir.next();
}
```

The operations facilitating the iteration (reset, next, current, at_end) are collectively called iterators. The reset and next operations are mutators—they modify the internal state of the object.

## Copying and Cloning

For objects that do not manage external resources, copying can be performed simply by assignment and initialization. Objects that have complex responsibilities need to supply their own functions for this purpose. We will discuss this in detail in Chapter 13.

An object can carry out copying in two ways: It can set itself to be a copy of another object, or it can return a copy of itself. The latter process is called *cloning*.

## Input and Output

An output operation simply renders the object onto some output device, such as a file, screen, or printer. The operation receives a handle to the output device as an argument. Output does not modify the object performing it.

An input operation similarly receives a handle to an input device. The input operation, when successful, overwrites all fields of the object with those settings read from the input device. If the input operation is not successful, it is desirable that the object be unchanged. If that cannot be achieved, care should be taken that it is at least in a well-defined state.

# *Design Hints*

## Too Many Operations?

Some basic classes, such as the string and stream classes, have about 50 operations. Most classes have far fewer. If your class has an unusually large number of operations, first check for cohesion. Are all operations really related to one abstraction? If not, split the class into two or more classes and distribute the operations over them. Then check for simplicity. Mark those operations that are primitive—that is, not decomposable into other operations. The other operations are then presumably for the convenience of the class user. Talk to some typical users. Try taking out operations and see who complains. Keep only those that are really appreciated.

## In How Many Ways Can the Class User Achieve a Task?

There has to be at least one way to achieve any task that makes sense with the class, and in most cases there should be exactly one way. That keeps it simple for the class user. However, sometimes you need to add operations that make a common task easier. When doing that, keep track of the number of ways in which a task can be achieved. Is there one that is obviously better? If not, programmers using the class can spend too much time agonizing over which way to choose.

## Is This Class Reusable in Another Context? Should It Be?

Some classes are built to be reused in a wide variety of different contexts, such as Date or string. Others are for a specific purpose, such as Mailbox.

A class with a wide usage range must be designed with a great deal of care. On the other hand, a class that has a specific purpose for only one project should concentrate on those services that are essential to get its job done. Some programmers overengineer classes by adding lots of operations that far exceed any reasonable future use. You should always keep reuse in mind, but not to the extent of gold-plating. Actually, reuse is often facilitated by keeping classes as simple as possible.

## On How Many Other Classes Does This Class Depend?

The fewer, the better. Any class that does input and output depends on the input/output device. A class that is geared toward terminal input and output may be difficult to use in a graphical user interface, where input and output go through dialog boxes. Consider the `Mailbox::print(int)` operation, which prints a message to standard output. Certain devices that deliver mail, such as some handheld communicators, have no notion of streams or standard output. The `Mailbox` class would be better off replacing `print` with an operation `get`, which simply returns a message, and leave it to another part of the system to render the message on the screen. Then `Mailbox` no longer depends on `ostream`.

## No Class Is Perfect

You will find inevitable conflicts in designing a class. The quest for a minimal interface competes with the desire for convenience. Naming and use of operations should be consistent but also reflect traditional use. We don't want a class with just one operation, but that one operation may not coherently fit anywhere else. As in any engineering task, it is the job of the class designer to understand the conflicts and to resolve them by making the necessary compromises.

# 5

# Object-Oriented Design

This chapter introduces a miniature version of a typical object-oriented design methodology. This approach is not intended to replace an industrial-strength methodology. It is our goal to provide the guidance of a formal method while reducing some of the cumbersome mechanics and detail. This makes it more appealing to complete program designs, even for small projects, rather than starting to code right away. We spend some time explaining the mechanics of the tools (when to use paper and pencil, when to use software, how to run a group discussion). Many of these points may be obvious, but we feel it is important that you are comfortable with the activities.

## *Description of the Mail Message System*

To walk through the basic steps of the object-oriented design process, we will consider the task of writing a program that simulates a telephone voice mail system, similar to the message system that many companies use.

In a voice mail system a person dials an extension number and, provided the other party does not pick up the telephone, leaves a message. The other party can later retrieve the messages, keep them, or delete them. Real-world systems have a multitude of fancy features: Messages can be forwarded to one or more mailboxes; distribution lists can be defined, retained, and edited; and authorized persons can send broadcast messages to all users. Some features deal with the physical characteristics of voice. An electronic mail message can be displayed as a page of text on a computer screen, and it is easy to glance at it and scroll forward and backward. For voice messages, scrolling is not so easy. Special commands are necessary to move back or skip ahead by a few seconds. (The system in use at my university has a particularly obnoxious feature: You cannot fast forward or delete a broadcast message from the university president until you have listened to it in its entirety.)

We would like to write a program that simulates a voice mail system but does not create a completely realistic working phone system. Few of us today have computers with easily programmable voice capture and storage. We will simply represent voice mail by text that is entered through the keyboard. We will also ignore the complexities of simultaneous access to the system by multiple users. Our simulation will handle sequential access events only.

Are we ready to start coding? Definitely not. We have some major decisions to make. What features will we actually implement? How will we distinguish simulated voice input from simulated input of telephone number keys (1 . . . 9, #, *)? How will we denote the acts of hanging up and picking up the receiver? Are there system limits on the length of a message, the number of messages per mailbox, or the number of mailboxes? How are mailboxes created and deleted?

A surprisingly popular approach, practiced both by students and industry programmers, is to start programming and to solve these problems as they come up. The result can be quite acceptable if produced by a single individual with a solid understanding of user needs, good judgment, and strong code organization. More likely, it will be an awful mess that is not intuitive to use and impossible to enhance and maintain. We are interested in a process that does not take chances but predictably delivers a good program.

The first formal step in the process that leads us toward the final product (the mail message program) is the analysis phase. Its role is to answer the questions we just raised. We will perform a sample analysis in the next section.

## Analysis of the Mail Message System

### Reaching an Extension

At the outset, the mail message system awaits the input of a four-digit extension number. Some numbers belong to active extensions; others do not. We will see subsequently how active extensions are created. If an inactive extension has been dialed, an error message is generated, and the system reverts to its initial state. If an active extension has been reached, the mailbox greeting is played. Unless changed by the owner, the greeting is this:

```
You have reached extension xxxx. Please leave a message now.
```

At this point, the caller can type in a message by entering the message text on the keyboard. At the end of the message, an "H" should be entered on a single line to denote hanging up the telephone. Only nonempty messages should be stored.

Alternatively, callers can press the "#" key to access their own mailboxes.

## Accessing a Mailbox

To restrict access to a mailbox to its owner, the system prompts for a passcode. After the mailbox owner has entered the correct password, he or she can retrieve messages from the mailbox or change mailbox settings. The user options menu is displayed:

```
You have n new messages and s saved messages.
Press 1 to retrieve your messages.
Press 2 to change your greeting.
Press 3 to change your passcode.
```

(The first command prompt is shown only when messages are pending.) When the caller presses "1" the system enters the message retrieval loop.

If the caller presses "2" to change the greeting, the system prompts to record a new greeting. If the caller presses "3" to enter a new passcode, the system prompts to enter a new passcode. Passcodes must be four digits long. Invalid passcodes cause an error message. On completion of a greeting or password change, the main menu is displayed again. If the user hangs up instead of entering a greeting or passcode, no change is recorded.

## Retrieving Messages

The first message is displayed. Then the message options menu appears:

```
Press 1 to delete the current message.
Press 2 to save the current message.
```

After the selection is processed, the next message is played. This cycle repeats until all messages are played. Then the user options menu appears again. At any time, the caller may hang up by pressing "H." New messages are played in the order in which they were received. After all new messages are played, the saved messages are played in the order in which they were saved.

## Adding New Mailboxes

When first started, the mail system has one special mailbox, with extension 9999 and passcode 1728, belonging to the administrator and no other active extensions. The administrator mailbox works the same way as all other mailboxes, but it has an additional option in the main menu:

```
Press 4 to add a new extension.
```

When the administrator presses "4" the system prompts to enter the new four-digit extension number and then prompts for a four-digit passcode. The extension is activated, and the main menu is displayed again.

## Simulation of Voice Data and Telephone Equipment

In our program, we need to simulate the three distinct input events that occur in a real telephone system: speaking, pushing a button on the telephone pad, and picking up and hanging up the telephone. We use the following convention for input: An "H" on a line by itself denotes hanging up the telephone. A sequence of keys "1" . . . "9" on a line with no other characters denotes a dialed number. A "#" or "*" on a line by itself denotes pushing one of the command keys on the pad. Any other text denotes voice input.

To quit the program, access mailbox 0000 by typing "0000."

## System Limits

We need to set some limits on system resources. The following limits are admittedly unrealistic, but they enable us to concentrate on the object-oriented features rather than memory management during the programming phase. We set limits of 10 active mailboxes in addition to the administrator mailbox, and as many as 20 new and 10 saved messages per mailbox.

Attempts to generate more active accounts are rejected. If a mailbox with 20 new messages is called, the message

```
You have reached extension xxxx.
The mailbox is currently full.
```

is displayed instead of the greeting, and no new message can be stored. If the saved message area is full, the mailbox owner can only discard new messages. Messages and greetings may be of any length. They may span multiple lines.

# CRC Cards

## Card Layout

An effective technique for discovering classes, functionality, and relationships is the so-called CRC card method, described by [Beck]. A CRC card is simply an A5 or A6 size index card (4″ by 6″ or 3″ by 5″ will do fine if you live in a nonmetric country) that describes one class and lists the class responsibilities (operations) and collaborators (related classes). Index cards are a good choice for a number of reasons. They are small, thereby discouraging you from piling too much responsibility into a single class. They are stiff and can be handed around and rearranged by a group of designers in brainstorming sessions. Of course, many people have used regular sheets of paper or documents in a multiwindow editor with good success.

You make one card for each discovered class. List any discovered operations on the front, together with any classes that are used in some way to carry out these operations. On the back you may list any data fields.

The front of the CRC card shown in Figure 5.1 indicates that we have discovered two operations of the mailbox: to get the current message and to play the greeting. The "get current message" operation collaborates with the Message and MessageQueue classes. That is, it needs to interact with message and message queue objects in some unspecified way.

## An Example of CRC Card Evolution

CRC cards are quite intuitive for an analyst "walking through" a sequence of steps that solve one task. Consider, for example, the behavior of the message system when a user sends a message to another user's mailbox. The scenario

```
                    Class: Mailbox

Operations (Responsibilities)   Relationships (Collaborators)
get current message                 Message, MessageQueue
play greeting
```

```
Fields (on back of card)
queue of new messages
queue of kept messages
greeting
extension number
passcode
```

**FIGURE 5.1**    Front and back of a typical CRC card.

begins when "someone" processes the dialing of an extension number. We need to specify a responsible agent and create a new index card, shown in Figure 5.2.

In our program we will have only one object of type `MailSystem`: "the" voice mail system. That is fine—top-level objects are typically the sole instance of their class. The `InputReader` is a class that can handle the separation of simulated telephone keys and message input.

The next logical step is to find the mailbox that belongs to the extension. This sounds like an appropriate task for the `MailSystem` class because the system knows where all mailboxes are. We add an operation (see Figure 5.3).

"Someone" has to find out whether the next step in the input is a message for the dialed extension or a login command. This could be done either by `MailSystem` or `Mailbox`. We let the "process dialing" function handle it

```
                        Class: MailSystem

Operations (Responsibilities)   Relationships (Collaborators)
dial extension                  InputReader
```

**FIGURE 5.2**  An initial CRC card for the mail system.

and give two separate operations, `receive message` and `login`, to the `Mailbox` class. The updated CRC cards are shown in Figure 5.4.

## Hints for Using CRC Cards

Try to keep cards physically close to their collaborators. The visual arrangement of the cards can give clues to simple or overly complex relationships. You should not be afraid to tear up cards or to erase, modify, or reorganize operations. Experienced designers will cheerfully admit that they rarely hit

```
                        Class: MailSystem

Operations (Responsibilities)   Relationships (Collaborators)
process dialing                 InputReader
locate mailbox                  Mailbox
```

**FIGURE 5.3**  Evolving the CRC card for the mail system.

| Class: MailSystem | |
|---|---|
| Operations (Responsibilities) | Relationships (Collaborators) |
| process dialing | InputReader |
| locate mailbox | Mailbox |
| | |
| | |
| | |
| | |
| | |
| | |
| | |

| Class: Mailbox | |
|---|---|
| Operations (Responsibilities) | Relationships (Collaborators) |
| get current message | Message, MessageQueue |
| play greeting | |
| receive greeting | Message, MessageQueue |
| login | InputReader |
| | |
| | |
| | |
| | |
| | |
| | |

**FIGURE 5.4** Updated CRC cards for the mail system and mailbox.

upon an optimal division of responsibilities at the first try and that a fair amount of trial and error is necessary even in seemingly simple cases.

Group discussion can be particularly successful with class design. Get two or three designers together. Here is a good way to "break the ice" and get started. Let all participants use the "noun and verb" technique described in Chapter 1 to come up with a pool of candidates for classes and operations. Then consider the first important task that comes to mind, and perform a scenario walk-through. Have one person play the protagonist, who proposes a responsible agent and a method for carrying out the task. Invariably the description will be somewhat vague, and the other participants find it easy to ask for clarification or to suggest different preferences. Rotate the protagonist role. You are done when all nontrivial tasks have been played through to the satisfaction of all participants.

Resist the temptation to add operations just because they can be done. Keep in mind that implementation details are not supposed to be prescribed in the design, but it is certainly fair to consider sketches of possible implementations. In fact, participants should criticize approaches that unnecessarily force a particular data structure. Conversely, belief in the validity of an operation is strengthened when it is shown that it can be carried out under two different plausible implementations.

You do not necessarily need a group of people for effective class discovery. If you work on your own, though, it helps if you have a "Jekyll and Hyde" personality and can play your own devil's advocate.

CRC cards are a good tool for discovering designs, but they are not particularly suited for documenting them. The visual arrangement and movement of the cards are ephemeral. As the design evolves over time, updating a stack of paper cards becomes inconvenient. For this reason, the cards are usually discarded after a design has been found. We will discuss more permanent documentation tools in the next sections.

In summary, index cards are a popular mechanism for discovering classes and operations. Making a new card for each class as the need arises and marking new operations on the cards are both easy. Scenarios can be "played out" by moving the cards around while tracing the control flow.

## CRC Cards for the Mail System Problem

Figure 5.5 shows a complete set of CRC cards for the mail system example. The solution presented here is only one of many possible divisions of responsibility.

# *Class Categories*

We cannot completely categorize classes, but we can determine that classes do fall into common patterns. The following patterns, which cover the most frequent cases, may be helpful in your class discovery process. A given class may fall into more than one of these categories.

## Tangible Things

These are the easiest classes to discover because they are visible in the problem domain. We have seen many examples: `Mailbox`, `Message`, `Document`, `Footnote`.

| Class: MailSystem | |
|---|---|
| Operations (Responsibilities) | Relationships (Collaborators) |
| process dialing | InputReader, Message |
| locate mailbox | Mailbox |
| create mailbox | Mailbox |
| | |
| | |
| | |
| | |
| | |
| | |

```
Fields (on back of card)
collection of mailboxes
administrator mailbox
```

**FIGURE 5.5**   A complete set of CRC cards for the mail system.

## System Interfaces and Devices

These are also easy to discover by considering the system resources and interactions of the system. Typical examples are DisplayWindow and InputReader.

## Agents

Sometimes it is helpful to change an operation into an agent class. For example, the "compute page breaks" operation on a document could be turned into a Paginator class, which operates on documents. Then the paginator can work on a part of a document while another part is edited on the screen. In this case, the agent class is invented to express execution parallelism.

| Class: Mailbox | |
|---|---|
| Operations (Responsibilities) | Relationships (Collaborators) |
| receive message | Message, MessageQueue |
| login | InputReader |
| get current message | Message, MessageQueue |
| delete current message | Message, MessageQueue |
| change greeting | InputReader |
| change passcode | InputReader |
| retrieve messages | |
| activate | |

```
Fields (on back of card)
queue of new messages
queue of kept messages
greeting
extension number
passcode
```

**FIGURE 5.5**   (*Continued*).

The InputReader class is another example. Rather than having the message read its input, the input reader gets text, which is used to construct the message. The Agent class decouples the Message class from input mechanisms and separates the abstraction levels of input processing and controlling message contents.

## Events and Transactions

Event and transaction classes are useful to model records of activities that describe what happened in the past or what needs to be done later. A low-level example is a MouseEvent class, which remembers when and where the mouse moved or a button was clicked. A high-level example is a Customer-Arrival class, which specifies when and where what kind of customer is scheduled to arrive.

| Class: AdminMailbox | |
|---|---|
| Operations (Responsibilities) | Relationships (Collaborators) |
| receive message | Message, MessageQueue |
| login | InputReader |
| get current message | Message, MessageQueue |
| keep current message | Message, MessageQueue |
| delete current message | Message, MessageQueue |
| change greeting | InputReader |
| change passcode | InputReader |
| activate | |
| create mailbox | MailSystem |

Fields (on back of card)
queue of new messages
queue of kept messages
greeting
extension number
passcode

**FIGURE 5.5**   (*Continued*).

## Users and Roles

User and role classes are stand-ins for actual users of the program. An `Administrator` class is an interface to the human administrator of the system. A `Reviewer` models a user in an interactive authoring system whose role is to add critical annotations and recommendations for change. `User` classes are common in systems that are used by more than one person or where one person needs to perform distinct tasks.

## Systems

System classes model a subsystem or the overall system being built. Their roles are typically to perform initialization and shutdown and to start the flow of input into the system. The `MailSystem` is a typical example.

| Class: Message | |
|---|---|
| Operations (Responsibilities) | Relationships (Collaborators) |
| play | |
| | |
| | |
| | |
| | |
| | |
| | |
| | |
| | |

| Fields (on back of card) |
|---|
| |
| |
| |
| |
| |
| |

**FIGURE 5.5**  *(Continued)*.

## Containers

Containers are used to store and retrieve information. An example is a
`Mailbox` that stores messages or an `Invoice` that stores items and quantities
ordered. At the design phase, you should not be overly concerned with the
low-level nature of a container (hash table or balanced tree), and you should
assume that the standard data structures (lists, queues, maps, and so forth)
are readily available.

## Foundation Classes

These are classes such as `String`, `Date`, `Vector`, `Matrix`, `Rectangle`, `Postal-
Address`, or `Semaphore`. They encapsulate data types with well-understood
properties. At the design stage, you should simply assume that these classes

| Class: MessageQueue | |
|---|---|
| Operations (Responsibilities) | Relationships (Collaborators) |
| length of queue | |
| get message at head | Message |
| remove message at head | Message |
| append message at tail | Message |
| | |
| | |
| | |
| | |
| | |

```
Fields (on back of card)
collection of mailboxes
```

**FIGURE 5.5**   (*Continued*).

are readily available, just as the fundamental types (integers and floating-point numbers) are. These classes can often be acquired from library vendors. They can be reused easily in many projects.

## Collaboration Patterns

Sometimes, classes group together to achieve a goal. The container/iterator pattern is characteristic. A container holds data, and an iterator can attach itself to the container and sequentially step through the data in the container. This way, data can be inspected one item at a time. Another common pattern is the model/view pattern, in which a so-called model holds information and one or more views can present the data in different formats. An example is a model class, holding financial data, with one

```
┌─────────────────────────────────────────────────────────────┐
│                      Class: InputReader                       │
├─────────────────────────────────────────────────────────────┤
│ Operations (Responsibilities)  Relationships (Collaborators)  │
│ type of pending input                                         │
│ get next item                                                 │
│                                                               │
│                                                               │
│                                                               │
│                                                               │
│                                                               │
│                                                               │
│                                                               │
└─────────────────────────────────────────────────────────────┘

┌─────────────────────────────────────────────────────────────┐
│ Fields (on back of card)                                      │
│ buffered input line                                           │
│                                                               │
│                                                               │
│                                                               │
│                                                               │
│                                                               │
│                                                               │
│                                                               │
│                                                               │
│                                                               │
└─────────────────────────────────────────────────────────────┘
```

**FIGURE 5.5** (*Continued*).

view displaying the information as a graph and another presenting it as a table.

# Recognizing Class Relationships

## Recognizing Association

Association is easiest to recognize. Simply look at the "collaboration" part of the CRC card. Collaboration implies association. For example, the `Mailbox` class collaborates with `Message`, implying an association between them. But the `Message` class does not use `InputReader`, suggesting that the classes are not associated.

## Recognizing Aggregation

Aggregation is the "has-a" relationship. It is fulfilled if each object of one class either contains or exclusively manages objects of another class. For example, each `Mailbox` has, or aggregates, `Message` objects.

We distinguish between aggregation and simple attributes. If an object consists of a field of a numeric basic type, such as integer or floating-point values, or of a foundation class, such as date or string, it is considered merely an attribute, not aggregation.

The fields that are noted on the back of a CRC card denote either attributes or aggregation. Of course, no concerted effort is made in the design phase to determine all fields of a class. You should therefore check to capture all aggregation relationships.

## Recognizing Inheritance

Inheritance is the "is-a" relationship. If every object of a class logically conforms to another class but has additional special properties, then the first inherits from the other. For example, the `AdminMailbox` class inherits from `Mailbox` because an administrator mailbox is a special case of a mailbox.

Sometimes inheritance is difficult to see because you did not yet discover a common base class. If you observe that several classes have shared responsibilities, check whether it is possible to define a base class that can assume those responsibilities.

Recognizing common base classes is particularly important for the implementation. Common code need be provided only once in the base class, and it is automatically inherited by the derived classes—hence the term *inheritance*. Chapter 7 describes how this code sharing is carried out in C++.

Here is an example for discovering shared behavior. Consider a computer system that can deliver faxes, voice messages, or electronic mail. The user sees a listing of the received messages on the screen, showing type, arrival time, and sender. Faxes can be printed, deleted, saved, and forwarded with attachments. Voice messages can be played over the computer speaker, deleted, saved, and forwarded with added recordings. Electronic mail can be displayed on the screen, deleted, saved, or edited and forwarded. What is the common abstraction, and what are its properties? The common abstraction is `Message`. A mailbox holds a collection of messages, which may be fax, voice, or e-mail. The mailbox can keep, delete, or forward them. Each message can be inspected and edited. Derived classes are `FaxMessage`, `VoiceMessage`, and `EmailMessage`. The method of inspection and editing is different for each of these classes, but the operational interface is the same.

# Class Diagrams

## Common Diagramming Conventions

Graphical presentation methods to convey design information are very popular, for a good reason. It is easier to extract relationship information by looking at a diagram than by reading documentation. On the other hand, there is a limit to the information contents of graphs (see [Tufte]). The best approach is to use the graph to convey an overview of the design and to use text for the details.

To express class relationships, some convention is required. We are all familiar with flowcharts that use rectangles for steps and diamonds for decisions. Of course, there is no logical reason why decisions couldn't be denoted by triangles or circles. The diamond is just the traditional choice. Unfortunately, there is no similar tradition for class diagrams. A number of diagramming conventions have been proposed, among them those described in [Booch], [Rumbaugh], and [Coad]. These notation systems are in active use, and software tools support each one of them. The notations are well thought-out and provide tools to express a large amount of detailed information in a graphical form. There are symbols for class relationship, object behavior under transactions, timing and scheduling, modules, and templates. For our modest goals, let's concentrate on class relationship notation only.

Unfortunately, the various notations differ greatly in their visual appearance. Figures 5.6, 5.7, and 5.8 show the same relationships, as drawn following the Booch, Rumbaugh, and Coad-Yourdon notations. Classes are easy to recognize—they are denoted by boxes or cloud shapes containing the class name and (if you like) the names of the major operations. The class relationships are frustrating to decipher. To the uninitiated, the small circles, squares, and diamonds used as annotations for connecting lines are completely meaningless. One author ([Martin], p. 121) recommends that "tools using strange diagrams are best avoided" and then explains his own diagrams, which look just as strange.

The sophisticated methodologies of [Booch] and [Rumbaugh] use many more diagrams to display other design information. Furthermore, a methodology is more than just diagramming rules. To avoid overwhelming the reader, we just use the most important subset, which is common to a number of methodologies.

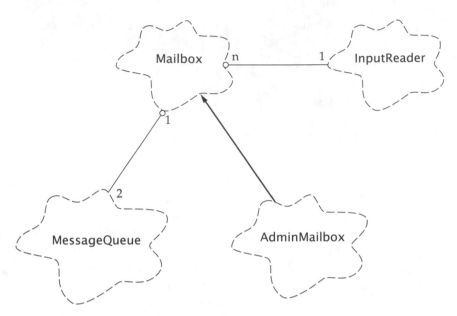

**FIGURE 5.6**   A class relationship diagram in the Booch notation.

## A Simple Subset of the "Unified Notation" Class Diagrams

In this book, we will draw all diagrams using the "unified notation" devised jointly by Booch, Rumbaugh, and Jacobson. This is a second-generation notation, developed to unify the Booch, OMT, and Objectory notations that Booch, Rumbaugh, and Jacobson had designed separately.

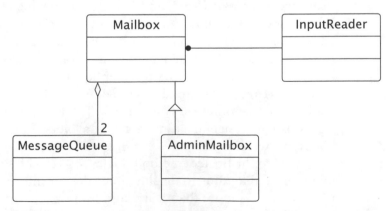

**FIGURE 5.7**   A class relationship diagram in the Rumbaugh notation.

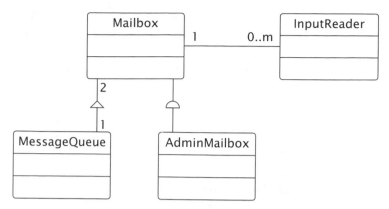

**FIGURE 5.8** A class relationship diagram in the Coad-Yourdon notation.

**FIGURE 5.9** A class in the UML notation.

**FIGURE 5.10** A class with data fields and operations.

This basic notation is fairly simple. Classes are drawn as boxes, which can contain the class name, and, when appropriate, the names of data fields and operations (see Figures 5.9 and 5.10). You usually do not list all data fields and operations, only the most important ones.

Classes are joined by three kinds of connections: association, aggregation and inheritance (see Figure 5.11).

To keep the diagrams readable for those who aren't notation enthusiasts, we extend the unified notation slightly. We write the relationships on the connectors, using this simple convention:

| *Annotation* | *Meaning* |
|---|---|
| uses | Association relationship |
| has | Aggregation relationship |
| is | Inheritance relationship |

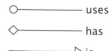

**FIGURE 5.11** Class relationships.

We make one slight change to the unified notation. The unified notation suggests to draw a line without adornments for the "uses" relationship. That makes it difficult to see which class is being used. Following the notation of Booch, we place a small circle at the class that uses the other class.

For the association relationship, you can use the generic term "uses," or you can describe the nature of the association in English. For example, if the `Mailbox` class uses the `InputReader` class to read input, you can annotate the connection with "read input".

Similarly, for the aggregation relationship, you can replace the generic term "has" with the name of the data field representing the aggregation. For example, if every `Mailbox` object has a datafield of type `MessageQueue` to store the new messages, you can replace the "has" annotation with "new messages".

If a class inherits from a base class, draw an arrow from the derived class to the base class (see Figure 5.12).

Amazingly enough, there has been some discussion about the proper shape of this arrow tip. Traditionally, Rumbaugh used a hollow triangle and Booch used an open arrow tip. This doesn't sound like something to get excited about unless you are a notation designer. Just use whatever arrow tip your graphics program can easily produce.

If a class contains objects of another class, we call this the aggregation or "has" relationship. It is denoted by a line with a diamond on the side of the "larger" class, the one containing objects of the other class. Many newcomers to the notation find it a little confusing that the diamond for aggregation is at the end of the larger class, the arrow tip for inheritance at the end of the smaller class (see Figure 5.13).

For the "has" relationship, we also write the cardinality on the end points of the connection. Common choices for the cardinality are as follows:

1:1

1:2

1:0 . . . 1

**FIGURE 5.12** Inheritance.

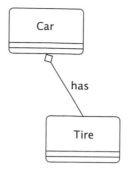

**FIGURE 5.13** Aggregation relationship.

1:* (any number ≥ 0)

1:1 . . . * (any number ≥ 1)

Note that for aggregation, this is always a "1:*x*" relationship. It makes no sense to have a "0 . . . 1:*" or "*:*" aggregation. Such a relationship needs to be expressed as a more general association.

While aggregation relationships are implemented as data fields, not all data fields should automatically be drawn as associations in a class diagram. For example, suppose the class Employee has a field _hiredate of type Date. You should not automatically draw boxes for the Employee and Date classes and join them by an aggregation line. Ask yourself "Does an Employee have a Date"? In one sense, of course, the answer is "yes." Every employee has a hire date. But you can carry this too far. Employee objects have data field _salary of type double. Does every employee "have a double"? That sounds ridiculous. In this case, neither the date nor the floating-point number are entities that are of interest outside the employee object. It makes more sense to describe them as *attributes* of the Employee class. Numeric fields should always be considered attributes, and the same holds for fields of class type when the class is a simple abstraction such as a string, Date, or Address. You can write the attributes into the second compartment of the class box, as in Figure 5.14.

In the unified notation, the association relationship is denoted by a line without any adornments on either side (see Figure 5.15). However, we will place a small circle at the side of the class that uses the other class.

The symmetry of the connector in the unified notation is a little unfortunate because we like to think of associations as asymmetric whenever possible. If class A is associated with class B, then class A must be aware of

| Employee |
| --- |
| double _salary<br>Date _hiredate |

**FIGURE 5.14** Attributes.

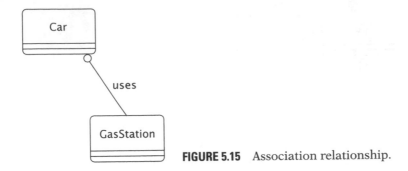

**FIGURE 5.15** Association relationship.

class B. But there is not necessarily a reason that class B needs to know about class A. For example, a Mailbox uses an InputReader, but the opposite is not true—the InputReader has no conception what objects request input from it.

Sometimes, an association indeed appears bidirectional on initial analysis. Consider a software system that processes the payroll of several companies. Clearly there is some association between companies and employees. That can be indicated by an unspecified association (see Figure 5.16).

Later, as the nature of the association becomes clear, you can be more specific. Companies *employ* employees. Employees *work for* companies (see Figure 5.17).

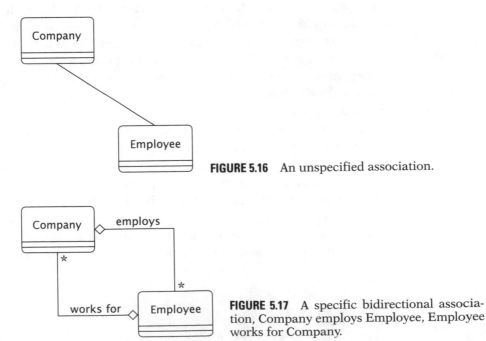

**FIGURE 5.16** An unspecified association.

**FIGURE 5.17** A specific bidirectional association, Company employs Employee, Employee works for Company.

As with aggregations, it is useful to write the cardinalities of association relationships at the ends of the connectors. Unlike aggregations, a many-to-many relationship can occur. For example, the relationship between companies and employees is many-to-many: every company has many employees, and an employee may have worked for more than one company.

If you have used the class browser in a development environment, you have seen class relationship diagrams that show just inheritance. Actually, as it turns out, inheritance is not the most important relationship to diagram. The most important relationship to control is the "uses" relationship. Recall that a class A uses another class B if any A operation needs to access a B object. In that case, any change in B could have a potential impact on A. For that reason, well-clustered usage relationships greatly increase the stability of a design.

## Diagramming the Mail System Design

We discovered the following class relationships:

- AdminMailbox inherits from Mailbox.
- A MailSystem has one AdminMailbox and $n > 0$ other mailboxes.
- A mailbox has two message queues.
- A message queue has $n > 0$ messages.
- MailSystem and Mailbox each use Message and InputReader.

Figure 5.18 displays these facts graphically.

## Object Message Diagrams

An object message diagram shows the flow of function calls or the flow of messages, as they are called in object-oriented circles, that result from the execution of a particular operation. Although it is overkill to render an object message diagram for every operation, drawing these diagrams for certain operations that are central to a system or that are particularly intricate can be useful.

Here are the rules for drawing the diagrams. Each object is represented by a rectangle with two compartments. (Recall that the rectangles denoting classes have three compartments.) It contains either the name of the class (Mailbox) or the name of the object, preceded by the name of the class (MessageQueue _new_messages) (see Figure 5.19).

An object message diagram should show the flow of control inside one operation. That operation is denoted by a line ending in the object that is responsible for carrying out the operation, labeled by the name

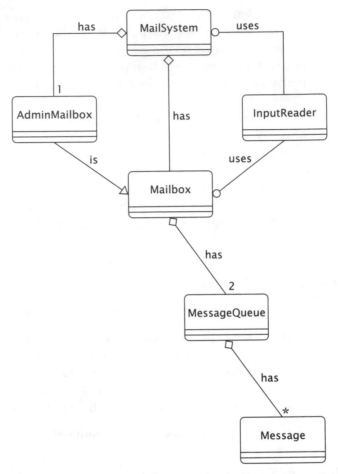

**FIGURE 5.18** The annotated Booch diagram for the mail system.

of the operation and an arrow indicating the direction of the flow (see Figure 5.20).

For example, let us complete an object message diagram for the process_dialing operation of the MailSystem class. Here is the sequence of actions in English:

**FIGURE 5.19** Object diagrams.

**FIGURE 5.20** Beginning of an object message diagram.

1. Read input.
2a. (If the input is 9999) Have administrator mailbox receive a message.
2b1. (If the input is another extension) Find the mailbox for that extension.
2b2. Have that mailbox receive a message.

This results in the object diagram shown in Figure 5.21.

In an object message diagram, each function call is symbolized by a line joining the calling object with the object responsible for carrying out that function. The name of the function, together with an arrow pointing to the responsible object, is written along the connector. The function calls are numbered sequentially (1., 2., . . .). To capture branches and loops, you must use a more complex numbering scheme (1, 2a, 2b1, 2b2, . . .), but this can get tedious very quickly. Ultimately, the purpose of an object diagram is not to show the same level of detail as the actual source code, but to show with which other objects an object must collaborate to carry out an operation. In fact, drawing object message diagrams can be very useful

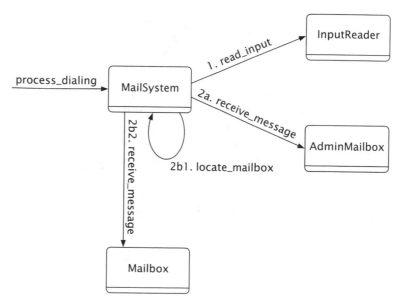

**FIGURE 5.21** Object diagram for `MailSystem::process_dialing`.

when you are trying to find the collaborators of a class in the CRC card process.

The lines in object diagrams can be tagged with markers to show how the objects that carry out the various functions are located. There are five possibilities:

F—data field of the object

P—procedure parameter

G—global variable

L—local variable

S—the object itself

Let us consider these possibilities in the following example. Suppose an object of class Car carries out an operation add_gas. It needs to get the gasoline from a GasStation object. How can the GasStation object be located? The simplest case is the most common one: the add_gas operation has a parameter of class GasStation.

```
void Car::add_gas(GasStation& station)
{   station.buy_gas(...);
}
```

This is described with the "P" tag (see Figure 5.22).

A less attractive alternative is that there is a global gas station (or a global array of gas stations).

```
void Car::add_gas()
{   the_gas_station.buy_gas(...);
}
```

This is described with the "G" tag (see Figure 5.23).

Perhaps every Car object contains a pointer to "its" gas station.

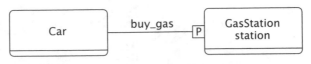

**FIGURE 5.22**   The parameter tag.

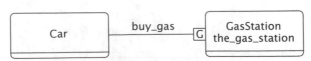

**FIGURE 5.23**   The global tag.

**FIGURE 5.24** The field tag.

```
void Car::add_gas()
{   _my_gas_station->buy_gas(...);
}
```

Then the gas station is a data field of the object and we use the "F" tag (see Figure 5.24). This would be a somewhat strange design, of course.

The next possibility is even stranger. [Riel] calls it the method of the wealthy: build and destroy a gas station.

```
void Car::add_gas()
{   GasStation* station = new GasStation();
    station->buy_gas(...);
    delete station;
}
```

In this case, `station` is a local variable and we use the "L" tag (see Figure 5.25).

This exhausts the possibilities for the `GasStation` object. It must be a parameter, a data field, a local variable, or a global variable. To see the use of the "S" tag, let us assume that the `Car` class has an operation `find_gas_station`. Then a `Car` object must first ask itself to find the nearest `GasStation`. For that operation, the "S" tag is used (see Figure 5.26). The `GasStation` is the return value of that operation and thus a local variable.

```
void Car::add_gas()
{   GasStation* station = find_gas_station();
    station->buy_gas(...);
}
```

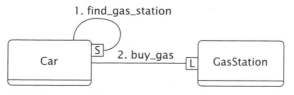

**FIGURE 5.25** The local tag.

**FIGURE 5.26** The self-reference tag.

Now that we have seen all possibilities with a contrived example, let us look at our mail system. When the process_dialing operation of the Mail-System reads input, it calls the get_input operation of the InputReader class. But which object of type InputReader actually carries out the operation? In this case, we have one global input reader that is accessible by both the mail system and the mailboxes. Thus we use the "G" adornment.

If the user entered the special number for the administrator mailbox, then the receive_messages operation is carried out by an AdminMailbox object. Which object? The administrator mailbox is a data field of the Mail-Message class, and therefore we use the "F" adornment. If the user enters another mailbox number, then the locate_mailbox operation is used to locate the mailbox. That operation is carried out by the same MailSystem object that does the dial processing; thus, it is a self-reference and we use the "S" symbol (see Figure 5.27).

The object message diagram of Figure 5.27 shows that there is one incoming message into the MailSystem object (namely the operation to be described) and a number of outgoing messages from the MailSystem object. No other operations are shown because we assume that all operations except for process_dialing are "black boxes." This kind of object message diagram is the easiest to understand, and we recommend that you restrict yourself to this simple form until you are very familiar with these diagrams.

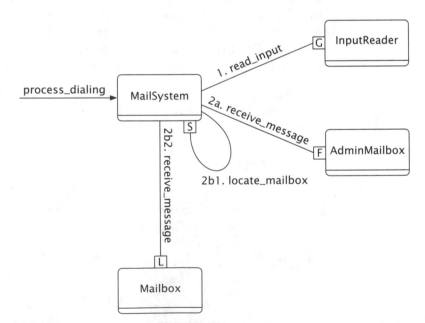

**FIGURE 5.27** The object message diagram of MailSystem::process_dialing with adornments.

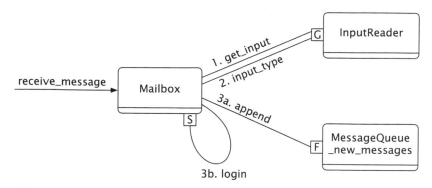

**FIGURE 5.28**   Object diagram for Mailbox::receive_message.

If you want to show how another operation, such as `receive_message`, is carried out, then draw a second diagram (see Figure 5.28).

It is possible to have one diagram show multiple call nesting levels. For example, in Figure 5.29, we show the `process_dialing` operation of the `MailSystem` class with a detail view of the `receive_message` operation of the `Mailbox` class.

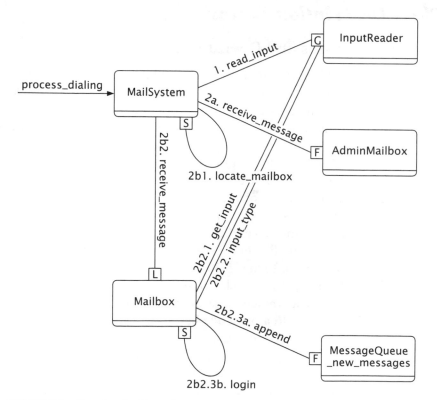

**FIGURE 5.29**   Two-level object diagram.

Showing multiple levels of calls leads to more complex diagrams that can be hard to grasp. You should use this feature with restraint, always keeping in mind the central point that you want to make with a particular diagram.

Class diagrams are very useful, and it is a good practice to draw diagrams showing the relationships between all classes. It is not a good idea, however, to draw an object message diagram for every single operation. Many operations yield trivial diagrams that are not worth rendering. You should focus on those operations that are particularly interesting and whose implementation is not obvious.

Object-oriented design experts use many more diagrams. Among them are use case diagrams, message trace diagrams, state diagrams, module diagrams, and process diagrams. These can all be useful, especially when designing large and complex systems. For systems of moderate scope, a complete set of class diagrams, supplemented by object message diagrams for key scenarios, is certainly sufficient.

# Class Description Forms

## Forms for Classes and Operations

CRC cards contain very limited information about classes: their names, the names of all operations, and the names of related classes. Class diagrams add information on the nature of the relationship. A more detailed description is necessary to aid the programmer charged with implementing the class.

The information is gathered in forms. ([Booch] calls them templates, but in the context of C++ templates mean something completely different.) You can think of a form as a questionnaire, asking about important features of the class. As with all forms, some fields may not apply to a particular situation and so can be left blank.

Actually, there is one form for the class and a separate form for each operation. Figure 5.30 shows the class form. For each operation, fill out a form like the one shown in Figure 5.31.

The implementation details for fields should be left as vague as possible. Should a passcode be an `int` or a `string`? Either way, it won't have an impact on the design, and the decision can be deferred. The nature of a link may be kept open, and during implementation a pointer, reference, handle, or other location mechanism may be selected. The exact nature of a collection (that is, whether it is an array, linked list, hash table) should not be specified.

| Name | |
|---|---|
| Base class(es) | |
| Purpose | |
| States | |
| Constructors | |
| Operations<br>*Mutators*<br><br><br><br><br><br>*Accessors* | |
| Fields | |

**FIGURE 5.30**  A class description form.

| Prototype | |
|---|---|
| Purpose | |
| Receives | |
| Returns | |
| Remarks | |

**FIGURE 5.31**  An operation description form.

## Preparing Forms

Some programmers like to plan everything with pencil and paper before starting to code. For those programmers it is best to make photocopies of the forms and fill them in by hand, as in Figure 5.32.

However, it actually makes a lot of sense to type the descriptions into the computer, using a programming editor. You can use a word processor, but if you do, don't bother with fonts or fancy boxes. The goal is to get an ASCII file that becomes the basis for code in the implementation phase. We assume that the implementation language will be C++. Use C++ syntax to describe functions, arguments, and fields, and use C++-style comments to bracket text sections.

| Name | Mailbox |
|---|---|
| Base class(es) | |
| Purpose | A mailbox contains messages that can be listed, kept or discarded. |
| States | empty \| full \| neither<br>inactive \| active |
| Constructors | default: makes inactive mailbox |
| Operations<br>*Mutators*<br><br><br><br><br><br>*Accessors* | receive_message(Message)<br>login( ): process password and commands<br>retrieve_messages( )<br>delete_current( )<br>change_greeting( )<br>change_password( )<br>activate(int extension, int passcode)<br>Message get_current( ) |
| Fields | MessageQueue _new_messages<br>MessageQueue _kept_messages<br>string _greeting<br>_extension<br>_passcode |

**FIGURE 5.32**  A class form for the Mailbox class.

The information in Figure 5.32 might look like this in an editor:

```
class Mailbox
/* PURPOSE: A mailbox contains messages that can be listed,
            kept, or discarded.

   STATES:  empty | full | neither
            inactive | active
*/
// CONSTRUCTION
   default // makes inactive mailbox

// OPERATIONS - Mutators
   receive_message(Message)
   login() // process passcode and commands
   retrieve_messages()
   delete_current()
   change_greeting()
   change_password()
   activate(int extension)
// OPERATIONS - Accessors
   Message get_current()
// FIELDS
   MessageQueue _new_messages
   MessageQueue _kept_messages
   string _greeting
   _extension
   _passcode
```

Figure 5.33 shows a form containing the information about an operation. When entered in a programming editor, the information should be formatted to look like this:

```
bool MailSystem::add_mailbox(int extension)
/* PURPOSE:  Add a new mailbox to the system.
   RECEIVES: extension - the extension number of the mailbox
   RETURNS:  true iff the operation succeeded
   REMARKS:  The operation may fail if the extension number is
             already in use or if there is no space to add
             another mailbox.
*/
```

The tabular form is easier to read, but the ASCII form is easier to convert to code, and the code will be modified as time goes on. We are, therefore, interested in code that is as self-documenting as possible. For small and medium-sized projects, it is feasible to keep most documentation in the code, thereby avoiding the considerable difficulty of keeping code and external documentation synchronized. At this time, a number of CASE tools are

| Prototype | Bool MailSystem: :add_mailbox(int extention, int passcode) |
|-----------|------------------------------------------------------------|
| Purpose | Add a new mailbox to the system. |
| Receives | extension – the extension number of the mailbox<br>passcode – the passcode number |
| Returns | TRUE if the operation succeeded |
| Remarks | The operation may fail if the extension number is already in use or if there is no space to add another mailbox. |

**FIGURE 5.33**  A form describing a class operation.

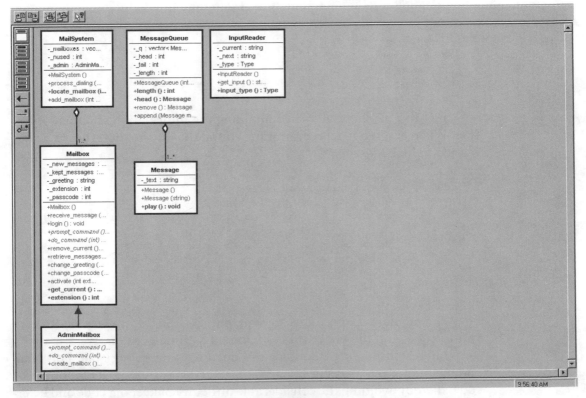

**FIGURE 5.34**  The Together/C++ tool inside Borland C++.

commercially available as well. These tools succeed to varying degrees in keeping the code and design documentation synchronized. Compiler vendors are beginning to integrate these tools into their development environments as well. For example, the professional version of the Borland C++ compiler ships with a *Together/C++* plug-in (see Figure 5.34). Changes in the code are automatically reflected in the design diagrams, and editing the diagrams in the Together/C++ CASE tool updates the code.

## C++ *Implementation*

In many cases producing a code outline from the forms described in the previous section is easy. Some issues need to be resolved in the coding phase:

- Specific data structures need to be selected for containers.
- Object links must be implemented as pointers, references, handles, or other mechanisms.
- Code must be written for all operations (of course).
- Additional private operations and data fields may need to be added to carry out these operations.
- Memory management functions may be required (see Chapter 14).

Here is the code for the `Mailbox` example form from the preceding section:

```
class Mailbox
/* PURPOSE: A mailbox contains messages that can be listed,
           kept, or discarded.
   STATES: empty | full | neither
           inactive | active
*/
{
public:
   Mailbox(); // makes inactive mailbox
   void receive_message(Message);
   void login(); // process passcode and commands
   void retrieve_messages();
   void delete_current();
   void change_greeting();
   void change_password();
   void activate(int extension, int passcode);
   Message get_current() const;
private:
   MessageQueue _new_messages;
   MessageQueue _kept_messages;
   string _greeting;
   int _extension;
```

```
      int _passcode;
};
```

Note that accessor functions are declared as const and that all data is in the private section. All comments are retained.

The comments describing operations should also be retained when the implementation code is added:

```
bool MailSystem::add_mailbox(int extension, int passcode)
/* PURPOSE:  Add a new mailbox to the system.
   RECEIVES: extension - the extension number of the mailbox
             passcode - the passcode number
   RETURNS:  true iff the operation succeeded
   REMARKS:  The operation may fail if the extension number is
             already in use or if there is no space to add another
             mailbox.
*/
{  if (_nused > NMAILBOX) return false;
   int i = locate_mailbox(extension);
   if (i >=0) return false; // duplicate
   _mailbox[_nused].activate(extension, passcode);
   _nused++;
   return true;
}
```

# Design Hints

## Consider Reasonable Generalizations

Every problem is just one instance in a larger range of similar problems. Permute the task that you are modeling in reasonable ways. What features might the next update contain? What features do competing products implement already? Check that these features can be accommodated without radical changes in your design.

## Minimize Coupling Between Classes

A class is coupled with another if there is a relationship (is, has, uses) between them. A class that is not coupled with any other classes contributes nothing to the system and can be dropped. Classes that are coupled with too many other classes are a sign of trouble ahead. The inevitable evolution of the highly coupled class will force changes in the other classes.

Reducing coupling can require major reorganization, discovery of new classes, and reassignment of responsibilities, but this is time well spent. Make every effort to minimize coupling at the design stage. Once you get to the implementation, it is too late to make substantial reductions in coupling.

## Challenge Counts of One

An essential advantage of object-oriented design is that it is just as easy to create multiple objects as it is to create one object. You should double-check all aggregations that specify a count of 1.

Does the word processor really edit just one document? Is there only one window on the screen? Does the mail system really have just one administrator mailbox? Does a message have just one sender? Sometimes, a count of 1 is an integral part of the problem to be solved. More often, it is just a temporary limitation that may need to be lifted later. Make sure that your design can withstand this generalization.

## Split Up Classes with Too Much Responsibility

Sometimes a top-level class such as MailSystem ends up with far too many operations because all commands are simply added to it. Rethink classes with too much responsibility and split them up.

## Eliminate Classes with Too Few Responsibilities

A class with no operations surely is not useful. What would you do with its objects? A class with only one or two operations may be useful. You should convince yourself that there is really no better way to distribute the responsibilities. If another existing class can carry out the task meaningfully, move the operations and eliminate the class.

## Eliminate Unused Responsibilities

Sometimes responsibilities seem natural for a class, but they are never used in the scenario walk-throughs. For example, someone may have suggested that a Mailbox operation "sort messages."

It makes little sense to implement an operation that is unused. It is not even a good idea to promise to implement the operation should there ever be a need for it. That promise may restrict the evolution of the class.

Nevertheless, the fact that an operation can be supported adds confidence that the design is strong and generalizable.

## Reorganize Unrelated Responsibilities

Does your class contain an operation that sticks out like a sore thumb, completely unrelated to the others? Move it to a different class, or add a new class that can handle it.

## Express Repeated Functionality with Inheritance

Is the same responsibility carried out by multiple classes? Check whether you can recognize this commonality by finding a common base class and have the other classes inherit from it.

## Keep Class Responsibilities at a Single Abstraction Level

Every software project exhibits a layering of abstraction levels. At the lowest levels, we have file systems, memory allocation, keyboard and mouse interfaces, and other system services. At the highest levels there are classes that tie together the software system, such as `MailSystem` or `Spreadsheet-Application`.

The responsibilities of a class should stay at one abstraction level. A class `MailUser` that represents a midlevel abstraction should not deal with implementing queues, a low-level responsibility, nor should it be concerned with the initialization of the system, a high-level responsibility.

## Names of Classes and Operations

Class names should be nouns, in the singular form: `Message`, `Mailbox`. Sometimes the noun needs to be prefixed by an adjective or gerund: `ConvexPolygon`, `ReceivingBuffer`. Don't use `Object` in the class name (`MailboxObject`)—it adds no value. Unless you are solving a very generic problem, stay away from generic names such as `Agent`, `Task`, `Item`, `Event`.

Names of operations should be verbs or short sequences of words containing one verb. In the first steps of design, operation names can be longer and informal: "get input from terminal." In the implementation, names should be shortened to one or two words. Take advantage of the added information given by the types of the arguments: "add message" can become `add(Message m)`.

Keep implementation names consistent. Don't mix `get_message` with `give_name`.

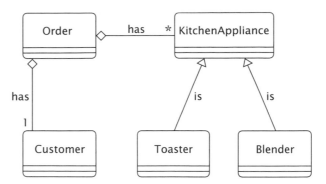

**FIGURE 5.35**  Kitchen appliance classes.

## Do Not Model Unrelated Behavior

It is a common trap to model behavior that is unrelated to the problem to be solved. Suppose you are designing software to process orders for kitchen appliances such as toasters and blenders. If you let the object-oriented design process run amok, you end up with classes Order, Customer, KitchenAppliance, Toaster, and Blender (see Figure 5.35). Clearly Kitchen Appliance is a base class; toasters and blenders are special cases of kitchen appliances, hence derived classes. Every kitchen applicance has a price and a manufacturer. In addition, toasters have a rich set of specialized attributes and behavior (number of slots, a toast operation).

But wait—the kitchen appliance hierarchy is *irrelevant* to our problem, namely to process orders and payments.

Beware of this overdesign trap. Just because you can model something doesn't mean you have to. Model only those aspects of a system that are relevant to your problem.

## Don't Model Unnecessary Aggregation

Use aggregation only if one object serves as a container for other objects, either by interacting with them or by managing an arrangement of them. The MessageQueue class in the mail system example actually manages the messages. Thus, it is a proper container for the messages, and aggregation is appropriate.

Does every gas station have cars? Of course it does. Should you therefore draw a "has" connection between the class GasStation and the class Car? Not necessarily. You should only model the aggregation if the gas station *interacts with* or *manages* car objects in some way. If the gas station does not need to interact with the cars, you should not store the collection of cars with the gas station object.

# 6

# Programming by Contract

As you have seen, the encapsulation features of C++ make it possible to produce dramatically more reliable code than you can produce in C or other
languages that don't monitor data access. The C++ compiler watches so that
no function can modify a data field without permission. Therefore, C++ can
guarantee the integrity of its data. Once we ensure that all constructors of a
class create only objects with valid state and that all mutator operations preserve the valid state, then we can never have invalid objects. Bertrand
Meyer, the pioneering designer of the Eiffel language, uses the metaphor of
a *contract* to describe these guarantees. Constructors promise to turn every
object into a valid state. Mutators promise not to produce invalid objects,
provided all objects are valid at the outset. Consequently, we can guarantee
that all objects are in a good state. No operation needs to waste a lot of time
checking for invalid objects. This chapter explores the ideas surrounding
the concepts of programming by contract.

## Preconditions

Consider a stack of floating-point numbers:

```
class Stack
{
public:
   void push(double);
   double pop();
   bool is_empty() const;
private:
   . . .
};
```

What should happen if a programmer using this class attempts to remove an element from a empty stack?

There are two ways to settle this question. The designer of the stack class may declare this behavior as an error. Users of the stack are plainly forbidden to pop an empty stack. Or, the designer of the stack class may decide to tolerate potential abuses and build in a robust failure mechanism, such as returning a zero value when pop is applied to an empty stack.

[Meyer], p. 115, views operations as agents fulfilling a contract. Contracts between persons or legal entities spell out responsibilities of two partners. The pop operation promises to deliver the correct result when applied to a nonempty stack. For an empty stack, you must read the fine print. Maybe pop promises absolutely nothing when applied to an empty stack; maybe it promises to handle the error gracefully.

Consider the contract you have with your bank. When you write a check that is not covered by the funds in your checking account, what happens? Depending on your agreement with the bank, it may refuse to pay the check, pay it by using money from another account (and charging you a fee), or use its discretion to do either.

As with all contracts, there is a price to pay for added services. Banks charge higher fees for accounts with overdraft protection. Stacks that check first if pop is applied to an empty stack penalize the legitimate user of pop every time—by making an unnecessary check. The important point is that both parties must understand the trade-offs. The terminology of pre- and postconditions serves to formalize the contract between a function and its caller. A precondition is a condition that must be true before the service provider promises to do its part of the bargain. If the precondition is not true and the service is still requested, the provider can choose any action that is convenient for it, no matter how disastrous the outcome may be for the service requester. A postcondition is a condition that the service provider guarantees upon completion. We will discuss postconditions in the next section.

For example, suppose you have a checking account without overdraft protection. A precondition for having your check paid is the presence of sufficient funds in the account. If you violate the precondition, the consequences may range from the uncomfortable (penalty charges) to the disastrous (a conviction for writing bad checks).

Here is an example of a precondition for an operation of a class.

```
class Stack
{
public:
    Stack();
    void push(double);
    double pop();
    bool is_empty() const;
private:
    int _optr;
    vector<double> _data;
};

Stack::Stack()
:  _sptr(0)
{}

double Stack::pop()
// PRECONDITION: !is_empty()
{  _sptr--;
   return _data[_sptr];
}

bool Stack::is_empty() const
{  return _sptr == 0;
}

void Stack::push(double x)
{  if (_sptr < _data.size())
       _data[_sptr] = x;
   else
       _data.push_back(x);
   _sptr++;
}
```

The pop operation makes *no promises* to do anything sensible when you call it on an empty stack. In fact, this particular implementation wrecks the stack and the program containing it. Not only is the return value random junk, but the stack pointer is now negative. As a result, a subsequent call to is_empty incorrectly reports the stack as nonempty, and a subsequent push operation overwrites memory that doesn't belong to the stack.

In this particular case, the precondition is probably not a sensible one. It seems far more reasonable to make a simple check than to risk corrupting data.

Consider another case, the strcpy function from the C library.

```
char* strcpy(char to[], const char from [])
// PRECONDITION: (1) to != 0 and from != 0
// (2) to points to at least strlen(from) + 1 characters
```

The second precondition is familiar to every C programmer. In fact, if you are not 100 percent sure that the `to` array is longer than the `from` string, you must use `strncpy` instead. The first precondition surprises quite a few beginning programmers, who assume that the function is "smart enough" to do nothing if either of the pointers is null.

You can argue about the wisdom of that first precondition—it probably made more sense when C was designed than it does today. The essential point of a precondition is that it needs to be *published* and understood by the party requesting the service.

In practice, the purpose of programming is not to apportion blame but to get the job done. It does not usually pay to write operations with lots of preconditions. Most operations should spend some time making consistency checks and gracefully performing some default action rather than creating real damage. [Koenig] describes a dialog between two programmers in which one asks the other what should happen if a certain condition fails and the other responds, "I don't care—that can never happen." The first programmer then asks whether he can corrupt the entire database file in that case, and the second programmer concedes that he does care after all. Corruption of the entire database is too great a risk to take. Failures that theoretically can never occur *do* happen with distressing regularity in practice.

In a few instances errors are very common, but the error check is also very expensive. Consider, for example, bounds checking of arrays. The "safe" vector template that accompanies this book generates code that checks every array access `a[i]`, in effect generating code

```
if (0 <= i and i < a.size())
  use a[i];
```

This is great for trapping programmer errors, but it is a major performance bottleneck. The vector template in the C++ standard takes the position that it is the caller who must ensure that `i` is within the correct range—indeed, chaos will ensue if it is not. As every programmer knows, memory overwrites and challenging debugging sessions are the consequence of violating the precondition that all subscripts are within the array bounds.

Is the arbitrary corruption of memory an adequate penalty for failing to live up to your contractual obligations? Would you enter a contract that gives you great rewards in most cases but a terrible punishment if you mess up, or would you prefer a different deal that asks less of you but gives you less performance? In real life there is no one answer—some people drive race cars, others sedans. Similarly, programmers must constantly make similar trade-offs between safety and speed. The notion of preconditions is valuable because it makes the trade-off visible and explicit. To use Meyer's metaphor, documented pre- and postconditions are a written agreement and thus superior to implicit understandings or verbal agreements.

# *Postconditions*

Of course, every operation promises to do "the right thing," provided that the precondition was fulfilled when it was called. For example, `Stack::pop` promises to return the most recently pushed element. Such a promise is called a postcondition.

In very simple cases, such as stacks, you can actually write a complete description of these postconditions. If a stack is not full and we push an element on a stack, then calling `pop` retrieves the same element:

```
!s.is_full() { s.push(x); y = s.pop() } x == y
```

Here we use the notation

```
C1 { A1 ; A2 ; ... ; An } C2
```

to mean the following: Provided that the condition `C1` holds, the actions `A1`, `A2`, . . . , `An` are carried out in sequence. Afterward, the condition `C2` holds. If `C1` does not hold, we make no further assertion. The logical conditions `C1` and `C2` cannot involve mutator operations—only accessors and logical comparisons. The actions can involve mutators and assignments.

You can give a complete, logical description of a stack in this fashion. Other data types, such as queues or sets, can be characterized in a similar way (see [Cleaveland], Chapter 13). However, this logical specification does not spell out any implementation strategy, and it is completely silent on the performance aspect of the operations. Many data structures can implement the same abstract data type, with varying efficiency trade-offs. And for more complex data structures, the logic descriptions get very cumbersome. For those reasons, complete specifications have not proven to have much practical use.

What is useful in practice is to spell out partial guarantees. For example, a postcondition of `push` is that afterward the stack is not empty.

```
void Stack::push(double x)
// POSTCONDITION: !is_empty()
{  if (_sptr < _data.size())
      _data[_sptr] = x;
   else
      _data.push_back(x);
   _sptr++;
}
```

Such a postcondition is useful if it *matches the precondition* of another operation.

```
s.push(x);
// now we are guaranteed !is_empty()
. . . (operations not involving s)
// now we need !is_empty()
y = s.pop();
```

As another example, the constructor has a postcondition.

```
Stack::Stack()
// POSTCONDITION: is_empty()
:  _sptr(0)
{}
```

The importance of preconditions cannot be overstated. Preconditions should be comparatively rare, and they need to be clearly advertised when they do exist. On the other hand, you should not go overboard with post-conditions. You may have seen code like this:

```
double sin(double x)
// POSTCONDITION: the return value is the sine of x --DON'T!
```

That comment is absolutely useless. Of course, the postcondition of any operation is that it computes the correct value. You should spell out only postconditions that are true *in addition* to the obvious job of the operation. Here is an example of a postcondition that may be useful to ensure that another part of the code is correct.

```
double sin(double x)
// POSTCONDITION: -1 <= return value <= 1 --MAYBE
```

Here is a more realistic example of such a postcondition: After opening a file stream, the get and put position are set to the beginning of the file.

```
void fstream::open(string name, int flags)
// POSTCONDITION: if !fail(), then tellg() == 0 and tellp() == 0
```

## Class Invariants

A *class invariant* is a logical condition that is true after the completion of every constructor and before and after every operation.

Consider again the `Stack` class, but with the added feature that popping an empty stack returns 0.

```
double Stack::pop()
{   if (_sptr == 0) return 0;
    _sptr--;
    return _data[_sptr];
}
```

This implementation fulfills the following invariant:

```
0 <= _sptr and _sptr <= _data.size()
```

Let us verify the invariant. We need to show the following:

1. At the end of every constructor, the invariant is true.
2. Provided the invariant is true at the beginning of every mutator operation, it is again true when the operation has completed.

We don't worry about accessor operations because they don't change the object state.

As a consequence we know that the invariant must be true upon entry and exit of all operations. The first point above guarantees that no invalid objects can be created. Thus, the first time a mutator is applied, we know the invariant is true at the outset. Thus, the second point guarantees that it is again true when the first mutator operation completes. By the same logic, the second mutator operation must preserve the invariant condition, as must all subsequent operations.

In the case of the stack, the constructor fulfills the invariant because it sets `_sptr` to 0 and `_data` to an empty vector. Next, let us look at `pop`. Because we assume that the invariant is true at the beginning of the operation, we have that

```
0 <= _sptr_in and _sptr_in <= _data_in.size()
```

Here we use the subscript `in` to denote the data field values when the operation starts. If $\_sptr_{in} > 0$, then $\_sptr_{out} = \_sptr_{in} - 1 \geq 0$. If $\_sptr_{in}$ is 0, then $\_sptr_{out} = \_sptr_{in}$. Either way, we have

```
0 <= _sptr_out and _sptr_out <= _data_out.size()
```

Thus the `pop` operation preserves the invariant. For the `push` operation, we have to look a little more closely. If $\_sptr_{in} < \_data_{in}.size()$, then $\_sptr_{out} = \_sptr_{in} + 1 \leq \_data_{in}.size()$. However, if $\_sptr_{in}$ equals _data$_{in}$.size(), then we push back another element. That is, _sptr$_{out}$ = _sptr$_{in}$ + 1 and _data$_{out}$.size() = _data$_{in}$.size() + 1. In either case, we can again conclude that

```
0 <= _sptr_out and _sptr_out <= _data_out.size()
```

Note that we don't need to check the is_empty operation. It is not a mutator, so we know it doesn't modify the data fields.

What benefit do we derive from all this algebra? We can now guarantee that the various vector accesses are always legal. For example,

```
double Stack::pop()
// class invariant: 0 <= _sptr and _sptr <= _data.size()
{   if (_sptr == 0) return 0;
    // logic: 0 < _sptr and _sptr <= _data.size()
    _sptr--;
    // logic: 0 <= _sptr and _sptr < _data.size()
    return _data[_sptr]; // guaranteed to be legal
}
```

(Look carefully at the < and <= signs.)

Working out the invariant had a real benefit: We didn't need to build in a test.

```
double Stack::pop()
{   if (_sptr == 0) return 0;
    _sptr--;
    if (0 <= _sptr and _sptr < _data.size()) // test not needed
        return _data[_sptr];
    else return 0;
}
```

Of course, this is a simple invariant, but it is very typical. Because of the closed nature of a class, you have complete control over all operations that modify the data fields. You can usually guarantee that certain values are within a legal range or that certain pointers are never null. Invariants are the appropriate tool for documenting such guarantees.

We distinguish between interface invariants and implementation invariants. Interface invariants are conditions that involve only the public interface of a class. Implementation invariants involve the details of a particular implementation. Interface invariants are of interest to the class user because they give a behavior guarantee for any object of the class. Implementation invariants can be used by the class implementor to ensure the correctness of the implementation algorithms.

The invariant that we discussed in the stack example was an implementation invariant. The notion of an integer index _sptr is meaningless if the stack is implemented as a linked list.

Interface invariants must be stated in terms of the public interface of a class. For example, an interface invariant of the Date class is that

```
1 <= day() and day() <= 31 and 1 <= month() and month() <= 12
```

This is true for our Date class because the constructor rejects bad dates, and the only mutator operation (advance) always creates valid dates.

Once the invariant is documented, we can rely on the properties of these operations and need not program unnecessary checks. For example, we can safely make a vector lookup:

```
vector<string> german_month_names(12);
. . .
cout << german_month_names[bday.month() - 1];
```

Formulating invariants also prevents you from implementing inappropriate operations. Consider this invariant of the Date class:

```
if month() is 2, 4, 6, 9, or 11, then day() <=30
```

Now suppose we had an operation set_day in the Date class. It would be an inappropriate operation because we could no longer guarantee the invariant. Consider this scenario:

```
Date d(20, 2, 1992);
d.set_day(31); // invariant condition violated
d.set_month(1);
```

After the first mutator, the invariant condition is violated. Of course, after the next operation, the condition is again true. But an invariant must be fulfilled after every class operation. (It can be temporarily violated during the execution of the operation, but it must be restored at the end.) Only then can we guarantee that objects never have a bad state.

Thus we have a choice—drop the invariant and make fewer guarantees about the state of Date objects, or drop the set_day and set_month operations.

Class invariants are meaningful only for classes with constructors. In the absence of a constructor, fields may be initialized with random values, and it is unlikely that any meaningful invariants can be established.

In practice, class invariants are a useful tool but not a complete guarantee against all problems. It is usually difficult to formulate a complete set of interface invariants that uniquely defines the abstract data type. A partial set of conditions that spells out the nonobvious conditions is more helpful to the class user. Similarly, the most useful invariant conditions for the class implementor are those that set out rules for the more subtle implementation aspects. Invariants that guarantee the validity of certain pointer variables or the range of certain index variables are often useful. They form a convenient checklist of conditions that every operation must restore.

## *A Refresher on Loop Invariants*

Before class invariants were known, computer scientists studied *loop invariants*, conditions that were preserved by loops. Although they are not directly related to class invariants, loop invariants can be a useful technique, and we present a short discussion here.

You have probably heard of the "binary search" algorithm and perhaps implemented it yourself. We have a *sorted* array of elements $a[0] \ldots a[n-1]$, that is

$$a[0] \leq a[1] \leq \ldots \leq a[n-1]$$

We are trying to find the position of a value $t$ in the array, that is, the position $p$ such that $a[p]$ equals $t$. If $t$ is not present in the array, then $p$ should be set to $-1$. The algorithm goes as follows. We keep a range that is initially the entire index range $(0 \ldots n-1)$. Then we compare the middle element with $t$ and either discard the top or the bottom half of the range. We continue until either $t$ is found or the range is empty. If $t$ occurs on more than one position, then we can return any one of them.

When you read this description, you are probably confident that you can implement this algorithm without too much trouble. In fact, why don't you give it a try?

Jon Bentley ([Programming Pearls, p. 36]) tells a sobering story. He has assigned this problem in courses at Bell Labs and IBM to *professional programmers*, giving them two hours to implement it in a language of their choice. After two hours, almost all participants would report that they had solved the problem to their satisfaction. This was carried out in several classes with more than 100 programmers. The result: upon close examination, 90 percent of the programs contained bugs. Of course, most of the bugs were off-by-1 errors or bad behavior in boundary cases.

A technique that ensures that a simple function works correctly in all cases would be nice to have. *Loop invariants* can sometimes give such a guarantee. Let us look at a solution of the binary search problem and see how a loop invariant can give us complete confidence that the solution is correct, without the need for any debugging.

```
int binary_search(vector<double> a, double t)
{   int low = 0;
    int high = a.size() - 1;
    while (low <= high)
    {   /* invariant:
            either t is not in a, or it is in a[low]...a[high]
        */
        int mid = (low + high) / 2;
        if (t == a[mid]) return mid;
        else if (t < a[mid]) high = mid - 1;
        else low = mid + 1;
    }
    return -1;
}
```

Notice the comment that states the somewhat complicated *loop invariant*. We will show the following facts about this condition:

1. The condition is true when the loop is first entered.
2. Provided the condition is true at the top of the loop, it is true at the bottom of the loop.

The first part is easy. Because at the outset, `low` is 0 and `high` is `a.size() - 1`, the range is the entire vector. The invariant condition thus is trivially true: if `t` is anywhere in the vector, it must be between `a[0]` and `a[a.size() - 1]`.

Now for the second part. Because the values for `low` and `high` change in the loop, let's label the values at the beginning of the loop as $low_{in}$ and $high_{in}$, the values at the end of the loop as $low_{out}$ and $high_{out}$. There are three possibilities in the loop:

If `t` equals `a[mid]`, then we return `mid`, obviously the correct answer.

If `t < a[mid]`, then $low_{out} = low_{in}$ and $high_{out} = mid - 1$. If `t` is not in a, then the invariant condition remains trivially true. If, however, `t` is in a, then we assume it is somewhere between `a[`$low_{in}$`]` and `a[`$high_{in}$`]`. That is because we assume the invariant to be true whenever we enter the loop. Now we also know that `t < a[mid]`, and because the array elements are sorted, `t` must hence be between `a[`$low_{out}$`]` and `a[mid - 1] = a[`$high_{out}$`]`.

If `t > a[mid]`, then $low_{out} = mid + 1$ and $high_{out} = high_{in}$. Again, if `t` is anywhere in a, we already assume that it is between `a[`$low_{in}$`]` and `a[`$high_{in}$`]`. Now we know it must be between `a[mid + 1] = a[`$low_{out}$`]` and `a[`$high_{out}$`]`.

Thus, we see that the invariant condition is true for $low_{out}$ and $high_{out}$ provided it is true for $low_{in}$ and $high_{in}$.

What good is it? Consider the point at which the loop is exited. There are two ways of exiting the loop. In the first case, we found t and obviously return a good value. In the second case, we exit the loop because low > high. In that case, the invariant condition is still true. That is, either t is not in the array, or it must be between a[low] and a[high]. But the latter range is empty, so we conclude that t was not in the array and we are correct in returning -1.

The loop transforms the settings of low and high into new settings, from $low_{in}$ and $high_{in}$ to $low_{out}$ and $high_{out}$. That transformation preserves the invariant—see Figure 6.1. As a result, we know that the invariant must be true when the loop exits, and with some luck we can deduce the correctness of the algorithm.

We can settle another aspect of this algorithm through the power of invariants. Is the vector access a[mid] always legal? We can show that it is, by analyzing another invariant.

```
int binary_search(vector<double> a, double t)
{   int low = 0;
    int high = a.size() - 1;
    while (low <= high)
    {   /* invariant:
            0 <= low and high < a.size()
        */
        int mid = (low + high) / 2;
```

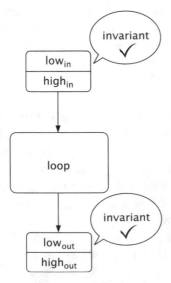

**FIGURE 6.1** Each iteration of the loop transforms values but keeps the invariant valid.

```
        /* note that low <= mid and mid <= high */
        if (t == a[mid]) return mid;
        else if (t < a[mid]) high = mid - 1;
        else low = mid + 1;
    }
    return -1;
}
```

In fact, it is very easy to see that this invariant must be true—at the beginning, 0 equals `low` and `low` can only *increase* in the loop. Similarly, `high` starts out as `a.size() - 1` and only decreases from then on.

Because the average `mid = (low + high) / 2` must lie between low and high, we can thus conclude that

```
0 ≤ low ≤ mid ≤ high < a.size()
```

Hence `a[mid]` is a legal array access. This *must* be true, *even in pathological cases,* for example, if a only has one or two elements.

When computer scientists first discovered these loop invariants, they were very hopeful that computer programs would routinely be proven correct by using invariants systematically. In practice, this has not worked out. As programs get larger, coming up with the invariants becomes harder. Instead of making errors in the program, computer scientists started making errors in the proofs. Nevertheless, invariants are a powerful technique for analyzing limited aspects of code. A few cleverly chosen invariants can often give you more insight and confidence than hours of debugging.

## Testing for Invariants and Conditions in C++

The C++ language supports no constructs to attach logical conditions to classes or operations for automatic checking. We will use conditional compilation and the `assert` facility. Checks against null pointers or range errors take little time to perform. Other invariants, such as the correctness of a date or the sortedness of an array, can be expensive to check. We must therefore have a way of turning checking on for testing and off for production code. (This technique has been described as akin to wearing a life vest while sailing close to the shore and throwing it overboard in the middle of the ocean. True enough, but the life vest is uncomfortable and there is no chance of being rescued anyway when washed overboard in the middle of the ocean.)

The simplest method for conditional check is the `assert` macro defined in the `assert.h` header file. Insert the code

```
assert(condition that should be true)
```

into your code, and if the condition fails, the program exits with an error message that contains the text of the condition, the name of the source file, and the line number in the file. For example,

```
assert(den != 0);
double x = (double) num / den;
```

To test for a class invariant, add a private operation

```
bool Class::check_invariants() const
```

that tests the invariant. As the invariant conditions are refined, they need to be updated only in one location. Then add the line

```
assert(check_invariants());
```

at the end of each constructor and at the end of each mutator operation. You may even wish to avoid generating code for the invariant check if assertion checking is turned off. To achieve that, surround both the declaration and the definition of the `check_invariant()` function with preprocessor directives

```
#ifndef NDEBUG
```

and

```
#endif
```

Similarly, pre- and postconditions of individual operations can be checked by adding `assert` statements at the beginning and end of operations. For example,

```
void Stack::push(double x)
{  assert(!isfull());
   _sptr++;
   _data[_sptr] = x;
   assert(check_invariants());
}
```

# Design Hints

## Typical Interface Invariants

The most common interface invariants are the following:

- Restrictions on state, as observed through accessors
- State change, caused by a mutator
- Relationships between two mutators

The invariant that a date is legal is of the first kind.

```
1 <= d.day() and d.day() <= 31
if month() is 2, 4, 6, 9, or 11, then day () <=30
```

Only accessors are used.

## Typical Implementation Invariants

Implementation invariants make statements about data fields. Common examples are assertions that an index is within certain bounds or that a pointer is not null.

Implementation invariants can spell out the relationships between several data fields. For example, in a linked list we may keep pointers to both a current element and its predecessor. The fields are related by the invariant

```
if _pre != NULL, then _pre->_next = _cur
if _pre == NULL, then _cur == _head
```

This is a subtle but important invariant, and it is well worth checking that it is preserved by each mutator operation.

## Typical Preconditions

A precondition is a condition that the class user guarantees when calling an operation. Preconditions fall into two categories:

- Validity of the arguments of the operation
- Compatibility between object state and the operation

Consider a hypothetical `File` class:

```
class File
{
public:
   void open(string name);
   unsigned char get();
   . . .
};
```

For this class, a precondition for `open` is that `name` corresponds to an existing file. Here we require that the argument of the operation be valid. A precondition for get is that the file has been previously opened. Here we require that the state of the object is not in conflict with the operation.

## Typical Postconditions

A postcondition is a condition that an operation guarantees on completion. Postconditions fall into two categories:

- A statement about the result
- The state of the object upon completion

For example, a postcondition of the get operation on a priority queue is that the returned item be smaller than all others held in the queue. This is a statement about the result.

The push operation of a stack has as postcondition a guarantee about the state of the stack: It is definitely not empty. These postconditions are valuable because they can turn into preconditions to other operations. After a push, we are assured that a pop may be applied to the stack.

## Preconditions Must Be Verifiable

Consider the File class of the earlier section, "Typical Preconditions." Would you want to use it? Consider that the precondition of the open operation is that the file name correspond to an existing file name. Because it is a precondition, the open operation is permitted to take any action if you invoke it with an illegal file name. It may terminate the program or just mess up in some way. Termination of the program (or continuation with flaky behavior) seems like a high price to pay for invoking the operation with an invalid file name.

A precondition is a strong contractual statement. The caller of the operation *must* fulfill it or lose the program. Suppose we are given another function to test whether a file with a certain name exists. Then we could invoke it first, before calling open, and be assured that the operation will succeed.

```
File f;
if (file_exists(filename))
{  f.open(filename);
   . . .
}
```

Not quite. Between the execution of file_exists and open, another process might have removed or renamed the file, causing our program to die.

We conclude that requiring the existence of a file is an *inappropriate* precondition for the open operation because there is no way for the programmer to *guarantee* its validity. We should drop the precondition, allow open to take any file name, and have it return the success or failure of the operation.

```
class File
{
public:
    bool open(string name); // no precondition
    unsigned char get(); // precondition: file open
    . . .
};
```

Contrast that with the precondition for get, namely that the file must be opened. This is objectively verifiable by the class user.

```
if (f.open(filename))
{ unsigned char ch = f.get();
    . . .
}
else
    // don't call get-it may terminate or corrupt your program
```

## Preconditions versus Defensive Programming

The advantage of a precondition is that it allows a more efficient implementation. Because the caller guarantees it, the operation need not spend time to check it. For example, the File::get operation may go right to the file buffer and get the next character without bothering to check whether the file is opened and its file buffer is correctly initialized.

Of course, if get is called on a file that has not been opened, the pointer to the file buffer is invalid, and accessing the file buffer through it either gives random results or causes a processor fault.

The alternative to a precondition is *defensive programming*, allowing the invocation of the operation on objects of any state, with any arguments. Then the operation must spend time checking the validity of the object and all arguments and then proceed only if they are in order.

We recommend the following approach. For infrequent operations, program defensively. The savings of not performing a check are not worth the risk of having the program die. For operations that are carried out frequently, especially in loops, such as putting elements into a container or getting input from a file, preconditions are effective. Formulate preconditions that the class user can verify.

As a class user, try to verify that the preconditions must hold for logical reasons. Monitor them during debugging. Measure the speed-up that results from dropping the check. If it is substantial, consider the remaining risk and make a decision to drop the check or to leave it in place in the release version.

# 7

# Inheritance

In this chapter we discuss the important class relation of *inheritance*. A class (the so-called *derived class*) inherits from another class (the so-called *base class*) if the derived class describes a specialized subset of those objects characterized by the base class. Liskov formulated the following *substitution rule* for inheritance: Any object of the derived class must be usable in place of a base-class object (see [Bar-David], p. 59). For example, a class `Truck` may derive from a class `Vehicle`. All operations that apply to vehicles (accelerating, determining the weight, obtaining the driver) also apply to trucks. But trucks are more specialized because they have operations that are not applicable to vehicles in general. For example, computation of road taxes applies to trucks but not to bicycles.

As we saw in Chapter 3, classes can be modeled in any language supporting structured data types. The support of class operations and encapsulation (private and public features) is a useful benefit of object-oriented language. However, the principal advantage that an object-oriented language offers is the direct support of inheritance as a language construct.

In the first two sections of this chapter, we will introduce a collection of classes for displaying graphics on the computer screen. This may seem a long digression, but it is worth the effort because classes representing graphical shapes lend themselves very well to the study of inheritance. We then learn how this collection of classes can be extended and organized through the inheritance mechanism.

## *Graphics Context*

Consider the task of drawing the words "Hello, World" and surrounding it with a box, as in Figure 7.1.

If you write the program using the Microsoft Win32 API, as explained in [Petzold], the code looks like this. Stock code for `WinMain` and the window procedure are omitted.

```
#include <windows.h>
#include <stdlib.h>
#include <string.h>
void paint (HWND hwnd)
{  PAINTSTRUCT paintstruct;
   BeginPaint(hwnd, &paintstruct);
   HDC hdc = paintstruct.hdc;
   String msg = "Hello, World";
   int msglen = msg.length();
   SIZE sz;
   GetTextExtentPoint32(hdc, msg.c_str(), msglen, &sz);
   int xwidth = sz.cx;
   int yheight = sz.cy;
   int xleft = 10;
```

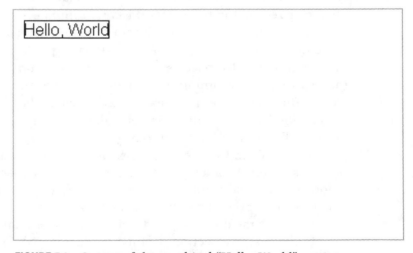

**FIGURE 7.1**  Output of the graphical "Hello, World" program.

```
    int ytop = 10;
    TextOut(hdc, xleft, ytop, msg.c_str(), msglen);
    int xdist = 5;
    int ydist = 5;
    SelectObject(hdc, GetStockObject(EMPTY_BRUSH));
    Rectangle(hdc, xleft - xdist,
        ytop - ydist,
        xleft + xwidth + xdist,
        ytop + yheight + ydist);
    EndPaint(hwnd, &paintstruct);
}
```

Of course, the code to achieve the same results on the Macintosh or with the X Windows system looks completely different. And the code in Java will look different again. Even for Windows 3.1, there are a number of small changes. This is a problem for any book that tries to give code examples for graphics programs.

As a first approximation, we might try to discover functions with common purposes on all graphics systems that we want to support, such as `setFont` and `drawRect`, and implement them as functions with common names. Each of these functions would call one or more functions that are specific to a particular graphics system. To some degree, this can be done. However, different graphics systems manage the graphics state, such as the current font or fill pattern, in different ways. What is required is a combination of data reflecting the current state, together with a collection of functions providing graphics services. As we know, these combinations of graphics operations and graphics states can be represented by classes. Such a class is usually called a *graphics context* or *device context*.

We supply a graphics context class, called `Graphics`, that has been implemented on top of Windows 3.1, Win32, DOS, and X11. Furthermore, the interface for this system has been purposely kept the same as that for the `Graphics` class in Java. (However, only the most important operations in the Java graphics context are supplied.) The code for the `Graphics` class and the various `Shape` example classes are available from the book's Web site.

Here is the interface of the `Graphics` class:

```
class Graphics
{
public:
    void drawLine(int xfrom, int yfrom, int xto, int yto);
    void drawOval(int xleft, int ytop, int xwidth, int yheight);
    void drawRect(int xleft, int ytop, int xwidth, int yheight);
    void fillOval(int xleft, int ytop, int xwidth, int yheight);
    void fillRect(int xleft, int ytop, int xwidth, int yheight);
    void drawString(string s, int xleft, int ybase);
    Color getColor()const;
```

**TABLE 7.1**  Standard Colors

| | | |
|---|---|---|
| black | green | red |
| blue | lightGray | white |
| cyan | magenta | yellow |
| darkGray | orange | |
| gray | pink | |

```
    void setColor(Color c);
    FontMetrics getFontMetrics() const;
    Font getFont() const;
    void setFont(Font font);
private:
    . . .
};
```

The classes `Color`, `Font`, and `FontMetrics` are related classes for color and font handling.

The `setColor` operation takes a parameter of type `Color`. You can either pick one of the 13 standard colors listed in Table 7.1 or specify a color by its red, green, and blue components.

To create a color object, you use the constructor `Color(r, g, b)`, where r is the red value `(0 - 255)`, g is the green value `(0 - 255)`, and b is the blue value `(0 - 255)`. To change the current color, call the `setColor (Color c)` operation.

To create a new font object, call the constructor `Font(name, style, size)`, where name is the font name (e.g., "Times Roman"), style is the style (e.g., `Font.PLAIN`), and size is the point size.

For example,

```
f = new Font("Helvetica", Font.BOLD, 14);
```

To measure a string, we need to use the `FontMetrics` class. The `stringWidth` operation of `FontMetrics` takes a string and returns its width in pixels. The `getAscent()` and `getDescent()` operations return the largest height of the characters in the font above the baseline and the largest depth of the characters in the font below the baseline (see Figure 7.2).

} ascent
} descent

stringWidth

**FIGURE 7.2**  FontMetrics measurements.

The code to display "Hello, World" in a box is then

```
void paint(Graphics& g)
{   string msg = "Hello, World";
    FontMetrics fm = g.getFontMetrics();
    int xleft = 10;
    int ytop = 10;
    int ybase = ytop + fm.getAscent();
    int xwidth = fm.stringWidth(msg);
    int yheight = fm.getAscent() + fm.getDescent();
    g.drawString(msg, xleft, ybase);
    g.drawRect(xleft, ytop, xwidth, yheight);
}
```

You don't need to construct an object of type Graphics. One will be supplied to you in the paint function. Simply place the code for drawing the desired picture in a function

```
paint(Graphics& g)
{
}
```

and link together with the file graphics.cpp in the Practical00 directory. That file contains the main function (or the analog to main called WinMain for Microsoft Windows programs).

## *Graphical Shapes*

### Points

We start with a simple class for points.

```
class Point
{
public:
    Point();
    Point(int x, int y);
    void move(int dx, int dy);
    void scale(Point center, double scalefactor);
    int x() const;
    int y() const;
    void plot(Graphics&) const;
    void print(ostream&) const;
    . . .
private:
    int _x;
```

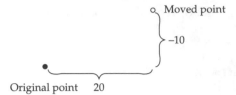

Original point    20

**FIGURE 7.3**   Moving a point.

```
    int _y;
};

inline int Point::x() const { return _x; }
inline int Point::y() const { return _y; }
```

Two operations move points around. The move operation is the simpler of the two. It has two parameters that specify by how much the point should be moved in x- and y- direction. For example, after

```
p.move(200, -10);
```

the point p has moved 200 pixels to the right and 10 pixels up (Figure 7.3).

Of course, the move operation is simple to implement:

```
void Point::move(int dx, int dy)
{   _x += dx;
    _y += dy;
}
```

This operation is most interesting when applied to a bunch of points. Figure 7.4 applies the same move(20, -10) operation to a cloud of points. As you see, the move operation simply shifts all points to a new location.

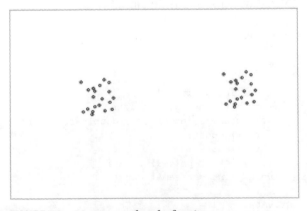

**FIGURE 7.4**   Moving a cloud of points.

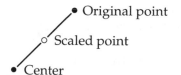

● Original point

○ Scaled point

● Center                    **FIGURE 7.5**   Scaling a point.

The second useful geometric operation that we will implement is scale. The scale operation has two parameters: a center point and a scalefactor. The effect of

```
p.scale(center, 0.5)
```

is to move the point p closer to the point center so that the distance between the two points is cut in half (see Figure 7.5).

The code for the scale function is a little more complex.

```
void Point::scale(Point center, double scalefactor)
{ _x = (int) (_x * scalefactor + center._x * (1 - scalefactor));
  _y = (int) (_y * scalefactor + center._y * (1 - scalefactor));
}
```

However, the algebra is not important for our purposes. You should just understand what this operation performs. Figure 7.6 shows the following:

■ A cloud of points
■ The cloud after applying scale(Point(200, 0), 0.25) to each point
■ The cloud after applying scale(Point(0, 0), 2) to each point

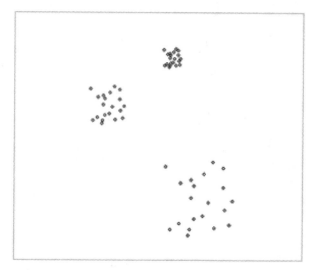

**FIGURE 7.6**   Scaling a cloud of points in two ways.

As you can see, scaling with a factor <1 moves the points closer to the center of the scaling. Scaling with a factor >1 moves them further away.

In the examples that follow, we will frequently use the move and scale operations because they do something interesting with points and other geometric objects.

Here is a simple program that keeps plotting and scaling a point.

```
void paint(Graphics& g)
{   Point p(50,50);
    Point center(200, 200);
    for (int i = 1; i <= 20; i++)
    {   p.plot(g);
        p.scale(center, 0.9);
    }
}
```

Figure 7.7 shows the output of this program.

## Rectangles

We will design a Rectangle class that holds the coordinates for a rectangle given by two corner points, as shown in Figure 7.8. We have two choices for the data layout: The first is to place the points inside the Rectangle class:

```
class Rectangle
{
```

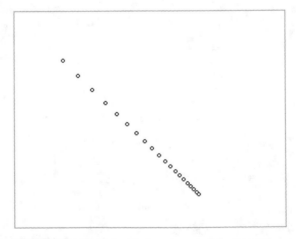

**FIGURE 7.7** Output of the repeated scale operation.

**FIGURE 7.8**  Specifying a rectangle from two corner points.

```
public:
    Rectangle(Point, Point);
    void move(int dx, int dy);
    void scale(Point center, double s);
    void plot(Graphics& g) const;
    . . .
private:
    Point _topleft;
    Point _bottomright;
};
```

The second is to place individual *x*- and *y*-coordinates:

```
class Rectangle
{
public:
    . . .
private:
    int _xleft;
    int _ytop;
    int _xright;
    int _ybottom;
};
```

As a rule of thumb, *always use the highest level of abstraction possible.* This leads us to adopt the first solution.

The Rectangle constructor looks like this:

```
Rectangle::Rectangle(Point p, Point q)
:   _topleft(min(p.x(), q.x()), min(p.y(), q.y())),
    _bottomright(max(p.x(), q.x()), max(p.y(), q.y()))
{}
```

Consider the implementation of the scaling operation. It is easy to compute the scaled rectangle. Just invoke the scale operation on the corner points, and the scaled corners describe the scaled rectangle (Figure 7.9).

```
void Rectangle::scale(Point center, double s)
{   _topleft.scale(center, s);
    _bottomright.scale(center, s);
}
```

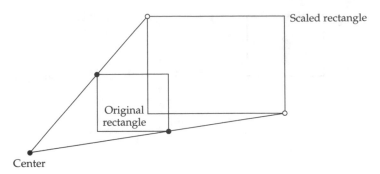

**FIGURE 7.9**  Scaling a rectangle.

This confirms the wisdom of our decision to use the higher abstraction, `Points`, rather than `numbers`, to implement rectangles. `Points` are smart—they knew how to scale themselves. Had we used numbers `_xleft`, `_xright`, `_ytop`, `_ybottom`, then we would have had to reinvent the algebra to compute the coordinates of the scaled rectangle. Instead, we were able to leverage the higher *functionality* of points.

## Polygons

We now turn to a class to display polygons. A polygon is a closed path specified by a set of corner points (Figure 7.10).

We were able to specify a rectangle by giving the corner points in a constructor. But a polygon can have an arbitrary number of corner points. Therefore, we will use the following interface:

```
Polygon q(4); // a quadrangle
q.set_corner(0, Point(130, 120));
q.set_corner(1, Point(95, 125));
q.set_corner(2, Point(90, 95));
q.set_corner(3, Point(120, 80));
```

**FIGURE 7.10**  A polygon.

That is, we supply the constructor only with the number of corners. Each corner point is set separately with the set_corner operation.

The corner points are stored in a vector

```
class Polygon
{
public:
   Polygon(int);
   void set_corner(int i, Point p);
   void move(double dx, double dy);
   void scale(Point center, double s);
   void plot(Graphics& g) const;
   Point corner(int) const;
   . . .
private:
   vector<Point> _corners;
};
```

We supply a constructor

```
Polygon::Polygon(int n)
: _corners(n)
{}
```

and an operation to set a corner.

```
void Polygon::set_corner(int i, Point p)
{  assert(0 <= i && i < _corners.size());
   _corners[i] = p;
}
```

The plot function simply joins adjacent points by a line.

```
void Polygon::plot(Graphics& g) const
{  for (int i = 0; i < _corners.size(); i++)
   {  int j = i + 1;
      if (j == _corners.size()) j = 0;
      g.drawLine(_corners[i].x(), _corners[i].y(),
         _corners[j].x(), _corners[j].y());
   }
}
```

This concludes the preparations that we need to make before we delve into inheritance. We will use the Point, Rectangle, and Polygon classes as the basic building blocks to build more sophisticated classes.

## *Implementing Inheritance*

### Inheritance for Code Reuse

Let us design a class to store triangles (see Figure 7.11).

Rather than replicating all code, we will take advantage of the existing polygon code. We use a new programming paradigm and *inherit* from the Polygon class.

```
class Triangle : public Polygon
{
public:
   Triangle(Point, Point, Point);
};
```

This code means that a triangle is a special case of a polygon. Triangles behave in exactly the same fashion as polygons, except for construction: You construct a triangle from three points.

All operations of polygons (such as plotting or scaling) are automatically applicable to triangles (Figure 7.12).

```
void plot(Graphics& g)
{  Point p(30, 20);
   Point q(5, 25);
   Point r(40, 10);
   Point center(100, 100);
   Triangle t(p, q, r);
   for (int i = 1; i <= 20; i++)
   { t.plot(g);
        // can plot because it is a polygon
     t.scale(center, 0.9);
     // can scale because it is a polygon
   }
}
```

We refer to Triangle as the derived class and to Polygon as the base class. The process of forming a derived class is called *derivation, inheritance,* or *subclassing* (see Figure 7.13).

**FIGURE 7.11** A triangle.

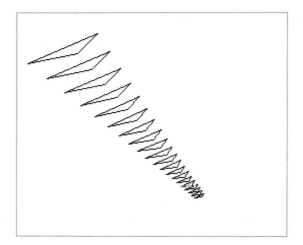

**FIGURE 7.12** Output of the triangle scaling program.

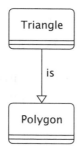

**FIGURE 7.13** Inheritance diagram

When inheriting from a base class, you need to declare only the *difference* between the derived and base classes. Reuse of the base-class operations is automatic.

The keyword `public` in the syntax for inheritance,

```
class Derived : public Base { /* ... */ };
```

is required for technical reasons. It is a common error to omit it. If you do, the compiler will complain about inaccessible base class operations. (If the keyword `public` is omitted, inheritance defaults to private inheritance. Private inheritance is not useful for object-oriented design and only marginally useful in some implementation scenarios. We do not cover it in this book.)

## Constructing Base Classes

We need to supply the code for the `Triangle` constructor:

```
Triangle::Triangle(Point a, Point b, Point c)
: Polygon(3)
{   set_corner(0, a);
    set_corner(1, b);
    set_corner(2, c);
}
```

The : notation is used to call the base-class constructor. Base classes are identified by their *type*, such as `Polygon`.

Compare this constructor with the recently discussed `Rectangle` constructor.

```
Rectangle::Rectangle(Point p, Point q)
: _topleft(p),
  _bottomright(p)
{}
```

Here the : notation is used to call the data field constructors. The data fields are identified by their *name*, such as `_topleft`.

In general, derived-class constructors may need to invoke both base-class constructors and data-field constructors. We will see examples of such constructors later in this chapter.

## Simulating Inheritance

C++ directly supports inheritance as a language construct. It is instructive to see what you must do to simulate the effect of inheritance with traditional means.

Instead of inheriting from `Polygon`, we can use aggregation. The polygon information can be stored in a data field.

```
class A_Triangle
{
public:
    A_Triangle(Point, Point, Point);
    void scale(Point center, double s); // must reimplement
    void plot(Graphics& g) const; // must reimplement
    . . .
private:
    Polygon _polygon;
};
```

The constructor is similar, but, of course, it needs to construct the data field, not the base class. Note that the set_corner functions are now applied to the explicit data field, not to the implicit argument.

```
A_Triangle::A_Triangle(Point a, Point b, Point c)
:  _polygon(3) // instead of Polygon(3)
{  _polygon.set_corner(0, a); // instead of set_corner(0, a)
   _polygon.set_corner(1, b);
   _polygon.set_corner(2, c);
}
```

All operation functions must be recoded to make them available to the new class!

```
void A_Triangle::plot(Graphics& g) const
{  _polygon.plot(g);
}

void A_Triangle::scale(Point center, double s)
{  _polygon.scale(center, s);
}
```

Of course, the recoding is completely trivial. The functions are just reapplied to the polygon object.

Real inheritance makes this recoding unnecessary. That is why inheritance is such a useful mechanism for enhancing an existing class.

## Adding Operations to the Base Class

Suppose we add a print function to Polygon:

```
void Polygon::print(ostream& os) const
{  os << "Polygon " << _corners.size();
   for (int i = 0; i < _corners.size(); i++)
   {  os << " ";
      _corners[i].print(os);
   }
}
```

For example, q.print(cout) prints

```
Polygon 4 (130, 120) (95, 125) (90, 95) (120, 80)
```

The Triangle class picks up this operation automatically. If inheritance is simulated, as in the A_Triangle class, an A_Triangle::print function must be added manually to track the increased functionality.

This is particularly important from a code management point of view. The fact that `Triangle` inherits from `Polygon` indicates that any operation that is applicable to polygons, whether it is implemented today or will be added at a later time, is applicable to triangles. Indeed, if an operation is later added to the `Polygon` class, it is then automatically available to `Triangle`, whereas in the simulation of inheritance the operation would have to be added manually to all simulated derived classes.

## Adding Data in the Derived Class

To display text on the screen, let us start with a simple `Text` class.

```
class Text
{
public:
   Text(Point, string);
   void scale(Point center, double s);
   void move(int dx, int dy);
   void plot(Graphics& g) const;
private:
   Point _start;
   string _text;
};

Text::Text(Point p, string s)
: _start(p),
  _message(s)
{}

void Text::plot(Graphics& g) const
{  gc.drawString(_message, _start.x(), _start.y());
}

void Text::scale(Point center, double s)
{  _start.scale(center, s);
}
```

Here the starting point is the *basepoint* of the string (see Figure 7.14).

This text class is fine for labeling figures, but it does have one problem. The position of the text is changed by the scaling operation, but the size of the characters is not.

**FIGURE 7.14** A Text object.

```
void plot(Graphics& g)
{  Point p(100, 100);
   Text t(p, "Hello");
   Point center(200, 200);
   for (int i = 1; i <= 20; i++)
   {  t.plot(g);
      t.scale(center, 0.9);
   }
}
```

Of course, we could have designed a better `Text` class. But let us take the point of view that the `Text` class exists already and cannot be changed. Perhaps it was written by a third-party vendor, and we don't own the source code. Or suppose it has been used in another application that doesn't require scalable text, and we want to share the code without upsetting that other application. Admittedly, for such a simple class, this is not a big consideration, but you can easily imagine realistic scenarios where you can't or won't change an existing class. Let us fix the deficiency by *deriving* from `Text` to obtain a class whose objects scale properly (see Figure 7.15).

```
class ScalableText : public Text
{
public:
   ScalableText(Point p, string s, int size);
   void plot(Graphics& g) const;
   void scale(Point center, double s);
private:
   double _size; // the font size
};
```

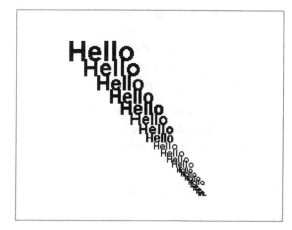

**FIGURE 7.15** Scaling scalable text objects.

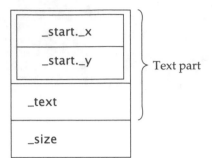

**FIGURE 7.16** Memory layout of a `ScalableText` object.

An object of type `ScalableText` has the data layout shown in Figure 7.16. Here is the constructor:

```
ScalableText::ScalableText(Point p, string s, int size)
: Text(p, s),
  _size(size)
{}
```

Note the construction of the base class (`Text(p, s)`) versus construction of the data field (`_size(size)`).

We will study the implementation of the `ScalableText` operations in the next section.

## Operations in Base and Derived Classes

A derived class `D` can take three actions with respect to an operation `f()` of a base class `B`:

1. The derived class can *inherit* the function `B::f()` without change.
2. The derived class can *replace* `B::f()` by a function `D::f()` performing a different action.
3. The derived class can *extend* `B::f()` by a function `D::f()` calling `B::f()` and performing other tasks.

We have seen an example for the first case: The `Triangle` class inherits the `plot` and `scale` operations without change. We will see examples for the other cases in this section.

### Extending a Base Class Operation

The `scale` operation of the derived class `ScalableText` extends the action of the corresponding base-class operation.

```
void ScalableText::scale(Point center, double s)
{  Text::scale(center, s);
   _size = _size * s;
}
```

The derived-class function calls the base-class function (`Text::scale`) and performs additional work. Note the scope resolution in the call `Text::scale`. This specifies that the `scale` operation of the base class `Text` should be invoked. (Recall that the base-class operation scales the starting point.)

It is easy to forget the `Text::`.

```
void ScalableText::scale(Point center, double s)
{  scale(center, s); // ERROR!
   _size = _size * s;
}
```

If it is omitted, then `scale` refers to the closest scale operation that the compiler can find. Because there is a `ScalableText::scale`, that operation is invoked, not `Text::scale`. The result is an infinite recursion.

## Replacing a Base Class Operation

In C++ a derived-class operation can perform any task whatsoever. There is no requirement that it call the corresponding base-class operation.

For example, we may not be happy that triangles are printed out as

```
Polygon 3 ...
```

In this case, we may wish to replace the base-class operation.

```
class Triangle : public Polygon
{
public:
   Triangle(Point, Point, Point);
   void print(ostream& os) const;
};

void Triangle::print(ostream& os) const
{  os << "Triangle ";
   corner(0).print(os); os << " ";
   corner(1).print(os); os << " ";
   corner(2).print(os);
}
```

Some object-oriented languages (such as the experimental language Beta) do not allow replacement because it alters the character of the derived objects. In such languages all operations must be either inherited or extended.

When you program in an application framework such as the Microsoft Foundation Classes (MFC), you commonly derive new classes from existing ones and redefine operations. You must then know whether your derived-class operation needs to call the base-class operation. The Microsoft Visual C++ compiler has a "wizard" that creates skeleton code that looks like this:

```
void Derived::f()
{  Base::f();
   // add your code here
}
```

The "wizard" knows whether a particular base-class function should be called before your code, after your code, or not at all.

## Access Rights to the Base Class

Consider again this operation:

```
void ScalableText::scale(Point center, double s)
{  Text::scale(center, s);
   _size = _size * s;
}
```

The following code would have saved a function call:

```
void ScalableText::scale(Point center, double s)
{  _start.scale(center, s); // ERROR
   _size = _size * s;
}
```

However, this code does not compile: ScalableText does not have the right to access the _start data field.

This appears to contradict the data layout diagram, according to which ScalableText has three data fields: _start and _text (inherited from Text) and _size (added in ScalableText). Nevertheless, _start and _text are private to Text and not accessible from classes deriving from Text.

It is important not to confuse the *presence* of the data with the *right to access* the data. If the derived class needs to access private base-class data, it must go through the public protocol, just like everyone else. Derived-class operations have no special privileges to access base-class data.

There is no difference between inheritance and aggregation in this regard. Consider the simulated inheritance

```
class A_ScalableText
{
public:
   . . .
private:
   Text _text;
};
```

Then _text._start is not accessible either.

# When Not to Use Inheritance

## Points and Circles

Recall that inheritance is used to model an "is-a" relationship. Use aggregation (data fields) for "has-a" relationships.

For example, each rectangle *has* two corner points. Each triangle *is* a polygon. A car *has* a tire (in fact, it has four, or five counting the spare). A car *is* a vehicle.

It is easy to get this wrong. For example, a popular C++ tutorial derives Circle from Point:

```
class Circle : public Point // DON'T
{
public:
   void plot(Graphics& g) const;
   void move(int dx, int dy);
   void scale(Point c, double s);
   . . .
private:
   int _radius;
};
```

This does little good—only one of the operations of Point (namely move) is applicable to Circle. Nothing of value is inherited, and, except for move, all operations need to be coded again. A circle *has* a center point—it isn't a point.

```
class Circle
{
public:
   void plot(Graphics& g) const;
   void move(int dx, int dy);
```

```
    void scale(Point c, double s);
    . . .
private:
    Point _center; // OK
    int _radius;
    . . .
};
```

The same tutorial goes on to derive `Rectangle` from `Point`. That doesn't work any better. In fact, it is downright weird.

```
class Rectangle : public Point // DON'T
{
public:
    void plot(Graphics& g) const;
    . . .
private:
    Point _other;
};
```

One of the corner points is stored in the base class; the other is a data field. None of the operations can be inherited. The implementations of the operations look very strange because of the asymmetry between the point stored in the base class and the point stored as a data field:

```
void Rectangle::move(int dx, int dy)
{   Point::move(dx, dy);
    _other.move(dx, dy);
}
```

## Lists and Stacks

Consider a linked list class with the following interface:

```
class List
{
public:
    List(); // makes an empty list
    void insert_head(int x); // insert at head
    int remove_head(); // remove from head
    void insert_tail(int x); // insert at tail
    int remove_tail(); // remove from tail
    int head() const; // return head
    int tail() const; // return tail
    int length() const; // number of links
    . . .
private:
    . . .
};
```

Some authors recommend using the linked list as the base class for a Stack class:

```
class Stack : public List // DON'T
{
public:
   void push(int x);
   int pop();
   bool is_empty() const;
};


void Stack::push(int x) { insert_head(x); }


int Stack::pop() { return remove_head(); }


bool Stack::is_empty() const { return length() == 0; }
```

This is not a good idea. A stack isn't a special case of a list. Some things you can do to a list make no sense for a stack. When using inheritance, the stack class inherits *all* operations of the list class, whether appropriate or not. The code

```
Stack s;
s.push(x);
s.insert_tail(y);
```

is legal but obviously makes no sense for a stack. The appropriate solution is to use aggregation, not inheritance.

```
class Stack
{
public:
   void push(int x);
   int pop();
   bool is_empty() const;
private:
   List _list;
};


void Stack::push(int x) { _list.insert_head(x); }


int Stack::pop() { _return _list.remove_head(); }


bool Stack::is_empty() const { return _list.length() == 0; }
```

## Students, Professors, and Staff

Here is an example from [Wiener and Pinson](for consistency, we replaced `char*` pointers with `string` objects). The purpose of this example is to model students, faculty, and staff at a university, presumably for a database application.

```
class DataRec
{  . . .
   string _lastname;
   string _firstname;
   string _street;
   string _city;
   string _state;
   string _zip;
};

class Student : public DataRec
{  . . .
   string _major;
   int _id_number;
   int _level;
};

class Professor : public DataRec
{  . . .
   string _dept;
   float _salary;
};

class Staff : public Professor
{  . . .
   float _hourly_wage;
};
```

Figure 7.17 shows the class relationships.

There are some real problems with this design:

■ Is a student or a professor a `DataRec`? Hardly. A student *has* a name and an address.

■ Is a secretary a special case of `Professor`? Hardly. Just because `Staff` can inherit the `_dept` field doesn't mean it should derive from `Professor`. And what good are the two fields `_salary` and `_hourly_wage` in `Staff`?

Here is a possible remedy.

■ The `DataRec` class seems artificial. Having two classes, `Name` and `Address`, is clearer.

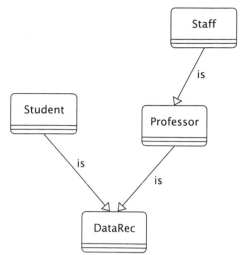

**FIGURE 7.17** Diagram for university classes.

■ Professors and staff members are both employees. A base-class `Employee` captures the common elements, such as the department. But professors are salaried employees, staff are not. (Admittedly, this is not realistic, but we are fixing the design, not the analysis.)

■ Students and employees are persons. Each person has a name and address.

This leads us to the classes and relationships shown in Figure 7.18.

```
class Name
{  . . .
   string _lastname;
   string _firstname;
};


class Address
{  . . .
   string _street;
   string _city;
   string _state;
   string _zip;
};


class Person
{  . . .
   Name _name;
   Address _address;
};
```

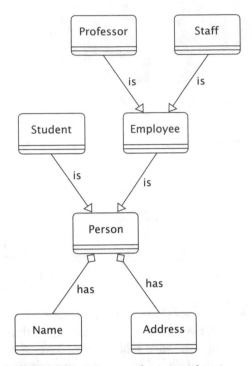

**FIGURE 7.18** Diagram for revised university classes.

```
class Employee : public Person
{  . . .
   string _dept;
};

class Staff : public Employee
{  . . .
   float _hourly_wage;
};

class Student : public Person
{  . . .
   string _major;
   int _id_number;
   int _level;
};

class Professor : public Employee
{  . . .
   float _salary;
};
```

## *Subobjects and Subclasses*

Each car *has* a motor. An individual motor is therefore a subobject of an individual car, as shown in Figure 7.19. We model this as aggregation.

```
class Car
{ . . .
private:
   Motor _motor;
};
```

Each car *is* a vehicle; in other words, the class of cars is a *subclass* of the class of vehicles, as shown in Figure 7.20. We model this subset relationship as inheritance:

```
class Car : public Vehicle
```

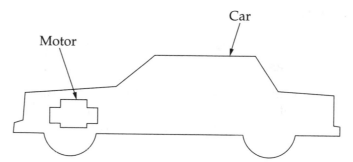

**FIGURE 7.19**   Aggregation means object containment.

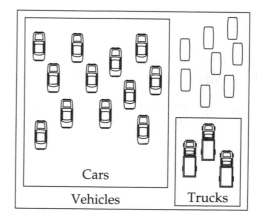

**FIGURE 7.20**   Inheritance means class containment.

Sometimes differentiating between "is-a" and "has-a" relationships is complicated by the language we use. We usually talk about objects when we mean classes, saying "*a* car" when we mean "*each* car" or the class of all cars.

Note that we look for the "is-a" relationship only between two *classes*. For example, "Chevrolet is a car" means that every Chevrolet is a car. That is a relationship between classes (the class of Chevrolets and the class of cars). But "Chevrolet is a division of General Motors" is a relationship between an object (the Chevrolet division) and a class (the divisions of General Motors).

Class derivation is often referred to as *subclassing*. Beginners are sometimes confused by that term because *objects* get *bigger* (or at least stay the same size) when performing subclassing. The "sub" prefix expresses the fact that the subclass models a smaller *collection* of objects. These more specialized objects are fewer in number but need a richer state to perform their operations and hence have a larger size.

# Design Hints

## Place Common Operations and Fields into the Base Class

Consider a class `Vehicle` with derived classes `Car` and `Truck`. Suppose we simulate cars and trucks moving along a road. Position, speed, and acceleration are common to cars and trucks, indeed all vehicles, and should be placed in the base class.

Consider the operation `update_position`, which computes the position after a time interval from the current position, speed, and acceleration. The laws of physics dictate that $s(t + \Delta t) = s(t) + v\Delta t + \frac{1}{2}a\,(\Delta t)^2$, independent of the kind of vehicle. Hence, this operation can be placed in the base class.

## Use Fields for Variations in State, Operations for Variations in Behavior

Suppose trucks have a maximum legal speed of 55 miles per hour, but cars may drive up to 65 miles per hour. Do not define operations this way:

```
double Car::max_speed() const { return 65; } // DON'T
double Truck::max_speed() const { return 55; } // DON'T
```

Instead, add a field `_max_speed` to `Vehicle` and a `Vehicle` accessor operation reporting its value. Set the field in the constructors of `Car` and `Truck`.

Reserve operations for variations in *behavior*. For example, the method for computing road tolls may differ for cars (with a charge per passenger) and trucks (with a charge depending on weight). Both `Car` and `Truck` need to define a `road_toll` operation.

## Derived-Class Operations Must Preserve Base-Class Invariants

An operation of a derived class must not put an object in a state that violates an invariant of the base class.

Here is an example: Consider the `Message` class holding an electronic mail message. Let `Message::lines()` compute the number of lines in the message by counting newline characters in the message text. A class `EncryptedMessage` derives from `Message`. Ignoring 2,000 years of better algorithms, we encrypt with the method known to Caesar, by adding a fixed number to each character.

```
string encrypt(string s, char key)
{   string r = s;
    for (int i = 0; i < s.length(); i++) r[i] += key;
    return r;
}
```

For example, `encrypt(Hello, 8)` is "Pmttw". The original string is retrieved with a key of `-8`. The constructor of `EncryptedMessage` first encrypts the string, then passes it to the `Message` constructor. The `Encrypt-edMessage::play` function first asks the recipient for the key, on which the sender and recipient presumably agreed. It then decrypts and displays the message.

The inherited `lines` operation produces nonsense results for encrypted messages because newline characters are no longer recognizable. The derived class has failed to preserve a subtle invariant of the base class, namely that newline characters in the message text denote line terminators.

It is actually difficult to come up with an example for this problem if all fields of the base class are private and all base-class operations preserve the class invariants. As long as the derived class must use the public interface of the base class, it has no better chance of violating the class invariant than any other client of the base class.

However, some programmers do access `protected` base-class data fields from the derived class. (See Chapter 11 for a discussion of the `pro-tected` attribute.) It is then important to ensure that the derived-class operations preserve the base-class invariants.

## Derived Classes Must Be Preserved
## by Inherited Operations

The objects of a derived class form a subset of the objects of the base class. The operations that the derived class inherits from the base class must map that subset into itself. In other words, the derived class must be closed under the inherited operations. If not, one or more operations transform derived-class objects into invalid objects. In that case, the derived class needs to redefine the offending base-class operations, or else we must conclude that inheritance is not an appropriate relationship for the classes involved.

Consider a class `Filename` deriving from `string`, describing a DOS file name. A DOS file name is a string containing a name, with up to eight characters, and an optional extension, with up to three characters, as in whatnot.cpp. Because `Filename` derives from `string`, any `string` operation can be applied to a `Filename` object. But there are plenty of `string` operations that, when applied to a `Filename`, yield a string that is not a legal file name. Just append more than 12 characters, or insert spaces or newlines. This shows that inheritance from `string` is not appropriate for the `Filename` class. Instead, `Filename` should use aggregation to gain a `string` field and define only those class operations that make sense for manipulating file names.

**8**

# Polymorphism

## *Conversion Between Base and Derived-Class Objects*

For plotting bar charts, we would like to display rectangles that are filled with a color, like the one shown in Figure 8.1. We will derive from the existing `Rectangle` class:

```
class FilledRect : public Rectangle
{
public:
   FilledRect(Point, Point, Color);
   void plot(Graphics& g) const;
private:
   Color _color;
};
```

`Color` is a class defined in the simple graphics package accompanying this book. A number of predefined colors (such as `Color::red`) are included; they should be self-explanatory.

Here is code for a simple bar chart, shown in Figure 8.2.

```
FilledRect rect1(Point(10, 70), Point(20, 20),
   Color::red);
Rectangle rect2(Point(20, 70), Point(30, 10));
FilledRect rect3(Point(30, 70), Point(40, 30),
   Color::blue);
Rectangle rect4(Point(5, 5), Point(45, 75));

rect1.plot(g);
rect2.plot(g);
rect3.plot(g);
rect4.plot(g);
```

This code isn't terribly useful. In a practical application the number and height of the bars vary at run time and are not known at compile time. In the next sections we will see how to write a program that can display an arbitrary mix of rectangles and filled rectangles.

Figure 8.3 shows the data layouts in a `FilledRect` object and a plain `Rectangle` object. Each `FilledRect` object inherits the `_topleft` and `_bottomright` fields from `Rectangle` and adds a `_color` field.

Note that derived-class objects have as least as many data items as objects from the base class because fields can only be added, not taken away, in the derivation process.

A derived-class object can be assigned to a base-class object. However, because the base-class object has fewer fields, some information is lost during such an assignment.

**FIGURE 8.1**   A filled rectangle.

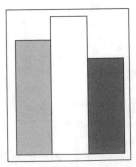

**FIGURE 8.2**   A bar chart.

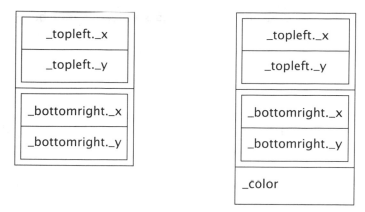

**FIGURE 8.3** Memory layout of base-class and derived-class objects.

```
FilledRect d(tl, br, Color::blue);
Rectangle b = d; // OK, but information lost
b.plot(g); // plots as Rectangle only
```

This information loss is often described as "slicing away" the derived class information (see Figure 8.4).

A derived-class object can be passed as an argument to a function that expects a base-class object. Because the function argument is a variable that can hold only base-class information, the additional fields are sliced away.

```
void plot(Rectangle r) { r.plot(g); }
FilledRect d(tl, br, Color::blue);
plot(d); // plots as Rectangle only
```

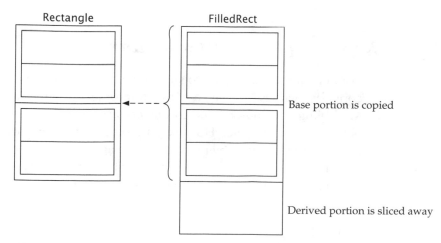

**FIGURE 8.4** Assignment from derived to base class.

Conversely, a base-class object cannot be assigned to a derived-class object.

```
Rectangle b(tl, br);
FilledRect d = b; // ERROR
```

The reason is clear: The derived-class object has more fields than the base-class object, and it is not obvious how the fields should be set.

It is common to have a mix of objects—some of the base class and some of a derived class. Storing such a collection is a problem. A simple array does not suffice. Suppose we use an array of base-class objects:

```
vector<Rectangle> rects(4);
rects[0] = FilledRect(Point(10, 70), Point(20,20),
   Color::red);
rects[1] = Rectangle(Point(20,70), Point(30,10);
rects[2] = FilledRect(Point(30,70), Point(40,30),
   Color::blue);
rects[3] = Rectangle(Point(5,5), Point(45,75));
for (int i = 0; i < rects.size(); i++)
   rects[i].plot(g);
```

This code is not useful. All objects are truncated to the base information only.

Conversely, you cannot use a vector of derived-class objects. In general, there may not be a unique derived class, and at any rate, base-class objects cannot be stored in derived-class vector entries.

We will see in the next section how this problem can be overcome by storing pointers to objects instead.

## A Quick Refresher on Pointer Syntax

Pointers are a mechanism to share ownership of objects. In C++, objects are copied as values. That is, a copy of an object has its own distinct identity. Modifying the copy has no influence on the original. In many cases, this behavior is desirable. However, in some situations objects need to be inspected or changed by more than one agent.

For any type X, there is an associated pointer type X*. For example, pointers of type Employee* are used for accessing Employee objects. Pointer variables are defined like this:

```
Employee* pe;
```

Actually, if you are a C programmer, you may be surprised to see the `*` grouped with the `Employee`, not the `pe`. The designers of the C language were proponents of the "declare it as you use it" concept. If `pe` is an `Employee` pointer, then `*pe` is an `Employee` object. The definition

```
Employee *pe;
```

was literally meant to read "pe is a thing such that `*pe` is an employee". That logic gave us a charming syntax for encrypting pointer definitions. For example,

```
int (*p) [10];
```

means "p is a thing such that `*p` is a thing to which you can apply `[n]` (with $n < 10$) and get an `int`". That is, `p` is a pointer to an array of 10 integers. We leave it to the reader to figure out how to define an array of 10 such pointers, or what

```
void (*p[10](int));
```

means. These make great questions for job interviews.

Today we know that "declare it as you use it" is a programmer-hostile concept. It is better to define variables by clearly *separating* the *type* and the *name* of the variable. In the case of a simple pointer definition, this is achieved simply by sliding the `*` to the left:

```
Employee *pe; // C style
Employee* pe; // preferred C++ style
```

Of course, the compiler doesn't care—you could omit all spaces or add more white space:

```
Employee*pe;
Employee
*
pf
;
```

The only pitfall occurs if two pointer variables are defined together. The definition

```
Employee* pe, pf; // DON'T
```

does not do what the code suggests—pe is a pointer, pf is an employee. In practice, this is not usually a problem because each variable ought to be initialized anyway.

```
Employee* pe = ...;
Employee* pf = ...;
```

For complex pointer types, you can simplify the syntax by using typedef.

There are three methods for obtaining pointer values. The & operator returns a pointer to an existing object; the new operator creates an object on the heap and returns a pointer to it; and the value NULL (or 0) denotes a pointer value that currently points to no object.

```
Employee joe("Joe Isuzu");
Employee* pj = &joe;
Employee* ph = new Employee("Harry Hacker");
Employee* pn = NULL;
```

Many C++ programmers simply write 0, not NULL, to indicate a null pointer. They both mean the same thing, of course. In fact, NULL is #defined as 0. Actually, it makes a lot of sense to stick to NULL because it carries more information for the human reader.

Storage obtained from the heap must be recycled, by invoking the delete operator, when it is no longer used.

```
delete ph;
```

The unary * operator transforms a pointer into the value to which it points.

```
Employee e = *ph;
```

This transformation is called *dereferencing* the pointer. Applying * to a NULL pointer or an uninitialized pointer has results that are random, disastrous, or both.

By copying a pointer, you gain two access paths to the same object.

```
Employee* p = new Employee("Harry Hacker");
Employee* q = p;
(*p).set_salary(40000); // sets Harry Hacker's salary
(*q).raise_salary(.10); // raises Harry Hacker's salary
```

The parentheses in the function call

```
(*p).f();
```

are necessary because the member access operator (.) binds more strongly than the pointer-dereferencing operator (*). That implicitly puts *p.f() in parentheses as *(p.f()), which is an error: p is a pointer, not a structure, and the "." operator cannot be applied.

Because pointers to class objects are so common, and because expressions like (*p)._x and (*p).f() are cumbersome to write and read, C++ has another operator, -> ("dereference and access member"). The code

```
p->_x
```

performs the same operation as (*p)._x, and

```
p->f()
```

is equivalent to (*p).f().

Many programmers initially find that the -> operator looks strange when used to invoke an operation.

```
Employee p = new Employee("Harry Hacker");
p->set_salary(40000); // sets Harry Hacker's salary
```

It somehow looks as if p pointed to the set_salary function. You should not think of -> as having any special "points to" meaning. When used with a function, -> simply calls the function with the implicit argument *p and the explicit argument 40000.

Other languages, such as Pascal, do not have the -> operator because they do not need it. In Pascal, pointer dereferencing (^) is a *postfix* operator, and p^.x accesses a member without the need for additional parentheses. This is a much more sensible syntax.

## Conversion Between Base-Class and Derived-Class Pointers

In C++ a pointer to a derived-class object can be converted to a base-class pointer:

```
FilledRect* pd =
   new FilledRect(tl, br, Color::blue);
Rectangle* pb = pd;
```

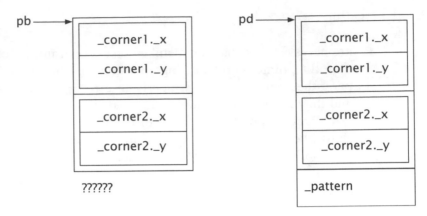

**FIGURE 8.5** Pointers to base and derived-class objects.

The memory layout, shown in Figure 8.5, makes it clear why this works. The base-class pointer is used only to access fields that are present in the base class. Those fields are also present in the derived class, in the same locations. The fact that there are other fields beyond is of no interest when using the base-class pointer.

This explains why operations can be inherited without recoding them. The base-class operation receives a pointer to a base-class object as its implicit argument, but it can equally well receive a derived-class pointer instead. For example, if the scale operation of Rectangle is called with the address of a FilledRect object, it simply transforms the fields in the Rectangle portion and leaves the others alone.

It is possible to convert a base-class pointer to a derived-class pointer. Of course, this makes sense only if it originated as a pointer to that derived class. Because of the inherent danger, such conversions always require a cast:

```
FilledRect*pd = ...;
Rectangle*pb = pd;
// ...
FilledRect*pe = static_cast<FilledRect*>(pb);
    // OK, because we remember
```

The cast mechanism forces the compiler to change the pointer type (but not the pointer value), although it is not necessarily safe to do so. Casts cannot always be avoided, but their use should be minimized. The results of dereferencing an improperly cast pointer are undefined and usually disastrous.

C programmers will find the syntax of the cast strange. In C, the syntax is

```
FilledRect*pe = (FilledRect*) (pb);
```

In C++, the (...) cast notation is slated for extinction. C++ provides four different cast operators: `static_cast`, `dynamic_cast`, `const_cast`, and `reinterpret_cast`. The `static_cast` operator is used to convert from one type to another where the conversion is portable (although not necessarily safe). The `dynamic_cast` operator is a safe cast that we will study in Chapter 10. Use `const_cast` to "cast away constness" (see Chapter 10). Finally, `reinterpret_cast` is used for nonportable casts such as conversions between numbers and pointers.

Pointers offer us a solution to the problem of storing a collection of related objects. While *objects* of base and derived classes may have different sizes, *pointers* to them have the same size. This is an important consideration that frequently comes up in C++ programs.

The following loop builds a vector of pointers and calls the plot function for each vector element.

```
vector<Rectangle*> rects(4); // a vector of pointers
rects[0] = new FilledRect(Point(10, 70), Point(20, 20),
   Color::red);
rects[1] = new Rectangle(Point(20, 70), Point(30, 10));
rects[2] = new FilledRect(Point(30, 70), Point(40, 30),
   Color::blue);
rects[3] = new Rectangle(Point(5, 5), Point(45, 75));
for (int i = 0; i < rects.size(); i++)
   rects[i]->plot(g);
```

Unfortunately, that code doesn't work. All rectangles come out plain (see Figure 8.6). The compiler translates the call `rects[i]->plot(g)` into a call to `Rectangle::plot` because the *static* (compile-time) type of `rects[i]` is `Rectangle*`.

We would like to select the appropriate plot function according to the *dynamic* (run-time) type of each `rects[i]`. In C++, this is possible by mak-

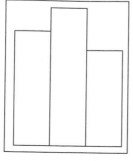

**FIGURE 8.6**   The fill colors are not plotted.

ing the `plot` function into a *virtual* function. Virtual functions are discussed in the next section.

# Dynamic Binding

## Static and Dynamic Binding

To enable the selection of the correct version of `plot` at run time, we make `plot` a *virtual* function. The compiler translates a virtual-function call into code that selects the correct operation at run time, depending on the actual type of the object making the call.

For example, if `plot` is a virtual function, the code

```
rects[i]->plot(g);
```

will call the correct version of `plot`, either `Rectangle::plot` or `Filled-Rect::plot`, depending on the actual contents of `rects[i]` for various values of `i`.

This call mechanism is more complex than a regular function call. It is referred to as *dynamic binding* or *dynamic dispatch*. The regular function call mechanism is called *static binding* because the actual operation to be executed is completely determined at compile time.

Static binding depends on the type of the *pointer* that invokes the operation. Dynamic binding depends on the type of the object. For example, in the call `rects[i]->plot(g)`, the type of `rects[i]` is `Rectangle*`. If `plot` is a nonvirtual operation, it is bound statically and `Rectangle::plot` is invoked. If `plot` is a virtual operation, then either `Rectangle::plot` or `FilledRect::plot` is invoked, depending on the object to which `rects[i]` points.

## Declaring Virtual Functions

To enable dynamic binding, the operation must be declared as `virtual` in the base class.

```
class Rectangle
{
public:
    Rectangle(Point, Point);
    virtual void plot(Graphics&) const;
    . . .
};
```

The keyword `virtual` is not replicated in the function definition.

```
void Rectangle::plot(Graphics& g) const
{   int xwidth = _bottomright.x() - _topleft.x();
    int yheight = _bottomright.y() - _topleft.y();
    g.drawRect(_topleft.x(), _topleft.y(),
        xwidth, yheight);
}
```

In the derived class, the keyword `virtual` is optional. It is, however, considered good style to provide the keyword for the benefit of the human reader.

```
class FilledRect : public Rectangle
{
public:
    FilledRect(Point, Point, Color);
    virtual void plot(Graphics& g) const;
    . . .
};
```

Once a function is defined as virtual, it remains virtual in all derived classes.

## Recognizing Dynamic Binding

Because C++ uses the same syntax for static and dynamic binding, it takes some effort for the compiler and, more importantly, the human reader to find out which mechanism is used for a particular invocation of an operation.

If an *object* invokes an operation, the call is always statically bound.

```
Rectangle r;
r.plot(g); // static binding, calls Rectangle::plot
```

If a *pointer* invokes an operation, the binding depends on the nature of the operation. If the operation has been declared as `virtual`, then the binding is dynamic. Otherwise the binding is static. In the following example, assume that `scale` is not virtual:

```
Rectangle* r;
r->plot(g);
    // dynamic binding, calls Rectangle::plot or FilledRect::plot
r->scale(p, 0.9); // static binding, calls Rectangle::scale
```

If a virtual function is invoked on the *implicit argument* of a class operation, the binding is dynamic. Consider this example:

```
class Window
{
public:
   virtual void paint(Graphics& g, Rectangle r);
      // repaint the part of the window inside r
   void scroll(int dx, int dy);
   Rectangle size() const;
   . . .
};

void Window::scroll(int dx, int dy)
{ . . .
   if (dy > 0)
   { // scroll window contents
      Rectangle s = size(); // static binding
      Point p = s.topleft();
      Rectangle r(p, Point(s.bottomright().x(), p.y() + dy));
      paint(g, r); // dynamic binding
   }
   else
      . . .
}
```

Note the call `paint(g, r)`. This invokes the virtual paint function. If the object invoking `scroll` is a plain `Window`, then `Window::paint` is called. But suppose that `GraphWindow` is derived from `Window` and inherits `Window::scroll`. Then the call

```
GraphWindow gw;
gw.scroll(0, dy); // static binding, calls Window::scroll
```

invokes `GraphWindow::paint` (see Figure 8.7).

Calling a virtual function inside any operation makes that operation more flexible. A part of its code adapts itself to the actual type of the calling

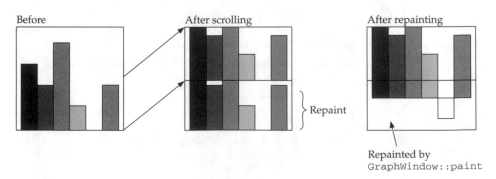

**FIGURE 8.7** Scrolling and repainting a window.

object. Whether the operation itself is virtual is immaterial. This is a powerful concept: It allows the base class to implement a general mechanism. The derived class merely needs to override specific subtasks, such as painting, that the base class cannot carry out.

To summarize, nonvirtual functions are always statically bound. Virtual functions are statically bound when they are invoked on an object and dynamically bound when they are invoked on a pointer or the implicit argument of an operation.

Unfortunately, finding out whether an operation has been declared as virtual can be tedious. Consider the following class:

```
class GraphWindow : public ChildWindow
{
public:
    void paint(Graphics& g, Rectangle r);
    . . .
};
```

Is `paint` a virtual function? Good coding style suggests that each redefinition of a virtual function must be tagged as virtual. But the C++ language does not require it, and not everyone follows the precepts of good style. The only way to find out for sure is to look at the parent class `ChildWindow`, its parent class `FrameWindow`, and its parent class `Window` to see whether any of them also defines `paint`, and if so, whether any of those definitions is tagged `virtual`. Only if no virtual ancestor is found anywhere can we be assured that `paint` is not a virtual function. This search process is less tedious if your compiler has a *browser,* a tool you can use to inspect the class hierarchy visually.

# *Polymorphism*

## Heterogeneous Collections

For a real chart we also want to add text, lines, bitmaps, or other graphical elements.

We would envision some code that builds up the elements of the chart in a vector. The chart can then be plotted with the code

```
for (int i = 0; i < rects.size(); i++)
    rects[i]->plot(g);
```

scaled to a different size with the code

```
for (int i = 0; i < rects.size(); i++)
   rects[i]->scale(c, 0.5);
```

and saved to disk with the code

```
ofstream of("chart.dat");
for (int i = 0; i < rects.size(); i++)
   rects[i]->print(of);
```

But what is the type of rects[i]? Its type needs to be a pointer to a class that supports virtual functions plot, scale, and print. No such type currently exists in our system, and we must introduce a new type that is the *lowest common denominator* of the objects we wish to display, scale, and save. We will call it a Shape.

Here is the definition for the Shape class.

```
class Point; // forward declaration
class Shape
{
public:
   virtual void plot(Graphics& g) const;
   virtual void print(ostream& os) const;
   virtual void scale(Point center, double s);
   virtual void move(int x, int y);
};
```

All other Shape classes are derived from it:

```
class Point : public Shape { ... };
class Rectangle : public Shape { ... };
class FilledRect : public Rectangle { ... };
```

The complete inheritance tree appears in Figure 8.8. Now we may store and manipulate our chart as a collection of Shape pointers:

```
vector<Shape*> shapes;
// construct chart
for (int i = 0; i < shapes.size(); i++)
   shapes[i]->plot(g);
```

The shapes vector is called a *heterogeneous collection* because it collects objects of different types. In contrast, a vector<Employee> collection is homogeneous. All elements are of the same type Employee.

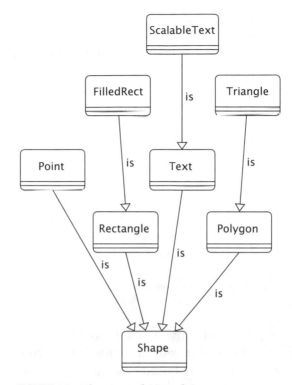

**FIGURE 8.8**   The Shape hierarchy.

## Forms of Polymorphism

The plot function in this code is an example for a *polymorphic* function. "Polymorphic" literally means "of multiple shapes." A polymorphic function is one that can result in different actions depending on context.

In C++, a function can be polymorphic for three different reasons:

- The same function name may be overloaded to denote several actual functions, leaving the compiler to pick the correct one. This is referred to as *overloading* or, occasionally, as *ad hoc* polymorphism.
- The name of an operation in a parameterized class, such as push_back in the vector tempate, stands for different actual functions in instantiated types, such as vector<Employee> or vector<Shape*>. Again, the compiler locates the correct version. Some authors refer to this process as *parameterized* polymorphism.
- Most importantly for object-oriented programming, a virtual function call can invoke any number of actual functions, but the actual selection occurs as the program runs. This is called *pure* polymorphism. In object-oriented programming, most people mean pure polymorphism when they talk about polymorphism.

## *Abstract Base Classes*

Consider the complete definition of the Shape class.

```
class Shape
{
public:
    virtual void plot(Graphics& g) const;
    virtual void print(ostream& os) const;
    virtual void scale(Point center, double s);
    virtual void move(int x, int y);
};
```

The Shape class has *no data fields* because it has no data in common with all derived classes.

The operations do nothing at all. Here is the plot operation.

```
void Shape::plot(Graphics&) const
{}
```

After all, what could it plot? (Note the syntax trick: When the name of a function argument is omitted, as with Graphics&, the compiler doesn't warn about the unused function argument.)

All Shape* pointers that are generated in the program actually point to real shapes, such as rectangles and text. The base-class Shape is only a unifying construction. The chart-drawing program is not expected ever to allocate actual shapes; in fact, such an allocation would be a conceptual error. Only objects of classes derived from Shape are allocated.

```
shapes[0] = new Rectangle(Point(...),Point(...));
shapes[1] = new Ellipse(Point(...), 5, 5);
shapes[2] = new ScalableText(Point(...), "C++");
```

A class that is never instantiated (that is, of which no objects are allocated) is called an *abstract base class*. Its only purpose is to serve as a base class for derivations and as a place holder for virtual functions.

We could modify the plot code to find out whether a Shape object had been accidentally created and plotted.

```
void Shape::plot(Graphics&) const
{ cerr << "Shape detected" << endl;
}

shapes[3] = new Shape;
    // ERROR:run-time error when plotted
```

Even better, we can tell the compiler that we have no idea how to plot a shape and that it does not matter because none are ever supposed to be created. We define `plot` as an *abstract* operation by appending " = 0" to the function declaration in the class definition. An abstract operation cannot have a definition. (In C++, abstract operations are often called *pure virtual functions*.)

```
class Shape
{
public:
   virtual void plot(Graphics& g) const = 0;
   . . .
};

shapes[3] = new Shape;
   // ERROR-cannot create object of abstract class
```

The compiler refuses to construct any object of a class with abstract operations. Of course, in the derived classes (`Rectangle`, `Ellipse`, and so forth) the `plot` function will be defined, and objects of those classes can be constructed.

Virtual functions of an abstract class are not necessarily condemned to do nothing. Functions can return a default response that is appropriate for many of the derived classes and can be overridden by others.

```
bool Shape::is_closed() const { return false; }
   // for flood fill test
```

This function can be retained by `Point` and `Text` and should be over-ridden to report `true` by `Rectangle` and `Polygon`.

It is often tempting to add *some* actual data into an abstract class to make it look more real and less naked. However, that is usually not a good idea. We could add a `Point` `_location` to the `Shape` base class, but this would be less than helpful for the `Polygon` class. Or we could add a `_color` field, but that would conflict with objects with more complex color descriptions, such as a bitmap.

## Simulating Virtual Functions with Type Tags

The classical solution to selecting an appropriate function at run time is to use type tags. Each value contains one field, at a well-defined location, specifying its type. The code contains branches like the following:

```
char type = ...;
switch (type)
{ case 'P':
      // scale a point
      break;
  case 'R':
      // scale a rectangle
      break;
  . . .
}
```

Let us sketch an implementation using type tags for the Shape hierarchy. We place a type tag in the base class T_Shape.

```
class T_Shape
{
public:
   void set_type(char);
       // called in derived-class constructors
   char type() const;
private:
   char _type;
};

char T_Shape::type() const { return _type; }

class T_Point : public T_Shape
{
public:
   void plot(Graphics& g) const;
   . . .
};

class T_Rectangle : public T_Shape
{
public:
   void plot(Graphics& g) const;
   . . .
};

class T_FilledRect : public T_Rectangle
{
public:
   void plot(Graphics& g) const;
   . . .
};
```

All objects are accessed as T_Shape* pointers. Once the type of an object is determined from the type tag, the pointer is cast to the correct type.

```
T_Shape* s = shapes[i];
switch(s->type())
{ case 'P':
      static_cast<T_Point*>(s)->plot(g);
      break;
  case 'R':
      static_cast<T_Rectangle*>(s)->plot(g);
      break;
  case 'F':
      static_cast<T_FilledRect*>(s)->plot(g);
      break;
  . . .
}
```

Obviously, this is tedious and error-prone. It is also a maintenance headache, as we will explain in the next section.

## Incremental Growth

Using virtual functions greatly improves program maintenance and growth. Consider the steps necessary to add a PieSegment to the object-oriented code with virtual functions.

- Derive a class PieSegment from Shape.
- Implement operations plot, scale, and so forth.
- Write code that constructs PieSegment objects.

The code can be placed in a separate file, compiled, and relinked with the existing code. *Not a line of existing code needs to be modified.* Calls such as

```
shapes[i]->plot(g);
```

now automatically work for PieSegment objects.

Contrast that with the effort required to add a T_PieSegment class to code using type tags.

- Write the T_PieSegment structure.
- Implement operations plot, scale, and so forth.
- Write code that constructs T_PieSegment objects.
- Look for all code performing an if or switch test on the type tag and check whether it needs to be updated.

Looking for all branches on the type tags is not too bad if they are all encapsulated in switch statements. But in real life, control logic involving type tags is often cluttered:

```
char t = s->type();
if (t == 'R' || t == 'F') // ...
else if (t >= 'a') // ...
// where does the T_PieSegment code go?
```

Inheritance and virtual functions enable a mode of programming in which the application code spells out the general mechanisms, but the individual objects are responsible for carrying out the detail instructions. It is then possible to add on new classes of objects that conform to the same protocol, perhaps even classes that were never envisioned by the original designers, without changing the application code.

# Inheritance and Invariants

## Class Invariants

Recall from Chapter 6 that a class invariant is a relationship between the data fields that must be true for all objects before and after every operation.

The derived class D must maintain all class invariants of the base class B. It can, of course, strengthen them.

Consider a class `BalancedTree` that implements a balanced binary tree. A tree is balanced if all leaves have depth d or d-1 for some integer d (see Figure 8.9).

Of course, any operations on the balanced tree must preserve this property—it is a class invariant. Derive from it a class `Heap`. A heap is a balanced tree with the added property that the element stored in each node is no larger than any of its children. In particular, the root of the tree contains the minimum element. Such heap structures (see Figure 8.10) are used for sorting and to implement priority queues. (This notion of "heap" has nothing to do with the free store for dynamic allocation, which is also commonly referred to as a heap.) See [Aho, Hopcroft, and Ullmann], p. 87, for more details on heaps for sorting.

The heap has an invariant that is stronger than the balanced-tree invariant. Its operations not only keep the tree balanced; they also keep all elements smaller than their children. `Heap` may therefore inherit from `BalancedTree`.

Derived classes must respect their base-class invariants for a good reason. If a derived-class operation destroys the base class invariant, other base-class operations may cease to function properly.

## Preconditions

Again, recall from Chapter 6 that a precondition of an operation is a condition that must be true before the operation can be called. The caller of the

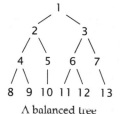

A balanced tree

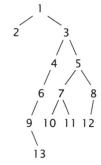

An unbalanced tree    **FIGURE 8.9**   A balanced and an unbalanced tree.

operation is responsible for making the call only when the precondition holds.

When a derived class redefines an operation f, its precondition must be *at most as strong* as the precondition of the base-class operation that it overrides.

The derived-class operation may be invoked dynamically through a base-class pointer. You must ensure at compile time that the derived-class operation can safely execute.

For example, suppose a class Manager derives from Employee. A precondition for the Employee::raisesalary function is that the percentage of the raise is not negative. Could we have a precondition of the raisesalary operation for managers that the percentage of the raise is always at least 5%? No. The precondition in the derived-class operation cannot be stronger than the precondition in the base-class operation. Suppose it was. The code

```
double raiseby = 0.02;
e->raisesalary(raiseby);
```

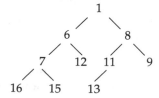

**FIGURE 8.10**   A heap.

would then appear to be correct because `raiseby > 0`, but if `e` actually pointed to a `Manager` object, then it would still be wrong. This conflicts with the concept that preconditions must be checkable by the programmer making the call. After all, a function is allowed to do anything, including terminate the program, if the precondition is not fulfilled.

In particular, if the base-class operation has no precondition, the derived-class operation may not have one either.

## Postconditions

When a derived class redefines an operation `f`, its postcondition must be *at least as strong* as the postcondition of the base-class operation. For example, suppose `Shape::plot` promises not to change the currently selected font in the graphics context (or to restore it if it has changed). Then all derived versions of `plot` must make the same promise.

# *Design Hints*

## Use Polymorphism, Not Type Information

Whenever you find code of the form

```
if (x is of type 1)
   action1(x);
else if (x is of type 2)
   action2(x);
```

think polymorphism. Depending on some property of x, a certain action was selected. Could it be that there are actually two kinds of x, each of which has a natural action associated with it? Then recognize the classes and make the action into a virtual function.

Code with virtual functions is much easier to maintain and extend than code with type tests.

## Move Common Behavior to the Base Class

Of course, if all derived classes provide an *identical* definition for an operation, it is an easy matter to move it to the base class. If *most* of them need one version of the operation, and a few need a different one, move the most common one to the base class and let only those that need a different one override it.

If the operations are *almost* identical, but not quite, see whether you can express the *difference* as a virtual function. Then move the code to the base class. The virtual-function call will reach the correct code in each derived class.

Consider, for example, an operation `Shape::floodfill` that plots a shape and fills its interior with a color. Here are some versions.

```
void Ellipse::floodfill (Graphics& g, Color c)
{ plot(g); // plot the shape
   Point p = _center; // find a point in the inside
   g.floodfill(p.x(), p.y(), c); // fill
}
void Rectangle::floodfill (Graphics& g, Color c)
{ plot(g); // plot the shape
   Point p = _bottomright; // find a point in the inside
   p.scale(_topleft, 0.9);
   g.floodfill(p.x(), p.y(), c); // fill
}
void Segment::floodfill (Graphics& g, Color c)
{ plot(g); // plot the shape
   // nothing to fill
}
```

To floodfill means to do the following:

- Plot the outline
- If it isn't a closed shape, give up
- Find an interior point
- Fill

Figure 8.11 shows these steps.

Here is the unified version in the base class.

```
void Shape::floodfill(Graphics& g, Color c)
{ plot(g); // plot the shape
   if (!is_closed()) return; // nothing to fill
   Point p = center(); // find a point in the inside
   g.floodfill(p.x(), p.y(), c); // fill
}
```

All specialized versions in the derived classes can be removed. The derived classes merely need to define `is_closed` and `center`. That means that the maintenance programmer who adds another derived class need not understand `floodfill` at all!

## Abstract Classes Can Have Concrete Operations and Fields

Abstract classes cannot be instantiated. That is, no object of an abstract class can be allocated. It is a common misconception that abstract classes

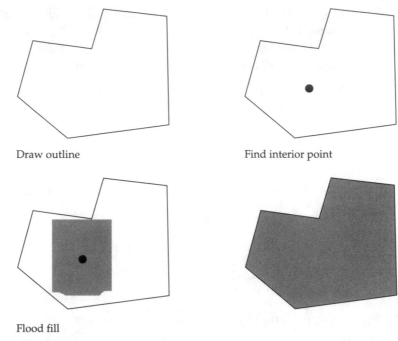

Draw outline        Find interior point

Flood fill

**FIGURE 8.11** `floodfill` of a shape.

have no data fields. That is not so; abstract classes can have data fields and operations. The reason they cannot be instantiated is that there is at least one virtual operation whose implementation has been deferred to a derived class. It would not be safe to have objects of that class around. If the deferred virtual function were invoked, the behavior would be undefined.

It always makes sense to move as much functionality as possible into a base class, whether or not it is abstract. Only those operations that cannot be implemented in the base class should be deferred.

Here is a typical example. A *chart* is a collection of shapes (rectangles, dots, pie segments, or whatever). A *bar chart* is a kind of chart; a *pie chart* is another kind of chart. Figure 8.12 shows the relationships between these classes.

We can store the shapes in the base class.

```
class Chart
{
public:
   void plot(Graphics& g) const;
   virtual void add_data(vector<double> data) = 0;
   void add_shape(Shape* s);
private:
   vector<Shape*> _shapes;
};
```

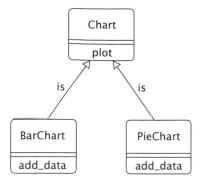

**FIGURE 8.12** Inheritance diagram of chart classes.

A bar chart derives from `Chart`. It has a specific `add_data` operation that knows about adding rectangles.

```
class BarChart : public Chart
{
public:
   virtual void add_data(vector<double> data);
};


void BarChart::add_data(vector<double> data)
{ int i;
   for (i = 0; i < data.size(); i++)
   {  double value = data[i];
      . . .
      add_shape(new Rectangle(. . .));
         // add another bar
   }
}
```

Similarly, the `add_data` operation of the `PieChart` class would add pie segments. However, the shapes are stored in the base class `Chart`. That class takes care of the plotting:

```
void Chart::plot(Graphics& g) const
{  int i;
   for (i = 0; i < _shapes.size(); i++)
      _shapes[i]->plot(g);
}
```

However, `Chart::add_data` is an abstract function. We only know how to add data to a specific chart, such as a bar chart or a pie chart. Therefore, `Chart` is an abstract class. But that doesn't mean it can't have data or operations. A chart does know how to do *something*, namely collect and plot shapes. But it doesn't know *everything;* hence, it is abstract.

# 9

# A Crash Course
# in Java

This chapter contains a very rapid introduction to basic Java, even more rapid than the C++ crash course in Chapter 2. As in Chapter 2, we cover basic types, strings, arrays and input/output. We also discuss the syntax for classes and inheritance in Java. This chapter focuses on the syntactic similarities and differences between Java and C++; later chapters will cover the differences in the object models of these two languages.

## *Types*

### **Numeric Types**

The numeric types in Java are similar to those in C++, with two exceptions: There are no `unsigned` types, and the sizes of all numeric types are fixed by the language and are not dependent on the implementation. Table 9.1 shows the types and their sizes.

In this chapter, we will refer to all these types as *numeric types*, although, strictly speaking, characters and Boolean values are not numbers.

**TABLE 9.1** Numeric Types in Java

| Type | Size |
| --- | --- |
| byte | 1 byte |
| boolean | 1 byte |
| char | 2 byte Unicode |
| short | 2 byte |
| int | 4 byte |
| long | 8 byte |
| float | 4 byte |
| double | 8 byte |

When we use this terminology, it turns out that all values in Java are either numbers or objects.

## Characters

In Java, characters have two bytes. Java uses the *Unicode* encoding scheme. Unicode can encode both regular ASCII characters (which have the top nine bits set to 0 and the remaining seven bits equal to the ASCII value) and characters from most written languages used today. A large fraction of the code space is devoted to the Chinese, Japanese, and Korean scripts. That doesn't actually mean that you can automatically display text in Russian or Chinese when you use Java. To display and print foreign characters, the operating system must also support Unicode and have the necessary fonts installed.

Unicode characters with codes outside the ASCII range are denoted as '\U*xxxx*', where *xxxx* is the four-digit hexadecimal Unicode value. For example, the Hebrew letter alef is '\U05D0'.

## Boolean Type

The Boolean type is called `boolean`, not `bool`, in Java. Unlike C++, there is *no* conversion between `boolean` and `int`. This protects the programmer against common errors such as these:

```
if (x = 0) . . .
   // C++, doesn't test whether x is zero
if (1 <= x <= 10) . . .
   // C++, doesn't test whether x is between 1 and 10
if (x && y > 0) . . .
   // C++, doesn't test whether x and y are greater than 0
```

All these expressions compile in C++ because the C++ compiler supports automatic conversions between integer and Boolean values. None of them compile in Java, and, of course, they shouldn't compile.

# *Arrays*

In our coverage of C++, we have used the ANSI C++ `vector` template for arrays because it supplied us with arrays that have two desirable properties:

- They are dynamic, that is, they grow on demand.
- They are strongly typed, that is, they hold elements of a specific type.

Unfortunately, in Java, we do not have that luxury. We have to give up one of these properties. Let us first look at the arrays that are built into Java.

## Built-in Arrays

Java has array types `T[]` ("array of `T`"), where `T` is any type. Arrays are *always* allocated on the heap:

```
int[] numbers = new int[n];
```

The size of the array can be any expression that is evaluated at run time. Unlike C arrays on the stack, the size need not be known at compile time. However, once the array is obtained, it cannot be resized. Java has no analog to the C++ `push_back` or `resize` operation.

Note that Java has no analog to a C style array on the stack

```
int numbers[6]; // C / C++
```

Instead, a C programmer ought to think of Java array allocations as the analog of

```
int* numbers = new int[6]; // C++
```

Don't worry about `delete[]`. Java does *garbage collection,* automatically freeing the memory of the array when it is no longer needed.

The length of an array can be obtained as

```
numbers.length
```

This is the analog of `v.size()` for vectors. Note, however, that there are no parentheses behind the `length`. Even though it looks like a data field, you cannot assign to it to change the array length. The Java documentation refers to it as a "read-only variable." It is the only variable of this kind, a somewhat incongruous feature.

The biggest difference between Java arrays and C++ vectors is that Java arrays have *reference semantics*. If you assign one array to another, both array variables refer to the *same array:*

```
int[] winning_numbers;
winning_numbers = numbers;
numbers[0] = 13; // changes both
```

Thus, an array variable in Java is just a reference to an array, whereas a vector variable in C++ denotes the actual vector. In C++, the assignment of vectors makes a *copy* of the object that is *initially* filled with the same values, but either vector can be changed independently of the other after the assignment.

```
vector<int> winning_numbers;
winning_numbers = numbers;
numbers[0] = 13; // doesn't change the other vector
```

In Java, the [] operator is checked at run time. When an invalid array index is supplied, a so-called *exception* is thrown that terminates the program unless it is explicitly handled in some other way. We will discuss exceptions in Chapter 16. The following invalid array accesses are all detected at run time:

```
int[] numbers = new int[6];
numbers[1000000] = 13;
numbers[-1] = 13;
numbers[6] = 13;
```

In contrast, the ANSI standard for C++ does not require that the [] operator check against bounds errors. Most implementations do not perform the check for performance reasons, and invalid bounds result in accessing or overwriting memory that belongs to other objects. These are among the most common C++ programming errors, so it makes a lot of sense to check against them, at least during debugging. For this reason, the version of the vector class is *safe* and checks for bounds errors.

C programmers are used to the so-called *array-pointer duality:* The name of an array is automatically converted to a pointer to the starting element, and the expression a[n] is equivalent to *(a + n), where a + n is the pointer to the nth element of the array. This is another fertile source of programming errors because it is all too easy to increment such pointers past the last element in the array, and Java does not support it.

# Vectors

The problem with Java arrays is that they don't grow on demand. Suppose you process input and want to store the input in an array. How much input will the user provide? There often is no way of knowing, especially if the input comes from a network connection, not from the keystrokes of a person. The traditional strategy of dealing with this is as follows:

- Make an array on the heap of what is normally a sufficient size.
- Keep a companion integer variable to indicate how full the array actually is.
- When the array turns out to be too small, make a larger one and copy over all the elements.

Here is a typical example:

```
String[] lines = new String[100];
int lines_size = 0; // companion variable
String line;
while ((line = in.readLine()) != NULL)
{  if (lines.length == lines_size)
   { String[] new_lines = new String(2 * lines.length);
      for (int i = 0; i < lines.length; i++)
         new_lines[i] = lines[i];
      lines = new_lines;
         // garbage collector will take care of old array
   }
   lines[lines_size] = line;
   lines_size++;
}
```

This code sequence is exceedingly common in Java code, just as it used to be exceedingly common in C++ code until vectors were introduced. That you need a pair of variables, the array and the companion integer, suggests that there really ought to be an object that knows both where the data is and how much of it is being used. The `java.util` library has a class `Vector` that implements this idea.

There is just one catch. Unlike C++, Java has no templates. In C++, you can have a `vector<T>` where `T` is any type; in Java, there is a single class `Vector` that must work for all types. It does that by storing values of type `Object`, the common base class of all Java classes. In Java, every type except for numbers and `boolean` inherits from `Object`. In particular, arrays and strings are descendants of `Object`. If you must make a vector of numbers, you use a *wrapper class* such as `Integer`, a class that stores an integer and is, like all classes, a descendant from `Object`. There are wrapper classes for all numeric types, and there is a wrapper `Boolean`.

When you insert elements into the vector, it is not a problem that the vectors store `Object` values. Every value is cast to the base class `Object`.

```
Vector v = new Vector();
v.addElement(new Integer(10));
   // grows vector and adds as last element
v.setElementAt("Hello", 0);
```

The `addElement` function is probably the most important function of the `Vector` class. It grows the vector size by 1 and inserts the element into the newly inserted slot. It is the equivalent of `push_back`. The `v.size()` operation returns the number of elements currently stored in the vector.

Because Java cannot overload operators, the designers of the `Vector` class were not able to use the `[]` syntax for vector access and instead had to supply a pair of functions `elementAt/setElementAt` to read and write a vector entry.

The syntax for `elementAt` is `v.elementAt(index)`. It returns the object that is stored at a specified index in the vector v.

The operation `v.setElementAt(obj, index)` puts a value in the vector v at the specified index.

When retrieving an object, then it must be *cast back* to its actual type.

```
String s = (String)v.elementAt(0);
```

Note that Java uses the old-style C cast notation

```
(type)expression
```

that is now obsolete in C++. However, unlike the casts in C, this type conversion is *checked:* If the result of `v.elementAt(0)` is not of type `String`, then the cast throws an exception, which normally terminates the program.

Thus, vectors have two drawbacks. They are inconvenient—the `v.setElementAt(obj, i)` and `obj = (Type)v.elementAt(i)` syntax is simply more cumbersome than a simple array access `v[i]`. And they are somewhat unsafe. It is possible to put in an object of the wrong type and then have the cast fail when the object is retrieved. In Java, this is the price to pay for flexible growth.

**TIP**

Here is a useful strategy that can often give you the best of both worlds—flexible growth and convenient and safe element access. If you first fill an array to its maximum size and then start using it, you can fill the elements into a vector and then convert the vector into an array. There is a special operation, `copyInto`, for this purpose:

```
Vector vlines = new Vector();
String line;
while ((line = in.readLine()) != NULL)
    vlines.addElement(line);
String[] lines = new String[vlines.size()];
vlines.copyInto(lines);
```
■

# *Strings*

As in C++, Java has a library type for strings. In Java, the type is String with an uppercase S. As in C++, + is the concatenation operator.

```
String greeting = "Hello, " + "World!";
```

If either argument of + is a string, the other is *converted to a string,* using the toString operation of its class

```
int errnum;
Socket s;
. . .
String message = "Error " + errnum + ": " + s;
```

This yields a string

```
Error value of errnum: value of s.toString()
```

In Java, strings are *immutable:* Once created, a string cannot be changed.

```
String greeting = "Hello";
greeting[4] = '!'; // ERROR
```

That allows sharing of strings in memory. C++ programmers find this initially quite uncomfortable. Keep in mind that only string *values* are immutable. You can change string *variables:*

```
greeting = "Howdy";
```

To edit a string, extract the substring you want to keep and concatenate with the new characters:

```
greeting = greeting.substring(0, 4) + "!";
```

Very occasionally, you need to do extensive editing of the same string. The most common case occurs when a string is assembled from characters arriving from an input stream. In that case, repeated concatenation is, of course, quite inefficient. Java has a `StringBuffer` class for editing strings. You make the string buffer from the string to edit (or you make a blank one). Then you edit the buffer. Finally, you convert the buffer back to a string object.

```
StringBuffer buf = new StringBuffer(greeting);
buf.setCharAt(4, '?');
greeting = buf.toString();
```

Note that charmingly the parameters (index, value) of the `setCharAt` function are the opposite order from those of the `setElementAt` function for vectors.

As all other objects in Java, strings are references.

```
String message = greeting;
  // now both point to the same string
```

Because strings are immutable, there is actually no problem with this arrangement. Because string objects are never changed, each string can safely have any number of references to it.

There is only one place in Java where the reference semantics of strings is noticeable and where it is a problem. When *comparing* two strings, the `==` operator tests whether the strings have identical *location*, not whether they have identical contents.

```
if (greeting == "Hello") . . . // Error
```

Instead, you must use `equals`:

```
if (greeting.equals("Hello")) . . . // OK
```

This can be a nasty pitfall.

The `<` `<=` `>` `>=` operators are not used for string comparison in Java (and, as we just saw, `==` and `!=` should not be used either). Instead, use the `compareTo` operation:

```
s.compareTo(t)
```

This code returns a negative integer if `s` comes before `t` in the lexicographic ordering, a positive value if `s` comes after `t`, and zero when the strings are identical.

To extract a substring, use the `substring` operation:

```
s.substring(m, n)
```

This code returns the substring of s starting at position m and ending at position n-1. It is identical to the C++ call

```
s.substr(m, n - m)  // C++
```

# *Classes*

## Class Definitions

Here is a typical Java class definition:

```
class Employee
{  public Employee(String n, double s)
   {  _name = n;
      _salary = s;
   }
   public double salary()
   {  return _salary;
   }
   public void raiseSalary(double percent)
   {  _salary *= 1 + percent / 100;
   }

   private String _name;
   private double _salary;
}
```

You can see the following differences between Java and C++:

■ public/private attributes are specified separately for each member.
■ Code for operations is always inside the class definition, not defined separately. That does *not* mean that the code is inline replaced.
■ There is no semicolon at the end of the class definition.
■ Accessor operations are not declared as const.

The first three differences are just details of the syntax. The fourth point is, however, a difference in semantics. Java cannot express the distinction between accessor and mutator functions. As we will see, a number of other conceptual distinctions can be expressed in C++ but not in Java.

## Objects

In Java, *all* objects must be allocated on the heap:

```
Employee harry
   = new Employee("Harry Hacker", 35000);
```

Think of this as the exact analog of the C++ code:

```
Employee* harry
   = new Employee("Harry Hacker", 35000); // C++
```

That is, an object variable in Java acts exactly like a pointer variable in C++. When you make a copy of the object in Java, the value is not copied. You merely establish a second reference to the same object (see Figure 9.1).

```
Employee boss;
boss = harry;
```

**PITFALL**

In C++, you often rely on the default constructor being called automatically:

```
Employee default; // C++, makes a default object
```

In Java, that same instruction merely makes a pointer variable. You must explicitly call `new` to make any object, even a default one:

```
Employee default = new Employee(); // Java
```
■

It is often said that Java has no pointers. That is not accurate: Java has no pointer *syntax,* but it has pointer *behavior* for all values except numbers.

Because Java cannot express the distinction between values and pointers, there is no need for distinguishing between the . and the -> operators for member access. In Java, you always use the . operator.

```
harry.raiseSalary(4.5);
```

Unlike in C++, in Java you never need to worry about memory management. The garbage collector automatically recycles the memory for

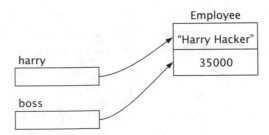

**FIGURE 9.1** Two object references to the same object.

those heap objects to which no variable points any longer. This is a great convenience for the programmer. Because a large percentage of errors in C++ programs arise from faulty memory management, this feature makes Java programs inherently safer than C++ programs.

Another safety feature is that Java object variables can never be invalid, as C++ pointers can be. In C++, it is all too easy to use a pointer that is uninitialized (and, hence, filled with a random value) or that points to an object that has already been deleted. In Java, all *local* variables must be explicitly initialized before they are used, or the compiler will flag the first use as an error. All other variables, including data fields in classes, are automatically initialized to a `null` pointer. Thus, all pointer values in Java are either `null` or a pointer returned by `new`. (You cannot take the address of a variable in Java.) Because the garbage collector will not delete an object if it has a pointer referring to it, having invalid pointers is not possible. When using a pointer to access a data member or call an operation, the run-time system checks if it is `null`. If it is, an exception is generated, which normally causes the program to terminate. If it is not `null`, then the pointer must be valid.

## Inheritance

The syntax for inheritance is similar to that in C++:

```
class Manager extends Employee
{  // additional operations and data fields
}
```

The : in C++ is replaced with the keyword `extends`. There is no private inheritance in Java; thus, you do not specify the keyword `public` as you would in C++.

Unlike C++, all classes in Java derive from a *cosmic base class* called `Object`. For example, the `Employee` class that was defined as

```
class Employee
{
}
```

implicitly derives from `Object` as if it were defined as

```
class Employee extends Object
{
}
```

This makes it possible to define generic classes such as `Vector` in the absence of templates.

Of course, you can assign derived-class values to base-class variables.

```
Manager carl = new Manager ("Carl Cracker", 110000);
Employee boss = carl;
```

If you have a base-class variable, you can find out if it actually points to an object of a derived type, using the instanceof operator:

```
if (boss instanceof Manager)
{   Manager m = (Manager)boss;
    . . .
}
```

Once you know that the variable actually refers to the derived class, you can cast to it, using the old-style C cast notation, (Manager)boss. However, this cast is *checked* at run time. If you perform an invalid cast such as (Rectangle)boss, then an exception is generated, which normally terminates the program.

In Java, all operations are dynamically dispatched by default—unlike C++, where dynamic binding had to be explicitly requested through the virtual keyword. If you do *not* want to have dynamic dispatch, you can declare an operation as final:

```
class Employee
{   public final double salary() { return _salary; }
    . . .
}
```

Functions declared as final can't be overridden in derived classes, and they give a hint to the compiler that it may make sense to use inline replacement instead of a function call.

You can declare a class as final. Then no other class can derive from it. In a final class, all operations are automatically final. This is often used for system classes.

```
final class StringBuffer { . . . }
```

In Java, abstract classes are tagged with the keyword abstract. (Recall that an abstract class is one that serves only as a base class and should not be instantiated.)

```
abstract class Shape { . . . }
```

Individual operations can be tagged as abstract to indicate that they are not defined in this class and must be defined in a derived class.

```
abstract class Shape
{  public abstract void plot(Graphics);
   . . .
}
```

If a class has an abstract operation or inherits an abstract operation from a base class, it must be tagged as abstract. Even if all operations are defined, the programmer can tag the class as abstract to prevent instantiation.

In C++, abstract operations are declared with the syntax

```
class Shape
{  virtual void print () const = 0; // C++
   . . .
}
```

Any C++ class is automatically abstract if it declares or inherits one or more abstract operations.

## Constructors

As in C++, the name of a constructor is the same as the name of its class. The biggest difference between Java and C++ constructors is that Java has no special initializer list syntax. Instead, all field assignments happen in the body of the constructor.

```
class Employee // Java
{  public Employee(String n, double s)
   {  _name = n; _salary = s;
   }
   . . .
}
```

In C++, you would use an initializer list:

```
Employee::Employee(string n, double s) // C++
: _name(n), _salary(s)
{}
```

The C++ syntax enables the constructor to bypass the default initialization of fields of class type. For example, the _name(n) directive constructs the name directly as a copy of n, whereas the alternative

```
Employee::Employee(string n, double s) // C++
{  _name = n; _salary = s;
}
```

would first construct _name as the empty string, then overwrite that string with n.

In general, constructing a default object has some cost. It may not even be possible to construct a default if there is no public default constructor. The field may be constant or a reference and therefore cannot be assigned to in the constructor body. The initializer syntax comes to the rescue in all these cases.

In Java, none of these issues apply. Java objects never contain any other objects, just references to other objects. They are initialized to `null` before entering the constructor body, which is essentially cost-free. Unlike C++, Java never calls the default constructor automatically for data fields.

**PITFALL**

In C++, any data field is initialized by its default constructor if no explicit construction is specified. For example, the _name field is set to the empty string by

```
Employee::Employee() : _salary(0) {} // C++
```

courtesy of the default constructor of the `string` class. However, in Java, all data fields are set to 0 or `null`, not a default object value.

```
class Employee // Java
{  public Employee() { } // _salary is 0, _name is null
   . . .
}
```

This is not what you want. You must explicitly call the default constructor of the data field to initialize it to a default object.

```
class Employee // Java
{  public Employee()
   {  _name = new String();
      _salary = 0;
   }
   . . .
}
```

Of course, in the case of strings, you can use _name = "" instead of _name = new String(). ■

Another role for the initializer syntax in C++ is to invoke the base-class constructor. In Java, there is a syntactical trick to achieve the same effect.

You use the keyword `super`, followed by the construction parameters for the base object.

```
class Manager extends Employee // Java
{  public Manager(String n, double s)
   { super(n, s);
   }
   . . .
}
```

The call to super must be the *first command* in the constructor!

If you don't call super in a derived class constructor, then the base class is constructed with its default constructor. (It is an error if the base class doesn't have a default constructor.) This is one of the few cases in Java where the default constructor is invoked automatically.

In C++, you can use *default arguments* to reduce the number of constructors.

```
class Employee // C++
{  Employee(String n = "", double s = 0);
   . . .
};
```

In Java, there are no default function arguments. Instead, you can have one constructor invoke another!

```
class Employee // Java
{ public Employee(String n, double s)
   {  _name = n;
      _salary = s;
   }
   public Employee()
   { this("", 0);
   }
   . . .
}
```

As in the case of the super syntax, the this keyword must be the *first command* in the constructor.

Finally, a data field can be explicitly initialized in the class definition.

```
class Employee // Java
{ . . .
   private String _name = "DEFAULT";
   private double _salary = Math.random();
}
```

These instructions are carried out before the constructor executes.

In detail, here is what happens when an object is constructed in Java:

1. All data fields are set to zero, `false`, or `null`.
2. If the constructor starts with the `this` construct, then it recursively calls the other constructor.
3. The base-class constructor is invoked, either with the parameters supplied in the `super` construct or with no parameters.
4. The data fields with initializers are set, in the order in which they appear in the class definition.
5. The constructor body is executed.

**PITFALL**

A surprisingly common error is the following:

```
class Employee // Java
{  public Employee(String n, double s)
   {  String _name = n;
      double _salary = s;
   }
   . . .
   private String _name;
   private double _salary;
}
```

Can you spot the error?
The line

```
String _name = n;
```

in the constructor body defines a new local variable _name that *shadows* the data field _name! After the constructor is finished, the local variables are forgotten and the data field _name is still `null`, as it was before entering the constructor.

In C++, you would never make this mistake because the initializer syntax has no place for a type name. For some reason, this error happens all the time to Java programmers. ■

# *Functions*

## No Global Functions

In Java, all functions must be operations of some class! There is no way to write a function such as

```
double sqrt(double x); // C++
```

In fact, in Java, the square root function is defined in the class `Math`. However, functions such as `sqrt` do not operate on objects—even in Java, `double` is not an object. Instead, you call the function as

```
y = Math.sqrt(x);
```

We will discuss these "object-less" operations and their implementation as `static` functions in Chapter 11.

In fact, even `main` must be a `static` function of some class. Here is the "Hello, World" function in Java:

```
class HelloWorld
{  public static void main(String[] args)
   {  System.out.println("Hello, World!");
   }
}
```

To run this function, you must tell the Java interpreter in which class it will find the `main` function. If you don't use an integrated Java development system but invoke the Java compiler from the command line, the command is

```
java HelloWorld
```

However, in this chapter we will be concerned only with Java applets that do not require static functions.

## Function Parameters

In Java, all function parameters are passed by *value*. There are no reference parameters. Thus, you could not write a function that swaps two numbers.

```
class Employee
{  . . .
   public void swapSalary(double s)
   {  double temp = _salary;
      _salary = s;
      s = temp; // no effect outside this function
   }
   . . .
}
```

If this function is called as

```
double x = 60000;
harry.swapSalary(x);
```

then the salary of `harry` is set to $60,000. But `x` is not set to the old salary of `harry`. That is not surprising in itself; in C++, the function would have the same effect because `s` is not a reference parameter. But in Java, there is no concept of reference parameters, so you cannot write such a function at all. You would need to make the old salary a return value. If a function has multiple return values (like the `jul2dat` function discussed in Chapter 3), then you must return an object with one data field for each return value.

This sounds like a drastic limitation, but fortunately it is not all that important in practice. Most interesting functions operate on *objects*, not numbers. Objects are still passed by value, but because object values are really pointers in Java, a function can change any object that is passed to it. Here is another contrived example:

```
class Employee
{ . . .
   public void swapSalary(Employee b)
   {  double temp = _salary;
      _salary = b._salary;
      b._salary = temp; // has effect outside this function
   }
   . . .
}
```

If this function is called as

```
harry.swapSalary(charley);
```

then the salaries of `harry` and `charley` really are swapped (see Figure 9.2).

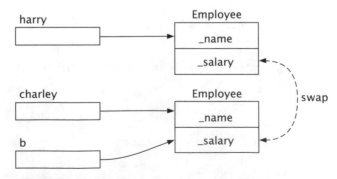

**FIGURE 9.2**  Methods can modify parameters.

**PITFALL**

Even though a function can *modify* any objects that it receives as parameters, it cannot *replace* them. Consider the following function:

```
class Employee
{ . . .
    public void swap(Employee b)
    {  Employee temp = new Employee(_name, _salary);
       _name = b._name;
       _salary = b._salary;
       b = temp; // no effect outside this function
    }
    . . .
}
```

If this function is called as

```
harry.swap(charley);
```

it makes a new `Employee` object and assigns it to the parameter variable b. But that does not change the actual parameter `charley` (see Figure 9.3). ■

Note that arrays are objects, and a function with an array parameter can change the entries of the array. However, the function cannot replace the array with one of a different size.

Function names can be overloaded in Java as in C++. Java is somewhat less aggressive in performing type conversions than C++ is to find a function

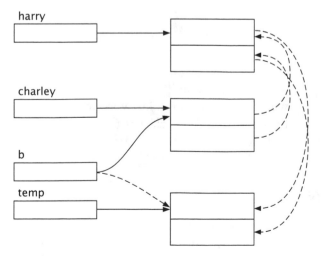

**FIGURE 9.3** Methods cannot replace parameters.

that matches a call. Naturally, it is never a good idea to write code that depends on the arcane matching rules anyway.

## Calling the Base-Class Function

In C++, you can pick which function you actually want to have called in an inheritance hierarchy by providing a scope resolution, such as

```
void ScalableText::scale(Point center, double s) // C++
{  Text::scale(center, s);
   _size = _size * s;
}
```

In Java, you cannot pick the function to be invoked. The function is solely determined by the run-time type of the implicit argument. But, of course, you cannot program

```
class ScalableText extends Text
{  public void scale (Point center, double s)
   {  scale(center, s); // Error
      _size = _size * s;
   }
}
```

That would make a recursive call to itself because the type of the implicit parameter is ScalableText. Instead, you use the keyword super to call the same function of the base class.

```
class ScalableText extends Text
{  public void scale (Point center, double s)
   {  super.scale(center, s);
      _size = _size * s;
   }
}
```

This is actually a little nicer than the C++ syntax, and some people wanted to add such a keyword to C++ as well. However, in C++, a class can have multiple base classes (see Chapter 18), and then super would not be well-defined.

## *Packages*

Java code is distributed over separate packages. There is a package java.util for utility classes and a package java.applet for classes that are needed to program applets, the Java programs that are embedded in a Web page. If you want to use a feature such as the `Vector` or `Applet` class, then you have two choices. You can refer to the class by its full name:

```
java.util.Vector v = new java.util.Vector();
```

Or you can use the `import` statement to import the name of the class:

```
import java.util.Vector;
```

After you imported a name, then you can use the short form:

```
Vector v = new Vector();
```

The directive

```
import java.util.*;
```

imports all names of the `java.util` package, which means that all names such as `Vector` and `Hashtable` defined in that package are available by their short names. To use the classes that were designed for this book, you must use the `COM.horstmann.practical00` package.

The compiler always looks into the `java.lang` package. You need not import it.

**NOTE**

C++ programmers usually confuse

```
import java.util.*; // Java
```

with

```
#include <java/util.h> // C++, but not the same meaning
```

These are really different mechanisms. The C++ directive is *required*. If you want to use a class or function that is specified in `java/util.h`, then you must include the header file (or repeat the class definition or function prototype). The Java mechanism is *optional*. Java will find all classes, provided you supply the full package name. The `import` directive is merely a convenience to allow the use of the short name. It is comparable to the *name space* mechanism described in Chapter 11. ■

## *Input and Output*

We will discuss files in greater detail in Chapter 13. Files in Java are rather complex—there are about 30 classes for input and output! In this section, you will just see how to do the basics—reading and writing numbers and strings.

The file System.out that is defined in the System class is an object of type PrintStream. You can also attach a print stream to a disk file by the following incantation:

```
PrintStream ps = new PrintStream(new
    FileOutputStream("output.dat"));
```

You can print numbers and strings to a PrintStream with the print and println operations. The println operation prints a newline after the output.

```
System.out.println("Hello");
ps.print(n);
```

There is no provision for formatted output (such as printf in C).

Input is not as convenient. The object System.in is tied to the standard input, but it is an InputStream, a class that can read only individual bytes. To read strings, you need to turn it into an object of type DataInput-Stream:

```
DataInputStream stdin = new DataInputStream(System.in);
```

You can open a disk file in the same way:

```
DataInputStream in = new DataInputStream(new
    FileInputStream("input.dat"));
```

The DataInputStream class has one useful operation: readLine. It returns the next input line or null at the end of the input.

To read a number, first read it in as a string and then convert it:

```
int age;
try
{ System.out.println("Please enter your age: ");
    String s = stdin.readLine();
    age = Integer.parseInt(s.trim());
} catch (Exception e) { age = 0; }
```

The trim operation returns a string with leading and trailing white space removed. The try/catch construction is used in C++ and Java to deal with exceptional conditions. We will discuss this important feature in detail in Chapter 16. Unlike the exceptions that are thrown as a consequence of programmer error (such as accessing a nonexistent array index), user input errors must be handled explicitly in Java. In this example, we set age to 0 if an error occurs. Instead, we could set an error flag or print a warning message.

Reading a floating-point number is even harder because there is no convenient parseDouble operation.

```
System.out.println("Please enter your salary: ");
String s = stdin.readLine();
double salary;
salary = new Double(s.trim()).toDouble();
```

You now know enough input and output commands to write simple programs. Look in Chapter 13 for more information on input and output.

## *Applets*

Java *applets* are graphical programs that can be displayed inside a Web browser. Our sample Java programs will be applets that show graphical shapes. An applet must extend the class Applet in the java.applet package. Minimally, it needs to override the paint operation to specify how the surface of the applet should be painted.

```
public class MyApplet extends Applet
{  public void paint(Graphics g)
   { // draw graphical shapes
   }
}
```

The Graphics object is used to issue drawing commands. You already know how to use it from chapter 7 since the Graphics class of the C++ graphics library for this book has the same interface as the Java Graphics class.

Put the code for the class in a file MyApplet.java. The Java compiler will compile it to a class file MyApplet.class. Then you must make an HTML file MyApplet.html that minimally contains the following tag:

```
<APPLET CODE="MyApplet.class" WIDTH=400 HEIGHT=400>
</APPLET>
```

If you view that file in a browser (such as Netscape or Internet Explorer), then the paint operation of the MyApplet class will be executed (see Figure 9.4).

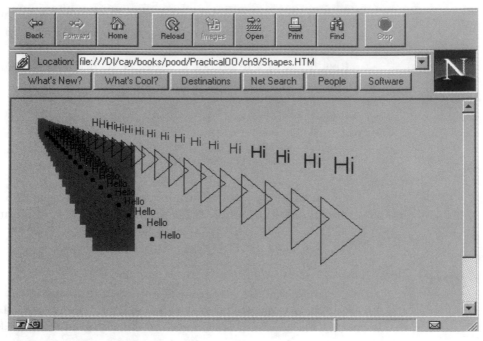

**FIGURE 9.4**   An applet running in Netscape.

**WEB**

Look at the code on the web page to see how to implement the graphical shapes (`Rectangle`, `Text`, and so on) in Java. There is also a sample applet scales and plots several shape objects.   ■

C H A P T E R

# 10

# The Object Models in C++ and Java

In this chapter, we begin our tour of the advanced features of C++ and Java. We have seen the basics: classes and encapsulation (`public`/`private`), inheritance, and polymorphism (`virtual` functions), in both C++ and Java, and found them to be similar in many ways. In this chapter we will contrast the object models in C++ and Java. There are many important differences between the languages, but because object models are inherently subtle, it actually helps to look at the underlying concepts from the vantage points of two languages that take different perspectives.

## *Objects, Pointers, and References*

### Reference Parameters

 The most obvious use for references is for functions that modify their arguments. In C++, however, references are common in a number of other contexts, discussed in this section.

219

When a function is called, the function parameters are allocated on the stack and initialized with the expressions in the function call. For large objects this process can be somewhat expensive. Giving the function a copy of the call argument is wholly unnecessary if that value is never modified. In that case, transmitting the location rather than the value suffices. That is just what references are designed to do. It is important to declare such references as `const` to convey that the reference mechanism is used for efficiency, not to modify the function argument.

For example, the function

```
void print(Employee e, ostream& os);
```

could be recoded as

```
void print(const Employee& e, ostream& os);
```

Neither the call nor the function code needs to be changed. However, all modules that use this function must be recompiled.

This transformation is obviously just an optimization strategy, and you may well wonder why the compiler cannot carry it out automatically. The compiler would merely have to check that the parameter is never changed in the function and that the cost of an added level of indirection for each access is less than the cost of making a copy. Unfortunately, this optimization would force recompilation of all modules that call the function. The standard programming environments compile each module in isolation, making such intermodule optimization infeasible. For this reason, it falls to the C++ programmer to perform this optimization manually.

 In Java, function arguments can never be passed by reference. As a consequence, a function can never change the value to which a function argument refers. If the argument is a numeric type, then the function cannot change that number. If the argument is an object, then the function can change the state of the object—Java has no notion of a *constant* reference. But the function cannot associate a new object with the argument, as discussed in Chapter 9.

## The Implicit Argument of an Operation

When an operation is invoked on an object, the implicit argument is transferred to the function, as are all explicit arguments. We know that the implicit argument must be a reference, not a value parameter, because an operation can modify its implicit argument.

```
Employee e;
e.raise_salary(0.05); // e modified
```

We normally have no need to refer by name to the parameter variable to which the implicit argument is bound because any names of class features used in the code of the operation are automatically applied to the implicit argument.

```
void Employee::raise_salary(double p) // C++
{ _wage *= 1 + p; // (implicit argument)._wage
}


class Employee // Java
{  . . .
   public void raise_salary(double p)
   { _wage *= 1 + p; // (implicit argument)._wage
   }
   . . .
}
```

Any fields of the implicit argument can be accessed. However, the value of the implicit argument is occasionally needed in its entirety—for example, to make a copy or to pass it to another function as an explicit argument. In such cases, its name is important.

In C++, every operation of a class has a pointer, called `this`, that points to the implicit argument. Thus, `*this` is a reference to the implicit argument.

```
Date Date::add_days(long n) const
/* PURPOSE: Return *this + n days
*/
{  Date b = *this;
   b.advance(n);
   return b;
}
```

The type of `this` in the `add_days` operation above is `const Date*`. In a mutator operation, such as

```
void Date::advance(long n)
/* PURPOSE: Add n days to *this
*/
{ . . .
}
```

the type of `this` is `Date*`.

It is something of a surprise that `this` is a pointer, not a reference. Consider the following operation:

```
long Date::days_between(const Days& b) const { /* ... */ }
```

The call

```
long n = d1.days_between(d2);
```

computes the number of days between d1 and d2. Both d1 and d2 are passed to the `days_between` function as constant references. However, inside the days_between operation, a *pointer* to d1 is referred to as `this` and a *reference* to d2 is referred to as b.

Most C++ programmers simply think of `*this` as an idiom for the implicit argument. It is a common trick to define away this inconsistency with the preprocessor statement

```
#define self (*this)
```

Actually, in some applications it is more natural to consistently use pointers, not object references, for variables and function arguments. Then `this` is quite natural as the name for the implicit argument. For example, consider an operation that tests whether two shapes meet (that is, have a nonempty intersection):

```
bool Shape::meet(const Shape* b) const { /* ... */ }
```

Because shapes are polymorphic, they are likely to be allocated on the heap. A typical call is

```
Triangle* t = new Triangle(...);
Rectangle* r = new Rectangle(...);
if (t->meet(r)) . . .
```

In this polymorphic situation, it is natural to pass both arguments as pointers. In the meet operation, the implicit and explicit arguments are then referred to as `this` and b, both of type `const Shape*`.

 In Java, the situation is much simpler. The implicit argument of every operation is called `this`, and it is an object reference just like any other object variable in Java. Note, however, that the add_days function of the Date class cannot be implemented as it is in C++.

```
class Date // in the COM.horstmann.practical00 package,
    // different from java.util.Date
{ . . .
```

```
public Date add_days(int n)
{  Date b = this; // ERROR
   b.advance(n);
   return b;
}
   . . .
}
```

Because all object variables in Java are references, the statement

```
Date b = this;
```

establishes a second reference, b, to the implicit argument. The line

```
b.advance(n);
```

would advance the date to which *both* b and this refer. That is not the intent. Instead, we must use

```
Date b = clone(); // or this.clone()
```

to set b to a copy of the implicit argument. We will discuss the clone operation later in this chapter.

By the way, the use of this to denote the implicit argument of an operation is completely unrelated to the use of this in a Java constructor, as discussed in Chapter 9.

```
class Employee // Java
{  public Employee(String n, double s)
   {  _name = n;
      _salary = s;
   }
   public Employee()
   {  this("", 0);
   }
   . . .
}
```

That usage is just a bit of keyword reuse.

## Returning References

A function can return a reference. It is not immediately obvious why this is useful. There are two applications. The most common case is an operation returning a reference to the implicit argument, *this.

```
Date& Date::advance(long n) // C++
/* PURPOSE: Add n days to *this
*/
{  . . .
   return *this;
}
```

This allows *chaining* of operations:

```
d.advance(30).print(cout);
```

The return value of advance, namely a reference to d, becomes the implicit argument of print.

 In Java, this idiom is also easy to achieve. Simply return this as the result of the operation:

```
class Date // Java
{  . . .
   public Date advance(long n)
   {  . . .
      return this;
   }
}
```

The chaining works exactly as in C++:

```
d.advance(30).print(System.out);
```

Some operations return a reference to a portion of their internal data. In general, this is not a worthwhile strategy. However, when building a general-purpose data structure such as the C++ vector template, some operations return references to give the user the same "look and feel" of the built-in arrays. For example, the vector template of ANSI C++ overloads the [] operator to return a reference to a vector element. That makes it possible to use the return value of the [] operator as an *lvalue*, on the left-hand side of an assignment such as

```
v[i] = 3.14;
```

(We will cover operator overloading in Chapter 12.)

As a simpler example that doesn't require operator overloading, we will consider yet another stack class. This stack has an operation top that returns the top element of the stack.

```
class Stack // C++
{
public:
```

```
    Stack();
    void push(double);
    double pop();
    double& top();
    bool is_empty() const;
private:
    int _sptr;
    vector<double> _data;
};

double& Stack::top()
{   if (_sptr > 0) return _data[_sptr - 1];
    static double z;
    z = 0;
    return z;
}
```

For example:

```
Stack s;
. . .
double x = s.top();
```

But since the function returns a reference, it can also be used on the left-hand side of an assignment:

```
s.top() = 3.14;
```

How does it work? The top function does not return a double value but the address of a double. The previous line stands for

```
* (returned address) = 3.14;
```

 There is no analog to this technique in Java. It is not possible to return a reference into an array. However, it is common in Java to return an *unintentional reference*. Consider this situation: An Employee class stores a hire date, and we have an accessor function returning that hire date.

```
class Employee // Java
{   . . .
    public Date hiredate() { return _hiredate; }
    . . .
    private Date _hiredate;
}
```

In C++, this function would be harmless—it would return a value that is a copy of the hire date. In Java, however, this function returns a reference to the employee's hire date, and the caller of the function can *use that reference to change the object.*

```
Employee harry = new Employee(...);
Date d = harry.hiredate();
d.advance(-365); // changes Harry's hire date!
```

This problem would not occur if the `Employee` object used the `Date` class in the `java.util` library instead of the `Date` class that is supplied in the code library for this book. The `java.util.Date` class has the property that *none of its operations are mutators.* Once a `java.util.Date` object is constructed, its state can never change. In that case, it is harmless to return a reference to such an object. However, a Java field accessor function should not return a reference to a data field of a class type with mutators. Doing so breaks the encapsulation of the class.

**TIP**

In Java, a field accessor function can safely return fields of numeric types or of classes without mutators, such as `String` or `java.util.Date`. However, when returning the values of other fields, you should first make a *copy,* using the cloning mechanism introduced later in this chapter. ■

 A common, and fatal, C++ programming mistake is to return a reference to a local variable:

```
double& Stack::top()
{  if (_sptr > 0) return _data[_sptr - 1];
   double z = 0;
   return z; // DON'T
}
```

All local variables go away when the function exits, and it makes no sense to return the address of a variable that no longer exists. For that reason, we declared z as `static` in the `Stack::top` function. Static local variables do not go away when the function exits but persist for the duration of the program. (They merely go out of scope when the function exits.)

For the same reason, it is not legal to return a reference to a constant.

```
double& Stack::top()
{  if (_sptr > 0) return _data[_sptr - 1];
   return 0; // DON'T
}
```

Because the `top` function returns a reference, it really must return the address of some memory location. Thus, the compiler will generate the following code:

```
double temp = 0;
return temp; // that is, return a reference to temp
```

`temp` is a local variable, so most compilers will issue a warning in this situation.

By the way, note that `return 0` does *not* mean that the `top` function returns a null pointer. When using references, you always program with objects, and the compiler turns them into addresses. Thus, all references are automatically addresses of objects that exist, at least at the time the reference is taken. There are no null references.

In C++, it is legal to return a reference to a new object on the heap, but it is extremely poor programming practice to do that.

```
double& Stack::top()

{  if (_sptr > 0) return _data[_sptr - 1];
   double* p = new double;
   *p = 0;
   return *p;
}
```

How can the allocated block be recycled to the heap?

 In contrast, in Java, it is very common to return a reference to a new object that was allocated on the heap.

```
class Segment extends Shape
{  . . .
   public Point intersect(Segment b)
   {  // compute intersection of this and b
     return new Point(x, y);
   }
   . . .
}
```

The garbage collector will automatically recycle the returned object when it is no longer needed.

## Copying Objects and References

 In C++, variables are used to hold object values, not to access objects. When an object value is copied into another variable, a copy of the object, distinct from the original, is created. Modifying the copy has no effect on the original.

```
Employee a("Joe User");
Employee b;
```

```
b = a;
b.raise_salary(0.05); // a is unchanged
```

This is not surprising to a programmer accustomed to the storage of structures in a language like Pascal or C. Both a and b have a collection of data fields, and the copy b = a makes a copy for each field.

In particular, it is the behavior we expect when generalizing from numeric types.

```
int a = 10;
int b;
b = a;
b += 15; // a is unchanged
```

Java takes a completely different point of view. Variables are not used for object storage but for object access. The objects themselves are stored in dynamic memory, and object variables hold their addresses. This is particularly convenient when managing collections of objects from different classes. All variables have the same size; hence, arrays and other containers can be built easily. Dynamic binding of operations (virtual function invocation) is the default.

The drawback is that a copy of a variable creates only another access to an existing object rather than a new object. To force a copy, a special clone operation must be called. This takes some getting used to, and it introduces a distinction between number types and class types.

The C++ object model, in which objects are values and copies create new objects, is well suited for abstractions that are conceptually like basic types, such as complex numbers or strings. It is less convenient for handling inheritance because it requires the use of pointers to express polymorphism.

The Java object model, in which objects are references, is particularly convenient for expressing polymorphism. Fundamental classes, such as Date or Point, can be awkward in Java. Conceptually, these simple types have a similar "look and feel" to numeric types, and it is not intuitive that a copy is just another reference. It is a very common programming error to accidentally modify an object by making a copy and modifying it.

**TIP**

It is a good idea to make classes that conceptually should have value semantics, such as dates or points, *immutable*. That is, the classes have no mutator operations. Once constructed, these objects always keep the same value. In that case, it does not matter if you make a copy by value or by reference. All references to an immutable object have the same value. In Java, this is carried out for quite a few of the basic types, such as `String`, `java.util.Date`, and the numeric "wrapper" classes `Integer`, `Double`, and so on, which we will discuss later. Whenever possible, consider making your own "value-like" classes immutable as well. In the library accompanying this book, the `Date` and `Point` classes violate this rule; we put more emphasis on compatibility between the C++ and Java libraries. ■

## Binding Variables to Objects

 When an object is stored in a variable, the object is said to be *bound* to the variable. For example, the C++ code

```
Employee e("Joe User");
```

binds an `Employee` object with name `"Joe User"` to the variable e (see Figure 10.1).

As the execution of the program progresses, other objects can be bound to e (see Figure 10.2).

```
e = Employee("Karl Schiller");
```

All objects bound to e have the same type, namely `Employee`. Although it is possible to assign an object of a derived type to e, that assignment copies only the `Employee` subobject into e. Any derived class information is sliced away.

```
e = Manager("Carol Smith"); // truncates object
```

In order to vary both the contents and the type of the objects bound to a variable, a pointer must be used in C++ (see Figure 10.3).

**FIGURE 10.1**   A C++ object variable.

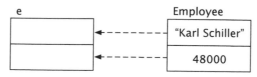

**FIGURE 10.2**   Changing the value of a C++ object variable.

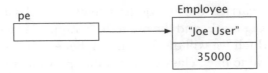

**FIGURE 10.3** A C++ pointer variable.

```
Employee* pe = new Employee("Joe User");
```

The variable pe is bound to an employee object, but at some later point in the computation it may be bound to another object of class Employee or any class derived from it (see Figure 10.4):

```
pe = new Manager("Carol Smith");
```

Two pointers can share an object (see Figure 10.5):

```
Employee* pf = pe;
```

Pointer variables can be bound to no object at all:

```
pe = NULL;
```

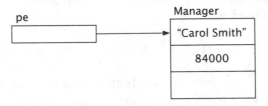

**FIGURE 10.4** Changing the value of a C++ pointer variable.

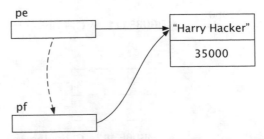

**FIGURE 10.5** Two pointers sharing an object.

This binding to no variable is possible only for pointer variables. Object variables are always bound to some object, even if it is an uninteresting default one.

C++ references are similar to pointers. They too can be bound to an object of a given class or any derived class thereof.

```
double salary(const Employee& e, Date from, Date to)
{ . . .
}
```

```
. . .
Manager m("Carol Smith");
double p = salary(m, d1, d2); // e bound to same object as m
```

There are a number of differences between references and pointers. First, references have the "syntactic sugar" of objects. That is, fields and operations are accessed with the dot (.) operator, not with ->. But there are more important conceptual distinctions.

As soon as a reference is created, it must be bound to an existing object. Once the binding is established, it cannot change for the lifetime of that reference. In particular, there is no null reference in C++.

References are most commonly used for function parameters. When a function with a reference parameter is called, the reference is bound to the object in the call. When the function exits, the binding terminates and the reference variable goes out of scope.

Object variables in Java are a mixture of references and pointers in C++. *They look like references but act like pointers.*

That is, there is no special syntax (like * and -> in C++) for derefencing or member access. But unlike C++ references, Java variables need not be initialized when they are defined, can point to different values during their lifetime, and can point to no object at all.

```
Employee pe;
pe = new Employee("Joe User");
pe = null;
```

## PITFALL

Superficially, Java objects actually look like C++ objects. In a couple of situations that superficial look commonly trips up C++ programmers. First of all, the definition

```
Employee e("Joe User");
```

is never valid in Java. You must use

```
Employee e = new Employee("Joe User");
```

More importantly, the definition

```
Employee e;
```

has completely different meanings in Java and C++. In C++, this defines an object variable e that is bound to an object built with the default constructor. In Java, this defines either an uninitialized pointer (if e is a local variable) or a `null` pointer (if e is a data field of a class). ■

## Casting Away constness

 We know that the `this` pointer of a C++ operation `X::f()` is of type `X*` when f is a mutator, and of type `const X*` when f is an accessor. If we make an assignment to a field in an accessor method, then the compiler generates an error message.

```
int Date::day() const
{   if (_day < 1)
        _day = 1; // ERROR
    return _day;
}
```

The assignment

```
_day = 1;
```

really means

```
this->_day = 1; // ERROR--this is a const Date*
```

Because `this` is a `const Date*` pointer, it is not permissible to change the object to which the `this` pointer refers.

Normally, this is not a problem. However, once in a while a C++ programmer must implement operations that are *logically* constant but not *physically* constant. Here is an example. Suppose we want to optimize the Date class to handle repeated `advance` operations very quickly, without calling the `dat2jul` and `jul2dat` functions every time.

```
void Date::advance(int n)
{   _day += n;
}
```

Of course, now the _day, _month, and _year fields need to be recomputed whenever they are required. The private `normalize` function performs this task.

```
void Date::normalize() const
{  if (_day < 1 || _day > 28)
    {  long j = dat2jul(1, _month, _year);
       int d, m, y;
       jul2dat(j + _day - 1, d, m, y);
       _day = d; // ERROR--see below
       _month = m;
       _year = y;
    }
}
```

This function must called before using the _day, _month, and _year fields:

```
int Date::day() const
{  normalize();
   return _day;
}
```

However, there is a problem with the `normalize` operation. It was declared `const` so that it can be called in the `const` operation `day`, but it modifies the _day, _month, and _year fields.

Actually, the `normalize` operation is *logically* constant. Calling `normalize` does not change the logical state of a `Date` object—it just changes the *physical* representation to a more convenient format.

There are two methods for overcoming this problem. The more traditional solution is to *cast away constness*. If p is a const X*, the expression `const_cast<X>(p)` yields p as a nonconstant X* pointer. (The expression `(X*)p` has the same effect, but it is less expressive—you should use `const_cast` in this situation.) Here is how we can write the `normalize` function.

```
void Date::normalize() const
{  if (_day < 1 || _day > 28)
    {  long j = dat2jul(1, _month, _year);
       int d, m, y;
       jul2dat(j + _day - 1, d, m, y);
       const_cast<this>->_day = d;
       const_cast<this>->_month = m;
       const_cast<this>->_year = y;
    }
}
```

Apparently, the designers of C++ found this solution so ugly that they came up with another mechanism to achieve the same goal. A data field can be tagged as mutable to indicate that it is permissible to assign to it, even through a constant pointer.

```
class Date
{  . . .
private:
   mutable int _day;
   mutable int _month;
   mutable int _year;
};
```

You use this construction whenever an object has multiple physical states to describe the same logical state, and you need to convert between physical states in accessor functions.

Another common example is a *cache*. Suppose you write a lookup table and for efficiency you cache the last three lookups because your experience has shown that a recently looked-up value has a good chance of being requested again. Then the lookup operation is logically constant because looking up a value in a table doesn't change the logical contents of the table. But it is physically not constant because lookups need to update the cache. The solution is to tag the data fields that implement the cache as mutable or to access them through const_cast<this>.

## The Multiple Uses of Pointers

 In C++, we have seen that mixtures of objects of different types must, in general, be allocated on the heap and that they must be accessed through pointers. However, there are other reasons to use pointers in C++. And, of course, in Java, all object variables are actually pointers. In either case, it is a good idea to distinguish between the various reasons *why* pointers are used in specific implementation scenarios.

In C++, there are three separate reasons to use pointers rather than objects:

1. For polymorphism (variation in type)
2. For sharing of objects
3. For zero/one relationships

We have seen many examples of using pointers for polymorphism to refer to an object of a base class or any of its derived classes.

Object sharing takes place when access to the same object is required in distinct parts of a program, either for efficiency or for controlled access. It is achieved by binding two or more pointer variables to the same object.

Pointers can be used to model zero/one relationships. A null pointer indicates no relationship; a nonnull pointer indicates a relationship with another object. It is this property of pointers that makes dynamic data structures such as linked lists possible. For each link, either there is a successor element, or there is not.

Also note that traditionally in C++ there was a fourth use for a pointer, to denote a position inside an array. With the advent of the `vector` template, that usage is no longer as important.

When pointers are used for polymorphism, objects are not usually shared, and having the flexibility of a zero/one relationship is usually not the intent. Unfortunately, you cannot simply see from the code what the intent of a pointer variable is. For example, consider

```
Employee* pe;
```

Which of the following is `pe`?

- A pointer to an object that may be an employee object or an object of a derived class
- A pointer to an employee record that is shared among different parts of the program
- A pointer that may either refer to an employee or be `null` to indicate that it currently has no association
- A combination of these

Of course, if the object was neither polymorphic nor shared nor potentially null, then a simple `Employee e;` would have sufficed.

**TIP**

If you mix two or more of the above interpretations (polymorphism, sharing, zero/one relationship) in a particular pointer variable (or any variable in Java), you should clearly document that fact. ■

Like pointers, C++ references are used to realize various design goals. A function may receive a reference to an object because the code of the function needs to modify that object, or it may receive a reference because the reference is cheaper to establish than a copy of the object. Both of these reasons are examples of object sharing. A reference may also be desired to realize polymorphism. For example, the salary function previously shown queries the object to compute pay information. The method for determining pay may differ between the base class and the derived classes. However, because there is no null reference, it is never possible to use references for zero/one relationships.

Because Java has no distinction between objects, pointers, and references, Java code is even less self-documenting than C++ code in this regard. It is always a good idea to clearly document, or at least clearly understand, the intentions for any Java variable:

- Is it intended to hold objects of a derived class?
- Is it intended to hold no object at all?
- Is it intended that there may be other references to the same object?
- Can the reference change after construction?

# Run-Time Types

## Testing for a Type Match

It is possible to find out whether a base-class pointer actually points to a derived class of a certain type. C++ provides the typeid operator for this test. (For the test to work properly, the class needs to have at least one virtual function.) The following code tests whether a Shape pointer actually points to a rectangle.

```
Shape* s;
if (typeid(s) == typeid(Rectangle*))
    // s points to a Rectangle object
else
    // s points to an object of some other class
```

The type match test looks interesting, but it is actually practically useless. In the previous code the test fails if s points to a FilledRect or some other class derived from Rectangle, even though conceptually a filled rectangle is a rectangle.

The purpose of inheritance is to build objects that act exactly like the base-class objects unless they themselves decide otherwise. Type matching defeats this.

We strongly recommend against testing for exact type matches because it is incompatible with inheritance. Use virtual functions instead. There is one legitimate use for type match testing—to write functions that test whether two objects have equal contents.

In C++, the typeid operator returns an object of a predefined class typeinfo. However, that class has only three useful operations: == and != operators to test two such objects for equality, and a name operation to return the name of the type. The code

```
cout << typeid(s).name() << endl;
```

can be useful for debugging.

Java has a similar mechanism. The `getClass` operation of the `Object` class (which is the root of all Java classes) returns an object of type `Class` that describes the object's class. In the initial version of Java, the `Class` class revealed only marginally more information than the C++ `type_info`. However, in Java 1.1, a set of operations, collectively referred to as *reflection,* was added to `Class`. These operations give a large amount of information about each class. We will discuss the reflection interface later in this chapter.

To get the exact class name of a Java object, invoke the `getName` operation on the class object. It yields a string spelling out the class name. You can print it out for debugging purposes.

```
Class c = s.getClass();
System.out.println(c.getName());
```

That feature can also be used for an exact type match:

```
if (s.getClass().getName().equals("COM.horstmann.practical00.Shape"))
    . . .
```

Again, keep in mind that the exact type match is not generally useful.

## Testing for Downcasting

Very occasionally, situations occur in which virtual functions are not flexible enough and a run-time type inquiry is required. Consider, for example, the task of computing the intersection of two geometric shapes that might be rectangles or polygons. In general, the intersection is a union of polygons, but the intersection of two rectangles is again a rectangle (see Figure 10.6).

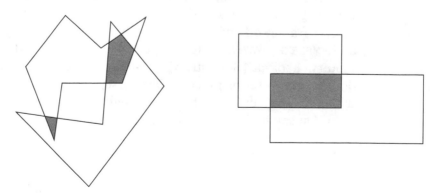

**FIGURE 10.6**   Intersection of rectangles and polygons.

In this case, we must know whether a Shape pointer actually points to a Rectangle or maybe to a class derived from it, such as a FilledRect. This test is sometimes referred to as a "kind of" test. If the test succeeds, we need to convert the Shape* pointer to a Rectangle* pointer to gain access to the rectangle features.

The process of converting a base-class pointer to a derived-class pointer, provided that some information is available that guarantees the correctness of the cast, is often referred to as *downcasting*. The term originates from the habit of many computer scientists to draw the root of the inheritance tree on the top (in complete violation of biological facts, except perhaps down under in Australia) and the derived classes further down.

In C++, downcasting is performed with the dynamic_cast operator. Suppose we need to find out whether a Shape pointer actually points to a Rectangle of some kind: a plain Rectangle, a FilledRect, or some other rectangle. The following code achieves this.

```
Shape* s;
// ...
Rectangle* r = dynamic_cast<Rectangle*>(s);
if (r != NULL)
    // r equals s and points to an object that is a Rectangle
else
    // s points to an object that is not a Rectangle
```

The dynamic_cast performs both the test and the type conversion. (For dynamic_cast to work properly, the base class must have at least one virtual function.)

It is possible to cast C++ references as well. Because there is no null reference, a failed reference cast causes an exception. See Chapter 16 for details.

Before C++ compilers supported safe dynamic casts, programmers were eager to use this feature. For example, in the Microsoft Foundation Classes framework, the programmer had to insert macros DECLARE_DYNAMIC and IMPLEMENT_DYNAMIC to generate the necessary code manually for type inquiry. Look at [Stroustrup], p. 442, for a description of how you can design such a set of macros. Of course, now that the language supports dynamic type inquiry, such macros ought to go away.

You can find the old-style cast notation

```
Rectangle* r = (Rectangle*)s;
```

in many existing programs, but this construction really should be avoided in new code. It makes sense only if you already know that s had to be a rectangle. In contrast, the `dynamic_cast` operator *checks* if s belongs to the Rectangle class or one of its derived classes. If you use the old-style cast (or the equivalent `static_cast<Rectangle*>`) and due to a programming error, s was not a rectangle pointer, then the program will likely crash when calling rectangle operations on the object to which s points.

 In Java, it is safe to use the old-style cast

```
Rectangle r = (Rectangle)s
```

(Note that you cast object references, not pointers, in Java.) If s is not a reference to a rectangle, then an exception is generated that normally causes the program to terminate. (See Chapter 16 for more information on exceptions.) That is bad, but not as bad as the random corruption that would be the result of a bad cast in C++.

To test whether s really points to a Rectangle object, or an object of a class inheriting from Rectangle, you use the `instanceof` operator. This operator takes two arguments, an object reference and the name of a type. It returns `true` if the object is an instance of that type or a derived type. For example, the test

```
if (s instanceof Rectangle)
   . . .
```

tests if s is a kind of rectangle. Once the test succeeds, you will likely want to apply rectangle operations, so you need to apply a cast:

```
if (s instanceof Rectangle)
{  Rectangle r = (Rectangle)s;
   . . .
}
```

This cast will not fail, of course, because it is preceded by a type inquiry.

Note that the C++ `dynamic_cast` is a combination of the Java `instanceof` test and cast.

## Shallow and Deep Copying

Suppose we want to make a copy of all entries in a C++ vector holding a collection of shapes. We can copy the pointers. Such a copy is called a *shallow* copy (see Figure 10.7).

```
vector<Shape*> fig1;
. . .
vector<Shape*> fig2 (fig1.size());
```

fig1

fig2

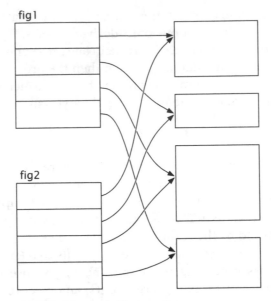

**FIGURE 10.7**  A shallow copy.

```
for(int i = 0; i < fig1.size(); i++)
   fig2[i] = fig1[i];
```

If the entries in `fig1` are changed, then the `fig2` pointers refer to the changed objects as well.

```
for(int i = 0; i < fig1.size(); i++)
   fig1[i]->rotate(p, a);
// fig2 also contains rotated shapes
```

That is often undesirable. Suppose that we really want to have a new set of objects. A virtual `clone` function is required that creates a new copy of an object:

```
class Shape
{
public:
   virtual void plot(Graphics& g) const = 0;
   virtual Shape* clone() const = 0;
   . . .
};
```

```
Shape* Point::clone() const { return new Point(*this); }
Shape* Rectangle::clone() const { return new Rectangle(*this); }
```

The statement

```
return new X(*this);
```

is roughly equivalent to

```
X* r = new X;
*r = *this;
return r;
```

However, it is more efficient to construct the new object directly as a copy of *this, rather than first using the default constructor, followed by assignment.

See Chapter 14 for more information on the process of constructing an object as a copy of another object of the same class.

The `clone` function can be used to make a true copy of each object, often called a *deep* copy (see Figure 10.8).

```
for(int i = 0; i < fig1.size(); i++)
  fig2[i] = fig1[i]->clone();
```

Because `clone` is virtual, the appropriate `clone` function is called for each object.

It is a good idea to plan for deep copies and include a `clone` function in an inheritance hierarchy. Of course, then each derived class must implement

```
Base* Derived::clone() const { return new Derived(*this); }
```

 In Java, the issue of shallow and deep copies is even more urgent. C++ copies objects by value, thereby making a deep copy. Only pointer copies are shallow. On the other hand, copies of object references in Java are always shallow.

To illustrate the issue, consider the following C++ code to make a square with center p  (see Figure 10.9):

```
Rectangle makeSquare(Point p, int w) // C++
{  Point a = p;
   a.move(-w / 2, -w / 2);
   Point b = p;
   b.move(w / 2, w / 2);
   Rectangle r(a, b);
   return r;
}
```

This function has two local variables a,  b of type `Point`. Each of them is initialized with a copy of p, then moved to the appropriate location (see Figure 10.10).

Now consider the same code in Java:

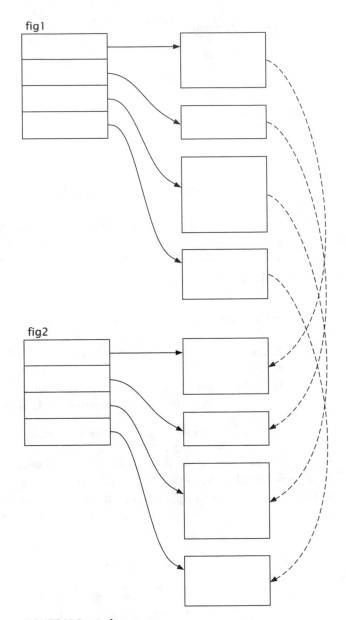

**FIGURE 10.8**   A deep copy.

```
public Rectangle makeSquare(Point p, int w) // Java, has bugs
{   Point a = p;
    a.move(-w / 2, -w / 2);
    Point b = p;
    b.move(w / 2, w / 2);
    Rectangle r = new Rectangle(a, b);
```

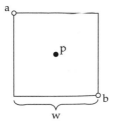

**FIGURE 10.9**   The action of the `makeSquare` function.

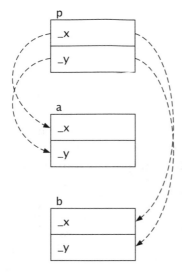

**FIGURE 10.10**   Memory layout of the `makeSquare` function in C++.

```
    return r;
}
```

This code will not work. Now the copies

```
Point a = p;
Point b = p;
```

are *shallow copies*. Both a and b refer to the same point (see Figure 10.11).
The operation

```
a.move(-w / 2, -w / 2);
```

moves the point to which a and p refer. The operation

```
b.move(w / 2, w / 2);
```

moves the same point back to the original place. The constructor

```
new Rectangle(a, b);
```

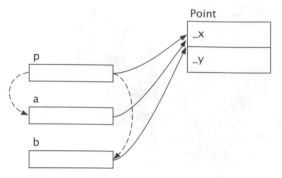

**FIGURE 10.11**  Memory layout of the makeSquare function in Java.

makes a rectangle of area 0, with the same point for the upper-left and lower-right corners.

Clearly, we need to make a and b refer to new points that have the same value as the point to which p refers. We must define a clone operation for the Point class and use it to obtain true copies of the center point:

```
public Rectangle makeSquare(Point p, int w) // Java
{  Point a = (Point)p.clone();
   a.move(-w / 2, -w / 2);
   Point b = (Point)p.clone();
   b.move(w / 2, w / 2);
   Rectangle r = new Rectangle(a, b);
   return r;
}
```

Note that the return type of clone is Object, so you must cast it back to the correct type.

Just as in C++, you must implement the clone function manually. Unfortunately, this is somewhat tedious. There is a clone operation in the Object base class that automatically copies all data fields, but that operation is not accessible by default. It is declared protected—see Chapter 11 for more details on the protected interface. And it checks that the cloned object belongs to a class implementing the Cloneable interface—see Chapter 18 for more details on interfaces. If not, the clone operation of the Object base class will throw an exception. Because the exception specification of the clone operation of the Object base class threatens to throw that exception, we must catch it, even if we are certain that we invoke clone legally. See Chapter 16 for more details on exception specifications and catching exceptions. As you can see, a full understanding of the clone operation requires knowledge of a number of advanced Java features. In this section, we will give a cookbook approach to implementing clone.

Here is how you would redefine `clone` for the `Point` class:

```
class Point implements Cloneable
{  public Object clone()
   {  try
      { return super.clone(); // clone all fields
      }
      catch (CloneNotSupportedException e)
      {  // can't happen–we are cloneable
         return null; // still must return something
      }
   }
   . . .
   private int _x;
   private int _y;
}
```

Clearly, this is completely mechanical. First, make sure that the class, or its base class, contains the `implements Cloneable` specification. If a base class (say `Shape`) is already `cloneable`, do not repeat that in the derived class. Then add the `clone` operation, exactly as in the `Point` example.

This simple version of `clone` works only if all data fields are numbers or immutable objects (such as strings). If they are mutable (such as `Point` objects), then you must *clone the field*. Consider the `Rectangle` class that has two `Point` data members.

```
class Rectangle implements Cloneable
{  public Object clone()
   {  try
      {  Rectangle r = (Rectangle)super.clone();
         r._topleft = (Point)_topleft.clone();
         r._bottomright = (Point)_bottomright.clone();
      }
      catch (CloneNotSupportedException e)
      {  // can't happen--we are cloneable
         return null; // must return something
      }
   }
   . . .
   private Point _topleft;
   private Point _bottomright;
}
```

That is, you must manually program `clone` to make a deep copy (see Figure 10.12). We will see in Chapter 13 how that process can be automated for certain classes, by using the Java *serialization* mechanism.

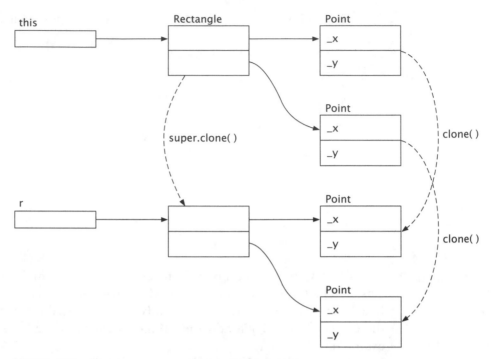

**FIGURE 10.12** Cloning a rectangle object in Java.

**TIP**

Forgetting to clone an object is particularly common when porting code from C++ to Java. Whenever a class has mutator operations, be sure to replace each assignment of objects

```
b = a; // C++
```

with

```
b = a.clone(); // Java
```

unless you are really sure that the subsequent code doesn't mutate b. The same holds for function calls. A call

```
f(a); // C++
```

should be changed to

```
f(a.clone())
```

unless you know that f won't change a. You really only know this for certain when a was passed by constant reference in C++. In C++, function argument variables are local variables that can be changed without modifying the input. In Java, invoking a mutator on an argument variable does, of course, change the input. ■

## Object Equality

 There are two concepts of object equality. Let us consider numeric types first. We may ask whether two integers have the same value:

```
int m, n;
. . .
if (m == n) ...
```

Given two C++ pointers to int, we may again wish to test whether the integers to which they point have the same value:

```
int* p;
int* q;
. . .
if (*p == *q) ...
```

Or we may want to know whether they have the same identity:

```
if (p == q) ...
```

The latter is interesting if we need to know whether changing *p also changes *q.

Reference values are compared like object values:

```
void f(int& r, int& s)
{ if (r == s) ...
}
```

To test whether two references have the same identity, compare their addresses:

```
if (&r == &s)
```

For a class object, testing equalities of values is often meaningful. For example, two points are identical if their *x*- and *y*-coordinates are:

```
bool Point::equals(const Point& b) const
{   return _x == b._x && _y == b._y;
}
```

Two rectangles are identical if their top-left and bottom-right corners are:

```
bool Rectangle::equals(const Rectangle& b) const
{   return _topleft.equals(b._topleft)
        && _bottomright.equals(b._bottomright);
}
```

Given two pointers to rectangle objects, it is now an easy matter to test whether they refer to the same object,

```
Rectangle* p;
Rectangle* q;
. . .
if (p == q) ...
```

or whether the objects to which they refer have the same value:

```
if ((*p) .equals(*q))
```

Or is it? If q points to a FilledRect, the call to equals will return true if its rectangle portion coincides with that of *p, even though intuitively a rectangle is never equal to a filled rectangle, and two filled rectangles are equal if their rectangle portions and fill pattern are.

More generally, we may want to test whether two arbitrary shape pointers point to objects of equal value—for example, to implement a set data structure that ignores duplicate values.

The simple answer is to make equals a virtual function. But the situation is not that simple: equals has two arguments, both of which vary in the type hierarchy. Virtual functions can select an operation based on only *one* argument, the implicit argument of the virtual-function call. While that is sufficient for many applications, it breaks down for equality testing. This is one situation where an exact type match is useful.

```
bool Rectangle::equals(const Rectangle& b) const
{   if (typeid(*this) != typeid(b)) return false;
    return _topleft.equals(b._topleft)
        && _bottomright.equals(b._bottomright);
}
```

Actually, it is very common to use an *overloaded operator* for equality testing. See Chapter 12 for details on overloaded operators. You simply call the function operator==, not equals.

```
bool Point::operator==(const Point& b) const
{ return _x == b._x && _y == b._y;
}
```

You can now use the == operator to compare two points.

```
bool Rectangle::equals(const Rectangle& b) const
{  if (typeid(*this) != typeid(b)) return false;
   return _topleft == b._topleft
     && _bottomright == b._bottomright;
}
```

The standard C++ container library (sometimes called STL) that we will discuss in Chapter 17 takes yet another approach to equality testing. If you want to insert objects into certain STL containers, you need to supply a *total ordering,* an overloaded < operator so that either a < b or b < a or a and b are equal. You typically use a lexicographic ordering on the key data fields. For example, for points you could use

```
bool Point::operator<(const Point& b) const
{  return _x < b._x || _x == b._x && _y < b._y;
}
```

This ordering makes no geometric sense, but it is a total ordering. Then STL automatically considers two objects identical if they fulfill the test

```
!(a < b || b < a)
```

 In Java, the == operator always tests for equality of references, *never* for equality of object content. We already saw that for strings. The test

```
s == t
```

tests if the string references s and t refer to the same string object. For example, the test

```
String oh = "o";
if ("Hello" == "Hell" + oh) . . .
```

will fail—the result of the concatenation is placed into a new memory location.

Instead, you must use the equals operation to compare strings: The test

```
if ("Hello".equals("Hell" + oh)) . . .
```

will succeed.

You should define an `equals` operation for all classes, especially for those classes that you want to insert into a container such as a hash table (see Chapter 17). The implementation is just as in C++:

```
class Point extends Shape
{  public boolean equals(Point b)
   {  return _x == b._x && _y == b._y;
   }
   . . .
}
```

```
class Rectangle extends Shape
{  public boolean equals(Rectangle b)
   {  if (!getClass().equals(b.getClass())) return false;
      return _topleft.equals(b._topleft)
         && _bottomright.equals(b._bottomright);
   }
   . . .
}
```

You really must make an effort to define these operations. If you don't, the class inherits the `equals` operation of the `Object` base class. That base class operation does the wrong thing and compares the object locations, not their contents.

## Virtual Constructors

Suppose we need to save a mixture of shape objects to disk. To be able to distinguish them when reading them back in, we first write the name of the type, then the actual object.

```
fstream out("shapes.dat");
for (i = 0; i < shapes.size(); i++)
{  out << typeid(shapes[i]).name() << " ";
   shapes[i]->print(out);
   out << endl;
}
```

A sample output would be

```
Point (30,40)
Rectangle (10,10) (50,60)
Ellipse (100,100) 10 20
```

When reading the objects back in, we first read the string describing the type. Now we would like to construct an object of that type, so that we can then call the virtual `read` function on that object to read in the object data.

The problem is to construct an object (e.g., `new Point`) from a string (e.g., `"Point"`). This task is often called *virtual construction* because it requires construction of objects of varying types at run time. Of course, constructors are never virtual—every constructor initializes an object of a specific type. Indeed, there is no C++ feature to carry out this task.

Here is how you can manually implement such a mechanism. Keep a correspondence between type names and default objects of that type.

```
map<string, Shape*> shapeTypes;
```

(We will discuss the map class in Chapter 17.)

Add an entry for every concrete class.

```
shapeTypes["Point"] = new Point();
shapeTypes["Rectangle"] = new Rectangle();
shapeTypes["Ellipse"] = new Ellipse();
. . .
```

When reading in the type name, find the matching default object and clone it.

```
fstream in("shapes.dat");
while (!in.fail())
{  string typename;
   in >> typename;
   assert(shapeTypes.find(typename) != shapeTypes.end());
   Shape* newShape = shapeTypes[typename]->clone();
   newShape->read(in);
   shapes.push_back(newShape);
}
```

That is, virtual constructors in C++ can be implemented by using a map from type names to default objects (sometimes called *exemplars*) and by cloning the matching exemplars.

 Unlike C++, Java has direct support for virtual construction. The `Class` class has a static function `Class.forName(s)` that looks up the `Class` object belonging to the string s. For example, `Class.forName("Ellipse")` returns the `Class` object that describes the `Ellipse` class.

Once you have a `Class` object describing the class, you can call its `newInstance()` operation to obtain a new object of the class, constructed with the default constructor. (An exception is thrown if the class does not have a default constructor.)

Thus, you can make a new object of a class whose name is stored in the string s as

```
Class.forName(s).newInstance();
```

The return type of newInstance is Object, and you may need to cast that to the appropriate type. For example, when reading in a shape, you would use the following code:

```
Shape newShape = (Shape)Class.forName(s).newInstance();
newShape.read(in);
shapes.addElement(newShape);
```

## Reflection

 The typeinfo class in C++ gives very little information about a type. It can reveal only the name and test if two types are identical. In Java 1.0, the Class class has only marginally more functionality. Besides giving the type name, it can also instantiate a new object of a type. This feature is used for virtual construction.

However, in Java 1.1, the capabilities of the Class class have been greatly expanded to support programs that can manipulate Java code dynamically. Examples of such programs are not just code browsers and debuggers, but also business tools such as form designers. If a Java program can find out about the properties of new classes, then users of such a program can drop in new classes at run time and have the program *reflect* on the newly added classes.

Here is a brief overview of the the most important parts of the reflection mechanism in Java 1.1. Three classes, Field, Method, and Constructor, describe data fields, operations, and constructors of classes. The getFields(), getMethods(), and getConstructors() methods of the Class class return arrays of the public fields, operations, and constructors that the class supports.

For example, this code writes out the signatures of all public operations that can be invoked on the object obj:

```
Methods[] operations = obj.getClass().getMethods();

for (int i = 0; i < operations.length; i++)
{  Method op = operations[i];
   Class retType = op.getReturnType();
   Class[] paramTypes = op.getParameterTypes();
   String name = op.getName();
   System.out.print(retType.getName() + " " + name + "(");
```

```
for (int j = 0; j < paramTypes.length(); j++)
{  if (j > 0) System.out.print(", ");
    System.out.print(paramTypes[i].getName);
}
System.out.println(");");
}
```

The complete mechanism is necessarily somewhat complex; because its use is limited to a narrow category of programs, we will not discuss all the details. For more information, see the online documentation at http://java.sun.com.

## Static and Dynamic Binding

### Determining the Binding of a Call

 Consider a call of an operation

```
x.f(); // C++
```

If x is an object, then its exact type is known at compile time. The call to f is always statically dispatched. That is, the compiler simply generates a call to X::f, where X is the type of x.

However, consider a call

```
px->f(); // C++
```

where px is an X* pointer. The *static type* of px is X*, but the object to which px points may well belong to a derived class. The pointer type of that actual object is called the *dynamic type* of px. Of course, the dynamic type is either equal to the static type or to a derived class thereof.

We usually wish to select the operation that is appropriate for the dynamic type. In C++ this is accomplished by a virtual function call.

Virtual function calls have a nontrivial overhead over regular function calls. The compiler therefore generates a regular function call whenever it can be assured that the static and dynamic type coincide; that is, when a call is carried out through an object. A virtual call is generated whenever the implicit argument is a pointer or reference.

```
Employee e("Joe User");
Employee* pe = new Manager("Carol Smith");
e.print(); // non-virtual call of Employee::print
pe->print(); // virtual call
```

```
double salary(const Employee& e, Date from, Date to)
{  double d = e.weekly_pay(...); // virtual call
   . . .
}
```

In particular, if one operation invokes another operation on its implicit argument, that call is virtual because the implicit argument is the *this reference of the operation.

```
void Employee::print_paycheck(Date from, Date to) const
{  double d = weekly_pay(...);
   // virtual call, this->weekly_pay(...)
   print();
   // virtual call, this->print()
   . . .
}
```

Occasionally, you must override the virtual call mechanism and call an operation of a specific class. This can be achieved by specifying the class name in the call. The most typical example is the invocation of the base-class operation in a derived-class redefinition.

```
void Manager::print() const
{  Employee::print(); // non-virtual call of Employee::print()
   . . .
}
```

Keep in mind that functions are dynamically bound only when they are declared as `virtual`. All other functions are statically bound. In Java, the situation is the exact opposite as in C++. By default, all functions are dynamically bound. To enforce static binding, functions must be declared as `final`. There are two reasons to use `final`. It potentially makes a function call more efficient. The Java compiler can inline replace very simple `final` functions such as

```
class Employee
{  public final double salary() { return _salary; }
   . . .
}
```

Then the call `e.salary()` can be inline replaced with the expression `e._salary` instead of having to make a function call.

And the class designer can ensure that no derived class supplies a different implementation.

```
class TransactionSecurityManager
{  public final boolean authorize(Transaction t)
```

```
   { . . .
   }
   . . .
}
```

This prevents the creation of a class

```
class RogueSecurityManager extends TransactionSecurityManager
{  public boolean authorize(Transaction t)
      // ERROR--can't redefine final operation
   {  return true;
   }
   . . .
}
```

In C++, it is possible to force static binding with the scope resolution syntax, for example, `Employee::print()`. That is not possible in Java. You can invoke the method of the direct superclass:

```
class Manager extends Employee
{  public void print()
   {  super.print(); // non-virtual call of Employee.print()
      . . .
   }
   . . .
}
```

You cannot go two levels up, though, as you could in C++. For example, suppose a class `Executive` inherits from `Manager`. Then there is no way of calling the `Employee.print` function on a `Executive` object.

Note that casting of the object reference has no influence on the dynamic selection of the operation.

```
Executive jean;
Employee e = (Employee)jean;
e.print(); // still calls Executive.print()
```

The dynamically selected operation is always the one that matches the *actual object;* the type of the reference invoking the operation is never significant. In particular, the following code is wrong:

```
class Manager extends Employee
{  public void print()
   {  ((Employee)this).print();
         // still calls Manager.print()
      . . .
   }
   . . .
}
```

The only way to call `Employee.print` is to use `super`. That is, `super` is *not the same as* `(BaseClass)this`. Instead, `super` is a keyword to turn off dynamic binding and statically bind to the superclass.

## Double Dispatch

As we have seen in the previous section, polymorphic equality testing is difficult because virtual functions allow run-time selection only on their first argument. For equality testing we were able to overcome that problem because equality is defined only on objects of the same type. The problem is more difficult if an operation is defined on arbitrary combinations of two polymorphic arguments.

Consider the task of computing regions on the screen. Regions are defined as unions and intersections of shapes. Intersections of rectangles are again rectangles (or empty), but unions of rectangles are not. Suppose the class `RectRegion` denotes unions of rectangles (stored as an array of their constituents), and `Region` denotes general regions, formed by unions and intersections of rectangles and ellipses (stored as tree structures). Figure 10.13 shows typical regions.

Table 10.1 lists the types of unions and intersections of the various regions.

The method of carrying out intersection and union depends on the type of both arguments. To compute the intersection of two rectangles, you compare their coordinates. To intersect a rectangle with a rectangle region, you intersect the rectangle with all rectangles in that region and form the union of the nonempty intersections (Figure 10.14).

Ideally, we would write separate virtual functions for each combination and rely on the virtual function mechanism to locate and execute the

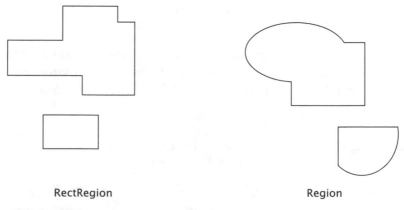

RectRegion                    Region

**FIGURE 10.13**  Regions.

**TABLE 10.1**  Unions and Intersections of Regions

| Intersection | Rectangle | RectRegion | Ellipse | Region |
|---|---|---|---|---|
| Rectangle | Rectangle | RectRegion | Region | Region |
| RectRegion | RectRegion | RectRegion | Region | Region |
| Ellipse | Region | Region | Region | Region |
| Region | Region | Region | Region | Region |
| **Union** | **Rectangle** | **RectRegion** | **Ellipse** | **Region** |
| Rectangle | RectRegion | RectRegion | Region | Region |
| RectRegion | RectRegion | RectRegion | Region | Region |
| Ellipse | Region | Region | Region | Region |
| Region | Region | Region | Region | Region |

correct one, whenever we need to intersect two shapes. But, as we have observed, virtual-function call

```
s->intersect(t);
```

looks only at the type of s to select an operation. You could resort to explicit type inquiry to find the type of t and then carry out the appropriate action. Explicit type inquiry, however, is always suspect and should be avoided.

Instead, we will use a technique called *double dispatch*. Consider, for example,

```
Shape* Rectangle::intersect(const Shape* t) const
```

which is executed as the result of the virtual-function call

```
s->intersect(t);
```

if s points to a rectangle. The trick now is to launch a virtual function on t to have the virtual function mechanism act on its type. Of course, just calling

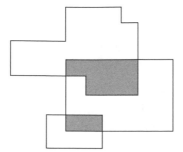

**FIGURE 10.14**  Intersecting a rectangle with a region.

```
t->intersect(s); // DON'T
```

would get us nowhere. Instead, we take advantage of the fact that we know that s must point to a rectangle, and call

```
t->intersect_rectangle(this);
```

Suppose t pointed to a rectangle region. This call then executes the function

```
Shape* RectRegion::intersect_rectangle(const Rectangle* r) const
```

In that function the types of both arguments are known: this (the original t) is a RectRegion*, and r (the original s) is a Rectangle*. We now have enough information to carry out the actual work.

That means for each of the types X, we have to define a virtual function

```
Shape* X::intersect(const Shape* t)const
{ t->intersect_X(this); }
```

and for each combination of types X and Y we define

```
Shape* Y::intersect_X (const X* r) const
{       // this is a Y*
        // r is an X*
        // now compute the intersection
}
```

Of course, several of the operations perform identical work, and common code can be factored out into (nonvirtual) procedures.

The double dispatch approach performs run-time resolution on two arguments, but at a cost. Suppose there are n classes, with base class B (in our example, n = 6). We require the following:

- A virtual function B::f(const B * ) const
- n virtual functions B::f_X(const X *) const
- n implementations X::f(const B * t) const { t->f _X (this); }
- n² implementations Y::f _X(const X * r) const that do the actual work of carrying out the operation involving X and Y objects.

Double dispatching works only for small and stable collections of classes. The code is difficult to maintain. The addition of a new class forces the addition of a new virtual function in the base class and 2(n+1) new implementations of operations.

Double dispatch is used only when functionality can vary with both arguments. Comparison operations such as equality testing should not be implemented with double dispatch. That would implement `n(n - 1)` operations that simply return `false`, and n operations that compute a nontrivial result when the argument types are identical.

We have indicated only a C++ solution for double dispatch. The exact same technique works for Java.

# Design Hints

## Use Objects Instead of Pointers When Possible

In C++, objects have more intuitive copy semantics than pointers. There is no need for dynamic allocation and deallocation. Use objects instead of pointers when you can.

You may need pointers for three reasons:

- Sharing
- Polymorphism
- Zero/one relationships

For example, consider a mailbox that holds messages. Should you use a `vector<Message>` or a `vector<Message*>`? Let us look at the reasons for pointers in detail. Can two mailboxes share the same message, to the degree that editing one necessarily affects the other? Are there different message types, derived from a base class `Message`? Does a slot in the mailbox need to differentiate between a blank message and no message at all (that is, is there a zero/one attachment)? If any one of these applies, use pointers; otherwise, use objects.

Of course, in Java, the issue is moot. You have no choice because all object reference variables act like pointers.

## Use References Instead of Pointers When Possible

C++ references have one essential advantage over pointers: They always refer to something. There is no null or uninitialized reference, thereby eliminating a whole class of programming errors.

You can use a reference to model an association that does not change over its lifetime. Reference parameters of functions are just one example. Over the lifetime of the function invocation, the reference parameter is bound to the argument of the call. An object may contain a reference to a file or a graphics context that it uses throughout its lifetime.

There is one additional requirement: You must be able to initialize the reference at the beginning of its lifetime. For reference parameters of functions, this is automatic. Reference fields of classes must be initialized in the constructor. If an object is to contain a reference to a file object, that file object must be supplied at construction and cannot be supplied (or changed) later.

## Don't Take the Address of an Object
## Except to Test for Identity

There is one legitimate reason to use the & operator: to test whether two pointers or references point to the identical object. All other uses are suspect.

Taking and storing the address of stack objects is not usually useful because stack objects are so short-lived. Taking the address of a field yields a pointer to the inside of an object and breaks the encapsulation.

Again, in Java, this is not an issue. There is no "address of" operator.

## Avoid Returning Pointers or References
## to Internal Fields

In general, C++ operations should not return pointers or references to data fields of objects. It violates the encapsulation. For example, the following would be an extremely poor idea:

```
class Date
{
public:
   int& day();
   . . .
private:
   int _day;
   . . .
};

int& Date::day() { return _day; } // DON'T
```

It sounds clever—day() can be used on the left-hand side of an assignment:

```
d.day() = 31;
```

There is essentially no difference between this setup and public data. In particular, it is impossible to change the data representation.

There is one exception to this rule. Containers like arrays, lists, vectors, and matrices commonly return references to the elements that they store.

This rule applies to Java as well, and with a vengeance. Consider the following class:

```
class Employee
{  public Date hireday() { return _hireday; }
   . . .
   private Date _hireday;
}
```

This function returns a *reference* to an internal object. If the Date class has a mutator method (such as the one in this book), then the encapsulation is broken: Anyone can modify the internal state of the object.

```
Date d = jenny.hireday();
d.advance(-1000); // give Jenny 3 more years of seniority
```

If the Date class doesn't have mutators, such as the one in the Java standard library, then it is safe to return a date reference. (However, the notion of being immutable is not necessarily stable. Mutators might be added to a class as it evolves.)

Otherwise, return a clone:

```
class Employee
{  public Date hireday()
   {  return (Date)_hireday.clone();
   }
   . . .
}
```

## Minimize Operations That Return Pointers to New Heap Objects

In general, C++ functions should not return pointers to newly allocated heap objects. Doing so requires that the caller capture the returned pointer and eventually delete it. This is a big burden to place on the caller.

However, an operation that computes a polymorphic result must build its return value on the heap. For example, to copy polymorphic objects, a clone operation must return a heap copy of *this. When reading in a polymorphic object from a file, the read operation must determine the exact type of the object described in the file, allocate a heap object of that type, and return it. The Shape::intersect operation must return a heap result.

In all three cases, the caller of the operation is responsible for eventually deleting the returned object.

Of course, in Java, we can be blissfully oblivious to this concern. Java objects are all allocated on the heap and automatically garbage collected.

## Never Return a Reference to a Stack or New Heap Object

In C++ code, never return a pointer or reference to a local stack object. The object is gone when the function exits.

Never return a reference to a newly allocated heap object. The syntax for deleting it is too unintuitive.

In general, only return a reference to an object that existed before the call of the operation. For example, returning `*this` is acceptable. For error handling, it is acceptable to return a reference to a static object.

## Avoid Type Inquiry

Whenever possible, use virtual functions rather than type inquiry. They lead to far more extensible and maintainable code.

Don't use the `typeid` operator or `getClass` operation except for equality testing. They are fundamentally incompatible with inheritance. Use `dynamic_cast` or `instanceof` when there is no good solution using virtual functions.

# Names: Scope, Access, and Conflict Control

When programming, you define certain constructs, such as classes, fields, operations, global variables, functions, types, and templates. We will collectively refer to these as *features*. Each feature is introduced in one place in a program, by giving a *name* and a *definition*. As an example of a feature, a class may be named Employee and defined to have certain operations and data fields. You later use the feature by referring to its name, Employee.

When a name is used in a program, the compiler needs to find out to which feature it refers. Most of the time, there is just one choice; however, it is possible to have multiple features with the same name in nested scopes. Then, rules decide which of them is meant by that name or if the name is ambiguous.

In fact, such ambiguity is a very real possibility in a program composed of many elements, written by many programmers and vendors. In this chapter, we will discuss techniques for guarding against unintended name conflicts.

Finally, when a name has been matched with a feature, that feature might still not be accessible, typically because it is not declared public. We will discuss the rules for access control in C++ and Java.

# Name Lookup for Variables and Functions

## Scopes

 In both C++ and Java, names are searched first in the local scope, then the scope of the class. Finally, C++ looks for names in the scope of the file if no match has been found in the local and class scopes.

Local scopes are nested and searched from the inside out:

```
void fun(string x, double y)
{  double x;
   . . .
   {  int x; // match
      . . .
      {  . . .
         x = 0;
         . . .
      }
   }
}
```

Function arguments are local names in the outermost local scope:

```
void fun(string x, double y) // match
{  . . .
   {  . . .
      {  . . .
         y = 0;
         . . .
      }
   }
}
```

If the variable is not found in any surrounding local scope, then the *class scope* is searched next. Of course, in the case of C++, that happens only inside operations of a class, not inside global functions.

```
class X
{  . . .
   void fun(double y);
   int x; // match
};

void X::fun(double y)
{  x = 0;
   . . .
}
```

If the class X derives from another class, all parent classes are also searched for a name match.

```
class B
{  . . .
   int x; // match
};

class X : public B
{  . . .
   void fun(double y);
};

void X::fun(double y)
{  x = 0;
   . . .
}
```

Just like variables, functions are looked up first in the class scope if they are invoked from another operation.

```
class X
{  ...
   void f(); // name match
};

void X::fun()
{  ...
   f();
   ...
}
```

If a match occurs, f denotes an operation with implicit argument *this in C++ or this in Java. (However, if f is a static class function, then it has no implicit argument. See the section on static functions later in this chapter.)

When looking for a matching function, the compiler looks at all functions in a given scope. (In C++, it does *not*, however, look into the base classes—see the discussion on hiding and overriding later in this section.) It then tries to find a unique function whose parameter types match the types of the values supplied in the call. Because both C++ and Java are willing to carry out certain conversions to achieve a match, the rules for matching are complex. We will not discuss the details. Instead, we strongly recommend that you do not use the same function name for two separate functions if there is a possibility of ambiguities.

In C++, the file scope is searched for a match if none has been found in the local or class scope.

```
int x; // a global variable
int g(); // a global function
. . .
void X::fun(double y)
{   x = 0;
    g();
    . . .
}
```

 Java has no file scope. All variables have local or class scope, and all functions have class scope.

Some programmers rely on the fact that the local scope is searched *before* the class scope to avoid prefixing data fields with an underscore. Consider the following code in a constructor:

```
class Employee
{   public Employee(String name)
    {   this.name = name;
    }
    . . .
    private String name;
};
```

That is, name matches the local variable and this.name matches the data field (in C++, you would use this->name). In constructors, this is handy because it lets you give meaningful names to the parameters, avoiding unsightly definitions such as this one:

```
Employee(String n) // huh? what is n?
```

Unfortunately, this is a somewhat dangerous strategy unless you have the iron will to prefix every data field with this. or this->. It is a surprisingly common error to accidentally introduce another local variable that matches a data field name and thus shadows it.

Consider this common mistake in a default constructor:

```
class Employee
{   public Employee()
    {   String name = "";
    }
    . . .
    private String name;
};
```

The programmer typed the String name by reflex, and the program compiles, but it initializes a local variable, not the data field.

The moral is this: The underscore prefix for field names may be ugly, but it is effective in making local scope and class scope disjoint.

## Accessing a Specific Scope

 In C++, you can always bypass the search in the local and class scope and refer to a global name by prefixing the name with the :: scope resolution operator.

```
void Window::message_box(string msg, string title)
{   // call global message_box function
    ::message_box(_handle, msg, title, MB_OK);
}
```

In this example, the :: operator selected the global message_box function.

Name lookup can be directed into the scope of a specific class with the scope resolution operator. This is commonly used to access a function in a base class:

```
class Manager : public Employee { ... };

void Manager::print(ostream & os) const
{   Employee::print(os);
    ...
}
```

 In Java, the situation is slightly different. You can use scope resolution to select a particular variable:

```
class B
{   public int x;
}

class D extends B
{   public double x;
    public void f() { B.x++; }
}
```

Naturally, it is not a good idea to add another variable of the same name in a derived class or to use public data fields. This example is used just to show the syntax.

You can also access static functions from another scope:

```
y = Math.sin(x);
```

However, to invoke an operation on an object, you have only one choice to select another scope, namely, to use `super`:

```
class Manager extends Employee
{  void print(PrintStream os)
   {  super.print(os);
      ...
   }
}
```

The syntax

```
Employee.print(os); // Error
```

is not legal for operations in Java—it is legal only for static functions. Casting the `this` reference is not helpful either: The call

```
((Employee)this).print(os); // doesn't call Employee.print
```

is still dynamically dispatched and finds the `Manager.print` function.

## Hiding Names

 Consider the following Java example:

```
class B
{  public void print(PrintStream os)
   { os.println(x);
   }
   . . .
   private int x;
}
```

```
class D extends B
{  public void print(PrintStream os)
   {  super.print(os);
      os.println(x);
   }
   . . .
   private double x;
}
```

As you can see, both B and D have a data field named x. This is perfectly legal. The field defined in D *hides* or *shadows* the one defined in B.

Although this is not a situation you would want to construct deliberately, it is, nevertheless, one that can arise in practice. Suppose the designers of B and D don't know about one another. The designer of D derives from B and adds another data field named x. Later on, the designer of B also happens to add another data field named x and ships the new version to the designer of D. Naturally, that programmer would prefer that an evolution of the base class does not break the derived class. Because the derived class data field hides the base class data field of the same name, they indeed don't conflict.

Now let us suppose the designer of D adds an operation f and an operation g that calls f.

```
class D extends B
{   . . .
   public double f(double n) { return n / 2; }
   public double g() { return f(1); }
}
```

Next suppose the designer of B adds a different operation, also called f.

```
class B
{   public int f(int n) { return n * 2; }
      . . .
}
```

Now D no longer compiles. The compiler complains about an ambiguity: The call to f(1) in D.g could match both the B.f(int) and the D.f(double) operations. This is unfortunate. Evolving the base class broke the derived class.

In Java, operations do not shadow one another as variables do. Because the two different versions of f have different parameter types, they represent completely unrelated functions.

Of course, if the base and derived class operations have the same name and the same parameter types, then the derived class operation *overrides* the base class operation. (Keep in mind that in Java all operations are "virtual" unless they are explicitly defined as final.)

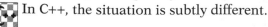 In C++, the situation is subtly different.

```
class B
{
public:
   int f(int n) { return n * 2; }
   . . .
};

class D : public B
{
```

```
public:
   double f(double n) { return n / 2; }
   public double g() { return f(1); }
   . . .
};
```

In C++, this code compiles, and the compiler picks `D::f` in `D::g`. This might be surprising because `B::f(int)` would seem a better match for the call `f(1)`. After all, 1 is an integer, not a floating-point number. Nevertheless, in C++, unlike Java, a function name always hides *all* functions with the same name in the base class. This avoids the problem that we saw in Java—in C++, adding a function in the base class will not break the derived class.

However, the C++ behavior is confusing, too. When you add a new function in a derived class, you are always shadowing all functions in the base class with the same name, regardless of the parameter types.

**TIP**

Inheritance and name overloading can conflict with each other. The rules for shadowing are different in C++ and Java. Whenever possible, do not use a function name in the base class as a function name in the derived class unless you want to override that function. In that case, of course, both functions have the same parameter types. ■

## Name Lookup and Access Control

In C++, name lookup is performed before access control. That is, first all names are searched, regardless of public or private attribute. Then the compiler checks whether the code has the privilege to access the found feature. Consider this situation:

```
class B
{
public:
   void f(int x) { cout << x << endl; }
   . . .
};

class D : public B
{  . . .
private:
   void f(double x) { cout << x / 2 << endl; }
};

int main()
{  D d;
   d.f(1); // Error
}
```

You might think that the call to d.f(1) would pick B::f(int). That is a public function, and it takes an integer argument. But the C++ compiler finds a function named f in the class D, the type of the implicit parameter of the call to f. It therefore looks at all functions called f in that scope. In this example, there is only one, namely D::f(double). It then finds that is a match because the integer 1 can be converted to a double by an implicit conversion.

After finding it an appropriate match, the compiler complains that D::f(double) is private and hence not accessible.

At first glance, it seems silly even to look at inaccessible features for name matching. However, programmers, in practice, often change operations from public to private or vice versa. If such a change could quietly change the meaning of an expression from one legal interpretation to a quite different one, undesirable consequences could occur. For example, suppose that the call to init in GraphWindow::open really intends to call Window::init from the base class, but then the designer of Window makes init private. It would not be desirable if that change simply altered the meaning of GraphWindow::open, invoking the global function init that happens to have the same name. Having the compiler generate an error alerts the programmer to the problem.

From a theoretical point of view, it is unsatisfactory that private features are used for name matching. Private features are a part of the implementation, not the interface. Making a public operation private or vice versa is really a change in interface. When the public interface changes, the class designer and users should expect changes in behavior.

 Indeed, Java does not use private functions for overloading resolution. Let us translate the example into Java:

```
class B
{  public void f(int x) { System.out.println(x); }
   . . .
}

class D extends B
{  private void f(double x) { System.out.println(x / 2); }
}

class Test
{  public static void main(String[] args)
   {  D d = new D();
      d.f(1); // calls B.f(int)
   }
}
```

The compiler ignores the private D.f(double) and picks the public B.f(int), which is the intuitive choice.

# Features with Class Scope

Of courses, classes define operations and data fields. In both C++ and Java, classes can define other features. Those features neither become a part of objects of the class, nor do they operate on such objects. They are just placed inside the class to take advantage of its scope. For example, by placing constants inside a class, their scope is restricted to that class, thereby avoiding name clashes.

## Class Scope Enumerations

Enumerated (enum) constants can be placed inside class declarations in C++:

```
class Date
{
public:
    enum Weekday
    { MON, TUE, WED, THU, FRI, SAT, SUN
    };
    . . .
};
```

Operations of the Date class refer to these constants simply as MON, TUE, and so forth. Because the enumeration is public, other functions can use them as well and must access them with the scope resolution operator

```
Date::MON
```

Enumerations can be private, in which case they are accessible only to the operations of the class defining them.

Enumerations in class scope are a powerful method for avoiding name clashes. Names of global constants are even more vulnerable to conflicts than names of functions because there is no possibility of overloading resolution. Even seemingly unique choices like SAT and SUN for weekday names can collide with names from quite different domains:

```
enum Workstation { DEC, HP, SUN, };
enum Test { SAT, GRE, GMAT, };
```

Moving enumerations into a class whose operations or clients are most likely to use them removes them from the global name space and minimizes the risk of conflicts.

Java has no enumerations, but it is still possible to define constants inside a class scope. Constants are tagged with the somewhat unsightly static final. (Java has reserved the keyword const but does not currently use it.)

```
class Date
{  public static final MON = 0;
   public static final TUE = 1;
   public static final WED = 2;
   public static final THU = 3;
   public static final FRI = 4;
   public static final SAT = 5;
   public static final SUN = 6;
   . . .

}
```

As you can see, this is less convenient than an `enum` in C++. You must come up with the numeric values for the constants yourself, and you don't get a new type. Instead you use `int` variables to hold weekdays.

As in C++, public constants can be accessed anywhere in a Java program by the scope resolution operator.

```
int trash_pickup = Date.WED; // same as Date::WED in C++
```

There is another curious usage of enumerations that are nested in a C++ class. In the past, it was not legal to initialize a static constant integer inside a class definition. (This was only recently permitted by the ANSI standard committee.) If the value of an integer constant is needed to specify the size of a buffer or other fixed-size array, then the constant can be defined in an anonymous enumeration.

```
class Stack
{  // ...
private:
   enum { SIZE = 20 };
   char _buffer[SIZE];
};
```

This solution is curious and really ugly, but it works and has become a standard idiom. We take advantage of the fact that `enum` constants can be given specific values.

The constant `SIZE` is not logically part of any enumerated type. For that reason, we did not give the enumeration any type name.

In Java, this problem does not arise because constants are initialized in the class definition and their value can be used elsewere in the class.

## Static Data

Consider the array

```
int days_per_month[12] =
{ 31, 28, 31, 30, 31, 30,
  31, 30, 31, 31, 30, 31
};
```

for use in a `Date` class. Suppose we want to restrict access to this array only to `Date` operations. We could make it a member:

```
class Date
{ . . .
private:
   int days_per_month[12];
   int _day;
   . . .
};
```

This approach would be very wasteful. Every instance of `Date` would have its own `days_per_month` array.

We want to have only one copy of the array that is shared among all `Date` objects, yet has the same access restrictions as regular `Date` members.

To declare such shared data, use the keyword `static`:

```
class Date // C++
{  // ...
private:
   static int days_per_month[12];
   int _day;
   // ...
};
```

```
class Date // Java
{  . . .
   private static int[] days_per_month;
   private int _day;
   . . .
}
```

This declares a single array that is not part of any `Date` object. It is accessible by all operations of the `Date` class.

In C++, the syntax for initializing a static variable is similar to that of defining an operation. The following definition must be included in the module implementing the `Date` class:

```
int Date::days_per_month[12] =
{ 31, 28, 31, 30, 31, 30,
  31, 31, 30, 31, 30, 31
};
```

In Java, the initializer can follow the static variable definition:

```
class Date // Java
{  . . .
   private static int days_per_month[] =
   {  31, 28, 31, 30, 31, 30,
      31, 31, 30, 31, 30, 31
   };
   private int _day;
   . . .
}
```

If the initialization is more complex, it can be contained in a *static initialization block:*

```
class Date // Java
{  . . .
   private static int days_per_month[];
   static
   {  days_per_month = new int[12];
      for (int i = 0; i < 12; i++)
      {  if (i > 0 && i % 5 == 0 || i % 5 == 3)
            days_per_month[i] == 30;
         else if (i == 1) days_per_month[i] = 28;
         else days_per_month[i] == 31;
      }
   }
   private int _day;
   . . .
}
```

A class can have multiple static initialization blocks. They are initialized exactly once, in the order they appear in the class, when the class is loaded.

Even though the declaration of static variables appears similar to that of data fields (except for the keyword static), they have nothing in common.

Data fields are parts of objects; static variables are not—there is a unique, per-class instance of each static variable.

In C++, global variables and static class variables behave identically except for name space control. Global variables are in the global scope and hence can clash with other variables of the same name. Static class variables are in the scope of the class and hence have their names protected. Java has no global variables, and you use static variables to simulate them.

The keyword static is somewhat unfortunate. It is an example of the keyword reuse that is common in C++ because the language designers are reluctant to add new keywords to a language in active use—any such keyword might clash with names that are already being used in programs.

Traditionally, static, when applied to local variables, makes the local variable persist when the function exits. The next time the function is entered, the same value is still there.

```
void f()
{  static int counter = 0; // a local static variable
   int n; // a local stack variable
   . . .
   counter++;
}
```

In this situation, the static keyword makes sense. The variable counter stays around, whereas the local stack variables are abandoned when the function exits. Thus, it really is more static.

Next, the same keyword was hijacked to express an entirely unrelated idea. A global variable or function is tagged as static to denote that it is private to the current module and cannot be used outside it.

```
static int current; // global variable, private to this module
```

In this situation, the static keyword makes no sense whatsoever. The variable current has the same lifetime as any other global variable.

Finally, the C++ designers decided to use the same keyword for shared variables in a class scope. Thus, static has three unrelated meanings in C++. There is no possibility for ambiguity—static refers to a local, global, or class variable.

In Java, there are no static local or global variables. The keyword static always denotes a shared variable.

## Static Functions

As we saw in the preceding section, global variables can be placed inside classes as shared variables, to group them where they logically belong and to remove their names from the global name space. The same is possible for functions.

Consider a function that tests whether a year is a leap year, for use in date arithmetic.

```
bool is_leap(int year)
{  if (year % 4 != 0) return false;
   if (year < 1582) return true;
   if (year % 100 != 0) return true;
```

```
   if (year % 400 != 0) return false;
   return true;
};
```

This function is not an operation of the `Date` class because it does not take an implicit argument. (Of course, we could write a different function, `bool Date::is_leap()`, to test whether the `_year` field of `*this` is a leap year.) Nevertheless, the function is logically related to the `Date` class. It can be inserted into the scope of `Date` by using the keyword `static`. Here is the C++ code. The keyword `static` is not repeated in the definition of the function—you need to look carefully at the function declaration inside the class definition to find out that the function is not a regular operation.

```
class Date // C++
{
public:
   static bool is_leap(int);
      . . .
};


bool Date::is_leap(int year)
{ . . .
}
```

Here is the Java code—the function is essentially the same except that the code is contained inside the class definition.

```
class Date // Java
{  public static boolean is_leap(int year)
   { . . .
   }
      . . .
}
```

As a public function, `is_leap` can be called by any other function. Functions outside the scope of `Date` must use scope resolution.

```
if (Date::is_leap(y)) . . . // C++
if (Date.is_leap(y)) . . . // Java
```

Static functions have no implicit argument and hence cannot access class fields without specifying an object. They can, however, operate on static data.

In Java, all functions must be defined inside a class. It is therefore quite common to have functions without a natural implicit argument implemented as static functions. For example, the `Math` class contains a large number of static functions:

```
double Math.sqrt(double)
double Math.sin(double)
double Math.atan2(double, double)
double Math.random()
. . .
```

None of these operates on objects of type `Math` (or any other class)—the `Math` class is just a convenient home for these functions.

Unlike global functions, static functions have the privilege of accessing private features of their class. In C++, this can be handy when writing comparison functions. For example, the standard C library function `qsort` requires a pointer to a comparison function to sort a C array. For greater efficiency, we may want to allow this function access to the private data. However, `qsort` requires a pointer to a regular function, not a member function. Here is the C++ code that shows how a static function can give you the access rights of a member function and the call properties of a regular function.

```
class Date
{
public:
   static int compare(const Date*, const Date*);
   . . .
};

int Date::compare(const Date* a, const Date* b)
{  int d = a->_year - b->_year;
   if (d != 0) return d;
   d = a->_month - b->_month;
   if (d != 0) return d;
   return a->_day - b->_day;
}

Date dates[100];
qsort(dates, 100, sizeof(Date), Date::compare);
```

## Nested Classes

In C++, a class can be nested inside another. This is most frequently done to hide a class that is relevant only for implementation:

```
class List
{
public:
   void insert(int);
   int remove();
   . . .
```

```
private:
   class Link
   {
   public:
      Link(int, Link* = NULL);

      int _info;
      Link* _next;
   };

   Link* _head;
};
```

This does not mean that every object of type `List` contains a subobject of type `Link`. Placing `Link` inside the scope of the `List` class merely hides the definition of `Link` from the outside world. Apart from visibility, there is no difference between nested classes and separately defined classes.

Although all data members of `Link` are public, they are known only to the `List` class because `Link` itself is declared in the private part of `List`. This is common and entirely permissible because the encapsulation of the `List` class is not compromised.

Operations of the `Link` class require two scope resolutions:

```
List::Link::Link(int i, Link* n)
: _info(i),
  _next(n)
{}
```

It is legal to declare a nested class inside its enclosing class and defer the definition:

```
class List
{ . . .
private:
   class Link;
   Link* _head;
};

class List::Link
{
public:
   Link(int, Link* = NULL);
   int _info;
   Link* _next;
};
```

That makes the enclosing class easier to read.

The 1.1 release of Java, which at the time of this writing is not yet final-ized, supports nested classes as well. However, they are called *inner classes*, and they are intended to be used for a different purpose than C++ nested classes.

In C++, the primary purpose for nested classes is namespace control. However, Java *packages* do a good job in namespace control already. There is no need to have a secondary structuring mechanism within packages. (The fact that the default visibility for data fields is the entire package suggests that the Java designers did not envision packages to be very large.)

However, inner classes in Java have an interesting feature: Their oper-ations are allowed access to the scope of the objects that instantiate them. We will cover inner classes in Chapter 19.

## Types in Class Scope

Nested classes define class types in the scope of a class. In C++, type defini-tions in class scope perform the same for type synonyms.

```
class Directory
{
public:
    enum { FILENAME_LEN = 80 };
    typedef char Filename[FILENAME_LEN];
    . . .
};
```

The type `Directory::Filename` can be used publicly, but it is guaran-teed not to conflict with other types named `Filename`.

## *Controlling Name Conflicts*

### Obtaining Unique Names

The traditional method a vendor takes to avoid name conflicts is to use a *prefix* for all classes and global variables and functions, such as **C**Window, **T**Edit, or **RW**HashTable. This technique is clearly limited. If both Rogue Wave and Roger Williams have the same bright idea to use RW as their ven-dor prefix, nothing is solved.

Alternatively, each vendor could choose a *unique* prefix, such as its tax ID number or its Internet domain name, to form prefixes like these:

```
COM_RogueWave_HashTable
Roger_Williams_149_16_2536_HashTable
```

Clearly, these long prefixes would be very awkward for the programmer. What is needed is a mechanism that guarantees unique names while retaining programmer convenience.

C++ and Java each have their own mechanisms for this purpose. C++ uses name spaces; Java uses packages. We will discuss both the C++ and Java mechanisms in this section.

Before studying the mechanisms, let us reconsider methods for obtaining unique names. Tax ID numbers are certainly unique within a given country, so a combination of the international telephone country code followed by a tax ID number might be a good unique identifier. The idea is to use a system where other bodies (such as the international telephone union or the national revenue collection agency) have already established unique identifiers.

Sun Microsystems recommends a different approach to generate unique package names. That method takes advantage of the fact that Internet domain names are unique. Write an internet domain backwards. (For some reason, they recommend capitalizing the first part, such as COM, EDU, CA, DE, etc.) Then append a name that is unique within your organization. Here are some examples:

```
DE.bmw.roadster.Z3
COM.horstmann.practicaloo
```

This seems like a good convention, and we will use it in this book, both for Java package names and C++ name space names.

## The C++ Name Space Mechanism

In 1993 a new language mechanism was added to C++ to provide unique (and therefore long) names in the object code of libraries that can be abbreviated to concise source code names.

Feature declarations are entered into a name space:

```
namespace COM_VendorA_Containers
{  template<class T> class List { ... };
   template<class T> class Queue { ... };
   ...
}
```

These declarations are imported into a program through a header file.

The implementor, that is, vendor A, must also wrap the implementation code in a name space block:

```
namespace COM_VendorA_Containers
{
    template<class T> T Queue<T>::remove() { ... };
    template<class T> int Queue<T>::length() const { ... };
    ...
}
```

This has the effect of generating object code in which all data and functions have long but unique names. It is assumed that the linker and dynamic link mechanism have no problems with long names.

Name spaces can contain the definitions of global variables and functions, types, classes, and templates.

Programmers can refer to these features by their full name, such as

```
COM_VendorA_Containers::Queue<Employee> q;
```

Of course, that is very awkward. An essential feature of name space is that shorter aliases are available. The easiest and safest method for simplifying access to a name space is to give it a shorter alias.

```
namespace Containers = COM_VendorA_Containers;
```

Now containers can be obtained by using the shorter alias as a prefix:

```
Containers::Queue<Customer> q;
```

It also eases the change from the container library by vendor A to a compatible library by another vendor.

The second method is to specify which features you would like to use. Their names are entered into the scope containing the using declaration and need not be qualified.

```
class Bank
{ using COM_VendorA_Containers::Queue;
    . . .
private:
    Queue<Customer> _waitingQueue;
    . . .
};
```

A using declaration can be inserted into any class scope, local scope, or file scope:

```
void f(double mean)
{   using COM_VendorA_Math::expdist;
    double x = expdist(mean);
    . . .
};
```

Finally, all names of a name space can be made available in a scope:

```
using COM_VendorA_Math;
void f(double mean)
{   double x = expdist(mean);
    . . .
};
```

However, that seems dubious. Name spaces are likely to be large and somewhat fluid because vendors tend to add new features periodically. Simply pouring the contents of one or more name spaces into a scope seems to invite name collisions.

## The Java Package Mechanism

 You have already worked with several Java packages, such as `java.util` for utility classes and `java.applet` for classes that are needed to program applets, the Java programs that are embedded in a Web page.

Packages are the Java equivalent of name spaces in C++.

If you want to use a feature such as the `Vector` or `Applet` class, then you have two choices. You can refer to the class by its full name:

```
java.util.Vector v = new java.util.Vector();
```

Or you can use the `import` statement to import the name of the class:

```
import java.util.Vector;
```

After you import a name, then you can use the short form:

```
Vector v = new Vector();
```

The directive

```
import java.util.*;
```

imports all names of the `java.util` package. That means, all names such as `Vector` and `Hashtable` defined in that package are available by their short names.

The * in the `import` directive can apply only to a single package. You cannot use

```
import java.*; // Error
```

or

```
import java.*.*; // Error
```

The compiler always looks into the `java.lang` package. You need not import it. The compiler also always looks for the default package with no name. This is where the classes for your own programs are located unless you explicitly put them into another package.

If you import packages, you get short names for all classes that do not conflict with another. However, if you import both `java.util` and `java.sql` and want to use the `Date` class, then you must be specific *which* `Date` class you want. There are two, namely `java.util.Date` and `java.sql.Date`.

And, of course, if you use the code with this book, there is a third `Date` class, namely `COM.horstmann.practicaloo.Date`. Here a flaw of the Java mechanism becomes obvious—having shorter aliases for long package names or being able to restrict the scope of the `import` clause to less than the whole source file would be desirable. This control is possible in C++, but not in Java.

## Access Control

We have seen that C++ and Java classes can control the access to their class features with the public and private attributes. As we know, data should always be private to a class, but we can decide to make operations, static functions, enumerations, nested classes, and types either public or private.

In certain circumstances, this simple access control mechanism is too restrictive. It distinguishes only between two sets of clients: the class's operations and all other code. Occasionally it is desirable to grant access to private features to some, but not all, other functions.

### Friends

 In C++, a class may name another function or another class as its *friend*. That gives the named function, or all operations of the named class, the right to access all private features. This is a dangerous mechanism, and it should be used only when absolutely necessary.

Consider the following pair of `Link` and `List` classes.

```
class Link
{
private:
    Link(int, Link* = NULL);
    int _info;
    Link* _next;
    friend class List;
};

class List
{
public:
    void insert(int);
    int remove();
    . . .
private:
    Link* _head;
};
```

The `Link` class declares that `List` is its friend. Hence, all `List` operations (insert, remove, and so forth) may access the private features of `Link`. In this case, `Link` has *no* public features, and only `List` operations can manipulate links. The effect is very similar to a `Link` class that is nested inside `List`. The nested class is generally the superior solution. However, if two classes, say `List` and `Queue`, share the same links, then the link class cannot be nested in either. Instead, it must be a global class that declares both `List` and `Queue` as friends:

```
class Link
{ . . .
    friend class List;
    friend class Queue;
};
```

If a class wants to give access permission to a global function or a single operation of another class, it must name it as a friend.

```
class Vector
{  . . .
    friend Vector Matrix::multiply(const Vector&) const;
    friend int compare(const Vector&, const Vector&);
    friend ostream& operator<<(ostream&, const Vector&);
};
```

In this example, three functions are permitted access to the private fields of the `Vector` class. The `Matrix::multiply` operation, which multiplies a matrix with a vector, can be implemented more efficiently if it has access to the internal representation of vectors. The compare function is not declared as an operation on Vector objects because it is intended for use in certain templates that require a global function. A better solution would be to make compare a static function of Vector. As we will see in Chapter 12, it is possible to map operators (+, *, ==, <<) to functions. The operator<< function implements the printing of a vector onto a stream, and for efficiency it is allowed access to the private vector data.

Use the friend mechanism with caution. Overused friendship is often a sign of poor class design.

Java has no friend mechanism. Instead, closely collaborating classes can be placed in the same *package*. We will discuss this approach in the next section.

## Package Visibility

 In Java, related classes are put together into packages such as java.lang, java.util or the COM.horstmann.practicaloo package for the code with this book.

In addition to public and private visibiity, Java has another visibility mechanism, *package visibility*. Somewhat surprisingly, this is the *default* mechanism. If you don't declare a data field or member function as public or private, it is automatically accessible to all operations of all classes in the same package.

For example, to implement a linked list, you would add both the List and the Link class into the same package and give the data fields of the Link class package visibility, simply by declaring them neither public nor private.

```
class Link
{  int _info; // package visibility
   Link _next; // package visibility
}

class List
{  public void insert(int) { . . . }
   public int remove() { . . . }
   . . .
   private Link _head;
}
```

Because the insert and remove operations of the List class belong to the same package as the Link class, they can access the _info and _next fields of the Link class. That is fine—we don't need to write cumbersome accessors and mutators. However, *every other class* in the same package can also access these fields, and that can become a problem over time.

This is an unfortunate default. Here is an example to illustrate this point. At the time of this writing, the `Window` class in the `java.awt` package contains a data field `warningString`:

```
package java.awt;
class Window
{  . . .
   String warningString;
}
```

If a window has a warning string, it is displayed at the bottom of the window (see Figure 11.1).

Browsers use this warning string to tag windows that are popped up by Java applets on Web pages. Without such a warning, a hacker might find out

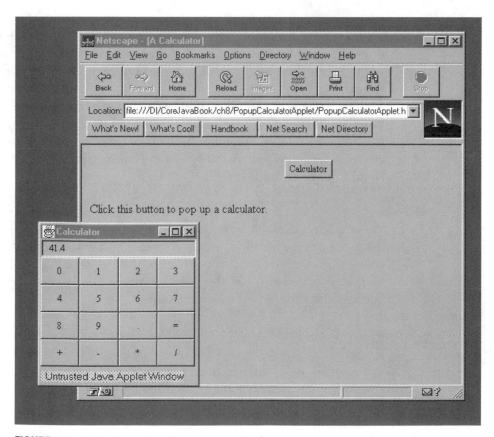

**FIGURE 11.1**   Warning string in a popup window.

what the logon prompt in a certain company looks like, entice the users in that company to visit his or her Web page, and have an applet on that page pop up an imitation of the logon prompt. Unsuspecting users might think that their connection was terminated and try to log in again. The applet would then capture the name and password. To avoid any such shenanigans, the browser tags all windows popped up by an applet.

If you look closely, you will find that the warningString field is not private. Thus, any other class in the same package can modify it. And it is possible to smuggle other classes into a package. Just try it: Make a directory \myclasses\java\awt, add a class

```
package java.awt;
class WarningChanger
{  public static void change(Window w)
   {  w.warningString = "Trust me!";
   }
}
```

into that directory, and add the directory \myclasses to the CLASSPATH.

Actually, the class loaders of browsers specifically disallow the loading of new classes into the standard packages, so this particular attach will not work. But it does point to the fact that package visibility is not a desirable feature.

In this particular case, there was actually no reason to give package visibility to the warningString field—no other class in the java.awt package accesses it. In all likelihood, the programmer simply forgot to add the private tag. Package visibility is rarely necessary—the designers of Java should not have made it the default.

**TIP**

Make a special effort to declare all data fields of a class as private. The default, package visibility, is rarely useful and could potentially be a safety concern. In the great majority of cases, the private keyword is omitted not to give other classes in the same package the access right, but simply because the programmer was in a hurry. ■

## Protected Features

 The operations of a derived class have no more right to access the private features of its base class than any other code does. For example, consider a base class Chart, which stores an array of numbers, and a derived class, PieChart:

```
class Chart
{
public:
   virtual void plot(Graphics& g) const = 0;
   . . .
private:
   vector<double> _val;
};


class PieChart : public Chart
{
public:
   virtual void plot(Graphics& g) const;
   . . .
};
```

The plot operation of PieChart cannot access the _val field of the base class Chart. The obvious solution is, of course, to supply a public operation Chart::value(int) const to obtain the data values. Then everyone, not just charts, gets to see these values. Another solution is to make PieChart a friend of Chart, but that is not a good idea. Other chart types, such as BarChart, will be derived from Chart. Making them all into friends does not work in general; a base class cannot know all classes that may derive from it.

It can occasionally be useful to consider operations of derived classes as more privileged than other code and to give them special access privileges. This is achieved with *protected* access control. A protected feature of a base class is accessible by the operations of all derived classes. For example, if the _val field is declared protected instead of private, then the operations of PieChart and BarChart can access (and modify) it.

Protected data is actually never a good idea. We will study a protected operation:

```
class Chart
{
public:
   virtual void plot(Graphics& g) const = 0;
   . . .
protected:
   double value(int) const;
private:
   vector<double> _val;
};
```

Now classes that derive from Chart can find out about the data stored in the chart, but no other code can.

```
void PieChart::plot(Graphics& g) const
{  . . .
   double s = value(i);
   . . .
}

int main()
{  PieChart pc;
   . . .
   double s = pc.value(i); // ERROR
   . . .
}
```

As an added security measure, class operations can use protected features only on objects *of their own class.*

```
void RogueChart::spy(BarChart& bc)
{  . . .
   double s = bc.value(i); // ERROR
   . . .
}
```

In using protected features, the belief is that derived classes have a better understanding of a base class and thus can be trusted more than others to access data or to call operations with the right arguments and in the right order. This is a somewhat dangerous assumption because a class has no influence over who derives from it.

 In Java, protected features can be used *both* by derived classes and by all other classes in the same package.

## Impact on Encapsulation

Loosening access control can compromise the encapsulation of a class. If a C++ class names a single function as a friend, this is not a problem. The friend function is listed in the class definition and thus becomes part of the interface. If the class implementation is changed, the friend function must track the change, just like all other functions declared in the class definition.

However, if a C++ class declares another class as a friend, it agrees that all operations of the friend class, whether they exist now or will be added later, have access to all private features. This should be carried out only to join closely related classes, such as Link and List. If the private section of the class granting friendship is modified, all operations of the friend classes must track the change.

When granting friendship, it is possible to enumerate all functions that are granted access to the private features. These are the explicitly named friend functions and all operations of friend classes. In contrast, it is impossible to enumerate all functions that are allowed access to protected features. Any class may derive from the base class that grants protected access, and the base class code contains no trace of the derivation.

For this reason, protected data fields are a bad idea. Determining what code must be changed when the data representation is modified is impossible. Protected data fields have another problem: Monitoring that the derived-class operations preserve the base class invariant is more difficult.

On the other hand, protected operations can be helpful in distinguishing the interface that is of interest to class users from the interface that is necessary to refine the class behavior through derivation. Because a class has no control over who will derive from it, protected operations should be written with the same care as public operations.

Finally, the package visibility in Java is not a desirable feature. Packages grow over time, and programmers can even smuggle new classes into existing packages. Therefore, there is very little control over the functions that can access features with package visibility. Java programmers should avoid this construct whenever possible and tag all operations and data fields explicitly as `private` or `public`. The few exceptions, where a number of collaborating classes must share data or functions, should be clearly documented.

# Separate Compilation

## Compilation Units

In practice, placing all source code for a program into a single file for compilation is not feasible. Compiling large programs is slow. Compilers have limits on the sizes of internal tables. Having more than one programmer work on one file at a time is awkward.

For that reason, programs are broken up into compilation units. Traditionally, compilation units are individual source files. (Implementations that are not based on files are possible in principle.)

In C++, each source file is translated into a single object file. The linker combines the object files to an executable file, resolving all references to data and functions that are defined in one compilation unit and used in others. In between these two is a separate control mechanism to produce the code for instantiated templates.

In Java, each source file is translated into a collection of class files. The Java compiler produces one class file for each class in the source file. These files contain the *byte codes,* instruction for the Java *virtual machine.* There is no linker. The Java interpreter simulates the virtual machine, which is started by specifying a single class name. The `main` function of that class is executed, and all other classes are loaded on demand. These classes can be loaded from the local file system or the network, depending on the *class loader*. For example, the class loader in a Java-aware browser loads applet classes from the host containing the ambient Web page.

## Declarations and Definitions

In C++, we distinguish between declarations and definitions. A *declaration* advertises the existence of a feature, such as a variable or function with a given name and type. The *definition* specifies the actual implementation. Variable definitions allocate space and optionally provide initialization. Function definitions specify the function code.

Definitions must be unique in a program, but the same feature can be declared multiple times, even in the same compilation unit.

The following are definitions:

```
int x;
Employee harry("Harry Hacker");
int sq(int x) { return x*x; }
```

The corresponding declarations are these:

```
extern int x;
extern Employee harry;
int sq(int);
```

Variable declarations require the keyword `extern` to distinguish them from definitions.

Declarations for classes and enumerations simply advertise the name:

```
class Date;
enum Color;
```

The definitions give the complete descriptions:

```
class Date
{
public:
   Date();
   void advance(long n);
   . . .
};
enum Color { RED, GREEN, BLUE, ... };
```

The class *definition* contains *declarations* of the operations that themselves are defined elsewhere.

```
void Date::advance(long n) { ... };
```

The name of the keyword notwithstanding, `typedef` *declares* types

```
typedef unsigned int Handle;
```

There are no type definitions in C++.

**TIP**

Many programmers are confused about the distinction between declarations and definitions in C++. It is common to say "here I am declaring a variable," when in fact the variable is being *defined*. And, of course, it doesn't help that type declarations are called `typedef`. Use the following simple rule to differentiate between declarations and definitions:

If you can write it twice, it is a declaration. Otherwise, it is a definition. For example:

```
extern int x;
extern int x; // OK to write it twice--it is a declaration

int x;
int x; // ERROR--it is a definition.
```

■

## Linkage of Global Variables and Functions

Global variables and functions can be reached from other compilation units (provided their declarations are supplied), unless their definitions are explicitly made private to the file containing them, with the keyword `static`. These variables and functions are public:

```
int x;
int sq(int x) { return x * x; }
```

Any compilation unit that wishes to access them simply includes their declaration:

```
extern int x;
int sq(int);
```

Prefixing the definitions with `static` makes them inaccessible outside their source file.

```
static int x;
static int sq(int x) { return x * x; }
```

This holds only for global variables and functions that are declared outside any classes. Anything declared inside a class follows the access specifications given by the public and private sections of the class.

## Header Files

C++ provides no automatic mechanism to communicate declarations of features between the implementation module and the modules using them. Programmers must establish this correspondence through header files.

A module is distributed over two files. A header file (module.h) contains the following:

- Definitions of classes, templates, and enumerated types
- Declarations of type synonyms (`typedef`)
- Declarations of global variables
- Declarations of non-inline global functions
- Definitions of inline constants and functions

The source file (module.cpp or module.c) includes its own header file and supplies the following:

- Definitions of shared class variables and global variables
- Definitions of non-inline operations and functions

These may be wrapped in `namespace` blocks, both in the header and source file.

Any module that wishes to use the features of another module includes that module's header file. A header file contains the definitions of those features that all client modules must know in detail for compilation. When the compiler merely needs to be assured of the existence of a feature, only the declaration is supplied in the header file.

In particular, the code for functions that are not inline replaced is given in exactly one source file. The header file communicates the existence of the function to all clients. The code for inline functions must be supplied in the header file because each client module must perform the inline replacement. Similar to inline functions, template code must be accessible to all clients to permit instantiation of the class and its operations, and hence it is placed in header files.

## Header File Design

The cardinal rule for header files is that they should be self-reliant. If a header file defines a feature that depends on the interface given in another header file, it should include it.

**FILE**

```
manager.h:

#include "employee.h"
class Manager : public Employee { . . . };
```

■

The clients of the manager module just want to include manager.h, not the collection of headers on which manager.h happens to depend.

If no detailed knowledge of a class is required, a header file may just declare its name rather than pull in another header. This happens when only pointers or references to a class are involved.

**FILE**

```
manager.h:

#include "employee.h"
class ostream; // no need to include iostream.h
class Manager : public Employee
{
public:
   void print(ostream&) const;
   ...
};
```

This speeds compilation, and it may even be necessary to break circular dependencies.

■

As a consequence, the same header file may be included more than once during compilation of a module. The compiler will read in a header file repeatedly because there is the theoretical possibility that the second parsing gives different results—a changed preprocessor variable might affect conditional compilation. Of course, any header files that are designed to provide a changed set of declarations when parsed twice ought to be taken out and shot.

Header files, however, contain definitions of classes, templates, and inline functions. Definitions may not be repeated. To guard against multiple inclusion, the contents of header files are surrounded by directives:

```
manager.h:

#ifndef MANAGER_H
#define MANAGER_H
header file contents
#endif
```

■

## Automatic Header File Generation

Many programmers find it tedious to distribute the code of a module into two files. All interface changes force update of both the header and the source file. The code library contains a tool that extracts header files automatically from source files, thereby cutting in half the number of files with which a programmer needs to deal. For historical reasons that tool is called mdgen, short for *m*odule *d*efinition *gen*erator.

Even though mdgen is not part of standard C++, quite a few programmers have used this tool and found it extremely convenient. Here is a brief outline of how it works—for more information, download the entire package from the Web site for this book.

When using mdgen, the programmer must tag the items that should be exported to the header file. For example,

FILE

```
sample.cpp

EXPORT
#include <iostream.h>

EXPORT int x;

EXPORT inline int sq(int x) { return x * x; }

EXPORT double sq(double x) { return x * x; }

EXPORT class Employee
{
public:
   Employee(string, double);
   . . .
private:
   string _name;
   double _salary;
};
```

■

Run the mdgen program from the command line:

```
mdgen sample.cpp
```

This produces a file sample.h with the following contents:

**FILE**

```
sample.h

#ifndef SAMPLE_H
#include <iostream.h>

extern int x;

inline int sq(int x) { return x * x; }

double sq(double x);

class Employee
{
public:
    Employee(string, double);
    . . .
private:
    string _name;
    double _salary;
};
#endif
```

■

This header file is ready for inclusion in other source files. Note that the mdgen tool is smart enough to copy the body of tagged inline functions into the header file, but it extracts only the declarations of functions that are not inline.

The EXPORT tag is #defined to be the empty string by the header file mdgen.h. It is just used by the mdgen tool to locate the features to be extracted. (Some compilation environments use the tag EXPORT for another purpose. Then use MDGEN_EXPORT instead.)

The purpose of this tool is to cut in half the number of files the programmer needs to inspect and administer. If you find this goal attractive, have a look at mdgen.

## Separate Compilation in Java

C and C++ are somewhat unique in forcing the programmer to manage the header files that tell one compilation unit about the features of other compilation units. Most other programming languages, such as Pascal or Ada, leave this task to the compilation environment. (In fact, the technique of the preceding section shows that this task can be automated in C++ as well.) Java does not follow the C++ model of programmer-generated header files. Instead, the compiler automatically looks inside the class files of any classes that are referenced in a compilation unit to discover the features of those classes. For example, if you compile a file that defines a class extending `java.applet.Applet`, then the compiler searches all directories on the *class path* for a subdirectory `java/applet` and for a file `applet.class` in that subdirectory.

In many compilation environments, the `CLASSPATH` environment variable lists the base directories from which the compiler will search for package directories. For example, to use the classes in this book, you might set the class path to

```
SET CLASSPATH=C:\java\lib;C:\PracticalOOBook;.
```

To find the `applet.class` file, the compiler will look into the following directories for classes:

```
C:\java\lib\java\applet
C:\java\lib\java\lang (because java.lang is always imported)
C:\java\lib (because the default package is always imported)
C:\practicaloobook\java\applet
C:\practicaloobook\java\lang
C:\practicaloobook
.\java\applet
.\java\lang
.
```

Here `.` is the current directory. To confuse matters more, the compiler also looks into **ZIP** or **JAR** files that are stored in any class path directory.

If the compiler finds a unique file with the name `applet.class` in any of these places, then it reads that file, which contains both the description of the class and its operations, and the compiled code of the operations.

If the compiler doesn't find such a class file, it won't give up quite yet. It will look for the following:

- A file `Applet.java` in all packages
- A class `Applet` in *all* `.java` files in the current package

If it finds one, it will compile that .java file to get an Applet.class file.

Once the class path has been set correctly, this entire mechanism is transparent to the user. However, if you write code that you place in your own package, that code must be located in a subdirectory whose path matches the package name. For example, the code for the COM.horstmann.practicaloo package must be located in the COM\horstmann\practicaloo subdirectory of one of the directories of a class path.

## Design Hints

### Don't Pollute the Global Name Space with Constants

In C++, it is possible to define global constants, but it is not a good idea. Even the most unlikely sounding name for a global constant invites a name conflict. Is WM_SIZE the window message for resizing or the size of the widget map? Place all constants inside classes (WindowMessage::SIZE, WidgetMap::SIZE). That way, you have a conflict only if two class names clash. When that happens, you are in trouble anyway, and you must rename the classes, or better, use name spaces.

Of course, in Java, this is not an optional activity. All constants must be placed inside classes.

### Eliminate Global Variables

Global variables can usually be eliminated by making them static variables of an appropriate class. Of course, being data, they should always be in the private section of the class. If necessary, add public static functions to inspect and update the variables.

In Java, there are no global variables. The equivalent to global variables are static variables in a class. As with all variables, it is best to declare them private and, if necessary, add static accessor and mutator functions.

### Try to Change Global Functions into Static Functions

In C++, it is a good idea to avoid global functions. Try to find a good home for them. Often there is a class that is closely related to their functionality. If the function is private to the module (declared as static), place it in the private section of the class; you gain the benefit of access to the class implementation, should you need it. If the function is public (not `static` and declared in the header file), place it in the public section of the class; you gain the benefit of name control. The function is now known to the public as `classname::f()`.

Of course, in Java, this is a requirement, not an optional step.

## Use Nested Classes for Auxiliary Abstractions

Some classes need auxiliary abstractions in their interfaces. For example, list iterators are objects that can be attached to linked lists to inspect their contents. An `Iterator` class can be defined in the public section of the `List` interface. It is known to the outside world as `List::Iterator`, eliminating any confusion with iterators from other container classes.

Implementation classes that are of no interest outside a class should be defined as nested classes in the private section. Typical examples are the links of a linked list or the nodes of a tree.

The following list interface shows both public and private nested classes.

```
class List
{
private:
   class Link
   {
   public:
      Link(int, Link* = NULL);
      int _info;
      Link* _next;
   };
public:
   class Iterator
   {
   public:
      Iterator(const List&);
      void reset();
      void next();
      int current() const;
      bool at_end() const;
   private:
      Link* _current;
   };
   void insert(int);
   int remove();
   . . .
private:
   Link* _head;
};
```

## Don't Grant Friendship Lightly

Declaring a single function (typically an operator function) as a friend of a class is perfectly acceptable. That function becomes a part of the class interface, and it is easy to gauge the impact of change in the private representation.

A class should declare another class as a friend only if it intends to be completely subordinate to that other class. For example, a Link class may declare List and Queue as friends because the sole purpose for links is to be carriers of information for lists and queues. But Date should not declare Employee as a friend. There is no telling how Date and Employee will evolve over time.

## Don't Use Protected or Package Data

The rationale for encapsulating class data is that the data representation is subject to change over the lifetime of a class. By making data private, it is possible to enumerate all operations that need to be updated when such a change occurs. Protected data is accessible to all derived classes. A base class cannot tell who derives from it. A class cannot control who joins it in the same package. The impact of a change in protected or package data can therefore not be gauged in the class code. For this reason alone, protected data and package data are bad ideas.

Furthermore, a base class can control the preservation of its class invariants by ensuring that its constructors and mutators respect them. If a derived class can mutate the base class fields directly, this control is lost. Implementation invariants can be subtle, and it is not a good idea to blindly trust all derived classes to understand them.

Here is a slightly contrived example. Let us define operations of the Text class that return the height and width of the text shape. Unfortunately, those dimensions are not known until the text is first plotted because they depend on a graphics context. We will initialize them with −1 because they can't be negative, but they could be 0 for the empty text. We set them in the plot operation if they have not previously been set.

```
void Text::plot(Graphics& g) const
{  if (_xwidth == -1)
   {  FontMetrics fm = g.getFontMetrics();
      _xwidth = fm.stringWidth(_text);
      _yheight = fm.getAscent() + fm.getDescent();
   }
   g.drawString(_text, _start.x(), _start.y());
}
```

Independently, the `ScalableText::scale` operation will scale the dimensions. The fields have been declared protected, making the access legal.

```
void ScalableText::scale(Point center, double s)
{  Text::scale(center, s);
   _size = _size * s;
   _xwidth = _xwidth * s; // protected access
   _yheight = _yheight * s;
}
```

This is incorrect. Scaling should not be performed if _xwidth is -1.

Of course, in this simple case it is easy to spot the problem and to fix it, but subtle properties of data fields are surprisingly common in real classes. It is not a good idea to assume that they are properly understood by the open-ended collection of operations of all derived classes, as they may come into existence over time.

The situation for package visibility is similar. It is not a good idea to assume that the open-ended collection of operations in a package, as it evolves over time, can correctly manage a data field.

# 12

# Operator Overloading

In this chapter, we discuss the C++ feature of *operator overloading*. To overload an operator means to give a new meaning to an operator, such as + or == or <<, when that operator is used with user-defined types. Code with overloaded operators is often more concise and easier to read than the equivalent code using function calls. However, it cannot be denied that operator overloading, when improperly applied, can lead to very confusing code.

Java does not permit the overloading of operators because supporting this feature would have made the language and the compiler considerably more complex.

## *Defining Overloaded Operators*

### The Reason for Overloading

C++ allows the redefinition of operators such as + – * / for user-defined data types. This is especially convenient for fractions, currency values, units of measurement, and so on. Of course, it is an essential feature for heavy-duty mathematics programming with complex numbers, vectors, and matrices.

Here is a simple example that avoids the use of mathematics. Consider the operation d.add_days(n), which returns a new date, n days away from d. We can overload the + operator to denote the same meaning:

```
Date finish = start + 100; // finish is start + 100 days
```

This seems quite pleasant. Similarly, we can overload the – operator to compute the number of days between two dates.

```
Date start;
Date finish;
. . .
long ndays = finish - start;
```

In C++, operators are overloaded by defining special operator functions.

```
class Date
{
public:
   . . .
   Date operator+(long n) const;
   long operator-(const Date& b) const;
};

Date Date::operator+(long n) const
{  long j = dat2jul(_day, _month, _year);
   int d, m, y;
   jul2dat(j + n, d, m, y);
   return Date(d, m, y);
}

long Date::operator-(const Date& b) const
{  long j1 = dat2jul(_day, _month, _year);
   long j2 = dat2jul(b._day, b._month, b._year);
   return j1 - j2;
}
```

Note that we are *not* defining operator+ to add two dates; you can add only a long integer to a Date object. For example, you can add 100 days to January 1, 1997, but you cannot add January 1, 1997 to June 16, 1959.

The compiler translates the + and - operators in expressions involving Date objects to calls of the operator+ and operator- functions. For example,

```
n = d1 + (d3 - d2);
```

becomes

```
n = d1.operator+(d3.operator-(d2));
```

Actually, the operator functions are normal functions and can be called explicitly, as in the call above. Of course, nobody would seriously do that. The only reason to overload operators is to have a convenient way of invoking the functions.

# Syntax Rules for Operator Overloading

## Operators That Can Be Overloaded

Essentially, all operators may be overloaded. Here is a complete list:

```
+ - * / % ^ &
! = < > += -= *= /= %=
^= &= |= << >> <<= >>= == !=
<= >= && || ++ -- -> ->*
[] () ,
```

Both the unary and binary forms of + - * & can be overloaded. For example, the binary minus is invoked as a - b, the unary minus as -a.
Only the following operators cannot be overloaded:

```
. .* :: ?:
```

No new operators can be created. Sorry, none of these operators are allowed:

```
|x|
y := x
y = x ** 2
```

An operator function must have *at least one* argument of class type. It is not possible to redefine operators applying just to numeric types (int, double, ...) or to pointer types (char*, X*, ...), or to define new operators for these types.

## Precedence and Associativity

Precedence and associativity (left-to-right or right-to-left grouping) are the same for overloaded and standard operators. For example, it is not a good idea to overload ^ to denote raising a fraction to a power

```
Fraction Fraction::operator^(int) const;
```

because the low precedence of the ^ operator will be surprising to most users. The operators in the expression

```
a ^ 2 + 1
```

bind as

```
a ^ (2 + 1)
```

Stick with the pow function—it is boring but predictable.

## Increment and Decrement

The compiler will not automatically transform

```
v += w;
```

into

```
v = v + w;
```

Instead, an operator+= function must be defined. That is just as well because a user-provided += operator can usually be coded more efficiently.
Similarly,

```
x++;
```

is not automatically equivalent to

```
x = x + 1;
```

Operator functions must be specifically defined if the use of ++ and − is desired. As an added complexity, there are both a prefix form (++x) and a postfix form (x++) of these operators. A slightly bizarre mechanism is utilized to map the operators to two different functions. Two overloaded versions of operator++ can be defined:

```
Date Date::operator++(); // prefix increment
```

and

```
Date Date::operator++(int); // postfix increment
```

The int argument should be ignored—a 0 is always passed.

## Implementing Overloaded Operators
## as Global Functions

Most operators can be defined either as operations of a class or as regular functions. The exceptions are

```
= -> () []
```

which must be operations. For example, date subtraction can be implemented as either

```
long Date::operator-(const Date&) const
```

or

```
long operator-(const Date&, const Date&)
```

The compiler translates

```
d - e
```

into either

```
d.operator-(e)
```

or

```
operator-(d, e)
```

Of course, defining both versions is wrong. As a rule of thumb, you should implement operators as operations of the class of the first argument whenever possible.

# *Type Conversions*

## Type Conversion on Operator Arguments

Consider a Date class with a constructor that can make a string into a Date object.

```
class Date
{
public:
   Date(string);
```

```
    long operator-(const Date& b) const
    . . .
};

Date bday("June 16, 1959");
```

The `Date(string)` constructor can convert a string into a date in an assignment.

```
bday = "January 1, 1997";
  // that is, bday = Date ("January 1, 1997")
```

The same `Date(string)` conversion is automatically carried out in arithmetic expressions that involve a `Date` and a `string` object:

```
long n = deadline - "January 1, 1997"
```

In this expression, the compiler realizes that there is no `Date::operator-(string)`, but that it can use the `Date::operator-(const Date&)` if it converts the string to a date. Thus, it carries out the operations

```
long n = deadline.operator-(Date("January 1, 1997"));
```

However, the seemingly similar expression

```
long n = "January 1, 1997" - deadline
```

is not legal: `operator-` is an operation of the `Date` class, so the first argument must be a `Date` object. The compiler does not perform a type conversion

```
Date("January 1, 1997").operator-(deadline) // not done
```

The implicit argument must match the class type; no conversion on it is ever attempted.

This makes `operator-` strangely asymmetric. To avoid that, we can make `operator-` into a function with two explicit arguments:

```
long operator-(const Date& a, const Date& b);
```

Now either argument can be converted from a string to a date.

## Defining Type Conversions

As we saw in the previous sections, constructors that accept a single argument also serve as type conversion functions. For example, a constructor

```
Date(string)
```

can automatically convert a string into a `Date`. Such constructors are the preferred method for defining automatic type conversions.

However, a different method is required in two cases:

- When the target type is not a class
- When the target type is a class that you have no authority to modify

Consider, for example, a type conversion from dates to strings. Because the `string` class is a system class that you cannot modify, you cannot define a constructor `string(Date)`. Instead, you must add a *type conversion operator* to the `Date` class:

```
class Date
{
public:
   . . .
   operator string() const;
}

Date::operator string() const
{  char buffer[20];
   sprintf(buffer, "%d/%d/%d", _month, _day, _year);
   return string(buffer);
}


. . .


Date bday(16, 6, 1959);
string harry = "Harry Hacker";
cout << harry + "'s birthday is on " + bday;
// harry + "'s birthday is on " + bday.operator string();
```

## Conversion to a Truth Value

The stream classes have a conversion `istream` → `void*` that can be used to test the stream state.

```
istream::operator void*()
{  if (the state is not fail)
   return this;
else
   return NULL;
}
```

The actual returned pointer is immaterial, as long as a nonzero pointer is returned on success.

A typical usage is

```
cin >> x;
if (cin) // operation was successful
```

It would appear to be simpler to define an `istream::operator bool` instead of a conversion to `void*`. For historical reasons, C++ allows conversions from `bool` to `int`. Having an automatic conversion from streams to integers would give legal but unintended meanings to many expressions. For example, the erroneous

```
int x;
cin << x; // NO-meant cin >> x
```

would compile! But it wouldn't compile to anything useful. It would mean a bitwise left shift of `cin.operator bool()` by x bits. That is a nasty little problem because humans expect the compiler to find syntax errors, not to translate them into a spurious meaning. The `void*` type doesn't suffer from this problem because the only legal operators on `void*` are comparison and assignment. For this reason, a conversion to `void*` is a common idiom for testing the state of an object.

# Commonly Overloaded Operators

## The << and >> Operators

The << and >> operators are probably the most commonly overloaded operators. Have a closer look at the C++ "Hello, World" program.

```
#include <iostream>
int main()
{  cout << "Hello, World" << endl;
   return 0;
}
```

Here `cout` is the `ostream` object attached to standard output. The << operator is overloaded to take an `ostream` on the left and another type on the right. The previous program uses

```
ostream::operator<<(const char[])
```

There are other << operators to output other data types:

```
double x = 3.14159;
cout << x;
```

This uses

```
ostream::operator<<(double)
```

Note that the << operators are not const. The calls change internal details in the ostream structure.

Of course, the header file iostream contains the definition of the class ostream and the declaration of cout.

The << operators can be *chained:*

```
double x = 3.14195;
cout << "The value of pi is approx. " << x;
```

This works because all << operators *return the stream reference they receive:*

```
ostream& ostream::operator<<(const char s[])
{  // print s
   return *this;
}
```

Dissecting the previous statement yields:

```
cout << "The value of pi is approx. " << x;
```
⎣_____⎦
            cout

The first call to operator<< prints the string and returns (a reference to) cout. The second call cout << x prints the floating point number.

It is easy to enhance the stream facility to read and print new data types:

```
ostream& operator<<(ostream& os, const Date& d)
{  os << d.month() << "/" << d.day() << "/" << d.year();
   return os;
};
```

Now Date objects can be printed like any other values:

```
Date bday;
cout << "Birthday: " << bday << endl;
```

Note that we cannot make the operator<< function into an operation of the Date class—its first argument is ostream&, not Date. We cannot make it into an operation of the ostream class either—we don't have the right to modify that class. This is one example where an overloaded operator must be implemented as a regular function.

To read dates in from an input stream, we define

```
istream& operator>>(istream& is, Date& date)
{  char ch1, ch2;
   int d, m, y;
   is >> m >> ch1 >> d >> ch2 >> y;
   if (ch1 != '/' || ch2 != '/' || is.fail()) . . . // error
   date = Date(d, m, y);
   return is;
}
```

We have left error handling open. When there is an input error, the error state of the stream should be set. We will discuss this in Chapter 13.

## The = Operator

The = operator is overloaded for classes that require special handling when copying their contents. The most common case is a class with a pointer to the heap. Under the default meaning of assignment, a copy of the object simply gets a copy of that pointer (that is, a shallow copy of the heap information). However, C++ users generally expect that assignment

```
b = a;
```

makes a deep copy of the object. This is achieved by overloading `operator=`. We will study this in Chapter 14.

## The < Operator

A number of containers in the standard C++ library, such as `set` and `map`, require that the objects inserted into the container can be compared with the < operator. Furthermore, < is required to be a total ordering, that is, if neither

```
a < b
```

nor

```
a > b
```

then a and b must be identical.

Of course, such an operation is supplied by overloading `operator<`:

```
bool Date::operator<(const Date& b) const
{  if (_year < b._year) return true;
   if (_year > b._year) return false;
   if (_month < b._month) return true;
   if (_month > b._month) return false;
   return _day < b._day;
}
```

Once you supply an `operator<`, the standard library automatically defines the `>`, `<=`, and `>=` operators, using the following logic:

```
a > b       b < a
a <= b      !(b < a)
a >= b      !(a < b)
```

**PITFALL**

Be absolutely sure that you define `operator<` only to denote a total ordering. Consider the following example. We consider one line segment smaller than another when the first one has a shorter length.

```
bool operator<(const Segment& a, const Segment& b) // bad idea
{ return a.length() < b.length();
}
```

This is a bad idea. If you ever insert `Segment` objects into a container such as a `set`, then two objects s and t will be considered identical whenever neither s < t nor t < s, that is, whenever s and t have the same length. Remedy: Use < for total orderings only.                                    ■

## The [] Operator

The `[]` operator is overloaded for the vector template in the standard library. Another interesting example is given by an associative array or map.

```
class Map
{
public:
   void add(string, double);
   double operator[](string);
private:
   class Pair
   {
   public:
      string _key;
      double _value;
   };

   vector<Pair> _assoc;
};
```

Pairs of strings and floating-point values can be inserted in the associative array. Values can be retrieved by their keys.

```
Map a;
a.add("Harry Hacker", 3.3);
x = a["Harry Hacker"];
```

The map template in the standard library works in just this way—it lets you specify arbitrary types for the keys and values.

## The () Operator

There are two good reasons to overload the () operator:

- To implement function evaluation on objects that behave in some way like functions
- To take advantage of the fact that () is the only operator that can take an arbitrary number of arguments

When using the algorithms of the standard C++ library, objects that act like functions are often needed. We will discuss these algorithms in detail in Chapter 17. Here is a simple but typical example. The count_if algorithm counts how many elements in a container fulfill a certain condition.

```
vector<Employee> staff;
. . .
count_if(staff.begin(), staff.end(), condition, counter);
```

The algorithm computes condition(e) for all objects e in the container, incrementing counter whenever that computation yields true:

```
for (p = staff.begin(); p != staff.end(); p++)
{  Employee e = *p;
   if (condition(e)) counter++;
}
```

Here condition can be any entity for which condition(e) makes sense. That is, condition can be either a pointer to a function or an object of a class that has an overloaded operator()(Employee) or operator()(const Employee&).

Here is an example of such a class that is useful to count the number of employees whose salary is at least a certain amount:

```
class SalaryAtLeast
{
```

```
public:
   SalaryAtLeast(double s);
   bool operator()(const Employee& e) const;
private:
   double _minSalary;
};

SalaryAtLeast::SalaryAtLeast(double s) : _minSalary(s) {}

bool SalaryAtLeast::operator()(const Employee& e) const
{  return e.salary() >= _minSalary;
}
```

To count the number of employees with salary of at least $100,000, we use the following code:

```
SalaryAtLeast atLeast100k(100000.0);
count_if(staff.begin(), staff.end(), atLeast100k, counter);
```

The algorithm then computes `atLeast100k(e)` for every employee `e` in the container.

Occasionally, `()` is overloaded to take advantage of the fact that it can take more than one argument. A matrix class may overload `()` to access an element whose row and column index are specified as the arguments to `()`.

```
class Matrix
{
public:
   Matrix(int, int);
   . . .
   double operator()(int r, int c) const;
private:
   vector<double> _coeff;
   int _nrow;
   int _ncol;
};

Matrix m(5, 5);
. . .
double x = m(3, 4); // calls Matrix::operator()(3, 4)
```

# Design Hints

## Avoid Surprises and Confusion

The C++ language enforces no semantics on overloaded operators. It is possible to define `operator+` to denote addition of vectors and subtraction of matrices. Naturally, that is not a good idea. In general, it is best to stick to established mathematical conventions.

It is best to avoid cute or cryptic interpretations of operators. Abuses are common in published code.

```
Stack s;
s += 5; // DON'T-use s.push(5)
x = s--; // DON'T-use x = s.pop();
```

It is counterproductive to replace perfectly obvious function names like push and pop with cryptic operators += and -- that are, to say the least, mysterious to the uninitiated. Here is a surprisingly common example of an obscure device—can you guess what it does?

```
List lst;
ListIterator it(lst);
int* p;
while (p = it()) cout << *p << endl;
```

The expression it() is not a function call but the application of the () operator on the object it. That operator is implemented to return a null pointer if the iterator is at the end of a list or otherwise to return a pointer to the current list item and advance the iterator. Redesigning the iterator interface is strongly suggested:

```
List lst;
ListIterator it(lst);
while (!it.at_end()) { cout << it.current() << endl; it.next(); }
```

Or, if you feel compelled to use overloaded operators, possibly

```
while (it) { cout << *it << endl; it++; }
```

## Supply a Complete Set of Operators with Natural Interactions

When supplying + and - operators, also supply unary + and - as well as += and -= operators. Of course, the following relationships should hold:

- $a = a + b \Leftrightarrow a \mathrel{+}= b$, but the latter may be more efficient.
- $a - b = a + (-b)$
- $-(-a) = +a = a$

## Minimize Type Conversions

If too many automatic type conversions are provided, the compiler can, surprisingly often, attach some unambiguous meaning that the programmer never intended. According to [Murray 1989], bidirectional automatic type conversions (such as string→Date and Date→string) are particularly suspect.

## Choosing Between `operator` Functions and Class Operations

When you can choose between defining an operator as an operation of a class or as a regular function, you should generally favor the class operation. It clearly makes the operator a part of the interface, and you get access to the implementation should you need it.

There are exceptions, though, in the following cases:

■ The type of the first argument of the operator is not a class.
■ The type of the first argument is a class that you have no authority to modify.
■ Type conversion is desired on the first argument.

Then you must use a regular function for the operator. If access to the internal representation of either argument is required, make it a friend.

For example, the addition of an integer and a date must be a regular function:

```
Date operator+(long, const Date&);
```

The left-hand side type, `long`, is not a class.
The insertion operator to print a date must be a regular function.

```
ostream& operator<<(ostream&, const Date&);
```

It cannot be an operation of `ostream` because you cannot modify the `ostream` class.

## Beware of Constructors with a Single Integer Argument

Constructors with a single argument are type converters, whether this is appropriate or not. Suppose a class `Queue` has a constructor `Queue(int n)` to make a queue with n slots. Now look at this code:

```
Queue a(100); // a queue with 100 elements
. . .
a = 5; // Oops...meant a.insert(5);
```

The assignment a = 5 compiles to the type conversion

```
a = Queue(5);
```

That sets a to a newly constructed queue of five elements. The old queue contents are lost.

This behavior is very surprising to most users, to say the least. There are two remedies. Some class libraries introduce a class Size just for the purpose of specifying sizes in constructor arguments:

```
Queue a(Size(100));
```

Because the compiler refuses to carry out two user-defined type conversions automatically, this solves the problem of inadvertently invoking the constructor. However, the better approach is to use a new keyword explicit that was recently introduced into the C++ language. A constructor marked as explicit is *never* used for implicit type conversions.

```
class Queue
{
public:
    explicit Queue(int);
    . . .
};


. . .

Queue a = 10; // error--requires implicit conversion
Queue a(10); // OK--uses explicit constructor invocation
Queue a = Queue(10); // also OK
```

Of course, here we see poor language design in action. It sounded like a clever idea to make one-argument constructors serve double duty as type converters. It saved the language designers the trouble of adding yet another language concept. By the time they recognized the problems caused by this decision, it was too late. They had to introduce another keyword, something they had strenuously avoided at first. They also no longer had the opportunity to do it right, that is, to introduce type conversion as a separate concept. Programmers had written immense amounts of code that would have to be modified if one-argument constructors were no longer implicit type converters. Instead, the standards committee came up with the band-aid solution of tagging some constructors with the explicit keyword.

# 13

# Streams
# and Persistence

C programmers use the functions defined in the stdio library to perform input and output. C++ replaces stdio with the iostream library. That is the library that we have used in this book exclusively. Users familiar with the C library may feel some reluctance to switch; it is indeed possible to write C++ code that uses stdio for all input and output. Nevertheless, the iostream library, despite its warts, is ultimately a superior design and should be used by C++ programmers.

Java programmers do not have a choice of libraries. The java.io package contains the classes for Java input and output classes. As you will see, this package has an elegant design that makes it quite extensible. However, little attention has been paid to making the library usable in common cases. We will describe a number of classes to improve this situation. The source code for these classes is available on the book's Web site.

Finally, we will discuss persistent storage, the saving and restoring of objects and pointers between them. In C++, there is no language solution for persistent storage, but many class libraries implement a mechanism. We will look at the serialization mechanism of the Microsoft Foundation Classes (MFC), which is characteristic of third-party persistence solutions.

Starting with version 1.1, Java offers very convenient and comprehensive support for persistence. That mechanism will also be explained in this chapter.

# Stream Classes

## Base Classes for Input and Output

Both C++ and Java use the concept of a *stream*. In Java, a stream is simply a source or target of bytes. In ANSI C++, the stream classes are actually parameterized by a type. The default streams are sequences of characters. For example, `istream` is actually a synonym for `basic_istream<char>`. Sixteen-bit Unicode characters can be read from a `basic_istream<wchar_t>`. (The type `wchar_t` describes a 16-bit Unicode character.)

The most common streams are, of course, files. Other sources or targets of bytes can be accessed through streams in C++ and Java, such as the characters in a string or memory block or the bytes in a network socket. The power of the stream abstraction means that programmers can treat these in the same way as files.

In C++, every class for reading input derives from `istream` and every class for writing output derives from `ostream`. A function with an `ostream&` argument can write output to an arbitrary destination, for example, a file or a memory block. The `<<` operators and other operations for writing output are defined for the `ostream` class.

The `ostream` class, in turn, inherits from the base class `ios`, which is responsible for maintaining the format and error state and for communicating with a *buffer*. Buffering parks characters in a buffer, to send them to an output device in a chunk, or holds characters in a buffer, as they are delivered by an input device. This is necessary for reasonable performance when interacting with files or devices such as network sockets.

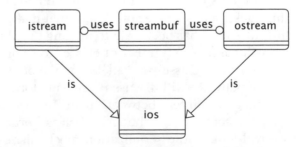

**FIGURE 13.1** Input and output stream classes.

Any class that derives from `ios` also interacts with a class derived from `streambuf`. That class defines virtual functions `overflow` and `underflow` to write more characters to a particular target when the buffer is full or to read more characters from a particular source when the buffer is empty. Figure 13.1 shows a class diagram of these classes.

The *formatting* of output that is common to all output streams is handled in `ostream`. Here, formatting means to convert objects into streams of characters. For example, numbers are written as sequences of characters `'1'`, `'2'`, ..., `'9'`, `'-'`, and so on. The mechanics of the buffering is done by the `streambuf` base class, and sending characters to a particular target is done in the `overflow` operation of a class derived from `streambuf`.

Generally, these details are of no interest to the programmer using streams. However, library builders love this setup: It lets them write new output stream classes that send characters to other targets simply by defining new stream buffer classes. They don't have to reinvent the formatting mechanism. We will show an example of such a custom `ostream` class later in this chapter. To summarize, the stream library is designed to separate two concerns:

- *How* is an object represented as a sequence of characters (formatting)?
- *Where* are the characters sent to (buffering and transmitting)?

Naturally, everything we said for output streams holds equally well for input streams in C++. The `istream` class also derives from `ios`. Classes derived from `istream` supply their own classes derived from `streambuf`, whose `underflow` operation gets new characters from the input device.

 Java uses a very different mechanism to separate formatting, buffering, and the ultimate destination or source of the bytes.

There is an abstract class `OutputStream` with just a handful of operations, to write a single byte, to write an array of bytes, and to close the stream. Concrete classes such as `FileOutputStream` and `ByteArrayOutputStream` derive from `OutputStream`. Their `write` operations are defined to send bytes to a file or a memory block.

However, these classes do not support any operations that a programmer might want to use, such as writing numbers or strings. For that, you need a `PrintStream`. A `PrintStream` is an *adapter*. You supply some other stream in its constructor.

```
FileOutputStream fout = new FileOutputStream("output.dat");
PrintStream pout = new PrintStream(fout);
```

The `PrintStream` does no actual streaming; it does formatting. Its various operations take numbers, strings, and other objects, translate them into sequences of bytes, and send the byte sequences to the stream that was supplied to the constructor.

You want both formatting *and* buffering? Very well, if you insist:

```
PrintStream pout = new PrintStream(new BufferedOutputStream(new
    FileOutputStream("output.dat")));
```

In Java, this chaining of streams is called *filtering*. You can apply as many filters as you like (see Figure 13.2).

The *first* class of the filter chain should be the one with the operations to write or read numbers and objects. The *last* class of the chain should actually send or receive bytes. The intermediate classes can do other work such as buffering or encryption.

This approach is very flexible; it is easy to write more filters. In fact, we will write a filter in this chapter to handle formatted input and output of numbers, a facility that is strangely missing from Java. However, for the user of the input/output library having to stitch together every stream from bits and pieces is a pain.

## Text and Binary I/O

 In C++, the ubiquitous >> and << operators write and read numbers and strings as *text*. For example, the integer 100 is written as the sequence of characters '1' '0' '0'. In contrast, binary output would write the integer 100 as the sequence of bytes 0x00 0x00 0x00 0x64 (or 0x00 0x64 on a 16-bit processor or 0x64 0x00 0x00 0x00 on a processor with little-endian byte ordering). Because binary input and output is inherently processor-dependent, it is not generally recommended, and there is not much support for it. But it is clearly more efficient to use binary I/O, and binary I/O of records of identical type makes random access easy.

Here is how you write a number in binary in C++:

```
double x;
out.write((char*)&x, sizeof(x));
```

You read it in with

```
in.read((char*)&x, sizeof(x));
```

**FIGURE 13.2**  A sequence of filters.

**PITFALL**

Never use `read` and `write` for objects. Most objects contain embedded pointers (in particular, if they have data fields of type `string` or `vector<T>` and the like). Saving the current value of a pointer makes no sense. When the file is read back in, the memory layout of the program will be very different. But even if an object contains no visible pointers, it may well contain invisible ones that are placed by the compiler. Every object of a class with virtual functions has a pointer to a table of all virtual functions. If that pointer is saved to disk and restored in the next program run, then the next virtual function call will cause disaster. Instead, overload `<<` and `>>`.   ■

 In Java, the situation is exactly opposite from that in C++. There is some support for text output, as long as you are not fussy about formatting, and no support at all for reading a text file back in. Binary I/O is supported, and the implementation is very careful to make the resulting files processor-independent.

To write a value in text format, use a `PrintStream` and the `print` or `println` operation.

```
PrintStream out;
Employee harry;
. . .
out.println(3.14);
out.print("Harry: ");
out.println(harry);
```

When printing a string, the output is in ASCII, not in Unicode! Only the less significant byte of each character is printed.

When printing an object, such as `out.println(harry)`, then the `toString` operation is applied to the object, and the resulting string is printed. The cosmic base class `Object` defines `toString` to yield a string containing the object type name and address, so it is a good idea for derived classes to override this operation to produce a string that lists all data fields of the object.

However, there is simply no input stream version of `PrintStream`. We will develop a suitable analog later in this chapter. To read a number, you must read a character at a time, place the characters into a string, and convert the string to a number.

Binary input and output is quite easy in Java. You need a `DataInput-Stream` or `DataOutputStream`. Then use one of the following operations:

```
readInt       writeInt
readShort     writeShort
readLong      writeLong
```

```
readFloat       writeFloat
readDouble      writeDouble
readBoolean     writeBoolean
readChar        writeChar
                writeChars
```

For example,

```
DataOutputStream out = new DataOutputStream(new
   FileOutputStream("output.dat"));
out.writeDouble(3.14);
out.writeChars("Harry");
```

The most important feature of these operations is their processor independence. The sizes and formats of the Java types are strictly defined. For example, `int` is always a 4-byte 2's complement binary number, `float` is always a 4-byte IEEE-format floating-point number. And the order in which the bytes are written to the stream is always fixed to be the big-endian or network byte ordering. If the processor uses little-endian byte ordering, it is the job of the read and write functions to reverse it. Thus, two Java processes on different processors can always safely communicate through data input and output streams.

Reading and writing numbers and individual characters are simple. Support for strings is not as good, however. To save a string, first save its length and then write its characters with the `writeChars` operation.

```
String s;
. . .
out.writeInt(s.length());
out.writeChars(s);
```

To read it back, read in the length, then read the characters into a *string buffer* object. A string buffer is an array of characters that can be turned into a Java string. Using a string buffer is more efficient than concatenating each new character to a string because each of the intermediate strings would need to be built up and then garbage collected.

```
int len = in.readInt();
StringBuffer b = new StringBuffer(len);
for (int i = 0; i < len; i++) b.append(in.readChar());
String s = b.toString();
```

Note that this method saves the characters in Unicode, that is, each character occupies two bytes.

It would have been nice if the designers of the data input and output stream classes had given us a `readString`/`writeString` pair of operations that does exactly that.

**TIP**

Sometimes, you need to read ASCII text input a line at a time. Somewhat paradoxically, you can use the `DataInputStream` for this purpose, even though normally `DataInputStream` is intended for binary, not text input. One operation, `readLine`, returns a complete input line as a `String`. Each byte of the input is made into a Unicode character by setting its top byte to zero. A `null` reference is returned at the end of input. This is just what is needed to read ASCII input a line at a time. Here is some typical code used to read a Web page a line at a time.

```
URL url = new URL("www.horstmann.com");
InputStream is = url.openStream();
DataInputStream in = new DataInputStream(is);
String s;
while ((s = in.readLine()) != null)
{ process s;
}
```

■

## Files

Getting a C++ file stream for reading or writing with the default attributes is very simple. You supply the file name in the constructor of an `ifstream` or `ofstream`. Because `ifstream` inherits from `istream` and `ofstream` inherits from `ostream`, you can use the usual stream operations with file streams.

```
#include <fstream>
ifstream is("input.dat");
ofstream os("output.dat");
int n;
while (is >> n) os << n << endl;
```

`fstream` files are opened for both input and output. Note that the class `fstream` does *not* derive from `ifstream` or `ofstream`, but from `iostream`. That is, you can use the operations for input and output (such as >> and <<) on `fstream` objects, but you cannot bind an `fstream` object to an `ifstream&` reference.

When opening the file, you can set different attributes; for example,

```
ofstream os("output.dat", ios::noreplace);
```

The attributes listed in Table 13.1 can be specified when opening a file.

**TABLE 13.1** Attributes for opening a file in C++

| Attribute | Purpose |
|---|---|
| in | Open for reading |
| out | Open for writing |
| ate | Open and seek to end of file |
| app | Append each write at end of file |
| trunc | Truncate to zero length |
| nocreate | Fail if file doesn't exist |
| noreplace | Fail if file exists |
| binary | Open in binary (nontext) mode |

File streams can be opened and closed explicitly:

```
fstream fs;
fs.open("file.dat", ios::in ios::out ios::binary);
. . .
fs.close();
fs.open("file2.dat",ios::in);
```

*Random access* is supported as well. Unlike the fseek/ftell interface in C, there are two positions, the *get pointer* for the next read and the *put* pointer for the next write. The seekg and seekp operations move the get and put pointer. The tellg and tellp operations tell their current offset from the beginning of the file.

```
fs.seekg(-1, ios::end); //one before the end of file
long n = fs.tellg();
```

The second argument of seekg/seekp is one of the following:

- beg—seek from beginning of the file
- cur—seek from the current position
- end—seek from the end of the file

Actually, these random access functions are defined by the istream and ostream classes, not by fstream. Other streams, such as string streams, also support seeking. If you try to seek on a stream that doesn't support it, for example, if you read keystrokes from cin, then the stream is set to a failed state.

 In Java, the FileInputStream and FileOutputStream classes yield streams that can read characters from files and write characters to files. Supply the file name in the constructor. Java has no destructors—remember to close the file when you are done!

```
FileInputStream fin = new FileInputStream("input.dat");
. . .
fin.close();
```

Unlike the C++ streams, the Java file streams have no useful operations to read or write data. You must use an adapter:

```
DataInputStream in = new DataInputStream(fin);
```

To get a file with both read and write access, you use a `Random-AccessFile`. This class has no relationship whatsoever with any of the other Java stream classes—because Java has no multiple inheritance, it cannot derive both from `InputStream` and `OutputStream`. Therefore, it derives from neither. Instead, it implements the `DataInput` and `DataOutput` interfaces that declare the read/write operations of the `DataInputStream` and `DataOutputStream` classes. (We will study Java interfaces in Chapter 18.)

**TIP**

If you write a function whose parameter is a `DataInputStream`, declare the parameter as a `DataInput` instead. That way, you can still use all the `read` operations, but you can pass a `RandomAccessFile` object to the function. For example,

```
class Employee
{  . . .
   void read(DataInput in) { . . . }
}
```

■

To open a random-access file, supply the file name and the string `"r"` to open the file for reading or `"rw"` to open it for reading and writing.

```
RandomAccessFile in = new RandomAccessFile("input.dat", "r");
RandomAccessFile inOut = new RandomAccessFile("inout.dat", "rw");
```

Of course, random-access files support random access. The `seek` operation moves the file position to an offset, always counted from the beginning of the file. You tell the current position by invoking the `getFilePointer` operation. As in C, there is no distinction between get and put positions.

```
inOut.seek(100); // sets file pointer
long n = inOut.getFilePointer(); // like tell in C
```

The designers of this library do have the special ability to keep programmers on their toes by staying away from trite and predictable naming pairs like seek/tell or setFilePointer/getFilePointer.

## String Streams

Writing generic code that can process characters that come either from files or from other sources is often useful. One such source can be the characters in a string. Both Java and C++ let you declare special streams that can interface with strings.

 We are showing here the stringstream classes that provide streams for C++ string objects. Not all compilers support these yet; an older strstream class is available that interfaces to char[] arrays.

To send characters to a string instead of a file, use an ostringstream. When you are done writing to the stream, you can get the string containing all the written characters with the str operation.

```
#include <sstream>
Date bday;
ostringstream out;
out << "Birthday: " << bday << endl;
string b = out.str(); // contains "Birthday: 16/6/1959\n"
```

To read characters from a string rather than a file, use an istringstream. Supply the string in the constructor.

```
string input = "12/3/1945";
istringstream in(input);
int day, month, year;
char ch1, ch2;
in >> day >> ch1 >> month >> ch2 >> year;
```

String streams are very useful for processing input. Input from human users is notoriously unreliable. It is generally necessary to gather the input a word or line at a time and then analyze it. After the input is placed in a string, an istringstream is a convenient mechanism for parsing and reading numerical values.

A stringstream can be used for both reading and writing.

C programmers will recognize string streams as the stream equivalent of the C functions sprintf and sscanf.

 In Java, streams don't read and write sequences of characters but sequences of bytes. Thus, the equivalent of C++ string streams are byte array streams. To send characters to a byte array, use a ByteArrayOutputStream. When you are done writing, you can get the sequence of bytes as a Byte[] array with the `toByteArray` operation or as a `String` (with the top byte of each character set to 0) with the `toString` operation.

```
Date bday = new Date(1959,6,16);
ByteArrayOutputStream bout = new ByteArrayOutputStream();
PrintStream out = new PrintStream(bout);
out.print("Birthday: ");
out.println(bday); // uses Date.toString()
String b = out.toString();
```

It sometimes happens that some data (for example, an image) is already in a memory block, but you have a function that insists on reading it from a stream. Then use a `ByteArrayInputStream` to turn the memory block into an input stream.

```
byte[] imageBytes;
. . .
ByteArrayInputStream in = new ByteArrayInputStream(imageBytes);
Image img = imageLoader.getImage(in);
```

To read characters from a string instead of a byte array, use a `String-BufferInputStream`.

```
String input = "12/3/1945";
StringBufferInputStreaam sbin =
   new StringBufferInputStream(input);
TextInputStream in = new TextInputStream(sbin);
int d = in.readInt();
```

## Advantages of the C++ Stream Library over the C `stdio` Library

C programmers are generally bewildered when they first see the C++ `iostream` library. It seems to offer nothing beyond the C `stdio` library other than a different notation. After all, the `stdio` library can read and write from strings and files and perform random access.

The C++ `iostream` library has two principal advantages over the C `stdio` library. It is always safe to use, and the operations for input and output can be extended to new types.

The C `stdio` library uses two functions, `printf` and `scanf`, to write to standard output and read from standard input, as well as related functions for arbitrary files and strings. These functions make use of a special C feature: They can take a variable number of arguments of arbitrary type. Of course, the functions must then interpret the bytes on the stack correctly. The first argument, the format string, is used for this purpose. The format string contains embedded codes specifying the variable types and formatting information.

```
int n;
double x;
printf("Count: %6d Average: %10.4f", n, x);
```

In this example, `%6d` means that the next variable to be printed is an integer, to be printed in decimal in a field that is six characters wide. The code `%10.4f` specifies a floating-point number, a field width of 10, and four digits after the decimal point.

The format string is undeniably convenient. It gives a concise visual picture of the output. Unfortunately, it is not very safe. A common bug is a mismatch between the format string and the actual arguments:

```
printf("Count: %6d Average: %10.4f", x, n);
```

The compiler cannot detect this bug—it knows nothing about `printf` except the prototype

```
int printf(const char*, ...);
```

Even more insidious is the following code:

```
int n;
double x;
scanf("%f %d", &x, n);
```

This code yields weird results. There are two mistakes. First, the `&` is missing from `n`, but an address is needed for storing the number. Second, the correct format to read in a double is `%lf`, for esoteric and historical reasons.

Stream operators are safe because the compiler picks the correct `operator<<` or `operator>>` function. A mismatch is impossible because there is no separate format string:

```
cout << "Count: " << n << " Average: " << x;
cin >> x >> n;
```

Especially for output, the drawbacks are clear. The output is harder to visualize because it is broken up into little pieces. Furthermore, there is no specification of the format, such as field width and floating-point precision. In the next sections, we will learn how to address the latter problem and, unfortunately, exacerbate the former in the process.

The second advantage of the C++ stream library is extensibility. It is not (easily) possible to extend `printf` to print other data types, such as fractions or vectors. To code

```
Date d;
printf("Birthday: %D", d);
```

it would be necessary to rewrite `printf` and recognize a new `%D` code. However, it is easy to enhance the stream facility to read and print new data types, just by adding more `operator<<` and `operator>>` functions. This process was explained in Chapter 12.

## Creating a New Stream Class in C++

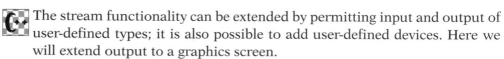 The stream functionality can be extended by permitting input and output of user-defined types; it is also possible to add user-defined devices. Here we will extend output to a graphics screen.

As we saw previously, the stream package divides the responsibility of printing data into two parts: formatting (in `ios`, the common base class of all stream classes) and buffering (in `streambuf`).

New buffer types can be derived from a base class `streambuf`. Two virtual functions, `overflow` and `underflow`, specify the device-dependent actions of emptying the buffer when it is full and filling it up when it is empty.

For simplicity, we will perform no buffering and define `overflow` to transmit the character that caused the overflow (in other words, every incoming character) to the graphics screen.

We derive a new buffer class:

```
class GraphicStreambuf : public streambuf
{
public:
   GraphicStreambuf(Graphics& g);
protected:
   virtual int overflow(int c);
private:
   Graphics& _g;
   FontMetrics _fm;
   int _xnext;
   int _ynext;
};
```

The `overflow` function puts the character c on the graphics screen, at position (xnext, ynext), and advances that position. We are not actually doing buffering, and the `overflow` function will be called every time a character is ready for printing. It simply displays the character.

```
int GraphicStreambuf::overflow(int c)
{   string s;
    switch(c)
    {   case EOF:
            break;
        case '\n':
            _xnext = 0;
            _ynext += _fm.getAscent() + _fm.getDescent();
            break;
        default:
            s = (char)c;
            _g.drawString(_xnext, _ynext, s);
            _xnext += _fm.stringWidth(s);
            break;
    }
    return 1;
}
```

We derive a new stream class from `ostream` and place a `Graphic-Streambuf` field inside it; see Figure 13.3.

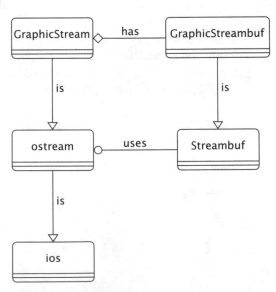

**FIGURE 13.3**   The stream class hierarchy, showing the added classes.

```
class GraphicStream : public ostream
{
public:
   GraphicStream(Graphics&);
private:
   GraphicStreambuf _buffer;
};
```

The constructor informs the `ostream` base class of the location of the buffer:

```
GraphicStream::GraphicStream(Graphics& g)
:  _buffer(g),
   ostream(&buffer)
{}
```

This stream class can be used like any other output stream:

```
void paint(Graphics& g)
{  GraphicStream out(g);
   out << "Hello, World " << endl << 3.14;
}
```

Figure 13.4 shows the output of this program.

This is quite amazing and is a tribute to the modular and extensible nature of the streams package. We were able to hijack the formatting layer completely and link our own destination into the buffering layer.

## Formatted Output

The C programmer is used to a wealth of formatting options in `printf`. All those options, and a few more, are available in the C++ stream library, but the access method is different and, frankly speaking, not very convenient. In

```
Hello, World
3.14
```

**FIGURE 13.4**   Output of the graphic stream.

the next section, we will introduce a manipulator that makes C++ formatting as easy as C formatting.

Java has *no* support for formatted output. The Web site for this book contains a handy class to add formatted output to Java, and we describe the design of this class in this section.

## C++ Formatted Output

### Field Width

The field width specifies the minimum number of characters for printing a value. If the character representation is shorter than the field width, spaces (or other fill characters) are inserted at the left or right, depending on the alignment.

There are two ways to set the field width: through a stream operation and through a stream manipulator. A manipulator is an object of some kind that is sent to a stream using the overloaded << or >> operator and that effects some state change in the stream object rather than character output.

Using stream operations is straightforward but requires breaking up the output statement:

```
cout.width(4);
cout << '(' << 12 << ',' << 34 << ')';
```

Manipulators are sent with the objects to be printed:

```
#include <iomanip.h>
cout << '(' << setw(4) << 12 << ',' << 34 << ')';
```

Both commands print

```
(  12,34)
```

Unlike all other formatting commands, the field width affects only the next number or string to be printed and then reverts to zero. Individual characters like '(' are not affected.

The field width specifies the minimum field size. Larger items are printed at their full width:

```
cout << setw(4) << 32000;
```

prints 32000, not 2000. It is better to have the correct output poorly formatted than the wrong output looking pretty.

The accessor `cout.width()` and the mutator `cout.width(n)` return the current width. In theory, this allows you to save the width and restore it later. In practice, this is rarely important because the width usually is zero. Of course, manipulators are inserted into the stream and cannot return the previous value.

### Fill Character

The fill character can be changed from the default (space) to any other character. Again, both operator and manipulator are provided:

```
cout.fill('*');
cout.width(4);
cout << 12;
```

and

```
cout << setfill('*') << setw(4) << 12;
print **12.
```

The fill character, like all other formatting attributes except field width, remains set until changed. The accessor `cout.fill()` and the mutator `cout.fill(c)` return the current fill character. Restoring the fill character to its original state (which may or may not be the space character) after changing it is good practice. The same holds for all other format attributes except field width.

### Alignment

Normally, values are right-aligned in their field. This is fine for numbers but not usually for strings.

The alignment is set through one of the many *flags* defined in the `ios` class. (`ios` is an abbreviation for "input/output state".) That class is a base class for both `istream` and `ostream`.

```
cout.setf(ios::left);
cout.width(10);
cout << "Month" << ':';
cout.setf(ios::right);
cout.width(4);
cout << 12;
```

or

```
cout << setiosflags(ios::left) << setw(10)
    << "Month" << ':'
```

```
<< setiosflags(ios::right) << setw(4)
<< 12;
```

print

```
Month : 12.
```

There is also a strange option, `ios::internal`, that distributes the fill character between the sign and the number. It is useful only if the fill character is 0.

```
cout << setiosflags(ios::internal)
   << setw(6) << setfill('0') << -12;
```

prints −00012.

### Integer Format

Integers can be formatted in decimal, hexadecimal, or octal formats.

```
int n = 12;
cout << hex << n << ' ';
cout << oct << n << ' ';
cout << dec << n << endl;
```

prints c 14 12. To show the base and print the letters in uppercase, use

```
cout.setf(ios::showbase ios::uppercase);
```

Now the same numbers print as 0XC 014 12.

Instead of the manipulators, you can also use `ios` flags `dec`, `oct`, and `hex`.

```
cout.setf(ios::hex);
```

### Floating-Point Format

By default, floating-point numbers are printed in a general format that uses scientific notation when necessary to show the significant digits (six by default).

```
cout << 123.456789 << ' ' << 123456789;
```

prints 123.457 1.23457e+008. (You can get an uppercase E by setting `ios::uppercase`).

You can explicitly choose either scientific or fixed format with the `ios` flags `scientific` or `fixed`.

```
cout << setiosflags(ios::fixed,ios::floatfield);
cout.setf(ios::scientific,ios::floatfield);
```

To reset to general format, you must use

```
cout << resetiosflags(ios::floatfield);
cout.unsetf(ios::floatfield);
```

To see a + sign for positive numbers, use `ios::showpos`. (This also works for integers.) To see trailing zeroes, use `ios::showpoint`. For example,

```
cout.setf(ios::fixed ios::showpoint ios::showpos);
cout << 123.456;
```

prints `+123.456000`.

You can change the precision from the default six:

```
cout << setprecision(10) << 1.2345678;
```

or

```
cout.precision(10);
cout << 1.2345678;
```

prints `1.2345678`. In general and scientific format, the precision denotes the number of significant digits; in fixed format, it denotes the number of digits after the decimal point. (Not all implementations handle this correctly.)

```
double x = 123.45678;
cout << setprecision(2) << x << ' ';
cout << setiosflags(ios::fixed,ios::floatfield) << x;
```

prints `1.2e+002 123.46`.

The accessor `cout.precision()` and the mutator `cout.precision(n)` return the current precision.

## Output Operations That Respect Format State

Output routines for user-defined types should respect the format state. Consider the case of printing dates. The following states are relevant:

- Field width
- Fill pattern
- Alignment

Preformatting the output into a string and then sending the string to the output stream is easier. The stream will then apply width, alignment, and fill pattern to the string without further ado. To format to a string rather than directly to a stream, we use a *string stream*.

```
ostream& stream& operator<<(ostream& os, const Date& d)
{  ostringstream s;
   s.flags(os.flags()); // set same flags
   s.setw(0); // in case it was set in os
   s << dec; // in case it was set to base 8 or 16 in os
   s << d._month << "/" << d._day << "/" << d._year;
   os << s.str();
   return os;
}
```

## A Critical Examination of the Format State Interface

Stream format state is an excellent example how muddleheadedness can creep into a library interface. Consider the name mismatches between operators and manipulators shown in Table 13.2.

It probably started out harmlessly enough with width and fill. Then someone added setf (why not setflags?) and unsetf. The manipulators then were named with set to distinguish them from the operators. Giving them different names is not strictly necessary but perfectly reasonable. But using set as a prefix is foolish because it conflicts with setf (should the manipulator be called setsetf?) Probably setw was chosen over the longer setwidth because it is so common. It would be difficult to conceive of a charitable explanation for resetiosflags instead of the consistent unsetiosflags.

**TABLE 13.2**  Comparison of Attributes, Operators, and Manipulators in C++ Streams

| *Attribute* | *Operator* | *Manipulator* |
|---|---|---|
| Width | width | setw |
| Fill character | fill | setfill |
| Set flags | setf | setiosflags |
| Reset flags | unsetf | resetiosflags |

All format attributes, except for field width, persist until changed. It is not clear why field width is treated differently from, say, floating-point precision.

The C interface, although perhaps cryptic, does manage to present the options as they are relevant to the programmer, not the library implementor. The field width and precision, surely the most important attributes, are communicated concisely. To print a plus sign and leading zeroes in a decimal integer n, the C programmer writes `"%+06d"`. The `iostream` equivalent is unbelievably cumbersome:

```
cout << setiosflags(ios::internal|ios::showpos|ios::dec)
    << setfill('0') << setw(6) << n;
```

Another problem is general floating-point format. There really ought to be a flag `ios::general` for general floating-point format in addition to the flags for fixed and scientific format, just as there is a flag `ios::dec` for decimal integers in addition to hexadecimal and octal format.

In the next section, we will program a *manipulator* that will look very sensible to C programmers—it sets the format state of the stream, using the familiar C `printf` style syntax. Here is how you can use that manipulator:

```
cout << setformat("%+06d") << n;
```

## Formatted Output in Java

 In Java, there is, oddly enough, no provision at all for formatting numbers. If you want to write numbers in dollars and cents, you are simply out of luck. The code accompanying this book contains an implementation of a `PrintfStream` adapter that implements all features of the `printf` function in C and makes them accessible to Java, for example,

```
PrintfStream out = new PrintfStream(System.out);
out.print("%10.2f", amountDue);
```

The implementation of this stream adapter is simple, except for the tedious part of programming the actual formatting options. This is done by several static functions whose code we omit. As all stream adapters do, we derive from `FilterOutputStream`.

```
class PrintfStream extends FilterOutputStream
{  public PrintfStream(OutputStream out)
   {  super(out);
   }
   public print(String fmt, double x)
```

```
    {  write(formatDouble(fmt, x));
    }
    public print(String fmt, int x)
    {  write(formatLong(fmt, x))
    }


    . . .
    private static byte[] formatDouble(String fmt, double x)
    private static byte[] formatLong(String fmt, double x)
    . . .
}
```

## Reading Text Input in Java

 As another convenience for the Java programmer, we provide an adapter that can read input from a text file. The interface is purposefully kept the same as that of the DataInputStream. We call the class TextInputStream. The code for the actual reading functions is complex, and we omit it here.

```
class TextInputStream extends FilterInputStream
    implements DataInput
{  public TextInputStream(InputStream in)
    {  pbin = new PushbackInputStream(in);
        super(pbin);
    }
    public int readInt() { . . . }
    public double readDouble() { . . . }
    public char readChar() { . . . }

    private PushbackInputStream pbin;
}
```

All read operations skip leading whitespace. In particular, readChar reads the next nonwhitespace character.

The stream adapter is easy to use, of course:

```
TextInputStream in = new TextInputStream(System.in);
int n = in.readInt();
double d = readDouble();
```

## *Manipulators for C++ Streams*

 We have seen a number of manipulators (endl, setw(n), and so forth) for formatting output. In this section, we will see what they are and how they work. Understanding how manipulators work is not central to using streams. Because the technique is complicated, you may want to skim over this material at first reading. The technique is interesting because it shows how to design objects that manipulate other objects.

## Function Pointers

We need to review the C syntax for function pointers now. Addresses of functions can be stored in variables and passed as function parameters. This is useful whenever an algorithm needs to leave the details of a computation open until its invocation.

Sorting is the traditional example. A sorting algorithm such as quick-sort picks elements to compare and then rearranges them in some way until the sorting is complete. Except for the method of comparison, the algorithm is completely independent of the objects to be sorted. Sort functions are often written to carry out the comparison and rearrangement logic in a generic way, with a pointer to a specific comparison function passed as a parameter. Here we sort an array by ZIP code, the numerical (five-digit) postal code used in the United States:

```
int compare_zip(const Address& a, const Address& b)
{ return a.zip() - b.zip();
}
vector<Address> labels;
sort(labels, compare_zip);
```

A function name that, like `compare_zip`, is not followed by parentheses denotes a pointer to that function. This is actually a pointer to the starting address of the function code in memory.

The syntax to describe such a function pointer is awkward because the pointer-dereferencing operator (`*`) has a lower precedence than the function call operator (`()`). It is always best to make a type definition:

```
typedef int (*AddressCompFun)(const Address&, const Address &);
```

Then the prototype of the `sort` function is simply

```
void sort(vector<Address>&v, AddressCompFun c);
```

Without the type definition, the prototype is

```
void sort(vector<Address>&v,
    int (*c)(const Address&, const Address &));
```

This expression rightly strikes fear in the hearts of C++ programmers.

Invoking a function through the function pointer is simple:

```
if ((*c)(v[i], v[j]) < 0) ...
```

This code executes the function whose starting address is stored in c.

Function pointers are useful when a wide variation of behavior needs to be specified for fixed object types. Virtual functions are a better mechanism to express a *narrow* range of behavior variation for related object types.

## Manipulators Without Arguments

The endl manipulator, like every stream manipulator that does not take an argument, is a function that eats a stream reference and returns it:

```
ostream& endl(ostream& os)
{   os << '\n';
    os.flush();
    return os;
}
```

An ostream is prepared to accept a pointer to such a manipulator function:

```
typedef ostream& (*OManip)(ostream&);
ostream& ostream::operator<<(OManip m)
{ return (*m)(self);
}
```

The stream permits the manipulator to act on itself.

## Manipulators with an Argument

Manipulators that take an argument are more difficult. Consider the setw manipulator that takes an integer argument. This manipulator acts on the ios class, the common base class of istream and ostream. It sets the width of either the next input field or the next output field.

The obvious extension of the previous method does not work:

```
ios& setw(ios& s, int w)
{   s.width(w);
    return s;
}
. . .
os << setw(10) << x;
```

The expression setw(10) is illegal because the setw function takes two arguments. (We were lucky with functions taking a single argument—omitting the argument resulted in a legal object, a function pointer.) Instead, the value of the expression setw(10) must be an object that the stream can accept.

There are two possibilities for setting this up. We can define a class setw with a constructor setw(int), or we can define a function setw(int) that returns an object of some class. The second approach is preferred because it introduces only a new function for each manipulator, not a new class. We will need to introduce a class as well, momentarily, but it can be shared among manipulators.

The setw(int) function needs to return an object of some class. That class is shared among all manipulators with one integer argument. It is designed to remember the following:

- The action to take on the stream
- The integer argument

Here is the class definition: Actually, it is a template because the type of the stream can vary (ios, istream, ostream), as can the type of the argument. In this case, think S as ios and T as int.

```
template <class S, class T>
class Manipulator
{
public:
    typedef S& (*Action)(S&, T);
    Manipulator(Action, T);
friend S& operator<<(S&, const Manipulator&);
friend S& operator>>(S&, const Manipulator&);
private:
    Action _action;
    T _value;
};
```

The overloaded >> operator applies the stored action on the stream object, using the stored value as the second argument.

```
template <class S, class T>
S& operator>>(S& s, const Manipulator& m)
{   (*m._action)(s, m._value);
    return s;
}
```

The setw(int) function returns a specific manipulator, specifying the width-setting action and the integer width to be set. The width-setting action is given by a function, named `do_setw`, with two arguments. It invokes the width operation of the `ios` class.

```
ios& do_setw(ios& s, int n)
{  s.width(n);
   return s;
}
```

Now we are ready to implement the original `setw(int)` function:

```
Manipulator<ios, int> setw(int n)
{  return Manipulator<ios, int>(do_setw, n);
}
```

Let's work through an example in detail.

```
cin >> setw(4);
```

1. `setw(4)` returns an object of type `Manipulator<ios, int>` that contains the `do_setw` function pointer and the integer 4.
2. `operator>>(ios& s, const Manipulator<ios, int>& m)` is called, where `s` is `cin` and `m` is the manipulator object returned by `setw`. It calls `do_setw(cin, 4)`.
3. `do_setw` calls `cin.width(4)`.

The ANSI standard does not require this exact technique. As a consequence, different implementations of C++ have different names for the manipulator template.

## Implementing a Manipulator for Easier Formatting

We would like to implement a `setformat` manipulator that can set the format state of a stream in a more convenient way. The actual work of translating C format codes into C++ format actions is done in

```
ostream& do_setformat(ostream& s, string n)
```

For example, a format string `"%8.2s"` is translated to

```
s.width(8);
s.precision(2);
```

The code for `do_setformat` is somewhat tedious and we omit it here. Note that it is just a regular function, not a manipulator. To turn it into a manipulator, we simply define

```
Manipulator<ostream, string> setformat(string s)
{  return Manipulator<ostream, string>(do_setformat, s);
}
```

Now we can use this manipulator to simplify stream formatting:

```
cout << setformat("%8.2s") << x;
```

# Error Handling

## Stream Error State in C++

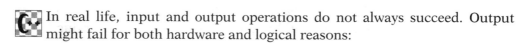 In real life, input and output operations do not always succeed. Output might fail for both hardware and logical reasons:

- A disk is full.
- A printer is disconnected.
- The file pointer has been set to an improper position.

Likewise, input might fail for a number of reasons:

- There is a physical problem with a device (for example, a disk has a bad sector).
- The end of file has been reached.
- The characters on the input stream are not in the expected format.

The error state of a stream keeps track of these problems. Each stream has three state bits, depending on whether the error originated in the device, the buffer, or the formatting layer:

- `eofbit`—end of file (or other device error)
- `badbit`—stream buffer error
- `failbit`—formatting failure

A stream buffer error results when a stream is not attached to a physical file or device or if the attached file or device has an error.

Five operations report on these states:

1. `good()`—No error and no end of file encountered.
   "The next operation might succeed."
2. `fail()`—An error condition has been encountered.
   "The previous operation has failed."
3. `bad()`—Stream buffer error has been encountered.
4. `eof()`—End of file has been encountered.
5. `rdstate()`—All state bits are returned.

These operations are somewhat confusing. It is important to note that `good()` does not mean `!bad()` or even `!fail()`, and that `fail()` does not simply return the value of `failbit`.

To say it outright, `good()` is pretty worthless. The `good()` operation won't reliably report on the success of the last operation because it fails if a value was read successfully but was followed by the end of file. You can't use `good()` as a predictor for the next operation. Even if the stream is happy now, it could still fail before it completes reading the next input. The `eof()` function is not all that useful—it is false if nothing but unread white space precedes the end of the file. Call it only after input has failed. The distinction between a stream buffer error and another error is not usually of great interest, and older implementations of the stream library make other uses of `badbit`. Therefore, `bad()` is rarely called.

It is best to test the state of a stream *after* attempting to read from it.

```
int n;
cin >> n;
if (!cin.fail())
    // n successfully read
```

Because `!fail()` is the most useful information, it can also be accessed through the conversion *stream* → `void*`.

```
cin >> n;
if (cin)
    // n successfully read
```

Errors on output are usually easy to handle. You may choose to test for them and refuse to perform more output if an error occurs, or you may just perform the output and let the lower-level routines refuse to actually send the characters.

Errors on input are much more bothersome. Every programmer must cope with end-of-file handling and detection of improper input formats. Here is a function to read dates and cope with error conditions.

```
istream& operator>>(istream& is, Date& dt)
{   char ch1, ch2;
    int d, m, y;
    is >> m >> ch1 >> d >> ch2 >> y;
    if (!is.fail() && ch1 == '/' && ch2 == '/')
    {   dt = Date(d, m, y);
        return is;
    }
    is.clear(ios::failbit | is.rdstate());
    return is;
}
```

There are two possible causes for errors. The / characters may be missing, or the integers surrounding the / are not present. When an error is encountered, the function sets the `failbit`. The code for doing this is unbelievably clumsy. An operation, strangely called `clear`, sets all error state bits. We retrieve the current error flags with an operation called `rdstate`, set the fail bit, and then store the result.

Note that the parameter `dt` is unchanged if the read operation fails. This is the correct behavior. It would have been wrong to make this operator a friend of `Date` and use

```
is >> dt._day; // WRONG
```

If input had failed later, `dt` would be *partially* overwritten.

## Stream Exceptions in Java

In C++, the error model is simple: As soon as there is a problem, the stream object turns into a bad state. That is pretty hard to overlook because no further operations succeed on a stream in a bad state. In contrast, if a C function like `scanf` fails, it merely returns an error code and further input operations still succeed, making it possible for the program to continue and do the wrong thing after an input error.

 Java has a different way of dealing with stream errors: It stops normal processing and throws an exception. (We will study exceptions in Chapter 16.) This, too, is hard to overlook.

Essentially, all Java stream operations, such as opening a file stream or reading a number from a stream, have the potential of throwing an `IOException`. Generally, the function that performs a low-level operation in the middle of a file ought not to be concerned about unexpected I/O failures; it ought simply to propagate them to a more competent handler. This is done by tagging the operation with the `throws IOException` specifier.

```
class Employee
{  public void read(DataInput in) throws IOException
   {  . . .
   }
   . . .
}
```

Unlike other exceptions such as `ArrayIndexOutOfBoundsException`, you must either advertise the possibility of IO exceptions or explicitly handle them. Until you learn about exception handling in Chapter 16, you should simply do that for all operations that perform input.

Is it better to signal an input error by an exception or by turning the stream to a failed state? Actually, there is no correct answer. Consider the end of the file. Every file must come to an end, so it sounds pretty drastic to terminate the current operation (and possibly the entire program if the exception is not caught) when the end of file is reached. The C++ way—setting the stream to a testable failed state—seems more sensible. However, suppose you read a *structured* file such as a file in HTML format. You simply would not expect the file to come to an end before the final </HTML> tag, and it makes perfect sense to abort the entire reading process when an *unexpected* end of file is encountered. Thus, programmers have different error-handling needs for different kinds of applications.

# *Persistence*

A persistent object is stored in a file or other permanent medium rather than in computer memory. A program can save persistent objects, interrupt the computation, and reload the same data at a later time. In fact, the data can be reloaded by a different copy of the same program or transported to a different computer for further processing.

C++ does not have built-in support for persistence, but the support can be supplied in a library. We will discuss the design of a typical persistence library now, namely that of the Microsoft Foundation Classes.

## Persistent Pointers

 Simply saving and restoring pointer values is meaningless. A pointer is a memory address, and it is, in general, impossible to reload an object into exactly the same location at which it is located when it is saved.

To see the complexities involved, consider the following example. A person has name and age. A vehicle has an owner and a driver, each represented as a pointer. Pointers are necessary for sharing information: One person can own several vehicles. The driver of one vehicle can be the owner of the same vehicle or another.

```
class Person
{
public:
   . . .
private:
   string _name;
   int _age;
   . . .
};
```

```
class Vehicle
{
public:
   Vehicle(Person*);
   void drive(Person*);
   . . .
private:
   Person* _owner;
   Person* _driver
};
```

We generate two person and two vehicle objects, as shown in Figure 13.5:

```
Person* joe = new Person("Joe", 41);
Person* carl = new Person("Carl", 19);
Vehicle car(joe);
Vehicle truck(joe);
car.drive(carl);
truck.drive(joe);
```

Now we want to save both vehicles and restore them some other time. We use the MFC CArchive class here—it uses the familiar << for writing data, but it has some strange syntax for opening the archive.

```
// in the File|Save handler

CFile file;
file.open("vehicles.dat", CFile::modeWrite | CFile::modeCreate);
CArchive archive(&file, CArchive::store);

archive << car;
archive << truck;

archive.Close();

// in the File|Load handler

CFile file;
file.open("vehicles.dat", CFile::modeRead);
CArchive archive(&file, CArchive::load);

archive >> car;
archive >> truck;
archive.Close();
```

Consider saving car. It contains two pointers: one to joe, its owner, and one to carl, its driver. We must save these Person objects in order to

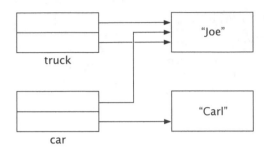

**FIGURE 13.5** Relationships between vehicle and person objects.

restore the Car object successfully. Now look at truck. Because we already saved joe, we must be careful not to save additional copies, but instead save each pointer as an instruction to restore it as a pointer to that object, wherever it will be in memory when the objects are read back in.

Let us assume that all pointers point to heap objects and that all pointers point to the start of an object, not to a field inside. We number all objects that we save. When we save an object for the first time, we save the number, the type name, and the object data. Subsequent saving of pointers to the same object just stores the serial number.

For example, here is how the two vehicles will be stored. Of course, they are actually saved in binary, but this listing shows the concept.

```
Pointer to Object 1 Vehicle
    Pointer to Object 2 Person
        "Joe"
        41
    Pointer to Object 3 Person
        "Carl"
        19
Pointer to Object 4 Vehicle
    Pointer to Object 2
    Pointer to Object 2
```

When restoring a pointer, we read the number in. If it is one that we never encountered previously, we make a new object on the heap, remember the correspondence (number, heap address) and proceed to read the object. Subsequent reads of a pointer with the same number are mapped to the same heap address.

## Persistent Types

 If a pointer may point to either a base or derived-class object, then we need to know the object's actual type when restoring it.

To understand the problem better, let us refine the previous example. Suppose classes `Car` and `Truck` derive from `Vehicle`, and the `Vehicle*` pointers `car` and `truck` actually point to objects of the derived classes:

```
Vehicle* pcar = new Car(joe);
Vehicle* ptruck = new Truck(joe);

// in the File|Save handler

archive << ptruck;
archive << pcar;

// in the File|Load handler

Vehicle* pcar;
Vehicle* ptruck;

archive >> ptruck;
archive >> pcar;
```

Now we are writing *pointers* to the stream. Because the `archive` operation is virtual, the vehicles are saved as cars and trucks. Here is the contents of the output file.

```
Pointer to Object 1 Truck
    Pointer to Object 2 Person
      "Joe"
      41
    Pointer to Object 2
Pointer to Object 3 Car
    Pointer to Object 4 Person
      "Carl"
      19
    Pointer to Object 2
```

When saving a persistent pointer, the stream writes the type name of the object as a string. When reading it back, the stream reads the type name string. It then needs to have some way of creating an object of that type. The problem is that it needs to do this at run time, not at compile time.

For example, suppose we read the type name string `"Truck"`. We now need to allocate a new `Truck` object. But type names are a compile-time phenomenon; at run time, there are only bytes and machine instructions, not types, much less type names.

Every persistence mechanism therefore needs to build a correspondence between type names and functions to make new objects of those types. MFC builds up a table in which each class has one entry containing the following:

- The class name string
- The size of an object of the class
- A "schema number," selected by the programmer, to differentiate between different versions of the same class
- A pointer to a function that creates a new object of the class on the heap, using the default constructor
- A pointer to the table entry of the base class

When a type name is read in from the input file, that string is searched in the class information table. A new default object of that type is created by calling the function in the table. Then the virtual `Serialize` function is called. To make all this work, the MFC programmer must do a certain amount of work when writing a class that can be archived:

- Derive the class from `CObject`.
- Add a macro `DECLARE_SERIAL` to the end of the class definition.
- Add a macro `IMPLEMENT_SERIAL` to the same module that contains the definition of the class operations.
- Write an operation `archive` that can save and restore the state of the object.

The `DECLARE_SERIAL` macro automatically generates the declarations for the `Serialize` operation, the `CreateObject` operation that creates a new default object on the heap, and certain other operations required by MFC for serialization. The `IMPLEMENT_SERIAL` macro automatically generates, among others, the table entry, the implementation of the `CreateObject` operation.

Here is how you use these macros. The `DECLARE_SERIAL` macro has a single argument, the name of the class. The `IMPLEMENT_SERIAL` macro has three arguments, the name of the class, the name of the base class, and the schema or version number.

```
class Person : public CObject
{
public:
    . . .
    DECLARE_SERIAL(Person);
private:
    . . .
};

IMPLEMENT_SERIAL(Person, CObject, 1);
```

We also must implement the `Serialize` operation. It is completely mechanical; it just saves or loads the data members.

```
void Person::Serialize(CArchive& archive)
{  // call base class
   CObject::Serialize(archive);
   if (archive.IsStoring())
      archive << _name << _age;
   else
      archive >> _name >> _age;
}
```

This must be carried out for *all* classes that you might want to store persistently. Again, the work involved is purely mechanical. If the compiler, or the run-time type information, was more expressive, then the unsightly macros and mechanical Serialize functions would not be necessary.

## Persistence in Java

 Persistence in C++ is a complex affair because every vendor has set up a different solution for it, each with its own set of arcane macros and mandatory functions in each class that wants to participate in the serialization. In contrast, serialization in Java is wonderfully simple, starting with Java version 1.1.

You need not do any work to prepare Java objects for serialization. You simply use the writeObject method of the ObjectOutputStream class to save an object, the readObject method of the ObjectInputStream class to read it back in. Note that the return value of readObject is Object, and you must cast it to the class of the object in the archive (or one of its base classes).

```
Person joe = new Person("Joe", 41);
Person carl = new Person("Carl", 19);
Car car(joe);
Truck truck(joe);
car.drive(carl);
truck.drive(joe);

ObjectOutputStream out = new ObjectOutputStream(new
   FileOutputStream("vehicles.dat"));
out.writeObject(car);
out.writeObject(truck);
out.close();

ObjectInputStream in = new ObjectInputStream(new
   FileInputStream("vehicles.dat"));
Vehicle v = (Vehicle)in.readObject();
Truck t = (Truck)in.readObject();
in.close();
```

As in the case of C++, the objects are *serialized:* the serial number, type, and contents of every newly encountered object are written to the stream. When an object is encountered again, only its serial number is written. When reading, this process is reversed.

However, unlike C++, Java *automatically* knows how to write and read all objects: All data fields are saved and restored.

There are a few times when it is not desirable to have a data field serialized explicitly. For example, fields in a `Window` object that are nominally of type `int` refer to window handles or pointers, and they make no sense if the object is read again later in another program run. Java offers a number of ways for the programmer to overcome this. By marking the field as `transient`, it is simply not saved or restored. Or the programmer can supply special functions

```
void writeObject(ObjectOutputStream out)
void readObject(ObjectInputStream in)
```

to implement a nonstandard mechanism for saving and restoring objects of a particular class. At the time of this writing, the details of these mechanisms are not completely determined.

**TIP**

The `writeObject`/`readObject` operations are so convenient that you should consider using them as the general mechanism for saving objects in file. Many systems have a top-level class that contains (directly or indirectly) all objects in the system. By simply saving that one object and restoring it later, you can implement persistence very easily. ■

# Design Hints

## Polymorphic Output

 Polymorphic output is easy to arrange. Have all classes derived from the common base class implement a virtual `print(ostream&)` operation. Then add a `<<` operator as follows:

```
ostream& operator<<(ostream& os, const Base& x)
{   x.print(os);
    return os;
}
```

Because `x` is a reference, the `print` function is bound dynamically, printing the derived-class object to which `x` refers.

Using polymorphism for << means that it is not necessary to define a separate << operator for each derived class.

It is also common to add a second overloaded version to print pointers.

```
ostream& operator<<(ostream& os, const Base* p)
{  if (p != 0) p->print(os);
   return os;
}
```

That way, the object to which a pointer p points can be printed either as os << *p or as os << p.

## Polymorphic Input

 For input, it is a good idea to have a virtual read function and define

```
istream& operator>>(istream& is, Base& x)
{  x.read(is);
   return is;
}
```

But this is not as polymorphic as you might like: You already have to know what to expect in the input, create a blank object of that type, and have it read from the stream.

True polymorphic input means that we create a new object, of the type that is actually present in the input stream, and then read it in. This cannot be the operation of a class because there isn't yet an object on which to act.

There must be a way to find out the type of the next object in the input stream, so that the format of the contents can be properly parsed. Typically, the output routine first writes the type name and then the contents.

```
vector<Shape*> figure;
for (int i = 0; i < figure.size(); i++)
   os << typeid(*figure[i]).name() << " " << *figure[i];
```

To reverse this process, we read in the type name and then have to find a way to get an object of that type. Chapter 10 discusses a systematic way of doing that, by keeping a map of type names and exemplar objects. For simple class hierarchies, an ad hoc approach works (barely).

```
istream& operator>>(istream& is, Shape*& x)
{  string name;
   is >> name;
```

```
        if (name == "Rectangle") x = new Rectangle;
        else if (name == "FilledRect") x = new FilledRect;
        else if (name == "Polygon") x = new Polygon;
        . . .
        else x = NULL;
        if (x != NULL) x->read(is);
        return is;
}
```

Each class must have a default constructor because we first must make an object before we can fill it by reading the data.

An alternative is to give each class a constructor that takes an `istream&` argument. That is conceptually very clean—we express the fact that objects can be constructed from the data found in a stream.

```
x = new Rectangle(is);
```

This scheme has only one added complexity: If input fails, be sure to initialize the object to some default state (or raise an exception).

## Dealing with Failure

Input can and will fail—it will certainly fail at the end of the file, but it might fail before the end because of an unexpected error in the input format. Of course, human input is completely unpredictable. Even computer files do get corrupted occasionally.

There is no way to test for failure except by doing it and seeing whether it worked. In Java, of course, failure to work means an exception has been thrown. In C++, check for failure *after* each read. You may then check for `eof()` to see whether the reason for failure is the end of the file or a formatting problem.

If you expect to read a certain input pattern but it is not present, report a format error by turning on the `failbit`. You may as well stop reading. All other input operations will do nothing because the stream has now failed.

Before committing to change a value, be sure that all input operations have been successful. Changing half of an object and then leaving the other half unchanged is definitely rude, and it also may produce an object that doesn't conform to the class invariant.

Once an input stream has failed, it is very hard to "unfail" it. You can clear the `failbit` and take your chances, but that is pretty useless in practice. If you cannot tolerate failure, read the input file as a sequence of strings and then parse the strings.

For output operations, error handling is not nearly as important. The major reason for output failure is a device failure (disk full, printer out of paper) about which you cannot do anything in an output routine. When the buffering layer detects the failure, the stream state is set to failure, and all further output is ignored. You can slightly speed up the process by checking for failure at the beginning of the output routine. Of course, after all output is completed, you must check whether the stream is still happy. If not, report the failure to the client that requested the output.

C H A P T E R

# 14

# Memory
# Management

The topic of memory management has little relationship to the theme of object-oriented programming. Many advanced programming languages, such as Java, employ garbage collection, automatically reclaiming memory that is no longer used. However, even the best garbage collection methods are computationally expensive. C++ has no garbage collection capabilities, and the programmer is responsible for allocating and deallocating memory. C++ does provide a substantial amount of support for *encapsulating* memory management, freeing users of classes that consume memory from the error-prone task of actively managing it. Some knowledge of the C++ memory management model is necessary to implement robust C++ classes.

This entire chapter discusses C++ memory management only; Java users are fortunate—they never have to think about memory. In Java, all objects are allocated on the heap with new, but programmers never need to worry about deallocating any memory. The garbage collector automatically reclaims any memory that is no longer referenced. It is true that the garbage collector is necessarily somewhat slow. However, experiences in Java have been generally very good. For the type of applications for which Java is typically used, the garbage collector overhead is not a problem because it is overshadowed by the waiting time for human input and network connections. Java programmers should also think of the garbage collector as a *safety feature*. The mishandling of heap pointers in C++ is among the most serious programming errors in C++, and those errors are notoriously difficult to debug. Commercial tools, such as BoundsChecker and Purify, can detect and pinpoint many of these errors in running programs. Such tools are indispensible to fix memory allocation bugs after they have been introduced. In this chapter, we will learn about the special memory management support functions provided by C++. When conscientiously applied, they can greatly reduce pointer errors in your code.

## The Free Store

### Memory Areas

C++ programs can allocate objects in one of three memory areas:

- The run-time stack
- The static data area
- The heap or free store

Local variables that are declared inside a function are allocated on the run-time stack. Their *visibility* and *lifetime* coincide, from the point of declaration until the end of the enclosing block. At the end of each block, all variables declared in that block are popped off the run-time stack. Of course, the values are not physically removed. Instead, a stack pointer is adjusted, and the memory area will soon be overwritten with other stack variables.

All variables that are declared outside of functions, as well as local and class variables that are declared as static, are allocated in the static data area. Their visibility depends on the declaration. Local static variables have the same scope as any other local variables. Global and shared class variables are visible in one or more modules. They come alive sometime before main starts and persist until after main exits. Unlike all other variables, static variables of nonclass type are guaranteed to be initialized with zero.

The stack and static data areas suffice to allocate data whose size and amount is known at compile time. However, most nontrivial programs cannot foresee the exact amount of run-time memory required for each data type because the generated data usually depends on user input or other external events. Any variable amount of data must be allocated on the heap or free store.

## Heap Allocation

The new operator is used to allocate an object on the heap. The syntax is

```
X* p = new X(constructor arguments);
```

A new object is allocated on the free store and constructed as specified. The constructor arguments can be omitted to invoke the default constructor or for a type without constructors. The allocated object itself has no name, but a pointer to it is returned.

All blocks that are allocated from new must be recycled to the free store when they are no longer needed. A memory block that is no longer accessible but has not been returned to the heap is called a *memory leak*. This is not a concern for programs that run very briefly and allocate little heap memory because the operating system reclaims all program memory on termination. But if a program with a memory leak runs sufficiently long, it will eventually exhaust the free store and cease to function properly. In writing reusable code, no memory leaks can be tolerated.

The delete operator is used to return a memory block to the heap. Its argument is a pointer to the object to be reclaimed.

```
delete p;
```

It is possible to allocate built-in arrays from the heap; however, that will never be done in this text because the array templates are a more convenient way of managing variable-size arrays. Refer to [Stroustrup], p. 175, for details.

The heap keeps a list of memory blocks that are available for allocation and their sizes. It is easy to corrupt this information by passing an address to delete that was not originally obtained from new or by continuing to write onto a memory block after reclaiming it with delete. (However, deleting a NULL pointer is safe and guaranteed to have no effect.)

```
Employee joe("Joe User");
Employee* pj = &joe;
Employee* ph = new Employee("Harry Hacker");
Employee* pk = ph;
Employee* pn = NULL;
delete pk; // OK
delete ph; // ERROR-deleting twice
delete pn; // OK-can delete NULL
delete pj; // ERROR-cannot delete pointer to stack
```

It is a good idea to obtain pointers from the heap only (with new) and never from the stack (that is, never with &). It is also a good idea to set a pointer to NULL after invoking delete to reduce the risk of deleting it twice.

```
delete ph;
ph = NULL;
```

Of course, this is not a complete safety guarantee. The same pointer value may be stored in a second pointer variable, and the programmer must still take care not to delete that value.

Corrupting the free list can lead to fatal consequences. Once the free list is damaged, a call to new may return a memory address that is already in use by another object. The resulting bugs tend to be difficult to reproduce, and the cause of the bug, namely the memory overwrite or faulty delete instruction, may well be far removed from the diagnosed symptoms. Encapsulating memory management is an important strategy to reduce the likelihood of such programming errors.

# Destructors

## Resource Management

Destructors are operations that are invoked automatically whenever storage for an object is reclaimed, just as constructors are automatically called when an object is created.

The construction and destruction activity is most easily envisioned for objects that exist on the run-time stack. When an object is allocated, space is set aside for it on the stack. At this point, the object has no well-defined value. Its storage is simply filled with the random bytes that happen to be on the stack as leftovers from previous program activity. It is the role of the constructor to turn the storage into an actual object, by initializing all data fields.

When program execution reaches the end of the block in which the object was allocated, the storage on the stack is abandoned. However, if a destructor is defined for the class to which the object belongs, the code of the destructor is executed first.

```
f(...)
{  ...
   {  ...
      List m;
      ...
   } // List destructor invoked on m
   ...
}
```

The purpose of the destructor is to relinquish any resources that the object may have acquired.

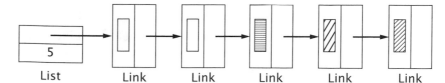

**FIGURE 14.1** A linked list.

The most common resource that needs to be managed with constructors and destructors is heap memory. Consider, for example, a linked list (see Figure 14.1) of integers.

```
class List
{   . . .
private:
   class Link
   {
   public:
      int _info;
      Link* _next;
   };
   Link* _head;
   int _length;
};
```

A `List` object merely contains a pointer to the first `Link`. The integers that are conceptually stored in the list are physically contained in the `Link` objects. These `Link` objects are allocated on the heap, as more values are added to the list. The `List` destructor recycles the links back to the heap when the `List` object goes out of scope.

Destructors can perform other actions besides returning memory to the heap. Common actions include closing files, releasing locks, and reducing use counts.

An alternative to destructors are cleanup operations that are invoked manually. However, this is error-prone, because it is easy enough to forget to call the cleanup operation or accidentally to call it more than once. In contrast, destructors are guaranteed to be invoked exactly once for each object.

Destructors are beneficial for code maintenance. Simple classes typically need no destructors. If a class evolves from a simple one to a more complex one, a destructor can be added. Existing code that uses the class need not be amended, just recompiled, and destructors are invoked automatically. If an explicit cleanup operation had been added instead, the existing code would have to be revisited to insert calls to that cleanup code.

## Implementing Destructors

A destructor of a class X has the name ~X(). Like constructors, destructors are declared in the class definition. While a class can have many constructors, it can have at most one destructor.

```
class List
{
public:
   List();
   ~List();
   . . .
private:
   Link* _head;
   int _length;
};


List::~List()
{  Link* p = _head;
   while (p != NULL)
   {  Link* pnext = p->_next;
      delete p;
      p = pnext;
   }
}
```

Much like default constructors, destructors are invoked automatically and cannot be called by the programmer. (Actually, there is a special syntax to invoke a destructor to make it available to builders of generic libraries, but this syntax should never be used in general programs.)

## Compiler-Generated Destructors

If one or more data fields or base objects of a class has a destructor, the compiler ensures that these data fields and base objects are properly destroyed. Consider a class containing a data field of class List:

```
class IndexEntry
{  . . .
private:
   string _phrase; // the phrase to index
   List _page_ref; // the pages on which _phrase occurs
   int _level; // the indentation level
};
```

Whether or not the IndexEntry class supplies a destructor, C++ ensures that the destructors of the string and List are invoked on the `_phrase` and `_page_ref` fields whenever an index entry object dies. Because `_level` is of type `int` and numeric types do not have destructors, no special action is performed for that field. If no `IndexEntry` destructor is provided, the compiler will generate one that invokes the destructors of the individual fields. If a destructor is provided, the instructions to destroy the `string` and `List` fields are appended to that destructor.

## Destruction and Deletion

A destructor is invoked whenever the memory that an object occupies is abandoned. For an object on the stack, this happens on exit from the block in which the object is allocated. An object on the heap is destroyed when the memory block that it occupies is deleted.

```
Employee* pe = new Employee(...);
. . .
delete pe; // Employee invoked on *pe
```

It is common that the destruction triggers more deletions. Suppose a linked list is allocated on the heap and later freed:

```
List* pl = new List;
pl->insert(...);
. . .
delete pl;
```

The `List` destructor is invoked on the `List` object to which `pl` points, and afterward the memory block in which that object resides is recycled to the free store. But the `List` destructor itself calls `delete`, this time on all `Link` objects that the linked list manages. In our example, the `Link` class has no destructor, and no special activity takes place before the links are reclaimed.

This example makes it clear that we must be careful to distinguish between destruction and deletion. *Destruction* is the cleanup that occurs before the storage used for an object is abandoned, regardless of whether the storage is part of the stack, heap, or static data area. *Deletion* is the reclamation of storage to the heap. Deletion always involves destruction of the block to be reclaimed.

## Virtual Destructors

Destructors can be declared as virtual. In fact, any class from which another class is derived ought to have a destructor and declare it as a virtual operation.

How does a class know whether another class will derive from it? If a class has any virtual function at all, it clearly intends to be a base class. If the class already has a destructor, be sure to make it virtual. If not, just add a virtual destructor that does nothing.

However, if a class has no virtual functions, making the destructor virtual is costly. It increases the size of each *object* by one pointer (to a table of virtual functions). For efficiency reasons, a virtual destructor is not usually added to classes like Date, List, or string, which have value semantics and are not envisioned as base classes for derivations.

Consider the following example:

```
class Employee
{
public:
    Employee(...);
    virtual void print(ostream&) const;
    . . .
private:
    int _id; // identification number
    . . .
};

class Manager : public Employee
{
public:
    Manager(...);
    virtual void print(ostream&) const;
    . . .
private:
    . . .
    List _superv; // ID numbers of supervised employees
};

vector<Employee*> staff;
// construct staff members
staff[0] = new Employee(...);
staff[1] = new Manager(...);
. . .
// print staff information
for (i = 0; i < staff.size(); i++)
    staff[i]->print(cout);
// recycle all allocated memory
for (i = 0; i < staff.size(); i++)
    delete staff[i];
```

Because the static type of staff[i] is Employee*, the compiler will invoke the Employee destructor, regardless of the actual type of the object to which staff[i] points. This is a problem because the Employee destructor can clean up only a portion of the `Manager` object. In particular, the `_superv` list is not destroyed.

The remedy is to declare an empty virtual destructor in the base class.

```
class Employee
{
public:
    virtual ~Employee() {}
    . . .
};
```

The compiler-generated `~Manager()` is then automatically virtual as well, and the call

```
delete staff[i];
```

invokes the correct destructor, depending on the actual type at run time.

### Pointers Have No Destructors

Only objects are destroyed provided that their class supplies a destructor. Destructors are never automatically invoked on pointers.

```
void f(...)
{  Employee* pe = new Employee(...);
   Employee e(...);
   . . .
} // ~Employee destroys e; *pe is not destroyed
```

This is to be expected. More than one pointer may refer to the same object, and the object should be destroyed only when it is no longer accessible by any pointer. In C++, the programmer must explicitly invoke `delete` at the proper time.

Similarly, when a reference goes out of scope, no destructor is triggered.

```
void print(List a, ostream& os)
{ . . .
} // ~List destroys a; os is not destroyed.
```

## *Assignment Operators*

Destructors are very useful for guaranteed cleanup without programmer intervention. However, their automatic invocation introduces a serious problem. Consider the code:

```
List a;
a.insert(...);
. . .
List b;
b.insert(...);
. . .
a = b;
// b goes out of scope
```

Suppose the lists look similar to Figure 14.2 before the assignment. The assignment a = b sets a._head to b._head and a._length to b._length (see Figure 14.3). Note that the old links of a are no longer accessible. As b goes out of scope, the destructor frees all links (see Figure 14.4). The a._head pointer now points to an unallocated link. Any further usage of a is an error. Even worse, the destructor for a will delete the invalid a._head pointer and corrupt the free list. (Recall that deleting the same pointer twice corrupts the heap.)

This example shows two problems: The original list was not deleted when a was replaced by another list, and the b list was deleted twice. Destruction appears to be incompatible with assignment.

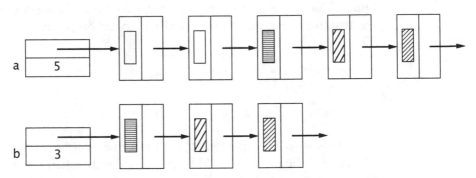

**FIGURE 14.2**   The lists before assignment.

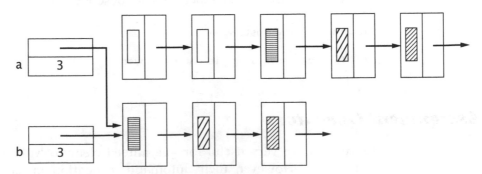

**FIGURE 14.3**   The lists after assignment.

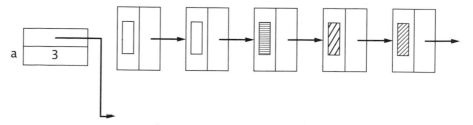

**FIGURE 14.4**  The lists after destruction of b.

In C++, this problem can be solved by overloading the assignment operator. As we saw in Chapter 12, it is possible to define the meaning for essentially all C++ operators by defining special `operator` functions. In this section we wish to define only the assignment operator, `operator=`. A user-defined assignment operator has to carry out two tasks:

- Free the memory of the left argument.
- Copy the memory of the right argument.

Here is the assignment operator for the `List` class:

```
class List
{
public:
   List();
   ~List();
   const List& operator=(const List& b);
   . . .
};

const List& List::operator=(const List& b)
{  // guard against assignment to itself
   if (this == &b) return *this;
   // destroy the left-hand side
   Link* p = _head;
   while (p != NULL)
   {  Link* pnext = p->_next;
      delete p;
      p = pnext;
   }
   // copy the right-hand side
   _length = b._length;
   p = NULL;
   Link* q = b._head;
   while (q != NULL)
   {  Link* n = new Link;
      n->_next = NULL;
      n->_info = q->_info; // copy information
      if (p == NULL) // first entry
         _head = n;
```

```
        else
            p->_next = n;
        p = n;
        q = q->_next;
    }
    return *this;
}
```

Note that the assignment operator takes two arguments: the implicit argument *this and an explicit argument b. It is customary to name the latter argument b or y, or even that, not a or x, to remind the reader that the first argument is implicit. The explicit argument is passed by constant reference (const List& b) and not by value (List b) to avoid copying the list.

The assignment operator returns a reference to the left-hand side to allow multiple assignments

```
c = a = b;
```

The protection

```
if (this == &b) return *this;
```

guards against the assignment

```
a = a;
```

in which case the left argument should *not* be cleared. (Nobody would assign a = a on purpose, but it might happen in a conditional expression or through an alias.)

Any class with a nontrivial destructor needs a user-defined assignment operator that makes proper copies.

# Copy Constructors

## Copying Function Arguments

In C++, objects can be copied with the assignment operator. Furthermore, objects can be copied into functions as arguments and out of functions as function results. These copies do not invoke the assignment operator, and they also conflict with destructors unless special action is taken.

In calling a function, all arguments of the call are copied into local variables of the function. These local variables are destroyed at the end of the function, just like any other local variables.

```
double average(List a)
{   double sum = 0;
    int n = a.length();
    . . .
    return sum / n;
} // ~List destroys a

List lst;
double avg = average(lst); // lst copied into a
```

It is helpful to look at the run-time stack. Before the call, lst is located on the stack, as in Figure 14.5. When the function starts, its local variables, a, sum, and n, are initialized. The parameter a is initialized as a copy of lst. That is, a._length is set to lst._length and a._head is set to lst._head, as shown in Figure 14.6.

When the function exits, all local variables are destroyed. Because numeric types have no destructors, sum and n are simply abandoned on the stack, but a is destroyed by ~List, deleting all links (see Figure 14.7). After the function returns, lst._head is no longer valid. Furthermore, when the

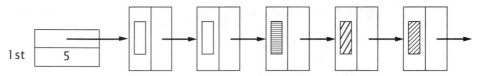

**FIGURE 14.5** The list before the function call.

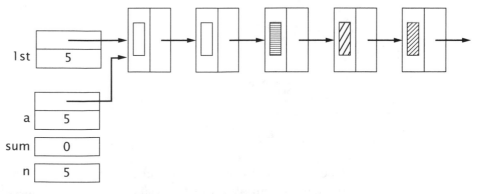

**FIGURE 14.6** The list at the beginning of the function call.

**FIGURE 14.7** The list after the function call.

~List destructor is invoked on lst, an invalid pointer is passed to delete, causing corruption of the free list. This situation is just as serious as the assignment problem discussed in the previous section.

You may well wonder why the compiler does not use the code defined in operator= to assign a = lst when the function starts. However, close inspection of the assignment code explains the problem. The assignment operator first frees the memory associated with the left-hand side of the assignment. However, the left-hand side, a, is completely uninitialized. In particular, a._head is a random pointer, and deleting it would be disastrous. The assignment operator can be used only to copy an object into another existing object, not to construct a new object.

In this situation, C++ requires the programmer to provide a so-called *copy constructor*, a constructor that initializes a new object as a copy of an existing one.

## Implementing Copy Constructors

A copy constructor for type X takes a single argument of type const X& and builds a new object as a copy of the constructor argument. Here is the code for the List copy constructor:

```
List::List(const List& b)
{  _length = b._length;
   Link* p = NULL;
   Link* q = b._head;
   while (q != NULL)
   {  Link* n = new Link;
      n->_next = NULL;
      n->_info = q->_info; // copy information
      if (p == NULL) // first entry
         _head = n;
      else
         p->_next = n;
      p = n;
      q = q->_next;
   }
}
```

Once a copy constructor has been defined, the compiler invokes it automatically to initialize function parameters with their call values.

Any class with a nontrivial destructor needs both a user-defined assignment operator and a user-defined copy constructor. When these memory management functions are defined, all destruction activity is matched by the appropriate copying actions.

Some data structures are very expensive to copy. Class designers can force class users to always copy pointers, not objects, by making the copy constructor and assignment operator *private*. The compiler then flags as an error any code that would require invoking either operation. No code should be supplied for these operations. This ensures that the linker will report an error if the class code itself invokes either operation.

**NOTE**

The copy constructor has the same purpose as the `clone` function in Java, namely to make a new object that is a deep copy of an existing object. However, `clone` returns a pointer to a new object on the heap; the copy constructor constructs a new object.

Once a copy constructor is provided, you can write a C++ `clone` function entirely mechanically:

```
class X
{
public:
   X* clone() const { return new X(*this); }
   . . .
};
```

## Factoring Out Common Code for Memory Management Operations

The code of the copy constructor is, of course, the same code as the second half of the assignment operator. In fact, the assignment operator can always be regarded as invoking the destructor on the left-hand side, then invoking the copy constructor to copy the right-hand side. However, constructors and destructors cannot be invoked explicitly, and it is customary to factor out the common code.

```
class List
{
public:
   List();
   List(const List& b);
   ~List();
   const List& operator=(const List& b);
   . . .
private:
   void copy(const List& b);
   void free();
};
```

```
List::List(const List& b)
{ copy(b);
}

List::~List()
{ free();
}

const List& List::operator=(const List& b)
{  if (this != &b)
   {  free();
      copy(b);
   }
   return *this;
}

void List::copy(const List& b)
{  _length = b._length;
   Link* p = NULL;
   Link* q = b._head;
   while (q != NULL)
   {  Link* n = new Link;
      n->_next = NULL;
      n->_info = q->_info; // copy information
      if (p == NULL) // first entry
         _head = n;
      else
         p->_next = n;
      p = n;
      q = q->_next;
   }
}

void List::free()
{  Link* p = _head;
   while (p != NULL)
   {  Link* pnext = p->_next;
      delete p;
      p = pnext;
   }
}
```

The advantage of splitting memory management code into copy and free is simplicity. However, you often have opportunities to make operator= more efficient by having it *reuse* existing memory rather than first freeing everything. For example, in the case of the linked list, the assignment operator could recycle the existing links, only allocating additional ones when needed and only deleting those that are not needed. Naturally, that makes the code for the assignment operator quite complex, but it is a worthwhile optimization.

## Copying Function Results

The copy constructor is used to copy function results out of the scope of a function into a temporary value in the scope of the caller. That temporary value is then used in further computations.

Consider a function that reverses a list without destroying its argument:

```
List reverse(List a)
{  List r;
    . . .
    return r; // List(const List&) copies r to scope of caller
} // ~List destroys r
 . . .
List u, v;
v = reverse(u);
print(reverse(u), cout);
```

When the result r is computed, the function ends and must pass the result to the caller. An unnamed temporary list object is constructed from r using the copy constructor. Then the list destructor destroys the local variable r. The unnamed temporary object is used in the computation; in this example, it is assigned to v or passed to print.

## Memberwise Copying and Assignment

As we saw in an earlier section, the compiler generates destructors, or enhances programmer-supplied destructors, to ensure that all data fields are properly destroyed. In the same fashion, copy constructors and assignment operators are automatically generated. These operations simply apply copying and assignment field by field, a process referred to as *memberwise copying*.

That is good news for users of classes with nontrivial copy semantics. Such classes can be used in "plug and play" fashion as building blocks for other classes. High-level classes can use data fields of any type without having to understand their mechanics of copying and destruction.

To understand how memberwise copying and assignment are carried out, consider again the IndexEntry example.

```
class IndexEntry
{  . . .
private:
   string _phrase; // the phrase to index
   List _page_ref; // the pages on which _phrase occurs
   int _level; // the indentation level
};
```

The copy constructor is used to construct a new object as a copy of an existing object, typically to copy it into or out of a function. It performs this copy individually on each field. The `string` and `List` copy constructors are used on the `_phrase` and `_page_ref` fields. Plain assignment is used on the `_level` field because the type `int` has no special copy requirements.

The analogous process is carried out in assignments. The assignment

```
IndexEntry a, b;
. . .
a = b;
```

is equivalent to the individual assignments

```
a._phrase = b._phrase; // uses string::operator=
a._page_ref = b._page_ref; // uses List::operator=
a._level = b._level; // plain copy of int values
```

For this reason, it is necessary to declare explicit copy constructors, assignment operators, and destructors only for low-level classes whose implementation directly manages some resource such as heap memory. Higher-level classes should rely on the compiler-generated memory management functions.

## Reference Counting

### Avoiding the Cost of Copying

Classes have destructors to free the programmer from the burden of having to remember when to relinquish a resource such as free-store memory. Classes that have destructors then need copying and assignment operations to ensure that each object has its own copy of the information because destructors cannot be allowed to clean up shared copies. But the cost of copying is substantial. Consider a function call

```
double average(List a)
{   double sum = 0;
    int n = a.length();
    . . .
    if (n > 0) return sum / n; else return 0;
} // ~List destroys a

List lst;
lst.insert(x);
. . .
avg = average(lst);
```

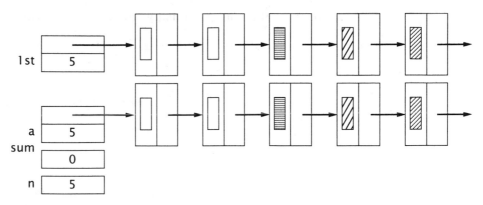

**FIGURE 14.8** A copy of the list is passed to the function.

When the parameter a is constructed as a copy of 1st, all links in 1st are copied, as in Figure 14.8. The information is then inspected (but not modified), and the copied links are destroyed at the end of the function. This is quite inefficient.

For function arguments, a constant reference can be used to avoid call by value and the cost of copying:

```
double average(const List& a)
{   double sum = 0;
    int n = a.length();
    . . .
    return sum/n;
} // ~List destroys a
```

Now the address of 1st, not a copy of the 1st object, is passed to the function, as shown in Figure 14.9.

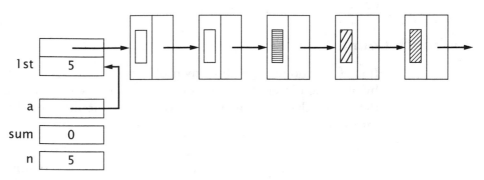

**FIGURE 14.9** A reference of the list is passed to the function.

However, that technique fails for function return values:

```
List reverse(const List& a)
{  List r;
   . . .
   return r;
   // List(const List&) copies r to temporary in scope of caller
} // ~List destroys r

List lst;
List rev = reverse(lst);
```

Transferring the result r out of the scope of the function into the scope of the caller involves a copy into a temporary, followed by the destruction of r. That is, all links of r that were built up in the computation are first copied, then deleted.

There is no easy way to avoid that copy. The function could be reformulated

```
void reverse(const List& a, List& result);
```

but this can make using the function less pleasant, and it is not an option for functions that define overloaded operators. We cannot have the function return a reference

```
List& reverse(const List& a); // DON'T
```

A reference to what? The function cannot return a reference to a local object because the stack of the function is popped when the function exits. Neither can we, in good conscience, return a reference to an object on the heap because the caller would then be obligated to delete that object when it is no longer needed.

Rather than trying to avoid the copy, we will learn how to reduce its cost.

## Reference Counts

It is often said jokingly that any problem in computer science can be solved by an added level of indirection. Indeed, this will help us manage objects that themselves must manage resources. We achieve that by separating the information into two classes:

- An access class, sometimes called a *handle*
- A representation class, containing a reference count and the object data

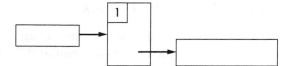

**FIGURE 14.10** The reference count after object creation.

The class user sees and copies only the access class. The representation class is invisible to the class user. Its class data is augmented by a field, called a *reference count*, that keeps track of the number of access objects sharing the same representation (see Figure 14.10).

When an access object is copied, the reference count is incremented, as in Figure 14.11. When an access object is destroyed, the reference count is decremented, as in Figure 14.12. Only when the reference count reaches zero is the representation object itself destroyed and the resources associated with the data released, as in Figure 14.13.

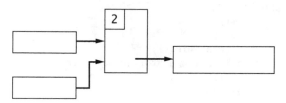

**FIGURE 14.11** The reference count after object copy.

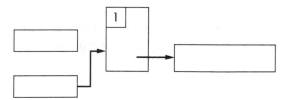

**FIGURE 14.12** The reference count after a destruction.

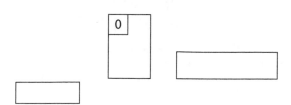

**FIGURE 14.13** The reference count after the last destruction.

## Implementation of Reference Counts

Let us implement a linked list class using reference counts. The list representation carries the reference count and the fixed list data:

```
class ListRep
{
private:
   unsigned _rc; // reference count
   Link* _head;
   int _length;
   . . .
friend class List;
};
```

The access class contains only a pointer to the data representation:

```
class List
{
public:
   List();
   . . .
   List(const List&);
   const List& operator=(const List&);
   ~List();
private:
   void copy(const List& b);
   void free();
   ListRep* _rep;
};
```

As described previously the copy and free functions are used to define the copy constructor, assignment operator, and destructor:

```
List::List(const List& b)
{  copy(b);
}

List::~List()
{  free();
}

const List& List::operator=(const List& b)
{  if (this != &b)
   {  free();
      copy(b);
   }
   return *this;
}
```

The `copy` and `free` functions manipulate the reference count field in the `ListRep` class.

```
void List::copy(const List& b)
{   _rep = b._rep;
    _rep->_rc++;
}

void List::free()
{   _rep->_rc-;
    if (_rep->_rc == 0)
        delete _rep;
}
```

The `ListRep` destructor is invoked only when all access objects sharing the list data are destroyed. It then deletes the links:

```
ListRep::~ListRep()
{   Link* p = _head;
    while (p != NULL)
    {   Link* pnext = p->_next;
        delete p;
        p = pnext;
    }
}
```

The `ListRep` constructor can be called only from `List`:

```
List::List()
{   _rep = new ListRep();
}
```

When a `ListRep` object is constructed, we set the reference count to 1:

```
ListRep::ListRep()
:   _rc(1),
    _head(NULL),
    _length(0)
{}
```

Note that the `List` class contains a single data field—a pointer to the list representation. Objects of type `List` are similar to pointers, but there is an important difference. Because constructors, assignment operators, and destructors can be defined for classes but not for pointers, list objects can automatically update the reference counts.

The `List` user need not be concerned with the fact that reference counts are used to manage lists. In fact, the `List` user never sees the `ListRep` class. All operations are declared on the level of the `List` class:

```
class List
{
public:
   List();
   void insert(int);
   int remove();
   int head() const; // peek at head
   int length() const;
   . . .
   List(const List&);
   const List& operator=(const List&);
   ~List();
private:
   . . .
};
```

The class implementor has to go to some degree of inconvenience to code the operations because all data fields must be reached by indirecting through the _rep pointer.

```
int List::length() const
{  return _rep->_length;
}
```

```
int List::head() const
{  assert(_rep->_head != NULL); // cannot peek empty list
   return _rep->_head->_info;
}
```

Naturally, this is not a major concern because it is outweighed by the benefits to the class user.

## Copy on Write

The reference count implementation discussed so far has one disadvantage. Suppose a copy of a list is made and then modified:

```
List a;
a.insert(x);
List b = a;
z = b.remove();
b.insert(y);
```

The changes to the copy b also affect the original list a! Because both a and b share the same data (with reference count 2), any modification through either list object affects the other. This seems unintuitive, and even though you might get used to it for simple lists, it really makes no sense when lists are used as building blocks for other classes. Consider, for example, an `IndexEntry` class:

```
class IndexEntry
{
public:
   . . .
   void indent();
private:
   string _phrase; // the phrase to index
   List _page_ref; // the pages on which _phrase occurs
   int _level; // the indentation level
};

void IndexEntry::indent()
{  _level++;
   _page_ref.empty();
}

IndexEntry a;
. . .
IndexEntry b = a;
b.indent();
```

The `a._level` and `b._level` differ by 1. We would expect that `a._page_ref` and `b._page_ref` also differ. But if the representations of the list are shared, the `empty()` operation empties both lists.

To overcome this problem, we will make a complete copy of the data in those operations that modify the object—that is, operations not declared as `const`. Of course, that copy is necessary only when the reference count is larger than 1.

A function `unique` performs the copy when necessary, by invoking the `ListRep` copy constructor.

```
void List::unique()
{  if (_rep->_rc == 1) return;
   _rep->_rc--;
   _rep = new ListRep(*_rep);
}

ListRep::ListRep(const ListRep& b)
{  _length = b._length;
   Link* p = NULL;
   Link* q = b._head;
   while (q != NULL)
   {  Link* n = new Link;
      n->_next = NULL;
      n->_info = q->_info; // copy information
```

```
      if (p == NULL) // first entry
         _head = n;
      else
         p->_next = n;
      p = n;
      q = q->_next;
   }
}
```

The `unique` function is called in all destructive list operations.

```
int List::remove()
{  assert(_rep->_head); // cannot remove from empty list
   unique();
   int r = _rep->_head->_info;
   Link* p = _rep->_head;
   _rep->_head = _rep->_head->_next;
   delete p;

   _rep->_length--;
   return r;
}
```

After the call to `unique`, the operation manipulates its own copy of the list data without disturbing any shared copies. This technique is called *delayed copy* or *copy on write* because copying is delayed as long as possible. Objects share the information for reading purposes, and copies are made only when necessitated by a write operation.

## Guidelines for Implementing Reference Counts

Reference counts and copy on write are sophisticated techniques, but once mastered, they can be implemented in a routine fashion. Use the following guidelines:

1. You need two classes, X and XRep.
2. The X class defines all interface operations.
3. The XRep class contains all data fields.
4. The X class contains a pointer XRep* _rep and no further data.
5. The XRep class has a reference count unsigned _rc.
6. The XRep class has a copy constructor that makes an actual copy of the class data (but is invoked only in `unique` when the reference count is greater than 1) and a destructor that releases any resources (but is called only when the reference count goes to 0).
7. The X class has private `copy`, `free`, `unique` operators that manipulate the reference counts and invoke the XRep destructor and `copy` constructor as needed. This code is completely routine.

8. The X class has a copy constructor, assignment operator, and destructor that call `copy` and `free`. This code too is completely routine.
9. The X operations access the data fields by indirecting through the `_rep` pointer. This is merely tedious.
10. All destructive operations must call `unique`.

If this is so mechanical, why doesn't the compiler do it for us for all classes? As we will see in the next section, reference counting is a very useful technique in many practical cases, but it is not a universal solution for memory management.

## Drawbacks of Reference Counts

Reference counting is an excellent storage management tool for many applications. It does, however, have three drawbacks.

Copying a reference-counted pointer consumes more time than copying a plain pointer. Updating the reference counts with every construction, copy, assignment, and destruction exacts a performance cost. (Using inline functions makes a measurable difference and is strongly recommended.) In some programming situations, manual deallocation of heap objects or manual release of other resources is not too hard to do, and the gain in performance may be important enough to forgo the added automation and security that reference counts provide.

Some objects can have a huge number of pointers to them, so you must be careful not to have the reference count "wrap around" beyond the largest representable value. Instead, these objects must be kept alive forever. Naturally, this situation is rare.

Most importantly, reference counts do not work for complex data structures. If there are cycles in the data structure, as in Figure 14.14, cycles

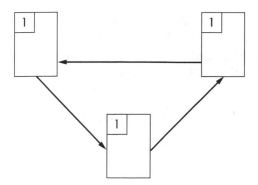

**FIGURE 14.14**   A self-supporting cycle.

of blocks may never be deallocated because they "support themselves," although there are no external references to them. In practice, such data structures do occur frequently—for example, in graphs or networks. Fortunately, in many other applications the nature of the problem guarantees the absence of cycles. For example, in a word processor, paragraphs may contain words, equations, graphs, or tables, which themselves may contain other objects, but because each object is made up of strictly smaller ones, no cycle can appear.

To perform automatic deallocation of arbitrary data structures without programmer intervention, full garbage collection is required. Some research has been undertaken to add garbage collection to C++, and commercial garbage collection facilities are available from third parties. However, there is no "official" support for garbage collection as part of the language, as there is in Java.

## Design Hints

### Agree on Responsibilities with the Class User

When you place a pointer as a data field in a class, you are taking on the responsibility of managing a resource: the memory to which the pointer points. You have to contract with the class user regarding the details. A number of contractual models are reasonable in different circumstances. The important part is that both the class user and the class implementor clearly understand their obligations. As class designer, you need to draft a contract that balances the user's need for convenience with the implementor's need for simplicity.

If the user gives you the pointer value as an argument to a constructor or operation, you must come to an agreement about whether you or the user will delete it. If you initialize the pointer, you must either automatically delete it in a destructor or give the user a public operation (such as `free`) to do it manually. If you supply a destructor, you must also supply a copy constructor and assignment operator or else extract the promise from the users that they will never make a copy of any object.

### Avoid Data Fields That Are Pointers

The simplest way of avoiding the morass of destructors, copy constructors, and assignment operators is to use data fields that already know how to copy and destroy themselves. If all data fields are of that kind, then the compiler generates a complete and correct set of all memory management operations automatically for you.

Use a `string` class, not a `char*` pointer. Use a `List`, not a `Link*` pointer. Use a `vector<X>`, not an `X*` pointer. And, the single most often overlooked possibility: Use an `X` object, not an `X*` pointer.

It is impossible to avoid pointers completely in all classes. There are three valid reasons for using them:

■ For sharing
■ For polymorphism
■ For zero/one relationships

## A Class That Has a Destructor Needs Both a Copy Constructor and an Assignment Operator

A class that has a destructor but no copy constructor is a recipe for disaster. If a user makes a copy, both the original and the copy are destroyed, usually causing a "double delete." Marshall Cline, the keeper of the list of frequently asked C++ questions on the Usenet C++ newsgroup, calls the three memory management functions of C++ "the big 3." If you implement one of them, you must implement them all. As Cline says, "It is not just a good idea—it's the law!".

If you decide to offer the class user the convenience of automatic cleanup by supplying a destructor, you must decide what to do for object copying. If you want to allow copying, implement the copy constructor. You can mechanically synthesize the assignment operator from the destructor and the copy constructor using the `free/copy` functions. Or, if copying is so costly or difficult that you want to prevent it, make the copy constructor and assignment operator private. For example, the copy constructor and assignment operator for the base class `ios` of all input/output streams are private—you cannot copy a stream.

## Polymorphic Types Must Have Virtual Destructors

If you delete a pointer that may point to a base- or derived-class object, the base-class destructor must be virtual to ensure correct cleanup of the entire object, not just the base part.

This is a difficult design requirement. How do you know whether a class will have derived classes? If the class has virtual functions, you are sure it has been designed to serve as a base class. Then make the destructor virtual if it exists, or otherwise add a virtual destructor that does nothing.

If a class has no virtual function, adding one or more virtual functions increases the size of *each* object by one pointer (to the so-called virtual function table). For classes that are small and unlikely candidates for derivation, such as Date, it seems worth the risk not to include a virtual destructor.

Conversely, if you derive from a base class, check that the base class has a virtual destructor.

C  H  A  P  T  E  R

# 15

# Parameterized
# Classes

Templates are the C++ mechanism for *generic programming*. We have already seen the `vector` template: `vector<int>` makes a vector of integers, `vector<Shape*>`, a vector of shape pointers. The designer of the `vector` template has to program the functionality of vectors for a *type parameter* `T`, and the *template instantiation* mechanism of the compiler binds `T` to an actual type such as `int` or `Shape*`.

Java does not have templates. For example, the Java `Vector` class stores `Object` references. That has two disadvantages. The user must always cast the return value from `elementAt` to the correct type:

```
Shape s = (Shape)figure.elementAt(i);
```

Clearly, this is a rich source of programming errors—it is easy to accidentally put an `Employee` object into a vector that was intended to hold shapes. Furthermore, the absence of type information makes the code hard to read. If a class has a data field

```
Vector elements;
```

you have no clue what kind of elements are being collected. There is, however, a good reason why the designers of Java decided against supporting type parameterization. As you will see in this chapter, templates are an enormously complex feature for compiler writers to implement. It is very easy to use templates—you have done it many times with the `vector` template. It isn't even all that hard to write them, but it is a real challenge for the compiler to pick the right templates and instantiate the needed operations. All of today's C++ compilers have many known template bugs and shortcomings. The decision of the Java designers not to include templates is therefore entirely understandable.

## Type Parameterization

If we want to find out how to implement a queue, we can consult a textbook on data structures and most likely will find code for a queue of integers. Of course, a queue of integers is rarely what you need in actual programming situations. We may need to implement a queue of customers. A mechanical change, replacing all `int` with `Customer`, yields a queue class that stores customers instead. Actually you must be somewhat careful. The `int` in

```
int Queue::remove()
```

must be changed to

```
Customer Queue::remove()
```

but

```
int Queue::length() const
```

should remain unchanged. Of course, queues of objects of entirely different types will be needed in other applications. To avoid the mechanical (and somewhat error-prone) process of adapting and editing existing code, a mechanism is desirable that lets us code the operations for a queue of objects of an arbitrary type, from which queues for specific types can be obtained. In C++, the *template* mechanism serves this purpose.

A generic `Queue<T>` template has a type parameter `T`. When that parameter `T` is replaced with an actual type, say `Customer`, a class `Queue<Customer>` results. The process of obtaining a class from a template is called *template*

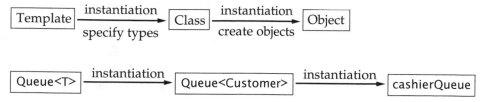

**FIGURE 15.1** Template instantiation.

*instantiation,* as shown in Figure 15.1. The class `Queue<Customer>` behaves like any other class. Objects of that class are declared in the usual way:

```
Queue<Customer> cashier_queue;
```

Parameterized types are useful for all containers, such as arrays, linked lists, queues, or hash tables. More generally, templates are useful for all constructs that generalize to arbitrary types.

## Using Templates

Using a template that has been implemented by someone else is very easy. Just plug in actual types for the type parameters to obtain a class, then use that class as you would any other. The `vector` template that was used throughout this book is a typical example. Other class templates are instantiated in the same way:

```
list<Shape*> display_list;
display_list.insert_tail(new Rectangle(...));

class Mailbox
{  . . .
private:
   Queue<Message> _msg;
};

void Mailbox::append(Message m)
{  _msg.insert(m);
}
```

It is the job of the compiler and linker to ensure that the code for all operations of the instantiated class is produced.

The instantiation type can be any legal C++ type.

```
Queue<int>
Queue<Message>
Queue<Event*>
Queue< list<Vehicle*> >
```

Note the spaces in the last example. Omitting the spaces between the > > yields a syntax error:

```
Queue<list<Vehicle*>> // ERROR
```

The >> is parsed as a shift operator—tokenization occurs before any syntactic analysis.

# Implementing a Class Template

## The Class Interface

The class interface of a parameterized class is the same as that of a regular class, prepended by the keyword `template` and a list of the template parameters. For the queue example, we need two templates: one each for the link and queue classes.

```
template<class T>
class Link
{
public:
    Link(T, Link<T>* = NULL);
private:
    Link<T>* _next;
    T _info;
    friend class Queue<T>;
};
```

```
template<class T>
class Queue
{
public:
    Queue();
    void insert(T t);
    T remove();
    int length() const;
private:
    Link<T>* _head;
    Link<T>* _tail;
    int _length;
};
```

The keyword `class` in

```
template<class T>
```

is a misnomer. `T` can be any type; it need not be of class type. For example, `Queue<Event*>` and `Queue<int>` are legal template instantiations, even though `Event*` and `int` are not classes. The designers of the language were merely reluctant to introduce another keyword such as `type` to describe this situation accurately.

## Implementing Parameterized Operations

Each operation of a class template is prepended by the `template` keyword. The class name is qualified with the template argument list.

```
template<class T>
void Queue<T>::insert(T t)
{   Link<T>*P = new Link<T>(t, _head);
    if(_tail) _tail -> _next = p;
    else _head = p;
    _tail = p;
    _length ++;
}
```

```
template<class T>
T Queue<T>::remove()
{   assert(_head != NULL);
    T t = _head->_info;
    Link<T>* n = _head->_next;
    delete _head;
    _head = n;
    if (_head == NULL) _tail = NULL;
    _length --;
    return t;
}
```

The placement of the `<T>` is somewhat confusing. They are almost always necessary, but they must be omitted for the names of constructors and destructors.

```
template<class T>
Queue<T>::Queue()
:   _head(NULL),
    _tail(NULL),
    _length(0)
{}
```

```
template<class T>
Queue<T>::Queue(const Queue<T>& b)
{ copy(b);
}
```

Templates for operations can be inline-replaced.

```
template<class T>
inline int Queue<T>::length() const
{ return _length;
}
```

## Default Values

Suppose we want the `remove` operation to return a "zero" element, rather than raising an exception, when it is invoked on an empty queue. We cannot simply return 0.

```
template<class T>
T  Queue<T>::remove()
{  if (_head == NULL)
       return 0; // DON'T
   . . .
}
```

If the type `T` is not an integral or pointer type, there may be no valid conversion from 0 to an object of type `T`. Instead, we may allocate a static object for this purpose:

```
template<class T>
class Queue
{
   . . .
private:
   static T _defval; // default value
};
```

```
template<class T>
T Queue<T>::remove()
{  if (_head == NULL)
       return _defval; // OK
   . . .
}
```

A static class variable is ideally suited for this purpose. If `T` is instantiated as a numeric or pointer type, `_defval` is guaranteed to be initialized with zero. If `T` is of class type, the default constructor is invoked to initialize it. It is reasonable to assume that the default constructor is most likely to construct a default object. If the class has no default constructor, then instantiation fails.

Static class variables must be both declared and defined. The definition template has the form

```
template<class T>
T Queue<T>::_defval;
```

**TIP**

Actually, quite a few compilers have trouble defining static data members. The workaround is to define a member function

```
template<class T>
const T& Queue<T>::defval()
{  static T _defval;
   return _defval;
}
```

Recall that a static *local* variable is initialized the first time the function is entered and that it stays alive until the program exits. ■

## Changing a Class to a Parameterized Class

Rather than developing a class template from scratch, it is usually easier first to write and debug an individual instantiation and then add the `template` keywords and type arguments. For example, start with a queue of floating-point numbers.

```
class Queue
{
public:
   void insert(double t);
   double remove();
   int length() const;
private:
   . . .
};
```

After testing, replace all `double` with `T` and prepend `template<class T>` before the definition of the class and of each operation.

**TIP**

If you use this strategy, don't start with a queue of *integers*. If you did, you'd have to think whether the `int` in `int Queue::length() const` needs to be replaced with `T`. ■

## *Template Parameters*

### Multiple Type Parameters

Templates can have more than one type parameter. A common example is a *map* or *associative array,* a data structure for storing associations.

```
Map<string, int> age;
age.set("Harry Hacker", 10); //associate "Harry Hacker" with 10
string name;
int a = age.get(name);
//find the integer associated with the string name
```

The map template depends on two types: the type of the key and the type of the value.

```
template<class K, class V>
class Map
{
public:
   void set(const K& key, const V& value);
   V get(const K& key) const;
   . . .
};
```

### Nontype Parameters

Besides types, templates can be parameterized by integer values known at compile time. Arrays of fixed size are the most useful application:

```
template<class T, int LO, int HI>
class FixedArray
{
public:
   T& operator[](int);
private:
   T _elements[HI-LO+1];
};

template<class T, int LO, int HI>
T& FixedArray<T, LO, HI>::operator[](int i)
{  assert(LO <= i && i <= HI);
   return _elements[i - LO];
}

FixedArray<Point, 1, 10> a;
```

These arrays are just like C arrays, but without the hassle:

- The [] operator performs range checking.
- The lower bound does not have to be zero.
- FixedArrays are copied by value.

Because the size of the array is known at compile time, it is allocated on the stack, without free store overhead.

## Default Parameters

Suppose we want to print the elements in a queue. By default, we want to use the << operator to print them, and the vast majority of users of the template will be happy with that choice. But perhaps there is no << for a particular type, or the user wants to substitute a different print function instead. Default template parameters let you make life simple for the majority of template users while still accommodating users with special needs.

A default argument is specified in the same way as the default argument for a function:

```
template<class T, class U = defaultU> . . .
```

Of course, in this case, we want to deliver a *function*, not a class, namely the operator<<. In principle this could be done by having a nonclass parameter of type ostream& (*)(ostream&, **const T&)** with a default value of operator<<. However, if the second parameter of operator<< happens to be just T, not const T&, then instantiation might fail. There is a useful trick to avoid this problem: Make a template for a class with no data and a single operation print that calls <<.

```
template<class T>
class Printer
{
public:
    void print(ostream& os, const T& t) { os << t; }
}
```

To print an element, the template code makes a default object of type Printer<T> and calls the print function.

```
Printer<T> p; // no data, just a print function
p.print(os, data);
```

Of course, this is just the default action. Here is the queue template with a default parameter.

```
template<class T, class P = Printer<T> >
class Queue
{  . . .
   void print(ostream& os) const;
}

template<class T, class P = Printer<T> >
void Queue::print(ostream& os)
{  Link* 1;
   for (1 = _head; 1 != NULL; 1 = 1->_next)
   {  T data = 1 -> _info;
      P p;
      p.print(os, data);
      os << endl;
   }
}
```

Because most users don't care about an alternative to << for printing, they can simply use the default:

```
Queue<Customer> q;
```

That is the same as

```
Queue<Customer, Printer<Customer> > q;
```

Thus, the class P in the print operation is Printer<Customer>:

```
Printer<Customer> p;
p.print(os, data);
```

The print command is inline replaced with

```
os << data;
```

Thus, we have succeeded in giving a reasonable default for most users.

A user who is not happy with the default must supply a different class with a print operation.

```
class EmployeePrint
{
public:
   void print(ostream& os, const Employee& e) { e.print(os); }
}

Queue<Employee, EmployeePrint> q;
```

It sounds like quite a bit of trouble to define a whole new class just to call a different function, but this strategy is not unusual. The ANSI C++ standard container library uses this device routinely to supply different functions to templates. In fact, it goes a step further and does not even give a meaningful name like `print` to the function to be supplied. Instead, it overloads the `()` operator.

Then the template code looks like this:

```
template<class T, class P = Printer<T> >
void Queue::print(ostream& os)
{  Link* 1;
   for (1 = _head; 1 != NULL; 1 = 1->_next)
   {  T data = 1 -> _info;
      P()(os, data);
      os << endl;
   }
}
```

The mysterious expression

```
P()(os, data);
```

means "make a default object of type P, then call the overloaded `()` operator with parameters os and data".

The default `Printer<T>` template overloads that operator to call `<<`:

```
template<class T> class Printer
{
public:
   void operator()(ostream& os, const T& L) { os << t; }
}
```

To supply a different action, write a new class with no data and an overloaded `()` operator:

```
class EmployeePrint
{
public:
   void operator()(ostream& os, const Employee& e)
   { e.print(os); }
}
```

This idiom is quite mysterious at first and takes some getting used to. In your own templates, you should probably use named functions like `print`, but if you use a template whose designer was enamored with `operator()` and you need to override a default, you have no choice but to master the idiom.

At this point, few compilers actually support template defaults, but since they are an essential feature of the ANSI C++ container library, this will surely change very rapidly.

## Function Templates

In C++, we can define templates of both operations and regular functions. The classical example for the latter is as follows:

```
template<class T>
inline T max(T a, T b)
{   return a > b ? a : b;
}

unsigned long x, y, z;
z = max(x, y);
```

For function templates, instantiation is much more difficult for the compiler than for class templates. There are no < . . . > to aid the compiler in the selection of the template. In fact, there may be any number of over-loaded nontemplate max functions defined as well, and the compiler may need to make a heroic effort to find the correct one.

A useful application for function templates is to define functions that operate on class template instantiations when an operation template is not appropriate. For example, consider this template to print the contents of a queue.

```
template<class T>
ostream& operator<<(ostream& os, const Queue<T>& q)
{   . . .
}

Queue<Customer> q;
os << q;
    // invokes operator<<(ostream&, const Queue<Customer>&)
```

The ANSI C++ library contains a large number of *algorithms* (such as sort or find_if) that are implemented as function templates. We will have a closer look at these algorithms in Chapter 17.

## Specialization

Occasionally, templates for classes or functions generate the correct code for almost all cases. It is possible to override the template-generated code by providing separate definitions for specific types.

For example, the max template

```
template<class T>
inline T max(T a, T b)
{   return a > b ? a : b;
}
```

does not work correctly on C character strings.

```
max("Harry", "Hacker")
```

instantiates max(const char*, const char*), which compares the addresses of the strings. To obtain lexicographic comparison in this case, we can supplement the template with a specialization:

```
const char* max(const char* a, const char* b)
{   return strcmp(a, b) > 0 ? a : b;
}
```

Specialization can be used either to correct the general template behavior in special circumstances or to supply *more efficient* implementations for certain types.

## Nested Templates

Templates can have operations that themselves depend on a template parameter. Here is a very typical example. C++ has a smart pointer template auto_ptr that we will examine in greater detail later in this chapter. A smart pointer of type auto_ptr<T> is similar to a T* pointer, except that the destructor of the object to which the smart pointer points is called when the smart pointer itself is destroyed.

Like all smart pointers, auto_ptr overloads the * operator to access the object to which the smart pointer refers.

```
template<class T>
class auto_ptr
{
public:
   T& operator*();
   ~auto_ptr() { delete _obj; }
   . . .
private:
   T* _obj;
};
```

Thus, smart pointers act almost like regular pointers.

```
auto_ptr<Employee> pe = new Employee("Harry Hacker");
(*pe).raise_salary(5.5);
```

There is, however, one major difference. The C++ compiler supports conversion between base-class and derived-class pointers, but there is no equivalent conversion between smart pointers. For example, objects of type `auto_ptr<Employee>` and `auto_ptr<Manager>` have no relationship to each other. An assignment

```
auto_ptr<Manager> pm = new Manager("Mary Moore");
auto_ptr<Employee> pe = pm;
```

will not compile. This is a major drawback that makes smart pointers unsuitable for object-oriented programming. To remedy this situation, the ANSI standard committee has recently added a *nested template* feature to C++. In our case, we will add a whole family of copy constructors to the `auto_ptr` template:

```
template<class T>
class auto_ptr
{
public:
   template<class D>
   auto_ptr(const auto_ptr<D>& pd)
   {  _obj = pd._obj;
      pd._obj = NULL;
   }
   T& operator*();
   ~auto_ptr() { delete _obj; }
   . . .
private:
   T* _obj;
};
```

Now, the code

```
auto_ptr<Employee> pe = pm;
```

will compile: it calls the constructor

```
auto_ptr<Employee>::auto_ptr(const auto_ptr<Manager>&)
```

The compiler has the thankless task of generating the code for this constructor if and only if it is actually needed.

Of course, the assignment

```
auto_ptr<D> pd;
. . .
auto_ptr<T> pt = pd;
```

should succeed only if D is actually a derived class from T. There is, however, nothing in the template that specifies that requirement. Let us see what happens when we try to abuse the feature and assign an auto_ptr<Rectangle> to an auto_ptr<Employee>. Then the compiler generates the copy constructor

```
auto_ptr<Employee>::auto_ptr(const auto_ptr<Rectangle>& pd)
{   _obj = pd._obj; // ERROR
    pd._obj = NULL;
}
```

It then reports an error: _obj is an Employee*, pd._obj is a Rectangle*, and you can't assign a Rectangle* to an Employee*. Thus, type errors manifest themselves in unsuccessful template compilations. Unfortunately, the compiler error message can be difficult to interpret—the compiler reports the error in the template code, and you must have some knowledge of the template to understand how to fix the error in your code.

Nested templates were invented specifically to make the Derived→Base conversion work for smart pointers. At this point, none of the major compilers supports this feature, but undoubtedly this will change in the near future. Equally undoubtedly, resourceful programmers will find new uses for this feature that will stretch the template instantiation mechanism to the breaking point.

# *Instantiation*

## The Instantiation Mechanism

The template mechanism is designed to be easy for the programmer to use, but it is definitely not easy on the compiler. When a class template is used, the compiler must locate the template definition and construct the layout for the instantiated class. When one class template uses another, as, for example, the Queue template uses the Link template, that template too needs to be instantiated. If there is a specialized version, it must be used instead of the general template.

Whenever a template operation or template function is used in a program, the compiler must locate the template code, generate code with the actual types, and place that code with the program's object code. Because a template function may well call other template functions, this code instantiation must be carried out recursively until all needed code is generated. Finally, some mechanism needs to be in place to make sure that multiple copies of the same instantiated code do not end up in the executable program.

Some compilers simply generate code for *all* operations of an instantiated class, whether or not they are used in a program. That eliminates the need for recursively determining which operations are actually needed, but it unnecessarily increases the size of the executable program.

## Instantiation Failure

In writing a parameterized class, the type parameters are not constrained. However, the code may not instantiate properly for some types. Suppose we attempt to build a queue of `ostream` objects:

```
Queue<ostream> osqueue;
```

A number of operations will fail to instantiate, among them this one:

```
ostream Queue<ostream>::remove()
{  . . .
   return t;
}
```

To return an `ostream` object, a copy constructor is required, but the copy constructor for `ostream` is private and hence not accessible.

This does not prohibit us from writing the `Queue<T>` template. It merely means that we cannot instantiate it with the type `ostream`. If instantiation is attempted, the compiler will refuse. This is called *instantiation failure*.

Actually, the instantiation strategy of the compiler affects the success or failure of instantiation. If the compiler generates code for all operations as soon as it instantiates a class, failure will occur immediately when an object of type `Queue<ostream>` is allocated. If the compiler instantiates code only for those operations that are actually used, instantiation fails only if the `Queue<ostream>::remove` operation (or another operation requiring a copy constructor) is called.

The ANSI standard requires that a compiler instantiate only those operations that are actually needed in a program. But that is not easy to implement, and several currently available compilers choose the simpler strategy of instantiating all operations when instantiating a class.

## Instantiation Requirements

The fact that we cannot build queues of ostream objects is not serious. To get objects into and out of containers, we must require that the objects have a copy constructor. (To queue streams, you can use a Queue<ostream*>.) This requirement is not an explicit part of the Queue template, but it is implicit in the code of its operations.

It is important to make the requirements for instantiations explicit by a comment in the template for the class definition:

```
template<class T>
class Queue
/* RECEIVES: T - any type supporting copy construction
*/
{
   . . .
};
```

Containers such as arrays and queues typically require support for copy construction (to get objects into and out of the container), assignment (to move items within a container), and default construction (to initialize empty slots).

Instantiation requirements can get more complex if objects in a container need to be identified. Consider the Map class:

```
Map<string, int> age;
age.set("Harry Hacker", 10);
. . .
age.set("Harry Hacker", 20);
```

The first insertion must add a new (*key, value*) pair. The second insertion with the same key must find out that the key is already present and change the associated value. This requires a mechanism for comparing keys.

```
template<class K, class V>
class Map
{
public:
   void set(const K& key, const V& value);
   V get(const K& key) const;
   . . .
private:
   vector<K> _key;
   vector<V> _value;
};
```

```
template<class K, class V>
void Map<K,V>::set(const K& k, const V& v)
{  bool found = false;
   for (int i = 0; !found && i < _key.size(); i++)
   { if (k == _key[i]) found = true;
   }
   . . .
}
```

The code for the set operation introduces an implicit requirement, namely that the type K support comparison with the == operation. If K is instantiated with string, this is not a problem. But K is more likely to be of some class type, for example

```
Map<Employee, double> salary;
```

If no operator== has been defined for the class Employee, instantiation will fail, perhaps surprising the user of the Map template.

To reduce surprises, it is important that the template document what it expects of its type arguments.

```
template<class K, class V>
class Map
/* PURPOSE:  a table of key/value associations
   RECEIVES: K - any type supporting copy construction and ==
             V - any type supporting copy construction
*/
{
   . . .
};
```

## Specifying the Behavior of Instantiation Types

For large maps, linear search is unacceptable. Binary search requires that the keys support a linear ordering. In writing the template, code must be chosen to make instantiation succeed for the largest number of cases.

We could require that K support an operation

```
int K::compare(const K& b) const
```

that returns a negative number if *this is less than b, zero if they are identical, and a positive number otherwise. The template code for the binary search can then use that operation:

```
if (_key[i].compare(k) < 0) ...
```

Alternatively, we can require that `K` support the < operator:

```
if (_key[i] < k) ...
```

Requiring an operation with a specific name (such as `compare` or `hash`) is a bad idea. It is then impossible to instantiate the template with nonclass types such as pointers. For example, instantiation of `Map<Employee*, double>` must fail because `_key[i].compare(k)` then invokes the dot operator on a pointer—a syntax error. Even for classes, adding new operations generally is not possible. Restricting the use of the `Map` template to those classes that already have an operation named `compare` is undesirable.

The second solution, requiring an overloaded < operator, is better because overloaded operators need not be operations and can be added without touching the definition of the key class. For example, if `Map<Employee, double>` is desired, it is easy to supply a suitable

```
bool operator<(Employee, Employee)
```

However, for nonclass types, < is already defined. In particular, for pointers it denotes comparison of their memory locations (provided they point to the same array). You cannot override this behavior through overloading. If we rely on the < operation for binary search, instantiation will succeed if `K` is a pointer type, but the generated code will be wrong.

A third possibility is to require that the user of the `Map` function supply a regular function, not an operation, with a specific name, say `compare`. The template code uses that function

```
if (compare(_key[i], k) < 0) ...
```

This makes using the template somewhat cumbersome—a specific function for comparing elements must be coded. To instantiate `Map<string, int>`, the user must supply

```
int compare(const string& a, const string& b)
{  if (a < b) return -1;
   if (a > b) return 1;
   return 0;
}
```

It also means that all maps with a given key type must use the same ordering. In practice, it might be desirable to compare employees lexicographically by name in some situations and by ID number in others. But there can be only one function

```
int compare(const Employee&, const Employee&)
```

in a program.

The possibilities we considered—requiring an operation with a fixed name, an overloaded operator, or a function with a fixed name—attempt to solve the problem of defining a total ordering for the key type on the template level, in a uniform way for all possible instantiation types. A template designer may decide that this is not reasonable and have the sort order defined on the class or object level instead.

A class-level solution requires specification of a comparison function for each instantiated Map class. This is best done through specialization. The class template declares, but does not define, a static function for comparison:

```
template<class K, class V>
class Map
{
public:
   static int compare(const K&, const K&);
   . . .
};
```

When the template is instantiated, a specialized definition of the function must also be supplied.

```
int Map<string, int>::compare(const string& a,
   const string& b)
{  if (a < b) return -1;
   if (a > b) return 1;
   return 0;
}
```

This comparison function is used for all maps of type Map<string, int>.

Note one advantage of this method—the name of the comparison function is now in the name space of the Map template, not in the global name space.

Alternatively, an implementation can provide a choice of comparison functions at the object level. Each instance of Map<K, V> can have its own comparison function. The comparison function must be supplied in the constructor:

```
template<class K, class V>
class Map
{
```

```
public:
   Map(int (*)(const K&, const K&));
   . . .
};

int comp_id(const Employee& a, const Employee& b)
{ return a.id() - b.id();
}

Map<Employee, Date> bday(comp_id);
   // construct with pointer to comparison function
```

# Smart Pointers with Reference Counting

## The `auto_ptr` Template

The ANSI C++ standard defines a template `auto_ptr<T>` that is similar to a `T*` pointer. However, when the template object is called, it calls `delete` on the pointer it contains. This is important to ensure that the destructor of the heap object gets called, even if an exception occurs. As we will see in Chapter 16, exceptions can prematurely terminate a function. Consider, for example, the code

```
Employee* pe = new Employee("Harry Hacker");
pe->raise_salary(5.5);
delete pe;
```

If the function `raise_salary` throws an exception, then the `delete pe` is never executed. However, the exception-handling mechanism guarantees that all destructors get executed, even when the normal control flow is interrupted by an exception. Thus, using an `auto_ptr<Employee>` object solves our problem:

```
auto_ptr<Employee> pe = new Employee("Harry Hacker");
pe->raise_salary(5.5);
```

The object `pe` is destroyed at the end of the block, and its destructor invokes `delete` on the pointer with which it was initialized.

In this simple situation, the `auto_ptr` template works well. There is a fundamental problem with it, however, that makes it difficult to use this template in most situations. Suppose you make a copy of the `auto_ptr`:

```
auto_ptr<Employee> pe = new Employee("Harry Hacker");
auto_ptr<Employee> pf = pe;
```

Both `pe` and `pf` will eventually be destroyed. Because the `Employee` memory block to which they point cannot be deleted by both of them, they cannot both own that employee object. Instead, copying and assignment *transfers ownership* of the object to the destination of the copy or assignment, and the source `auto_ptr` no longer owns it (see Figure 15.2).

This behavior is necessary to avoid deleting the heap object twice, but it is not attractive. A particularly unpleasant case arises when an `auto_ptr` is passed to a function.

```
void f(auto_ptr<Employee> a) { . . . }
auto_ptr<Employee> pe = new Employee("Harry Hacker");
f(pe);
pe->raise_salary(5.5); // ERROR!
```

When the function `f` is called, its parameter variable `a` is constructed from the `auto_ptr` `pe` and hence gains ownership of the `Employee` object on the heap. When `f` finishes, `a` is destroyed and the `Employee` object is deleted. The smart pointer `pe` contains only a `NULL` pointer, and the access `pe->raise_salary(5.5)` is a run-time error. Not so smart!

The problem with these pointers is, of course, that only one of them can own an object. If multiple pointers were allowed joint ownership of an object, the object should be deleted only when the *last* smart pointer owning it gets destroyed. That is, of course, just the method of reference counting

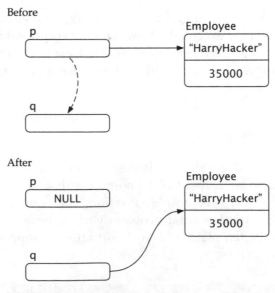

**FIGURE 15.2** Copying `auto_ptr` smart pointers.

that we described in Chapter 14. We will now implement a smart pointer template that carries out reference counting.

## How to Use the `rc_ptr` Template

In this section, you will see how to use the `rc_ptr` template that implements smart pointers with reference counting. The type `rc_ptr<X>` is a reference-counting pointer to X, a smart X*.

To make smart pointers behave like regular pointers, we overload the * and -> operators. To manage the reference counts, we supply the copy constructor, assignment operator, and destructor.

```
template<class X>
class rc_ptr
{
public:
    rc_ptr(); // makes null pointer

    // overloaded * and ->
    X& operator*();
    const X& operator*() const;
    X* operator->();
    const X* operator->() const;

    // equality test
    bool operator==(const rc_ptr<X>& b) const;
    bool operator!=(const rc_ptr<X>& b) const;
    bool operator==(int) const; // test for NULL
    bool operator!=(const rc_ptr<X>& b) const;
    bool operator!() const; // test for NULL

    // memory management functions
    rc_ptr(const rc_ptr<X>& b);
    const rc_ptr<X>& operator=(const rc_ptr<X>&);
    ~rc_ptr();
    void free();
private:
    . . .
};
```

This class implements a smart pointer to an object of type X. You can have multiple pointers to the same object, and the object is automatically destroyed when the last pointer to it goes away.

Here is how to use it. Don't call `new` to make a new object because `new` returns a dumb pointer. Instead, use the following syntax:

```
rc_ptr<Employee> pe;
new(pe) Employee("Harry Hacker");
```

This looks quite strange, except perhaps to Pascal programmers. It takes advantage of a rarely used feature, the so-called *placement syntax* for `operator new`. It is possible to overload the `new` operator to take several arguments. In this case, the operator

```
void* operator new(size_t size, rc_ptr<Employee>& p)
```

is called. It allocates memory, initializes p, and returns a pointer to the raw data that the `Employee` constructor then turns into an `Employee` object. Note that the caller of `new` doesn't specify the size; it is supplied by the compiler. The other parameter, in this case the `rc_ptr`, is written inside parentheses after the keyword `new`.

Once the smart pointer has been initialized with the curious placement syntax, it behaves like a regular pointer, thanks to the overloaded `->` and `*` operators.

```
cout << *p;
p->raise _salary(0.05);
```

You can copy the smart pointers; this simply increments the reference count.

```
rc_ptr<Employee> q = p;
```

When you are done with p, simply forget it. Don't call delete; that's for deleting dumb pointers. When p and all of its copies have gone away, the object memory is automatically recycled.

Actually, as we saw in Chapter 14, it is possible for reference-counted pointers to form self-supporting cycles. You can break such a cycle by calling `free`. The call

```
p.free();
```

decrements the reference count and sets p to a `NULL` pointer.

These smart pointers have a number of advantages over regular pointers. They are guaranteed to be initialized as either null pointers or pointers to a heap object. Objects are automatically freed when the last pointer to them has gone away.

Like regular pointers, these smart pointers also support the conversion from `Derived` pointer to `Base` pointer.

```
rc_ptr<Employee> pe;
rc_ptr<Manager> pm;
new(pm) Manager("Mary Moore");
pe = pm; // OK
```

This turns out to be a challenge to implement, especially if the compiler doesn't support nested templates.

You now know enough about reference-counted pointers to use them. In the next section, we will have a closer look at the implementation. The rc_ptr is not a part of the ANSI C++ standard. Unfortunately, the standards committee rejected suggestions to include a reference counted pointer template and merely agreed to support the much less useful auto_ptr template.

## Implementation

Reference counts are stored in a base class

```
class rc_base
{
public:
   void init() { _rc = 1; }
   void incref() { _rc++; }
   int decref { return --_rc; }
private:
   unsigned _rc;
};
```

The following wrapper class template wraps the object together with a reference count:

```
template<class X>
class rc_wrapper : public rc_base
{
private:
   X _obj;
friend class rc_ptr<X>;
};
```

For example, an rc_wrapper<Employee> object keeps the reference count in the base class and the employee data in the _obj data field of the wrapper. A smart pointer points to a wrapper (see Figure 15.3).

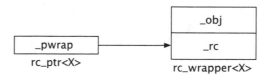

**FIGURE 15.3** A smart pointer pointing to a wrapper object.

To allocate a new object is tricky. The constructors of X do not automatically carry over to be constructors of rc_wrapper<X>. This is the reason for the trick with the placement syntax. Recall the invocation syntax:

```
new(p) Employee("Harry Hacker");
```

In the overloaded new operator, we allocate a block that is sufficient for a rc_wrapper<X>, initialize the reference count, and then return a pointer to the X portion of the block so that the constructor can be called. Here is the code:

```
template<class X>
void* operator new(size_t n, rc_ptr<X> p)
{  p.free();
   char* cp = new char[sizeof(rc_base) + n];
   p._pwrap = (rc_wrapper<X>*)cp;
   p._pwrap->init(); // initialize ref count
   return (X*)(cp + sizeof(rc_base));
      // return pointer to X portion
}
```

The X constructor then initializes the memory at the returned address to be an X object.

The default constructor makes a null pointer. Copy constructor, destructor, and assignment operator manipulate the reference counts in the usual way.

```
template<class X>
class rc_ptr
{
public:
   rc_ptr() : _pwrap(NULL) {}
   rc_ptr(const rc_ptr<X>& b) { copy(b); }
   ~rc_ptr() { free(); }
   const rc_ptr& operator=(const rc_ptr<X>& b)
   {  if (this != &b) { free(); copy(b); } return *this;
   }
   . . .
private:
   void copy(const rc_ptr<X>b);
   rc_wrapper<X>* _pwrap;
};
```

The copy function just copies the pointer and increments the reference count.

```
template<class X>
void rc_ptr::copy(const rc_ptr<X>& b)
```

```
{   _pwrap = b._pwrap;
    if (_pwrap != NULL) _pwrap->incref();
}
```

The `free` operation is more complex. If the reference count drops to zero, the memory must be freed. The `free` operation must first manually invoke the destructor on the `X` area of the wrapper object. Then it must recycle the wrapper memory.

```
template<class X>
void rc_ptr::free()
{   if (_pwrap != NULL && _pwrap->decref() == 0)
    {   char* cp = (char*)_pwrap;
        ((X*)(cp + sizeof(rc_base)))->~X();
            // call X destructor manually
        delete[] cp; // delete wrapper memory
    }
}
```

The overloaded operators give access to the object inside the wrapper. Note the curious unary `->` operator that returns a pointer to an object. The overloaded `->` operator is special and quite different from all other operators. The expression `p->m` means to get the result from `p.operator->()`, which should be an expression on which `->m` makes sense. The `->` is actually taken twice: `p->m` is `(p.operator->())->m`. For example, the call

```
pe->raise_salary(5.5);
```

first calls

```
pe.operator->()
```

This call returns an `Employee*` pointer, and the `->raise_salary(5.5)` is applied to the returned pointer.

Here are the overloaded `*` and `->` operators:

```
template<class X>
X& rc_ptr<X>::operator*()
{   assert(_pwrap != NULL); // cannot indirect through NULL pointer
    return _pwrap->_obj;
}
```

```
template<class X>
X* rc_ptr<X>::operator->()
{   assert(_pwrap != NULL); // cannot indirect through NULL pointer
    return &_pwrap->_obj;
}
```

The `const` versions of these operators perform the identical actions but act on `const rc_ptr<X>`.

Finally, we need to cover the hard question of the conversion of an `rc_ptr<Derived>` to an `rc_ptr<Base>`. If the compiler supports nested templates, then we can use the technique discussed previously in this chapter. Unfortunately, at the time of this writing, most compilers do not support nested templates. The following trick is used in the implementation of `rc_ptr` for this book.

We define the following three operations: an `operator const X*` that converts a smart `rc_ptr<X>` into a regular const `X*` pointer, a constructor that constructs an `rc_ptr<X>` from an `X*` pointer, and an `operator=` that can assign a regular `const X*` pointer to an `rc_ptr<X>`. The last two operators require that the pointer actually points into an `rc_wrapper<X>`.

```
template<class X>
class rc_ptr
{
public:
   . . .
   operator const X*() const
   { return _pwrap == NULL ? NULL : &_pwrap->_obj; }
   rc_ptr(const X* p)
   {  if (p == NULL) _pwrap = NULL;
      else
      {  char* cp = (char*) p;
         _pwrap = (rc_wrapper<X>*)(cp - sizeof(rc_base));
         _pwrap->incref();
      }
   }
   const rc_ptr<X>& operator=(const X* p)
   {  rc_ptr<X> b(p);
      return *this = b;
   }
   . . .
};
```

The point of converting first from a smart pointer to a regular pointer and then back is that the compiler will perform the `Derived*` → `Base*` conversion on regular pointers. Consider, for example, the following:

```
rc_ptr<Employee> pe;
rc_ptr<Manager> pm;
. . .
pe = pm;
```

The compiler translates this expression as follows:

1. Convert `pm` to a `Manager*` using the `operator const Manager*`.
2. Convert the `Manager*` to an `Employee*`, using the implicit `Derived*` → `Base*` conversion.
3. Use `rc_ptr<Employee>::operator=(const Employee*)` to move the pointer into `pe`.

If instead the target pointer is constructed as a copy of the source pointer, that is,

```
rc_ptr<Employee> pe = pm;
```

then the first two steps are the same, but in the third step, `pe` is constructed with the `rc_ptr<Employee>::rc_ptr(const Employee*)` constructor.

This setup solves our problem of providing an `rc_ptr<Derived>` → `rc_ptr<Base>` conversion, but unfortunately, there is a price to pay. The copy constructor and assignment operator with `const X*` parameters assume these are pointers that come from an `rc_ptr<Y>::operator const Y*`. If they don't, then the code will attempt to update reference counts that aren't there.

For example, the following code will compile but will crash:

```
rc_ptr<Employee> pe = new Employee("Harry Hacker"); // ERROR
```

This is very unfortunate. Programmers must be very careful to initialize `rc_ptr` objects only with the `new` placement syntax and never to mix smart and regular pointers otherwise. A true solution to this problem can be supplied only when compilers support nested templates.

# *Design Hints*

## Clearly State Requirements for Instantiation Types

Virtually all templates require that instantiation classes be copiable and have a default constructor. Nevertheless, the requirement must be stated. If your template requires that the type argument be a class and not a numeric or pointer type, state that. Some templates require that the class argument derive from a fixed base class such as `Persistent`.

Be explicit about any operations, functions, or operator symbols that must work on objects of the instantiation type. Many templates require that `os << x`, `x == y`, or `x < y` be defined.

## Minimize Dependencies on External Names or Operators

If your template performs output with << or comparison with <, it is useless for those operations that do not have << or < defined or, even worse, that have them defined to do something different from what you need in the template. The same holds for global functions like hash and compare. They can be defined only once. If you want to sort an array of employees in two ways, you cannot specify two global compare functions comparing employees.

If you compute a hash value with x.hash(), the template can be used only for class objects. If x is not an object, applying the hash operation is an instant syntax error. Even if x is of class type, the class may not have a hash operation. If the instantiator doesn't own the class, it is not possible to retro-fit it. Unless your template is intended only for objects that inherit from some common base class, never invoke any operation on the instantiation objects.

The best way to specify functions for comparison, hashing, printing, and other tasks is through function pointer arguments to the constructor or a specific operation (like sort). This is admittedly cumbersome for the user, but it maximizes the usability of the template.

## Consider Building a Separate Template for Pointers

We can build much more efficient container templates if we know that the entries must be pointers. It therefore makes a lot of sense to offer a second template for that purpose. PtrQueue<X> does just the same as Queue<X*>, just more efficiently.

The efficiency gain comes from two areas. Construction, copying, and destruction of pointers are trivial: initialize, copy bitwise, and forget. It is much more efficient to call memcpy to move an array of pointers than it is to invoke a copy constructor for each entry in an array. Furthermore, we can use inheritance and derive a PtrQueue<X> from a Queue<void*>. That way, the array operations are coded only once, for the void* container. The X* container just makes inline calls to the base. This can dramatically reduce code size.

However, void* pointers should be avoided in the debug version. They make it impossible for the programmer to inspect the contents of contain-ers during debugging. The best solution is to provide a debug version, with separate template code for each pointer type, and a release version, which maps to void*.

# 16

# Exception Handling

Both C++ and Java have sophisticated mechanisms for transferring control to an error handler after an error has been detected. The mechanisms are similar, but they have significant differences as well. We will discuss the advantages and disadvantages of both exception models.

## *Errors and Exceptions*

Programmers must deal with error conditions and exceptional situations. Several error types are commonly encountered.

- User input errors. A user enters input that does not follow the syntactic or semantic rules of the application. For example, the user may ask to delete a file name that does not exist, to drag the desktop into the trashcan, or to compile a program with syntax errors. An interactive program can typically inform the user of the problem and await further input. A program that reads data from a file, such as a compiler, must report the error to a file or the display terminal and then either abort or try to go on processing.

■ Device errors. Serial ports may be unavailable. A printer may be turned off. Such errors may cause a program task to be aborted or suspended until the problem is fixed. Devices may fail in the middle of a task. For example, a printer may run out of paper in the middle of a printout. It may be necessary for a program to abort just the print task and return control to the user, without exiting the program.

■ Physical limitations. Disks can fill up, and available memory can become exhausted.

■ Component failures. A function or class may perform incorrectly and deliver wrong answers or use other functions or classes incorrectly. Computing an invalid array index and trying to pop an empty stack are examples of this kind.

Most errors are unpleasant to handle. The programmer should not just abort the program with an assertion failure; the user may lose all work performed during the program session. Instead, the program must at least notify the user, save all work, and exit gracefully. The code that detects the error condition, however, is usually in no position to accomplish this. For example, the copy constructor of a linked list class may find that memory allocation fails because all memory is exhausted. Obviously, the list class has no information on how to shut down an application. The transfer of control from the point of error detection to a competent error handler is the central problem of exception handling.

## *Reaction to Error Conditions*

What should an operation do when it detects that memory is exhausted or when it is asked to do the impossible, such as popping a value off an empty stack? A number of strategies are available.

### Returning an Error Code

Some data types, such as pointers, offer an easy way of distinguishing valid from invalid data. Suppose a function reads shapes from a stream. When the end of the file is reached, no further shape is available. This situation can be communicated easily by returning either a pointer to a new shape or a null pointer:

```
Shape* read_shape(istream&);
```

Similarly, a function returning a string may return the empty string to denote failure.

It is more difficult to return an error code if there is no obvious way of distinguishing valid from invalid data. A function returning an integer cannot simply return 0 to denote error—the value 0 might be a perfectly valid value. A function reading employee records may not easily return a null employee at the end of the file.

```
Employee read_employee(istream&); // return what at end of file?
```

It is always possible to write functions to return an explicit Boolean error code and return any result through a reference parameter:

```
bool read_employee(istream&, Employee&);
```

Returning an error code is a good practice, especially for those operations that are known to fail eventually, such as reading data from a file or fetching elements from a queue.

## Ignoring the Error

Suppose a queue of integers is implemented as a fixed-size circular array:

```
class Queue
{
public:
   void add(int);
   int remove();
   bool is_full() const;
   bool is_empty() const;
   // ...
};
```

What should the add operation do if the queue is already full? Presumably the precondition of add is !is_full(), and the operation can do whatever pleases it. It may choose simply to do nothing. (Because this particular operation has no return value, we could change it to return true on success. Then again, if the caller didn't bother to check is_full() before adding to the queue, it isn't likely that the return value will be checked either.)

Doing nothing is not always easy, especially for functions that return a value. Consider the invocation of remove on an empty queue. The precondition of remove is !is_empty(), and the caller should always first check whether a queue is nonempty before removing a value from it. If the caller fails to do so, the remove function can return any value that it likes, such as 0 or INT_MAX.

For integers, such a value is usually easy to find, even though it is not distinguishable from a legal value. But suppose it is a queue of customers. The function cannot return 0 unless there happens to be a constructor `Customer(int)`. It could return whatever object the default constructor generates, if there is a default constructor.

Of course, in many situations doing nothing is not feasible. If the copy constructor of a list class finds that there isn't enough memory to form the copy, it cannot simply ignore the problem. After all, it isn't the class user's error if memory is exhausted.

Doing nothing when asked to do the wrong thing can be a reasonable strategy. During debug mode, an assertion failure can be triggered instead.

## Setting an Error Variable

A time-honored error-handling strategy is to set a global variable when an error is discovered. For example, mathematical functions in the standard C library set an integer variable `errno` to the constant EDOM or ERANGE if a domain error (such as `sqrt` of a negative number) or range error (over- or underflow) is discovered:

```
double sqrt(double x)
{  if (x < 0)
   {  errno = EDOM;
      return 0;
   }
   . . .
}
```

This is not a very useful mechanism. The error report contains only the type of error, not the name of the offending function or the value of the argument. Furthermore, if two errors occur in rapid succession, the second one will overwrite the reporting of the first one.

Properly monitoring the error variable is therefore dreadfully inconvenient. Each call to a mathematical function must be checked.

```
errno = 0;
y = sqrt(x);
if (errno != 0) . . .
```

In a correctly written program, domain errors on mathematical functions should never happen, or at least happen only in very exceptional situations. Monitoring an error variable requires that every call to a function that might report an error is complemented by a check against it, making the coding effort entirely disproportionate to the likelihood of the error.

## Printing an Error Message

Printing a message reporting an error is reasonable in student programs and for debugging only. Users of commercial software programs get extremely perturbed when a product emits error messages that are incomprehensible to them and whose remedy is beyond their power. What would you do if your game program notified you "Warning: Cannot add to full queue" and then kept on playing, maybe with one less game piece?

Of course, users may be asked to cure those error conditions that are within their power to remedy, such as closing a disk drive door, turning on a printer, or closing other applications or deleting unnecessary files to obtain more memory or disk space.

## Aborting the Program

When debugging a simple program, there is nothing wrong with printing a diagnostic message and aborting. For real products, though, a simple abort is unacceptable. A user who has spent hours creating data with a program cannot afford to lose all work when a program aborts spontaneously on an internal error condition.

At the very least, a program should save all work on disk and remove any temporary files before aborting.

## Jumping to an Error Handler

It is generally difficult to handle an error at the location of its discovery. When memory exhaustion is noticed in a constructor of a class, you cannot easily bail out and save all work right in that constructor procedure. Instead, the procedure must be abandoned, and error recovery must be initiated elsewhere.

C programs often use a nonlocal jump, implemented through the `setjmp` and `longjmp` functions, to transfer control to a body of code that can deal with errors and communicate with the program user.

However, these functions are incompatible with C++ because a `longjmp` simply abandons a portion of the stack without calling the destructors of stack objects. If those destructors merely close files and free memory, it is possible to use `longjmp` to go to a rescue point, save all work, and exit. But if some destructors manage other system resources that are not freed by the operating system on process death, that approach is not viable. Clearly, no retry is possible either.

C++ code should not use `setjmp` / `longjmp`. The C++ exception mechanism is the appropriate mechanism to transfer control to an error handler.

424 ■ CHAPTER SIXTEEN

## Raising a Signal

In many operating systems, processes can react to asynchronous error conditions such as a user abort request (by hitting [Ctrl+C], by killing a process, and so forth) or processor error (segmentation fault, illegal instruction, floating-point error). Using the `signal` function, a C program specifies a handler procedure to be called in such instances. (If no signal handler is specified, the program aborts.)

It is possible to raise a signal explicitly and transfer control to that error procedure, using the `raise` function, but this is not usually a good mechanism for error handling. There is very little a signal handler can do. Because it can be invoked asynchronously, the process may be in a completely unstable state, and it is doubtful whether the user's work can even be safely saved because the data structures may be left in the middle of an update, containing invalid references.

Signals should be used for their intended purpose only: namely, to handle catastrophic external events.

## Raising an Exception

C++ and Java have a convenient and safe mechanism to raise exceptions when errors are detected and to transfer both control and error information to code that is competent to deal with the situation. This exception-handling scheme will be discussed subsequently.

# *Exceptions*

## Raising an Exception

Both C++ and Java support the transfer of control out of a problem situation by throwing an exception.

When an error is encountered that cannot be handled at the point of detection, an exception can be raised with the command

```
throw e;
```

In C++, `e` can be any value, such as an integer or string,

```
throw "Stack underflow"; // not useful
```

but it is far more common to throw objects of special exception classes.

```
StackError e("Stack underflow");
throw e; // OK
```

Actually, rather than introducing a variable e that is never again used, you can just throw an anonymous object.

```
throw StackError("Stack underflow");
```

Throwing objects of error classes is the right thing to do for two reasons. As we will see shortly, error handlers specify the type of the exception object with which they are willing to deal. You can usefully provide a handler for StackError, but it is unlikely that a handler for int or strings can do more than report the error and give up. And error objects allow the program to carry an arbitrary amount of information conveniently from the locus of detection to the error handler.

 In Java, the object that you throw must belong to a class that is derived from Throwable.

```
Throwable e = new IllegalArgumentException("Stack underflow");
throw e;
```

Again, it is not common to define a separate variable. It is easier to simply throw the exception object without giving it a name:

```
throw new IllegalArgumentException("Stack underflow");
```

When a function throws an exception, a search for a handler is initiated. The function does not return in the normal way:

```
int Stack::pop() // C++
{  if  (_sptr <= 0)
      throw StackError("Stack underflow");
   _sptr--;
   return _s[_sptr];
}
```

If an empty stack is popped and the throw statement is executed, the function execution terminates immediately. It does not return any value. That is good; the programmer need not worry about supplying a fake return value.

The caller of a function that raises exceptions cannot rely on the function call succeeding. If an empty stack is popped, the operation does not return a value, and subsequent code is not executed.

```
n = stack.pop();
cout << n << endl; // never get here if stack is empty!
```

Instead, execution transfers to the error handler.

## Handling an Exception

Both in C++ and in Java, exception handlers are specified with `try` blocks:

```
try
{   code
}
catch (StackError& s)
{   // stack is empty, or other stack error
    // s contains error information
    handler code
}
```

The code in the `try` block is executed. That code may involve any sequence of statements, including loops or function calls. If anywhere during execution a stack error is reported, the code in the handler gains control.

It is not generally useful simply to wrap a `try` block around a function call that might raise an exception. Consider this call to `pop`.

```
try // DON'T
{   n = stack.pop();
}
catch (StackError s)
{   n = 0;
}
```

We can check for an empty stack with far less hassle:

```
if (!stack.is_empty()) n = stack.pop();
```

It is much more useful to check for errors that may occur anywhere in a subsystem:

```
try
{   read(is); // read in a file; parsing involves stack
}
catch (StackError& s)
{   message("Syntax error in input file");
    is.close();
}
```

This example illustrates the transfer of control from the point of detection to a point of competent handling. The stack module can report only a stack overflow. It cannot close the input file. The error handler is located at a point where it is clear that the cause of the error is an improper input file. The handler has access to the input file and perhaps a user interface and can report the problem in a way that makes sense to the program user.

## Handling Multiple Exceptions

A `try` block can handle multiple exceptions:

```
try
{  code
}
catch (StackError& s)
{  // stack is empty, or other stack error
   // s contains error information
   stack error handler code
}
catch (MathError& m)
{  math error handler code
}
```

If the code in the `try` block causes either a stack error or a math error, the appropriate handler is activated. If a different exception is raised, it must be caught by a handler elsewhere.

Exceptions are caught by their type—you *throw objects* and *catch classes.*

## Exception Hierarchies

 Because exception handlers specify the type of the exception they are able to handle, layering exception classes using an inheritance hierarchy is often useful.

For example, we can derive specialized error types from `MathError` (see Figure 16.1):

```
class DomainError : public MathError { /* ... */ };
class RangeError : public MathError { /* ... */ };
```

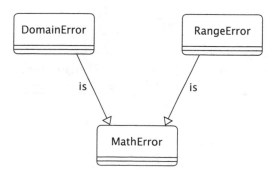

**FIGURE 16.1**   A hierarchy of math errors.

A domain error signifies an attempt to evaluate a function at an argument that is not in its domain, such as the square root or logarithm of a negative number. A range error denotes over- or underflow of the result.

```
try
{   code
}
catch (DomainError& e)
{   // a function was applied to an argument not in its domain
    domain error handler code
}
catch (MathError& e)
{   // some other math error
    generic math error handler code
}
```

All math errors that are not domain error type are handled by the second `catch` clause. In C++, you should catch exceptions by reference, to avoid truncation to the base class. It is then possible to access derived-class information by invoking a virtual function. Of course, in Java, you always catch a pointer to the exception object.

The ANSI C++ standard defines a hierarchy of number of basic exception classes that is a good starting point for your own hierarchy. That hierarchy is shown in Figure 16.2.

All errors that are the programmer's fault are derived from `logic _error`. Errors that are the cause of external effects are derived from `runtime_error`. That is, in principle, logic errors are always avoidable by

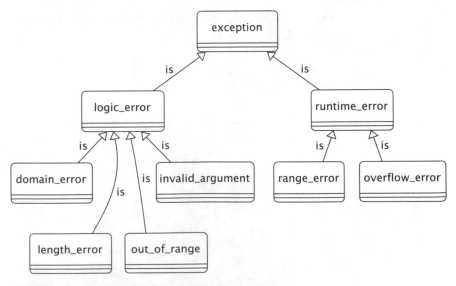

**FIGURE 16.2**   C++ standard exceptions.

first checking appropriate preconditions. Run-time errors may not be avoidable. For example, if a file comes to an unexpected end, perhaps because the network went down, then that should be classified as a run-time error. It wasn't the programmer's fault that the file wasn't read perfectly. But trying to pop an empty stack is a logic error—the programmer could have called `is_empty()` to test that there was an element to pop.

In other words, if a `logic_error` has occurred, there is no point in retrying the computation. The iron force of logic will dictate that it happens again in the same way. If a `runtime_error` occurs, then there is hope—maybe retrying the computation will work.

All standard exception classes have a constructor to supply a message string and an operation `what` that prints out that message.

```
try
{  code
}
catch(Exception& e)
{  cout << e.what() << endl;
}
```

It is a good idea to derive all exception classes from one of the standard exceptions:

```
class StackError : public logic_error
{
public:
   StackError(const string& s) : logic_error(s) {}
};
```

 In Java, the standard exception hierarchy is considerably more complex— Figure 16.3 only shows the most fundamental exception classes.

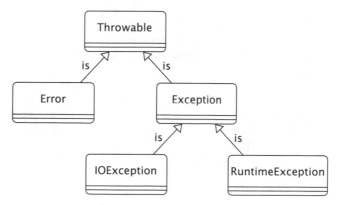

**FIGURE 16.3**  Standard exceptions in Java.

All exceptions derive from `Throwable`. There are two subcategories, `Error` and `Exception`. The `Error` hierarchy describes fatal conditions that are caused by internal errors in the virtual machine or class-loading mechanism. These are not of interest to the programmer because there is no remedy for them. The `Exception` hierarchy describes the exceptions that are under programmer control. It branches into two parts, the exceptions derived from `RuntimeException` and everything else.

The Java `RuntimeException` base class is the direct equivalent of the C++ `logic_error` class! That is, it describes logic errors, such as null pointer indirection or bad array indexes, that are the programmer's fault. You would derive your own logic error from this class.

```
class StackError extends RuntimeException
{  public StackError(String s) { super(s); }
}
```

The Java equivalent of the C++ `runtime_error` hierarchy are all exceptions that derive from `Exception` *but not from* `RuntimeException`. This includes, at the time of this writing, the important category of `IOException` and its derived exceptions, `SQLException` and seven other exceptions, that are quite technical and rarely used in practice. The exceptions that derive from `Exception` but not `RuntimeException` are often called *explicit exceptions* (see Table 16.1). As we will see soon, any function that throws an explicit exception must advertise that fact. The exceptions that derive from `Error` or `RuntimeException` are called *implicit exceptions*. They don't need to be advertised because they are either virtual machine problems (if they derive from `Error`) or logic errors that should be fixed instead.

**TABLE 16.1**    Explicit Exceptions in Java

| *Exception type* | *Usage* |
| --- | --- |
| `IOException` and derived classes | Used for input/output |
| `SQLException` and derived classes | Used for database access |
| `InterruptedException` | Used for multithreading |
| `AWTException` | Supposed to be used for window errors, but never thrown |
| `NoSuchMethodException` | Unknown purpose, never thrown |
| `ClassNotFoundException` | Thrown by `Class.forName` |
| `CloneNotSupportedException` | Thrown by `Object.clone` |
| `IllegalAccessException` | Thrown by `Class.newInstance` if the class has no default constructor |
| `InstantiationException` | Thrown by `Class.newInstance` if the class is abstract |

If you catch a Java exception, you can use the `toString` operation to get a descriptive text. Recall that `toString` is automatically invoked when an exception object is concatenated with a string. Furthermore, the `Throwable.printStackTrace` operation prints useful debugging information.

```
try
{ code
}
catch(Exception e)
{ System.out.println("Exception " + e);
  e.printStackTrace();
}
```

## Catch All and Rethrow

 Occasionally, you want to catch any exceptions that fly past a certain point, just to take some cleanup or protective action. Here is how you do it in C++.

```
try
{ code
}
catch(...)
  // some error occurred; this form will catch any exception
{ evasive action
  throw;
}
```

The `throw` command without an argument inside a `catch` clause throws the current error again. You should rethrow any caught error that you don't know how to handle (or better, not catch it in the first place).

 In Java, you instead catch the `Throwable` base class:

```
try
{ code
}
catch(Throwable t)
  // some error occurred; this form will catch any exception
{ evasive action
  throw t;
}
```

If an exception is not caught anywhere at all, the program is aborted. For that reason, many programs use this generic catch mechanism to catch any stray exceptions that managed to make it all the way to `main`.

## Stack Unwinding

In C++, the most important action of the exception-handling mechanism is the "stack walk." All objects on the stack between the throw and catch point (see Figure 16.4) are properly destroyed by invoking their destructors. This activity is of crucial importance. Normally, objects on the stack are destroyed when execution reaches the end of the block in which they are declared. But when an exception is raised, the linear flow of execution stops and control is transferred to the nearest handler that can catch the type of the exception object. In C++, stack objects are not simply abandoned when the stack between the `throw` and `catch` point is popped. Their destructors are invoked.

In particular, if an error (say, out of memory) is detected inside a constructor, all subobjects that have already been constructed are destroyed, rolling back the entire construction process.

If a destructor that is invoked while an exception is pending itself raises an exception, the program terminates. It is therefore highly recommended that destructors never throw exceptions.

There is a good reason for the great care that the C++ runtime system takes to invoke destructors during exception processing. After the exception is handled, the program may continue indefinitely. It is important that no resources are wasted, or they may eventually be exhausted.

The process of stack unwinding is quite complex, and the C++ runtime system spends a considerable amount of effort to maintain data structures

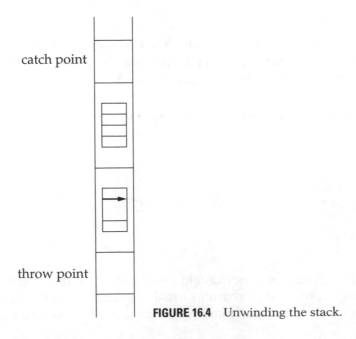

**FIGURE 16.4** Unwinding the stack.

that track which objects have been fully constructed or partially constructed at any given time, to enable their destruction in the event of an exception throw. This bookkeeping effort extracts a real performance cost, usually estimated to be about 5 percent of the total running time of a program, *even if no exception is ever thrown.*

 Java has no destructors, so it does not need to go through the effort of destroying stack objects when it transfers control from the `throw` point to the `catch` point. This makes the implementation of exception handling in Java much simpler and more efficient than in C++. Of course, sometimes it is necessary in Java to reclaim resources during exception processing. We will see how to accomplish that in the next section.

## Resource Acquisition and Release

 The possibility of exceptions places an added burden on the programmer, who can no longer rely on the linear flow of program execution. Consider, for example, the following code that uses the C `stdio` library:

```
FILE* fp = fopen("input.dat", "r");
f(fp);
fclose(fp); // may never happen
```

This code is wrong. The function `f` (or one of the functions it calls) may throw an exception and never return! In that case, the `fclose` command is not executed.

It would be technically correct to catch any and all exceptions, close the file, and rethrow what was caught:

```
FILE* fp = fopen("input.dat", "r");
try
{  f(fp);
}
catch( ... ) // some error occurred
{  fclose(fp);
   throw;
}
fclose(fp);
```

Applying this strategy in all similar situations would be extremely burdensome. Can you imagine having to code all pairs of functions that acquire and release a resource in this way?

```
fopen/fclose
new/delete
GetDC/ReleaseDC
CreateFontIndirect/DeleteObject
. . .
```

Exception handling is supposed to make programs simpler, not more complicated. And it is supposed to separate normal processing from error processing, not constantly intermingle the two.

The remedy is to *relinquish all resources in destructors*.

For example, the destructor of a file stream in the C++ iostream library automatically closes the file. Using an ifstream instead of a FILE* solves the problem.

```
ifstream fs("input.dat");
f(fs);
```

The file is closed when execution reaches the end of the enclosing block or when an exception terminates the function prematurely.

The same applies to memory allocation.

```
Employee* e = new Employee("Harry Hacker");
g(e);
delete e; // may never happen
```

Of course, it would be best if the pointer to the employee was encapsulated in some other object that had a destructor. But if it is not, it can be placed into a smart pointer such as the auto_ptr of the ANSI C++ standard or the more convenient rc_ptr that was developed for the library accompanying this book. These smart pointers were explained in Chapter 15.

```
auto_ptr<Employee> pe = new Employee("Harry Hacker");
g(pe);
```

The Employee object is deleted by the auto_ptr destructor. This occurs if the function g returns normally and the block containing pe is exited, as well as if the function g throws an exception and doesn't return.

The presence of exceptions therefore forces a programming style in which all resources are managed by constructors and destructors. All handles to those resources, and in particular all pointers to heap memory, should be fields of a class, not local variables of a function.

In Java, there are no destructors, so it is not possible to place resource deallocation into destructors. Of course, the overwhelming majority of C++ destructors are concerned only with memory management, and in Java, the memory management is already automated by garbage collection. However, occasionally it is necessary to close other resources such as files when an exception occurs. We can use the same strategy that we described for C++: catch all exceptions, relinquish the resource, and rethrow.

```
FileInputStream in = null;
try
{  in = new FileInputStream("input.dat");
   f(in);
}
catch(Throwable t) // some error occurred
{  if (in != null) // might be null if constructor didn't return
      in.close();
   throw t;
}
in.close();
```

Note that the code to close the file occurs *twice*, once in the catch clause and once after succesful exit from the try block. This is, of course, typical—no matter how we leave the try block, the file must be closed.

Java has a convenient shortcut for this situation. Any code placed in a finally clause is guaranteed to be executed, both when the try block completes normally and when it is interrupted by an exception throw.

```
FileInputStream in = null;
try
{  in = new FileInputStream("input.dat");
   f(in);
}
finally
{  if (in != null) // might be null if constructor didn't return
      in.close();
}
```

Resource deallocations belong inside destructors in C++, inside finally blocks in Java.

## Retry

Some programming languages provide special syntax to retry the statements in the try block after the problem has been cured in the handler. In fact, the Eiffel language forces the programmer either to retry or to propagate the exception outward. Giving up is not an option.

In C++ and Java, no special syntax for retry is provided, but it can easily be coded explicitly:

```
bool success = false;
while (!success)
{  try
   {  code
      success = true;
   }
```

```
      catch(Exception1 e1)
      {  handler code
      }
      catch(Exception2 e2)
      {  handler code
      }
} //(*)
```

When execution reaches the point (*), we are assured that the try block code has completed successfully. Of course, you should use this strategy only if it can be ensured that the code will eventually succeed. Another possibility is to try a number of times and give up after a certain number of tries:

```
bool success = false;
int ntries = 0;
while (!success)
{  try
   {  code
      success = true;
   }
   catch(Exception1 e1)
   {  handler code
   }
   catch(Exception2 e2)
   {  handler code
   }
   if (!success)
   {  // got here from one of the catch clauses
      ntries++;
      if (ntries >= MAXTRIES)
         throw runtime_error("retried and failed");
   }
}
```

Exception handlers in catch clauses should always do one of the following three actions:

- Reraise the current exception or raise a different exception.
- Retry the try block code.
- Cure the exception completely.

Ignoring the exception but failing to propagate it is never sensible.

## Exception Specifications

Exceptions bring a good deal of uncertainty to such mundane operations as calling functions. The function might throw an exception and never return in the normal way. If the function is supplied by a third-party vendor, the type of the raised exception might be unknown. Then no handler in the program will bother to catch it, and the program will terminate.

Knowing that certain functions never throw any exceptions or throw only exceptions of a certain kind would be useful.

 Both Java and C++ address this need, but they do it in completely different ways. In Java, a function *must* declare all *explicit* exceptions that it throws. Recall that explicit exceptions are those exceptions that are derived from `Exception` but not from `RuntimeException`. These are all the exceptions that might happen in a program because of runtime problems, not logic errors. The most commonly specified exceptions are input/output exceptions. Input and output, especially over a network, are inherently unreliable. Usually the functions that read and write individual objects can't do anything to remedy these errors, and they shouldn't even try. They should just let a competent handler catch the error. In Java, they must, however, advertise the possibility of the exception so that someone else will feel motivated to write such a competent handler at an outer level.

In Java, the `throws` specifier is used to declare which exceptions a function can throw. For example, the following function declares that it might throw an `IOException`.

```
class Employee
{  . . .
   public void read(DataInputStream in) throws IOException
   {  . . .
     double s = in.readDouble(); // can throw IOException
     . . .
   }
   . . .
}
```

If the `throws` specifier is omitted, the function will not compile: the `readDouble` operation declares that it might throw an `IOException`, and the `read` operation must either catch that exception or advertise to its caller that an `IOException` might "leak out." Because the `read` operation has no way of competently handling the `IOException`, it should just consent to having the exception propagated to a competent handler that might display an error message.

A function can advertise the possibility of multiple exceptions:

```
public void f() throws IOException, SQLException { . . . }
```

If a function has no `throws` clause, it guarantees that it throws no *explicit* exceptions.

You need not declare the possibility that a function might throw an *implicit* exception, that is, an `Error` or `RuntimeException`.

```
class Employee
{  int compare(Employee b) throws NullPointerException // NO!
   {  return _name.compareTo(b._name);
   }
   . . .
}
```

Sure, if someone calls `e.compare(f)` where `f` is `null`, then the function will be aborted because the access `b._name` generates a `NullPointer-Exception`. But if you have the foresight to observe that, you might as well fix the problem.

```
class Employee
{  int compare(Employee b)
   {  if (b == null) return -1;
      return _name.compareTo(b._name);
   }
   . . .
}
```

You should write code that throws no `RuntimeExceptions` rather than pondering what runtime exceptions your code might throw. But you cannot avoid explicit exceptions, and you must declare them with `throws` specifiers. In C++, exception specifications are *optional*. The syntax is slightly different, too. C++ uses `throw`, not `throws`, and the list of exceptions that a function throws is enclosed in parentheses. A function so tagged promises never to raise any exceptions except those in the list:

```
int f(istream&) throw (StackError, MathError);
```

A function may promise not to throw any exceptions.

```
int g(istream&) throw ();
```

A function without a `throw` specifier may throw any exception.

```
int h(istream&); // can throw anything
```

Unlike in Java, C++ exception specifiers are *not* enforced at compile time. Instead, they are enforced at run time. If an exception is detected in a function that is not of any of the types listed in the specifier list, the program terminates!

It is unfortunate that all functions without an explicit throw specifier are permitted to throw exceptions of any type. This makes it difficult to write functions with exception specifiers correctly, especially because exception handling is a new feature and existing functions are not declared with empty exception specifiers, even though they throw no exceptions. Consider this example:

```
int g(); // might throw any exception
```

It is now a real challenge to write a function correctly with exception specifications that calls g.

```
int f(istream&) throw (StackError, MathError)
{  g(); // might throw any exception
   more code // might throw StackError or MathError
}
```

This isn't a good idea. If g throws another kind of exception, then the program terminates! To correctly cope with this situation, we must add a third exception to the exception list. C++ provides a standard exception, bad_exception, for this purpose:

```
int f(istream&) throw (StackError, MathError, bad_exception)
{  try
   {  g(); // might throw any exception
      more code // might throw StackError or MathError
   }
   catch(StackError) { throw; } // caller will handle error
   catch(MathError) { throw; }
   catch(...) { throw bad_exception }
}
```

This is where the C++ programmer wishes that the compiler would enforce exception specifications at compile time. In Java, the programmer of g must list all exceptions that g throws, so the programmer of f who uses g can know with confidence what to expect, instead of having to catch all possible exceptions.

**TIP**

Many C++ programmers believe that the throw specifiers for functions are nothing but a documentation aid. Of course, they are useful for documenting what exceptions a function throws, but they are a documentation aid that is strictly enforced at run time. If the throw list is wrong and an unexpected exception is thrown, then the program terminates! That is a very real risk, and you need to defend against it. If you want to use exception specifications at all, you must be very disciplined. Supply exception specifiers for *every* function you write, and catch unexpected exceptions that may be thrown by functions. If you don't have that discipline, then don't use exception specifiers at all, not even as a documentation aid.  ■

 While the C++ approach of enforcing exception specifications at run time is somewhat dangerous, the Java approach of compile-time exception handling is not perfect either. Consider this situation:

```
class MyApplet extends Applet
{ public void paint(Graphics g)
   { FileInputStream in = new FileInputStream("input.dat");
        // ERROR!
     . . .
   }
}
```

The `FileInputStream` constructor might throw an exception. Normally, we could simply tag the function calling that constructor with a `throws IOException` specifier and hope that some handler will take care of it. However, that is *not an option* for the `paint` function. That function is inherited from `Applet.paint`, which throws *no* exceptions. Hence no function overriding it is allowed to throw an exception either. This is a common situation that forces the Java programmer to handle an exception even though this is not a good place for handling it.

There is then the overwhelming urge to *squelch* the exception:

```
class MyApplet extends Applet
{ public void paint(Graphics g)
   { try
     { FileInputStream in = new FileInputStream("input.dat");
        . . .
     }
     catch(Exception e) {} // eats all exceptions--bad style!
   }
}
```

Naturally, this is not good style. However, judging from looking at actual Java code, the strict compile-time exception checking in Java seems to encourage hurried programmers to do just that.

## Exceptions Should Be Exceptional

There is some temptation to use the exception mechanism as a convenient way of getting from one program point to another. This should be resisted.

Exceptions should be reserved for circumstances that are not expected to occur in the normal flow of a computation and whose occurrence creates a situation that cannot be resolved in the current scope.

Memory exhaustion is a good example where the exception-handling mechanism makes sense. You cannot predict when memory is exhausted, and at the point of detection it is rarely possible to do much about it. For that reason, it is the default behavior of the `new` operator to raise an exception (of type `bad_alloc`) when it cannot comply with a request for memory.

Contrast that with the detection of the end of a file from which data is read. All files must come to an end, and the code reading the file in should be prepared to cope with that. The code doing the reading may be expected to query the stream state. Of course, in reading a file of a known format, an unexpected end of file, perhaps caused by a disk error, can legitimately be converted to an exception, whose handler rolls back the entire reading process and reports a corrupted file.

Similarly, when taking data from a queue, you should test whether the queue is nonempty before removing an element. It is considered poor style simply to take the element and trap the exception that is raised when removal from an empty queue is attempted.

Here is another example. In Chapter 10 we discussed the `dynamic_cast` operator to test whether a base-class pointer actually points to a derived-class object:

```
Base* s;
. . .
Derived* r = dynamic_cast<Derived*>(s);
if (r != NULL)
    // r equals s and points to a Derived object
    . . .
else
    // s does not point to a Derived object
```

It is possible to cast references as well. Because there is no null reference, a failed cast throws an exception of type `bad_cast`. The test code is as follows:

```
Base& s;
. . .
try
{   Derived& r = dynamic_cast<Derived&>(s);
    // r equals s and refers to a Derived object
    . . .
}
catch(bad_cast)
```

```
{  // s does not refer to a Derived object
   . . .
}
```

Given that exceptions are supposed to be used for exceptional situations, this is a somewhat dubious strategy. The fact that `s` doesn't refer to the `Derived` object is not an error, just one branch in the control flow. A better alternative is to use `dynamic_cast<Derived*>(&s)` instead of `dynamic_cast <Derived&>(s)`.

Exceptions should be used to cope with unpredictable events only. If a problem can be predicted and handled in the current scope, a test should be coded instead.

## What Exceptions Should You Throw?

Because an unexpected exception can terminate the program, it is vitally important that your code minimize the number of exceptions it raises and that you clearly document the types of exceptions that can occur. Exception specifications are the proper tool for that.

Never use exceptions to return the result of a computation. The caller of a function can ignore a returned value without peril to the program, but an uncaught exception results in termination.

Low-level code should limit itself to reporting the following kinds of exceptions:

- Failure of precondition (for example, popping off an empty stack, inverting a singular matrix)
- Resource limitation (for example, out of memory, cannot allocate another font)
- Device failure (for example, drive door open, printer offline)

High-level code should translate these detail exceptions into subsystem failure.

This enables the caller of the high-level operation simply to retry or abandon the high-level operation rather than attempt to micromanage problems over which it has no control.

## What Exceptions Can You Catch?

There are two reasons to catch an exception:

- Catch those exceptions that you can handle.
- Catch and rethrow exceptions if you need to perform some action before a function terminates as an exception flies by it (but in this case

it is usually better to reorganize code to have the termination action invoked automatically in a destructor).

Never catch and eat an exception that an outer block would handle more competently.

When handling an exception, you have two choices. You can retry, perhaps after prompting the user to remedy the cause of failure (close the disk drive, turn on the printer, close other applications to provide more memory, erase a file to create more disk space), or you can give up. The latter is usually the only remedy when catching a failure of a precondition or a subsystem failure. There is very little you can do to fix, for example, popping a value off an empty stack. The cause could be external (for example, a corrupted input file) or programmer error. It may be possible just to abandon the current operation (for example, not to read in the file). Or the program may need to be terminated after all work has been saved.

# *Error-Handler Functions*

## Classes with User-installable Error Handlers

 An operation that finds an error condition can react to it in a number of ways. However, none of them may be appropriate in all circumstances. For this reason, classes often support user-installable handler functions. A default handler provides some action, usually printing a message and aborting the program. However, the user can install another function—for example, to record the error message in a file and continue processing or to raise an exception.

Here is a simple stack class with a user-installable error handler.

```
typedef void (*ErrorFun)(string);
class Stack
{
public:
   Stack();
   double pop();
   void push(double);
   bool is_empty() const;
   static ErrorFun set_handler(ErrorFun);
private:
   vector<double> _s;
   int _sptr;
   static void default_handler(string);
   static ErrorFun _errfun;
};
```

A handler can be installed with the set_handler function. This function returns the old handler, and it is considered good form to restore the original handler on completion.

```
ofstream errfile; // file for error messages
void report_handler(string s)
{  errfile << "Stack: " << s << endl;
}

ErrorFun old_handler = Stack::set_handler(report_handler);
. . .
x = s.pop(); // underflow calls report_handler
. . .
Stack::set_handler(old_handler);
```

The report_handler adds the error message and continues execution. Another plausible handler would throw an exception instead.

```
void except_handler(string s)
{  throw StackError(s);
}
```

Having a user-installable handler gives the user of the stack a choice between the drastic action of throwing an exception and the more limited action of logging the error and continuing execution.

The implementation of user-installable error handlers is straightforward. The stack class contains a static variable that holds the pointer to the current error function. That variable is initialized to point to a default handler:

```
void Stack::default_handler(string s)
{  cerr << "Stack: " << s << endl;
   exit(1);
}
ErrorFun Stack::_errfun = Stack::default_handler;
```

The set_handler function returns the old handler and installs a new one:

```
ErrorFun Stack::set_handler(ErrorFun newerr)
{  ErrorFun olderr = _errfun;
   _errfun = newerr;
   return olderr;
}
```

Whenever an error is detected, the error handler is called:

```
double Stack::pop()
{  if (_sptr <= 0)
   {  (*_errfun)("Stack underflow");
      return 0;
   }
   _sptr--;
   return _s[_sptr];
}
```

The pointer to the current handler and the `set_handler` function are static class functions of the `Stack` class. All stack objects share the same handler. It would also be possible to give each stack its own handler.

## Installing Handlers for Fatal and Unexpected Exceptions

 When an exception occurs and the stack is unwound, the destructors of all stack objects are called. If one of these destructors throws an exception, then the runtime mechanism cannot deal with two simultaneous exceptions and the program is terminated.

Actually, before the program terminates, it calls the *termination handler*. You can install your own function for this handler. The function cannot bring the program back to life, but it could write an error message and close vital files. You use the standard function `set_terminate` for this purpose. Your termination function *must* terminate the program; it may not return.

```
void terminator()
{  cout << "Goodbye cruel world!" << endl;
   exit(1);
}

int main()
{  set_terminate(terminator)
   . . .
}
```

If an unexpected exception is detected in a function with an exception specifier, then the program normally terminates as well. You can override that behavior by installing another handler with the `set_unexpected` function. Your handler must *either* terminate the program *or* throw an exception in the exception specification list.

A standard approach is to install a handler that throws `bad_exception` and to add `bad_exception` to the exception list of every function with an exception specification.

```
int f(istream&) throw (StackError, MathError, bad_exception)
{  g(); // might throw any exception
   more code // might throw StackError or MathError
}

void throw_bad_exception()
{  throw bad_exception;
}

int main()
{  set_unexpected(throw_bad_exception);
   . . .
}
```

Now if g throws an ACME_Exception, then f calls the handler installed by set_unexpected. That handler throws a bad_exception instead, which is listed in the exception list of f, so the program doesn't terminate.

## *Design Hints*

### Catch Only What You Can Handle

If you don't know how to handle an error, don't catch it. Presumably there is a more competent handler in an outer scope.

Of course, you may need to perform some cleanup not included in destructors, as an exception flies by. It is appropriate to catch an exception, do the cleanup, and rethrow the exception.

### Exceptions Are for Exceptional Circumstances

The punishment for an unhandled exception is the death penalty. Your program will die if one component throws an exception that nobody knows how to handle. Admittedly, you can shut up any exception with catch(...), but you have lost the entire computation and have a program that may still be very sick. This simple fact should discourage you from using exceptions if there is another reasonable alternative.

### Don't Rely on Exceptions If You Can Test

Don't rely on exceptions to report a failure that you could have tested. Test for an empty stack before popping an element. Don't just try to wait for the exception.

## Don't Throw an Exception If You Can Continue

If you must choose between throwing an exception and continuing the computation, continue if you can. If you implement a stack and must do something about popping off an empty stack, return a default value. It is inconceivable that the default return value could cause a greater harm than the exception. Obviously, the immediate caller of pop didn't care—it would have been a simple matter to call is_empty first. The other callers are likely to have even less knowledge of the situation. At any rate, what should they do with the information? All they get to know is that somewhere inside, a stack was empty although it shouldn't have been.

It would be nice if all code were perfect, but frankly, most large programs have large numbers of minor and major flaws. Some of them are perfectly harmless, and it makes more sense to keep the program going rather than have an uncaught exception kill it.

There are situations where you plainly can't continue. You are flat out of memory; you must get more information out of a file, but you can't because of a stream error; you are stuck in the middle of a constructor. Then exceptions are appropriate.

## Let Library Users Choose How They Want Errors Handled

If you build that stack class, your users will not agree how nonfatal errors should be handled. Some want them turned into exceptions; others want them ignored.

You must humor both kinds of customers. First, make sure that the class interface makes it possible for the class user to test the preconditions of all operations and that all operations that cannot guarantee success a priori report an error status. Now the user who does not wish to catch exceptions has all the necessary tools to avoid them.

Then give the user a chance to install an error handler. The default handler throws the exception, but the user may install a null handler to indicate willingness to handle all nonfatal errors.

## Constructor Failure

A constructor may fail for two reasons. The precondition may not be fulfilled; that is, it is being called with bad arguments. In that case, set the object to a default state and pass control on to the error handler. Some essential resource may not be available. This is not the caller's fault, and there is no good way for the caller to test for failure because constructors do not return values. This is a fatal error that should be turned into an exception.

## Don't Lose Resources During Exception Processing

The portion of the stack between the throw and catch point is abandoned before the exception is handled. All objects with destructors are properly destroyed, but pointers and handles to external resources are simply abandoned.

If possible, don't use pointers and handles on the stack but place them inside objects with proper destructors. If you don't have that luxury, you need to add code that catches any exception, relinquishes the resource, and rethrows the exception.

# 17

# Class
# Library Design

In this chapter we will look at the standard container class libraries in C++ and Java. The ANSI C++ standards committee agreed in 1995 to add the Standard Template Library (STL) that was developed by Alexander Stepanov and Meng Lee of Hewlett-Packard. This library provides several common container structures such as linked lists and red-black trees, as well as a large number of algorithms. We will study the architecture of this library; it is an important part of the ANSI standard, and somewhat less object-oriented than you would perhaps expect from a standard C++ library. We will then turn to the much more modest container library in Java, which has just a handful of data structures, and study the design and access mechanisms of the Java containers.

## *Containers*

### **Container Types**

A *container type* is an abstract type that specifies the protocol for insertion, removal, and traversal of elements in a container. Computer scientists and

449

library builders largely agree on what the standard canon of containers should be. Here is a description of the most common ones:

- A *stack* is a collection of elements with a single position for insertion and removal. Elements are inserted (or *pushed*) to the *top* of the stack and also removed (or *popped*) from the top of the stack. Thus, insertion and removal occurs in a "last-in/first-out" (LIFO) order.

- A *queue* is a collection of elements with one position for insertion and one position for removal. Elements are inserted to the *tail* of the queue and removed from the *head* of the queue. Thus, insertion and removal occurs in a "first-in/first-out" (FIFO) order. A typical example is the queue of customers at a checkout counter.

- A *deque* (double-ended queue) is a collection of elements with two positions for insertion and removal. Elements can be inserted and removed at either the head or the tail of the deque.

- A *list* is an ordered collection of elements. Elements can be inserted and removed at *any* position. The position of the elements in the list matters; elements stay at the positions in which they were inserted. For that reason, a list is often called an *ordered collection*.

- A *sorted collection* is a collection of elements that are inserted in any order, but are positioned in sorted order in the container. Of course, to sort the elements, there must be a way to compare them with each other. That is, given any two elements $x$ and $y$, either $x$ must come before $y$, $x$ must come after $y$, or $x$ and $y$ are indistinguishable from each other. Such a relationship is called a *total ordering*. For example, strings are totally ordered by lexicographic comparison, and employee records can be sorted by their name or ID number. Other types, however, have no natural total ordering, for example, circles in the plane. Note that elements don't have fixed positions in a sorted collection. When another element is inserted, the data structure can reorganize its contents.

- A *priority queue* is also a collection of elements on which a total ordering is defined. When you remove an element, you always get the smallest element. The other elements need not be in sorted order. Of course, a sorted collection can be used to implement a priority queue, but more efficient algorithms are known if you only need to repeatedly retrieve the smallest element, not visit all elements in sorted order. A typical use for a priority queue is an event queue in a scheduler. Events are sorted by the time stamp that specifies when they need to be executed. They are inserted into the priority queue in random order. The scheduler keeps removing the element with the lowest time stamp because it is the next one to be scheduled.

- A *set* is an unordered collection of elements. That is, the order in which elements are inserted may be different from the order in which they are kept in the container. Sets do not contain duplicate copies of elements. If the same element is inserted twice, only one copy is kept. Therefore, there must be some way of testing whether two objects are identical.

- A *bag* is an unordered collection of elements in which multiple copies of identical objects can be inserted. That is, unlike a set, a bag does not simply ignore efforts to insert multiple copies of identical objects. Instead, it stores a count for each element that tells how many times an element has been inserted and removed.

- A *map* (sometimes called *dictionary* or *associative array*) is an unordered collection of pairs (*key, value*). For each key, there can be only one associated value. Given a key, the associated value can be retrieved or removed. There must be some way to test whether two keys are identical, but no relation needs to be defined for the values.

- An *array* or *vector* is a special case of a map in which the key set is an interval of integers.

- A *graph* has a set of *vertices V* and a set of *edges E*. Each vertex is an element of some type (for example, a string or an object of type `City`). Each edge joins two vertices and also stores information of some type (for example, `double`). Vertices and edges can be inserted and removed, and there are many algorithms that compute interesting properties of graphs such as the shortest path between two vertices.

These types are *abstract* types. They can be implemented by any suitable data structure. For example, a sorted collection can be implemented as a plain binary search tree or as a balanced tree such as an AVL tree, red-black tree, or 2-3 tree. A set can be implemented as a linked list or, with better performance, as a hash table.

The distinction between the abstract types and the concrete implementations is confusing for those types with common names. Technically speaking, a *list* is the abstract type, and a *linked list* is its most likely implementation, as a sequence of cells linked by pointers. An *array* is an abstract type, almost certainly implemented as a *block* of consecutive elements in memory that is relocated when it needs to grow.

Most libraries of container classes present classes for the abstract types, such as `Set`, `Map`, and `SortedCollection`, internally realized with an implementation that is known to work well for most general purposes. Other libraries present classes for the concrete implementations, such as `LinkedList`, `HashTable`, or `AVLTree`, and leave it to the user to build higher-level structures out of them. The latter approach is less convenient. If a linked list is first chosen in an application that conceptually requires a set, and later the amount of data is so large that a change to a more efficient hash table implementation becomes necessary, some amount of painful surgery is required to make that transition.

Some libraries try to give users the best of both worlds—control over both the abstract data structure and the concrete representation—by supplying multiple implementations such as `QueueAsLinkedList` or `QueueAsCircularArray`. That way, only the type name needs to be changed to switch from one implementation to another. The access protocol to the container remains unchanged.

To improve performance and reduce allocation overhead, storing elements in a fixed-size block of memory can be useful. The size may be specified at compile time (through a template argument) or at construction time (through a constructor argument). Of course, as more elements are inserted into such a container, it fills up and further insertions become impossible. Strictly speaking, a stack made from a fixed-size array is not a proper implementation of the abstract type *Stack;* instead, it implements a *bounded stack.* Bounded containers have an added operation to test whether the container is full, in which case insertion of further elements is undefined, just as removal of elements from an empty container is undefined. Some libraries are careless about the distinction between bounded and unbounded containers. If your library gives you a `StackAsArray`, you should check whether the memory block has a fixed size (maybe with some magic default) or whether it relocates to grow on demand.

## Insertion, Retrieval, and Removal

Containers show great variety with respect to their insertion and retrieval protocols. Here we describe the access methods to these containers, using names for the containers and operations that are chosen to be intuitive, even though they differ from those used by the STL and `java.util` libraries.

Stacks, queues, and deques have specific locations at which elements are inserted—the top of the stack, the tail of the queue:

```
s.push(x);
q.insert(x);
```

Elements are removed from the top of the stack or the head of the queue:

```
x = s.pop();
x = q.remove();
```

The element at the distinguished positions (top of stack, head or tail of queue) can be inspected without removing it.

```
x = s.top();
x = q.head();
```

Arrays and maps require an *index* or *key* for insertion and lookup.

```
a[i] = x;
m.set(k, x);
x = a[i];
x = m.get(k);
```

You can remove an association from a map by specifying its key.

```
x = m.remove(k);
```

Strictly speaking, elements cannot be removed from an array, except from the ends. The key set of an array is a complete interval of integers.

Lists are more complex than the other containers because they support insertion by *position*. There must be some way of specifying a position into the list. Some list classes have a distinguished position, called a *cursor*, that can be moved to any position in the list. For those lists, insertion and removal occur at the cursor position (see Figure 17.1).

```
l.reset(); // set cursor to beginning of the list
l.next();  // advance to the second element
l.next();  // advance to the third element
l.insert(x); // insert between the second and the third element
```

Another popular approach is to use an object of a second class, a so-called *iterator*, to mark a position in a list (see Figure 17.2).

```
List<T> l;
. . .
List<T>::Iterator i = l.begin();
   // iterator points to beginning of list
i.next(); // advance to the second element
```

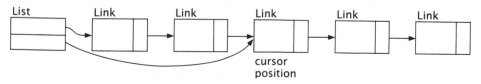

**FIGURE 17.1**  A list with a cursor.

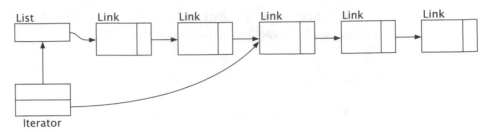

**FIGURE 17.2** A list with an iterator.

```
i.next(); // advance to the third element
i.insert(x); // insert between the second and the third element
```

The advantage of iterators is that they permit editing of the list at multiple positions.

Bags and sets are unordered; hence, no insert position can be specified. Sorted collections and priority queues arrange elements according to their sort position, and again no insert position is specified. You just insert the element.

```
b.insert(x);
```

It is often necessary to visit all elements in a container. Arrays can be traversed easily:

```
for (i = 0; i < a.size(); i++)
    do something with a[i];
```

This simple method does not work with any other container. Imagine doing something with all entries in a map. Maps have keys, but unlike an array, we do not know for which keys k there are entries m[k]. Obviously we cannot try all keys. Again, a cursor or iterator is required. For sorted collections, the iterator visits the elements in the sort order.

```
SortedCollection<T> s;
. . .
SortedCollection<T>::Iterator i = s.begin();
while (!i.at_end()) // prints in sorted order
{   cout << i.current() << endl;
    i.next();
}
```

For sets and bags, elements are visited in random order, not in sorted order.

Strictly speaking, you can't see any elements in a priority queue except the smallest one. You can inspect or remove the smallest element from a priority queue:

```
x = p.remove();
```

To remove an element from a sorted collection, or a set or bag, you must specify the element to be removed.

```
b.remove(x);
```

Or you can remove the element to which an iterator points.

```
x = i.remove();
```

Arrays, maps, and lists can return references to their elements. That lets you invoke mutator functions to change the element in place.

```
Map<string, Employee> staff;
staff["149-25-3649"].raise_salary(5.5);

List<Employee>::iterator i = staff.begin();
Employee harry("Harry Hacker");
i.current() = harry; // replace current element
```

For other containers, in particular sorted collections and sets, such in-place change is not possible. Those containers use intrinsic properties, such as sort order or equality with other elements, not an external position, to organize their stored objects. Changing an element's value may affect those properties and hence the position in the container.

## Traversal

If a linked list has a cursor, then it can be traversed by moving the cursor from the beginning to the end:

```
for (l.reset(); !l.at_end(); l.next())
   do something with l.current();
```

Using the list cursor for traversal has one drawback: It changes the state of the list by moving the cursor position. Consider the following operator function:

```
template<class T>
ostream& operator<<(ostream& os, const List<T>& l)
```

```
{ for (l.reset(); !l.at_end(); l.next()) // ERROR
      os << l.current();
   return os;
}
```

The cursor operations modify the list state and hence cannot be carried out on a const object. It is important that printing a list not modify its state. Consider the following test print in a code segment that relies on the correct placement of the cursor position:

```
List<int> l;
. . .
l.reset(); // swap first two elements
a = l.remove();
cout << l; // test printout
l.next();
l.insert(a);
```

We need a way of traversing the list without moving the list cursor. Two methods are available: function application and external iterators.

The implementor of a container can easily write code that visits each stored element to apply a user-provided function. With such a service, printing a list can be implemented as follows:

```
template<class T>
ostream& operator<<(ostream& os, const List<T>& l)
{  l.apply(print_fun, &os);
   return os;
}
```

Here print_fun is the function to be applied at each node.

```
template<class T>
void print_fun(const T& t, void* p)
{  (*(ostream*)p) << t;
}
```

Because the apply mechanism must cope with arbitrary traversal actions, it provides for an application function with two arguments: the currently visited element and a generic pointer to another argument. In our example, the stream argument is transported to the print function as a void* pointer. If more than one argument is required, a pointer to a separate structure containing all argument values must be used. (The unsightly void* pointers can be avoided by using another template if the compiler supports nested templates.)

The `apply` operation visits all elements without disturbing the list cursor:

```
template<class T>
class List
{
public:
   typedef void (*ApplyFun)(const T&, void*);
   void apply(ApplyFun, void*) const;
   . . .
};


template<class T>
void List<T>::apply(List<T>::ApplyFun f, void* p) const
{  for (Link<T>* n = _head; n != NULL; n++)
   (*f)(n->_info, p);
}
```

Function application is somewhat cumbersome because it is tedious to set up the auxiliary function. Furthermore, every node of the container is visited. It is not possible to stop the traversal when a particular element has been found. External iterators are better suited in that situation.

What happens if an iterator happens to point to a particular container element and that element is removed? What happens to an iterator if the list through which it iterates is destroyed? It depends on the library. Some libraries are careful and adjust all iterators if the container to which they point is edited. Others are sloppy and only caution the programmer that using the iterator after such situations will have disastrous effects.

Class library designers must decide whether iterators can be used only to inspect containers or also to modify their contents. For example, should the list iterator be able to support insertion and removal at the current position? It depends. If we want to use an iterator to traverse a const container, its constructor must take a const reference to the container:

```
template<class T>
List<T>::Iterator::Iterator(const List<T>&)
```

After all, the iterator will be attached to a const object:

```
template<class T>
ostream& operator<<(ostream& os, const List<T>& l)
{  for  (List<T>::Iterator it(l); !it.at_end(); it.next())
      os << it.current();
   return os;
}
```

If it is possible to carry out destructive operations like `it.remove()` through this particular iterator, the promise to leave the list unchanged can be broken.

There are two possible remedies:

■ A library may supply two iterator classes: one for inspection and one for mutation.
■ A single class can be provided, with two constructors, one taking a `const` reference, the other a non-`const` reference. The constructors set a flag to remember whether mutation is permitted. If a mutating operation is carried out and the flag is not set, an exception is raised.

The first approach uses a compile-time check, the second a run-time check.

Unordered containers, such as sets, bags, maps, and keyed collections, are traversed in a random fashion. These are often implemented as hash tables, and traversal just follows the vagaries of the hash function values.

In iterating through a priority queue, we may be assured that the first visited element is the minimum one. The remaining elements are visited in random order.

Of course, sorted collections are traversed in sort order. These containers are usually implemented as tree structures. Providing an iterator that steps through the tree in sorted order is actually quite difficult. Either each tree node must contain a pointer to its parent, which is inefficient, or each iterator must keep a stack of visited tree nodes. For trees, the `apply` mechanism is much more efficient. It is very easy to apply a function to all nodes in a tree, simply by visiting the tree in inorder traversal and applying the function to each visited node.

# The Standard Template Library

## An Overview of STL

STL, the standard template library, has two components: containers and algorithms. *Containers* are data structures that store values, such as linked lists, sorted trees, dynamic arrays and priority queues. STL *algorithms* act on these containers. They find elements or reorder or otherwise modify the contents of the containers. Having containers preprogrammed for you is, of course, a great help. It takes a certain amount of skill to implement a linked list, and most of us don't get it quite right on the first attempt. Using the STL list template can save hours of debugging. And the more sophisticated data structures in STL are sufficiently complex that most programmers would never bother implementing them manually.

The bigger win comes from the STL algorithms. They range from the mundane (remove adjacent duplicates) and predictable (sort) to the esoteric (random shuffle). Of course, writing code to randomly shuffle the entries in an array efficiently is not for the faint of heart, and it is great to have it done for you. But even the seemingly trivial algorithms make a lot of sense. Code that contains the `remove` template is easier to read than the explicit loop, and you are protected from silly index errors.

There is another aspect of STL that we will not discuss much in this chapter. STL is a *framework,* and new containers and algorithms can be added. Provided they follow certain conventions, they can work with the existing components.

Other commercial class libraries are available that are more convenient or more powerful than STL, but STL has two great advantages: It is free and it is portable. For those reasons, it makes sense for every C++ programmer to gain a working knowledge of STL.

STL has been adopted to become a part of the C++ standard. Many compilers are beginning to support STL now. In the long run, of course, STL will be included with every C++ compiler. Then it probably won't even be known as STL anymore; it will just become absorbed in the standard library.

The free implementation from Hewlett-Packard is available with the software accompanying this book, together with the *Safe STL* enhancement, a library that is fully compatible with STL but fine-tunes the containers and iterators to detect common programming errors. We will describe Safe STL in greater detail later in this chapter.

## Collecting Objects

Let us make a linked list of objects of type `Employee` and insert a number of employee records.

```
list<Employee> elist;
char* name[26] = { "Arthur Able", "Barry Baker",
   "Charlie Cracker", ... };

for (i = 0; i < 26; i++)
{  Employee e(name[i]);
   elist.push_back(e);
}
```

NOTE

According to the ANSI standard, the `list` template has two parameters: the type `T` of the elements and the type of an allocator for getting new elements. It is possible to allocate the memory for the links in another location than the standard heap. However, we will not use this feature at all in our examples. STL defines a class `allocator<T>` that allocates memory for objects on the heap, simply by calling `new` and `delete`. We always want to use just that allocator. It is supposed to be the *default argument* for the allocator parameter of the `list` template, which means you don't need to supply it if you just want the default allocation. Currently most compilers do not support default arguments of templates.

The original implementation from Hewlett-Packard simply did not use allocators at all. But other implementations, such as the one in Visual C++ 4.2, do, and because default template arguments are not supported, you must explicitly supply the allocator parameter in *every* STL template:

```
list<Employee, allocator<Employee> > elist;
```
■

First, the `list` template is instantiated to the type `list<Employee>`, then an object `elist` of that type is created. That list is filled with 26 employee objects. This is a doubly linked list in which every link has pointers to its predecessor and successor. There is no way to make a singly linked list in STL.

The list function `push_back` appends an object to the list. You might think that `append` would be a more natural name for that operation. The library is consistent and *all* containers call the append operation `push_back`. This makes more sense for some containers than others, of course.

The `push_back` operation stores a *copy* of the `Employee` object `e`, not just its address. That is, after `elist.push_back(e)`, there are two copies of the employee data, one in the variable `e` and one in the `elist`. This is no different from a vector. The assignment:

```
vector<Employee> evec;
evec[i] = e;
```

also stores a copy of `e` into the vector.

Of course, it is possible to make a list of pointers.

```
list<Employee*> pelist;
pelist.push_back(new Employee("Fred Foxtrot"));
```

However, note that a list of pointers has a major disadvantage over a list of objects. The destructor of the list object does not automatically delete the pointers. You must manually remove the pointers from the list and delete them before the list is destroyed.

## Traversing Containers

Once a list has been filled, we want to find out what is in it and perhaps modify the contents. In a C program, you do this manually by manipulating `Link*` pointers. That is a tedious and error-prone business. In STL, an *iterator* is an object that acts like a pointer into a data structure.

Here is the code to print all employee records in the list.

```
list<Employee>::iterator p = elist.begin();

while (p != elist.end())
{  Employee e = *p;
   e.print(cout);
   p++;
}
```

Every STL container defines a nested type *container*<T>::iterator. For lists, we therefore use `list<Employee>::iterator`.

Every container can produce two iterators, one pointing to the beginning and one pointing just past the end (see Figure 17.3). In our code, the iterator p is initialized with `elist.begin()` and is advanced until it equals `elist.end()`.

The ++ and * operators are overloaded for iterators: ++ advances the iterator to the next position in the list, and * returns the element of the link to which the iterator points. In STL, linked lists are always *doubly linked*, that is, each link has a pointer to its predecessor and successor. List iterators are *bidirectional*. The -- operator moves the iterator backwards. The ANSI standard requires that the -> operator is overloaded as well, but not all implementations support that yet. We will therefore write `(*p).print()`, but eventually `p->print()` should work with all compilers.

When we looked at the abstract properties of containers, we called the ++ operator next and the * operator current. In STL, the overloaded operators are supposed to remind you of pointers. In the theoretical model of iter-

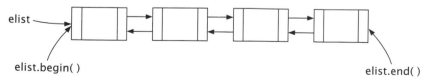

**FIGURE 17.3**  The begin and end iterator positions in a list.

ators, an operation `p.at_end()` would determine if an iterator was at the end of the container. However, the STL iterators do not know when they have reached the end! In fact, a common STL error is to run an iterator "over the cliff". Instead, we compare the iterator `p` against the iterator `elist.end()`. When they match, we are past the end.

Iterators are also used for editing the list. The following code inserts a new employee before the second element and then removes the element that originally was in the second position (see Figure 17.4).

```
p = elist.begin();
p++;
elist.insert(p, Employee("Kelly Kilo"));
elist.erase(p);
```

Note that the iterators `p` and `q` that are supplied in the `insert` and `erase` operations *must* point into the list that is the implicit argument of those operations. If not, very strange errors will occur, and the lists can get cross-linked. In the theoretical model, we assumed that `insert` and `erase` are operations on the *iterators*. That is, the iterator would know into which container it points and edit that container. But STL iterators do not know into which container they point.

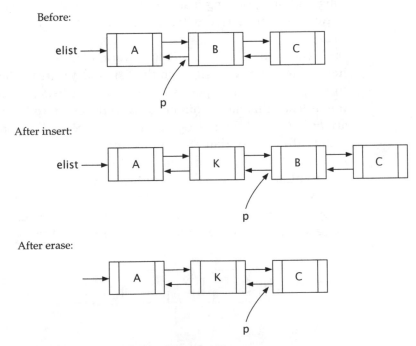

**FIGURE 17.4**  Editing a list through iterators.

## Sorted Collections

In STL, the name for such a *sorted collection* is, somewhat oddly, a `multiset`. Here we insert employee objects into a sorted collection in random order. When traversing the set, they are automatically sorted.

```
multiset<Employee> esort;

char* name[26] = { "Yolanda Yankee",
    "Fred Foxtrot", "Loretta Lima", ... };

for (i = 0; i < 26; i++)
{  Employee e(name[i]);
    esort.insert(e);
}

multiset<Employee>::iterator p;

for (p = esort.begin(); p != esort.end(); p++)
    (*p).print(cout);
```

**NOTE**

According to the ANSI standard, the `multiset` template has three parameters: the type `T` of the elements, the type of the comparison object, and an allocator for getting new elements. The type for the comparison object is supposed to default to `less<T>`, which in turn causes the elements to be compared by the < operator. And, as for lists, the allocator is supposed to default to `allocator<T>`. If your compiler doesn't handle default template arguments, you need to type

```
multiset<Employee, less<Employee>, allocator<Employee> > esort;
```

or, if you use the HP implementation that doesn't implement allocators,

```
multiset<Employee, less<Employee> > esort;
```

This is a hassle, of course, and a remedy is to use a `typedef`:

```
typedef multiset<Employee, less<Employee>, allocator<Employee> >
    Employee_multiset;

Employee_multiset esort;
Employee_multiset::iterator p = esort.begin();
```

■

How does the library know how to compare two employees? After all, `Employee` is a user-defined class. By default, objects in the sorted collection are compared with the < operator. If the `Employee` class already has an `operator<` member function, we need not do anything further. If not, we can define that operator for employees. Note that an operator need not be defined inside the class, so this can be done after the fact.

```
bool operator<(const Employee& a, const Employee& b)
{  return a.name() < b.name();
       // the names are objects of type string,
       // < compares strings in dictionary order
}
```

That is fine, but it lets us sort employees in only one way. Suppose we want to have another collection in which they are sorted by salary or hire date. Then we have to supply a comparison function, similar to the argument in the `qsort` function of the C library. The comparison function must return true if the first argument is less than the other, false otherwise.

```
bool sal_less(const Employee& a, const Employee& b)
{ return a.salary() < b.salary();
}
```

Then the type of the comparison object is no longer the predefined class `less<Employee>`, but it is a function pointer of type `bool (*)(const Employee&, const Employee&)`. Thus, the type of the container is

```
multiset<Employee, bool (*)(const Employee&, const Employee&)>.
```

The comparison function is passed as a construction parameter to the container object.

```
multiset<Employee, bool (*)(const Employee&, const Employee&)>.
   esalsort(sal_less);
```

That looks a bit overwhelming, of course.

## Maps

One of the most useful STL containers is the *map*, sometimes called a *dictionary*. Think of a map as an array, except that the array indexes aren't integers but objects of any type.

```
Employee e("Harry Hacker");

map<Employee, double> bonus;
bonus[e] = 500;
```

An essential feature of a map is that a key is associated with *exactly one* value, so you would expect that an `operator==` (or some other equality-testing function) is used to compare keys.

But in STL there is a catch: The key type must have a *total ordering*. That is, a comparison must be defined so that for any two objects either x < y, y < x, or x and y are identical. For example, the employee comparison by name is *not* a total ordering because two employees may have the same name. In this case, the remedy is easy: Compare them by their tax ID number instead. It makes no difference what ordering you use, as long as it is a total ordering.

Sometimes no good total ordering comes to mind for the key type. Consider a

```
map<Rectangle, Color> m;
```

It is easy enough to tell when two rectangles are the same, namely when they have the same left, right, top, and bottom. But how do you compare two that are different? Remember, we need a total ordering where for any two rectangles we determine that one is "smaller" than the other. You cannot compare them by their area. Two entirely different rectangles could have the same area. If you used comparison by area and inserted two rectangles that happened to have the same area, the second one would replace the first one.

In this case, you can use lexicographic ordering: First compare the left coordinates, and if they match, then compare the top, and if they match, then compare the right, and if they match, then compare the bottom. This is a pretty artificial sort ordering.

That you must come up with a total ordering for containers like map that are not intrinsically ordered is a pain. Other class libraries use hashing and equality testing, which is often more convenient for the class user. STL requires a total ordering for a reason: It wants to guarantee the performance of the operations. For example, key lookup in a map with $n$ entries is guaranteed to take no more than $\log_2 n$ comparisons, whereas a poor hash function can lead to up to $n$ comparisons instead. In a map with 1,000 elements, that makes a difference: guaranteed no more than 10 comparisons versus as many as 1000. But measurements have shown that hashing with a good hash function performs much better than the red-black trees used by STL. There was a proposal to add hash table implementations of sets and maps to STL, but it was rejected because of time constraints. Two different implementations are freely available by ftp from `butler.hpl.hp.com`.

## Collecting Pointers

All containers that we have seen so far collect objects, not pointers to objects. Collecting objects is easier than collecting pointers—you need not worry about allocating and deallocating additional memory. Of course, sometimes we need to collect pointers, for one of the following reasons:

- Polymorphism—for example, rectangles and circles derived from Shape
- Sharing—the same object may live in multiple containers
- Efficiency—to avoid the cost of copying large objects in and out of the container

For simple containers, this is not a problem. Here is a linked list of shape pointers.

```
list<Shape*> figure;
figure.push_back(new Rectangle(...));
```

For ordered collections, define the ordering relation to compare objects.

```
bool id_less(const Employee* a, const Employee* b)
{  return a->id() < b->id();
}

multiset<Employee*, bool (*)(const Employee*, const Employee*)>
   staff(id_less);
```

Could you use pointer comparison as a total ordering? That is, could you have a map<Shape*, Color> that just compares memory addresses? Unfortunately, you cannot. Pointer comparison p < q is only well defined when p and q point to the same array. For example, in the large memory model on a PC, only the offsets are compared, and it is possible to have two pointers with different segments and identical offsets that compare identically.

**PITFALL**

There is a real pitfall here. If you make a set

```
multiset<Employee*> staff;
```

then the compiler will cheerfully produce an ordered collection with a nonsensical ordering. Try out the following code on a PC in the 16-bit large and the 32-bit flat memory models:

```
multiset<Employee*> staff;
for(char c = 'A'; c <= 'Z'; c++)
{  Employee* pe = new Employee(c + ". Smith");
   staff.insert(pe);
}
cout << staff.size() << endl;
```

In 32-bit flat memory model, the size of `staff` will, of course, be 26. In the 16-bit large memory model, however, the size of the container will be 1! All pointers are allocated with different segment addresses but the same offset. Pointer comparison is only prepared to compare pointers into the same array, so it ignores the segments. All `Employee*` are considered the same!

That is, for pointers, the default comparison by the < operator is *always the wrong default.* ■

## Dynamic Arrays

We have already used the vector template extensively, as a replacement for C style arrays. STL offers a second array template, called a deque. (It has nothing to do with the data structure traditionally called *deque*. It is called a *deque* because it allows insertion and deletion of elements at both ends of the dynamic array in constant time.) The data structures differ in the growth behavior. A vector stores its elements in an array on the heap. If more space is needed, a new array is allocated and the existing elements are copied (see Figure 17.5). For large objects, that can be quite inefficient. Also, when the elements are moved, their addresses change and any pointers to them become invalid.

A deque allocates blocks of arrays instead (see Figure 17.6). When the deque grows, it just allocates more blocks. Because elements aren't copied, pointers into the deque don't become invalid! The drawback is an added level of indirection. (Of course, strictly speaking, STL doesn't require that a deque must be implemented as a collection of array blocks. But it guarantees that random access and insertion at the ends take constant time, which rules out relocation of the entire array.)

**TIP**

Use vectors if the size of the array doesn't change after construction, or if the contents are cheap to copy (such as pointers). Otherwise, use a deque. ■

To grow the dynamic array, you can simply append more elements to the end with `push_back`. Or you can grow the array by n elements with

```
a.insert(a.end(), n);
//It uses the default constructor to initialize the new elements
```

When using vectors, you should use the reserve member functions if you know the final size of the vector after a series of insertions. `v.reserve(n)` grows the vector, relocating if necessary, so that it can hold n elements without further relocations. The reserved space is left uninitialized until it is actually needed.

Before:

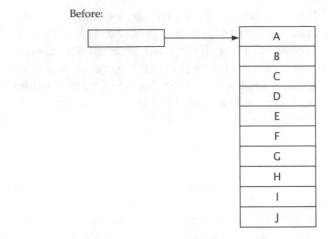

After relocation:

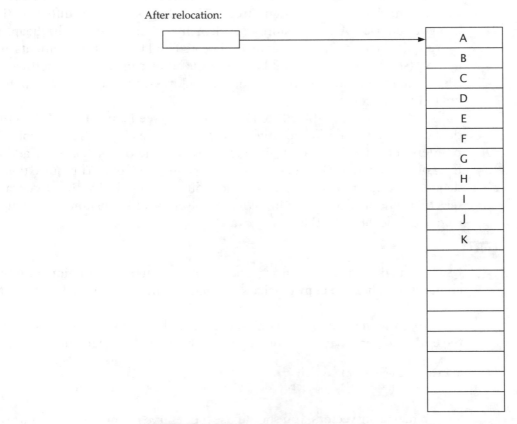

**FIGURE 17.5** Reallocating a vector.

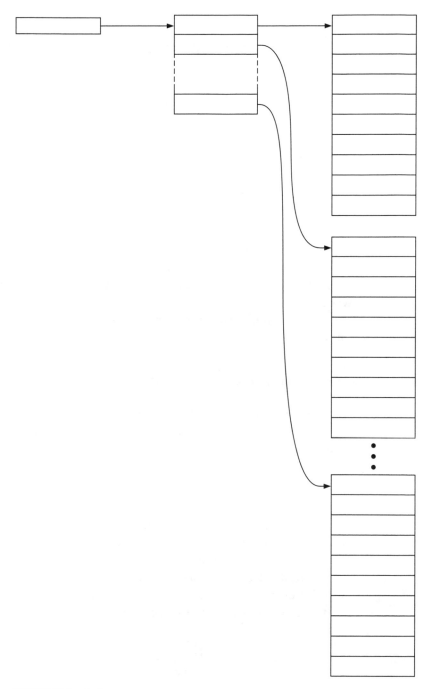

**FIGURE 17.6** A deque.

## Algorithms

Suppose you want to find a particular employee in a linked list. Of course, you can code the search by hand:

```
for (list<Employee>::iterator it = elist.begin();
     it != elist.end() && *it != e; it++)
   ;
```

But STL gives you an easier way, using the find algorithm:

```
list<Employee>::iterator it =
   find(elist.begin(), elist.end(), e);
```

Using the find algorithm instead of an explicit for loop, it is much easier to see the search range (from the beginning to the end of the container) and the object to match (e). There is absolutely no penalty in using the find algorithm—it is inline replaced into the exact same for loop you would write by hand.

Interestingly, the find template works equally well for *all* STL containers.

```
multiset<Employee>::iterator it =
   find(esort.begin(), esort.end(), e);
```

Amazingly enough, it even works for C arrays. You have to use the beginning of the array instead of begin() and one past the end of the array instead of end().

```
Employee staff[100];
Employee* it = find(staff, staff + 100, e);
```

In fact, making the algorithms work for both STL containers and C arrays was a major design decision of STL. That is why the STL iterators are so limited—they aren't allowed to know more than pointers into C arrays.

Actually, STL iterators are even more limited than C pointers. There is no null iterator. For eample, the find algorithm returns the second iterator (that is, past the end of the search interval) if the search failed.

```
list<Employee>::iterator it =
   find(elist.begin(), elist.end(), e);
if (it != elist.end()) // search succesful
   (*e).print();
```

The following code checks if there is a second copy of the employee in the list and removes the duplicate.

```
list<Employee>::iterator it =
   find(elist.begin(), elist.end(), e);
if (it != elist.end())
{  it++;
   it = find(it, elist.end(), e);
   if (it != elist.end()) elist.erase(it);
}
```

Of course, it would be nice to have an algorithm to remove all duplicates, but this is inefficient in general and STL doesn't provide it. If there is a total ordering on the objects, you can sort and then remove *adjacent* duplicates.

```
sort(elist.begin(), elist.end(), id_less);
unique(elist.begin(), elist.end());
```

That sounds good—sorting an arbitrary container such as a linked list can be tricky, and you probably don't want to implement that. Well, it turns out the designers of STL didn't either. The sort template requires *random access iterators*, and list iterators aren't random access. To sort a list, you must use its sort member function, and you can sort only on the ordering given by the < operator.

```
elist.sort();
unique(elist.begin(), elist.end());
```

Here is a list of useful algorithms. The last three require a random access iterator.

- for_each applies a function to each element.
- find locates the first element matching a given object; find_if locates the first element fulfilling a condition.
- count counts the elements matching a given object; count_if counts the number of elements fulfilling a condition.
- equal tests if containers have the same elements in the same order.
- copy copies elements from one container to another (possibly of a different type).
- replace/replace_if replaces all matching elements with a new one.
- fill overwrites a range with a new value.
- remove/remove_if removes all matching values.
- unique removes adjacent identical values.
- min_element/max_element finds the smallest and largest element.
- next_permutation rearranges the elements; calling it *n!* times iterates through all permutations.

- `sort` sorts the elements; `stable_sort` performs better if the container is already almost sorted.
- `random_shuffle` randomly rearranges the elements.
- `nth_element` finds the *n*th element, on average in linear time, without sorting the container. This is most useful to get the median or the second smallest/largest element.

There are lots of other algorithms, but most of them are of limited use or raw material for implementing other data structures.

## Other Containers

Table 17.1 gives a summary of all the containers that STL supplies, together with their key member functions.

Some of the standard container types, such as stacks and priority queues, are conspicuously absent from this list. Also, the `set` container doesn't actually have the typical set operations such as union and intersection. You can construct these data structures and operations out of STL building blocks.

For a *stack,* use the stack *adapter.* The construct

```
stack< list<Employee> > elstack;
```

gives a stack implemented as a linked list, whereas

```
stack< vector<Employee> > evstack;
```

**TABLE 17.1**   Containers that STL Supplies

| Container | Operation |
| --- | --- |
| all containers | size |
|  | insert/erase |
| vector | [] |
|  | push_back/pop_back |
|  | reserve |
| deque | [] |
|  | push_front/pop_front |
|  | push_back/pop_back |
| list | push_front/pop_front |
|  | push_back/pop_back |
|  | reverse |
| set/multiset | find |
|  | count |
| map/multimap | [] |
|  | find |

gives a stack implemented as a dynamic array. The role of the adapter is simply to map the familiar operations `push` and `pop` to the `push_back` and `pop_back` operations of the underlying container.

For a *queue*, use the queue adapter. Use

```
queue< list<Employee> > elqueue;
```

for a queue implemented as a linked list,

```
queue< deque<Employee> > edqueue;
```

for a queue as a dynamic array.

To implement a priority queue, use the `priority_queue` adapter. Here is a priority queue of events. The events are compared with the `evtcomp` function

```
priority_queue< vector<Event*>,
   bool (*)(const Event*, const Event*)> event_queue(evtcomp);
```

A *set* is a container that holds unique copies of objects, without regard to order, rejecting duplicates. As we already discussed, STL requires that you come up with a total ordering on the elements, not just some way of telling them apart. The usual set operations, such as union, intersection, and difference of sets, are not operations of the `set<T>` class. Instead, use the `includes`, `set_union`, `set_intersection`, `set_difference`, and `set_symmetric_difference` algorithms. For example,

```
set_union(a.begin(), a.end(), b.begin(), b.end(), c.begin());
```

computes the union of the sets `a` and `b` and puts the result into the set `c`.

A *bag* is just like a set, except it is possible to have multiple copies of the same element. Use the multiset template to implement a bag. The `count` member function tells how many copies of an element are present. The set algorithms (`set_union`, `set_intersection`, . . .) work correctly with multisets. For example, the union of two bags contains the maximum number of occurrences of elements in either bag.

STL has no *singly linked list.* Use `list` and ignore the backward links.

There is no *hash table* in STL because a hash table isn't really an abstract type. Use a multiset if you want to locate objects by an internal key, a multimap if the key is external to the object.

There is no *graph* class because all containers in STL support a *linear traversal:* Go from the beginning to the end and visit all elements in turn. There is no natural linear traversal for graphs; thus, STL doesn't support them.

## Advanced Features

STL contains a number of advanced features that aren't really necessary to use the library effectively. It is handy to have a reading knowledge of them so you can decipher other people's code.

*Function objects* are used to construct expressions that are inline replaced in comparison code. This is slightly more efficient, and arguably more elegant, than using a pointer to a function. Suppose we have a container of floating-point numbers and want to count how many are larger than 100,000. The boring method is to write a trivial function

```
bool gt_100k(double x) { return x > 100000.0; }
```

and pass it to count_if:

```
int n = 0;
count_if(c.begin(), c.end(), gt_100k, n);
```

count_if doesn't return the count. Instead, it increments n every time it finds a match.

Function objects let you build an object with an operator () that is inline replaced to do a computation. In our case, we do

```
count_if(c.begin(), c.end(),
   bind2nd(greater<double>(), 100000.0), n);
```

The comparison object constructed by bind2nd(greater<double>, 100000.0) is an object of a class whose name you don't want to know. Its sole mission in life is to have an overloaded () operator so that *comparison_object*(x) is inline replaced to x > 100000.0. That is nice. You don't have to come up with a trivial function, and having the comparison inline is a lot faster than calling a function.

In practice, this doesn't always work so well. Suppose we want to find out how many employees make more than $100K. We'd like to turn the test

```
e.salary() > 100000.0
```

into a comparison object. If salary had been a global function, there would have been a way of using other adapters to perform this feat, namely

```
compose1(bind2nd(greater<double>(), 100000.0), ptr_fun(salary))
```

But the ptr_fun adapter doesn't work for member functions.

Even when these adapter expressions do work, they are hard to understand and hard to write correctly. Therefore, it seems best not to use them.

Rather than using adapters, you can write a custom class

```
class Salary_gt_100k : public unary_function<Employee, bool>
{
public:
   bool operator()(Employee e) const
   { return e.salary() > 100000.0; }
};
```

Pass an object of that class, constructed with the default constructor, as the comparison object.

```
count_if(elist.begin(), elist.end(), Salary_gt_100k(), n);
```

That is a bit more work than just using a function pointer, but it inlines the comparison.

*Stream iterators* are an interface to input and output streams with the same syntax as container iterators. That way, they can be used in STL algorithms such as copy or merge. Here is a typical example:

```
copy(c.begin(), c.end(), ostream_iterator<double>(cout, " "));
```

This copies the floating-point numbers of the container c not to another container but to cout, separated by spaces.

It is a shortcut for

```
for (container::iterator it = c.begin(); it <= c.end(); it++)
   cout << *it << " ";
```

Similarly, there are input iterators. If you want to have a complicated way of writing

```
while (cin>>x) c.push_back(x);
```

then you can use

```
copy(istream_iterator<double>(cin), istream_iterator<double>(),
   inserter(c, c.end()));
```

**NOTE**

Use istream_iterator<double, ptrdiff_t> if your compiler does not support default template arguments. ■

Input iterators are always much more complicated than a simple input loop, so it makes little sense to use them.

Actually, these input and output iterators are curious objects. If oi is an ostream_iterator, then *oi = x causes x to be inserted into the stream. The expression oi++ has no actual meaning. You cannot simply skip a value in an ostream and leave it blank. Input iterators work similarly. This is probably stretching the concept of iterators quite a bit, but some people like it.

## Safe STL

STL has one excellent and innovative idea: a collection of algorithms that works on all containers. However, the designers of STL made the decision that these algorithms also need to work on plain C arrays and that, therefore, iterators need to mimic pointers into C arrays. That causes two major problems. First, C arrays are not objects. Instead, pairs of pointers are used to denote a range in a C array. Thus, all algorithms act on iterator pairs instead of containers. This is pointer-oriented programming, not object-oriented programming. More importantly, because pointers have no intelligence, neither do STL iterators. It is critical that the two iterators in an iterator pair point into the same container, but there is no way of testing that!

It is very easy to make programming errors with iterators. Consider this example:

```
it = find(c.begin(), d.end(), e);
```

By accident, we pass the beginning of c and the end of d to find. Provided that both c and d contain objects of the same type, the compiler cannot catch the error. When the program runs and c.end() is reached, dereferencing it likely leads to a program crash or other flaky behavior (see Figure 17.7).

You'd think nobody would ever be stupid enough to program like this. Actually, it happens all the time as the result of copying and pasting some code, then carelessly renaming the iterators in the copied code.

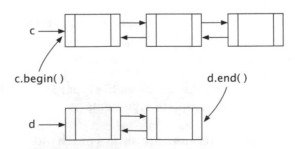

**FIGURE 17.7** Mismatched iterators.

Before

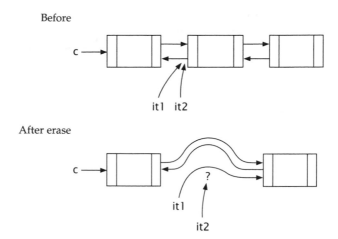

After erase

**FIGURE 17.8** Invalid iterators.

If you have multiple iterators into the same container, and if you change the container through a member function, then the iterators may become invalid. For example, if `it1` and `it2` both point to the same spot in a list `c`, then after `c.erase(it1)`, the iterator `it2` is invalid (see Figure 17.8).

For linked lists and containers implemented as trees, `insert` never invalidates iterators, and `erase` invalidates only those pointing to the erased element. For vectors, those operations that cause reallocation invalidate all iterators (see Figure 17.9).

To summarize, iterators are invalid in the following situations:

- Until they are initialized with a valid iterator
- At the end of a container
- When the container has gone out of scope
- When the container has been replaced with another by assignment
- When the container has been edited (depending on the edit)

You must keep track of that and not dereference an invalid iterator.

Note that no exception is thrown when you use an invalid data iterator. Either the program dies a horrible death right away, or it messes up the container in a subtle way and dies of its wounds later.

To overcome these problems, I wrote a *Safe STL* library, a modification of the part of STL that deals with containers and their iterators. The safe version is completely identical to the regular version, except that all iterators are tested whenever they are used. It makes a great debugging tool. This library is included as part of the code for this book.

Safe STL makes five kinds of checks:

Before:

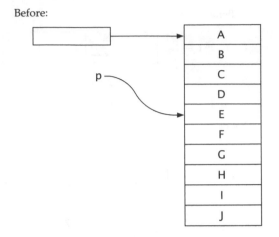

After relocation:

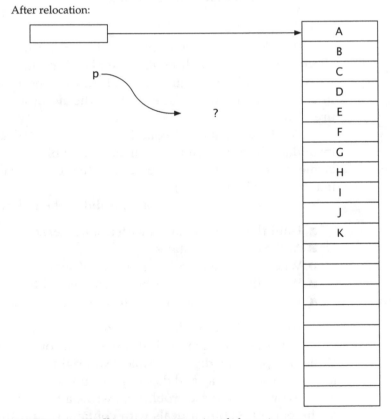

**FIGURE 17.9** Reallocating a vector invalidates iterators.

1. When an iterator is dereferenced, it must actually point to a container and not be past the end.
2. When an iterator is incremented, it must be valid. When an iterator is decremented, it must be valid or past the end.
3. To compute the difference between two iterators, or to compare two iterators, they both must point inside the same container.
4. When a container is accessed through an iterator (for example, `c.erase(it)`), then the iterator must point into that container.
5. When a container is edited, for example, by inserting and erasing elements, the iterators that point to the edit position are updated or invalidated.

Safe STL can detect these errors because its iterator implementation is more involved (and less efficient) than in plain STL. Every iterator has a pointer to the container into which it points (see Figure 17.10). That makes it possible to check if an iterator is valid and points to the correct container. Every container keeps track of all iterators that point to it. When the container goes out of scope, its destructor sets all those iterators to an invalid state. When a container is edited, it can update or invalidate all iterators that point to the edit position.

## Container Classes in Java

### Vectors and Stacks

 C++ has a rich set of containers and algorithms. In contrast, the `java.util` package offers just four container classes: `Vector`, `Stack`, `Hashtable`, and `Properties`.

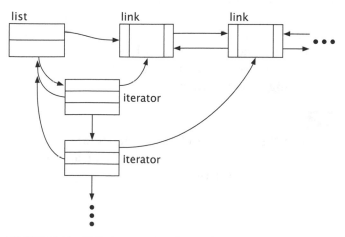

**FIGURE 17.10** Safe iterator implementation.

There is a fundamental difference between containers in C++ and Java. Because C++ has templates, containers are strongly typed: a vector <Employee> is different from a vector<Shape*>. Java has no parameterized types. Therefore, all Java containers store Object references. Unfortunately, this is error-prone: It is easy to accidentally insert an object of the wrong type into a container.

```
Vector staff;
staff.addElement(new Employee("Harry Hacker"));
staff.addElement(new Point(1, 2));
```

The error will manifest itself only when the element is retrieved and cast back to its expected type.

```
for (i = 0; i < staff.size(); i++)
{  Employee e = (Employee)staff.elementAt(i);
      // cast fails if object has wrong type
   e.raise_salary(5.5);
}
```

We have already used the Vector class extensively. The key feature of a vector is that it grows on demand, just like a C++ vector.

Because Java has no operator overloading, the elements of a vector cannot simply be accessed by the [] operator. Instead, you must use

```
e = (Employee)staff.elementAt(i);
```

to read an element and

```
staff.setElementAt(e, i);
```

to set an element. There is a certain amount of cruelty here—why couldn't the designers of this class have called these operations get and set? Element access in vectors may not be strongly typed, but it does require a lot of typing to access them.

**PITFALL**

The StringBuffer class has an operation setCharAt to set a character in the buffer. The parameters of setCharAt are in the opposite order from those of setElementAt! Use

```
b.setCharAt(i, c);
```

to set the ith character in a string buffer,

```
v.setElementAt(x, i);
```

to set the `ith` character in a vector.                    ■

A class `Stack` that supplies the familiar `push` and `pop` operations is derived from `Vector`. This is actually an example of poor object-oriented design. The `Stack` class does not just have the `push` and `pop` operations, but it also inherits all operations from `Vector` such as `setElementAt`, even though they make no sense for a stack.

## Maps

The map class in Java is called a `Hashtable`. You insert key/value pairs with the `put` function and retrieve the value that is associated to a key with the `get` function.

```
Hashtable map = new Hashtable();
map.put("987-98-9996", new Employee("Harry Hacker"));
Employee e = (Employee)map.get("987-98-9996");
```

If there is no value associated with a particular key, then the `get` operation returns `null`.

Keys must be unique. If you call `put` with a key that has already been used, then the existing associated value is replaced with a new one. The `put` function returns the old value—if it returns a non-`null` value, then you know that you replaced an existing one.

The `remove` operation removes a key/value pair from a hash table. It returns the value that is being removed or `null` if the key was not present.

```
map.remove("987-98-9996");
```

As the name suggests, Java maps are implemented as hash tables. Thus, it must be possible to compute hash codes for the key objects. The `Object` class has a `hashCode` operation that computes a hash code by scrambling out object memory address. This default is not very useful—objects with identical contents but different locations in memory have different hash codes. Other Java classes such as `String` redefine the `hashCode` operation to compute a hash code from the contents of the object. You should do the same for your own classes. Simply hash each data field and combine the hash values in some way. Here is an example:

```
class Employee
{  public int hashCode()
```

```
{  int h1 = _name.hashCode();
   int h2 = new Double(_salary).hashCode();
   return 13 * h1 + 17 * h2;
}
  . . .
private String _name;
private double _salary;
}
```

In addition to the hashCode operation, the equals operation must be correctly defined for the key type. After all, it is possible for two unequal objects to have the same hash code, and there must be a way to tell them apart. The Object class defines an equals operation, but it tests only if two objects have the same location in memory, not if their contents are identical.

You need to override the equals operation for any class that you want to use as key type of a map. Here is an example:

```
class Employee
{  public boolean equals(Object b)
   {  if (!b.instanceof(Employee)) return false;
      Employee e = (Employee) b;
      if (!_name.equals(b._name)) return false;
      if (_salary != b._salary) return false;
      return true;
   }
   . . .
   private String _name;
   private double _salary;
}
```

When both hashCode and equals are properly defined, then you can use the class as a key type:

```
Hashtable dept;
Employee harry = new Employee("Harry Hacker", 35000);
dept.put(harry, "Purchasing");
```

## Property Sets

The Properties class is a hash table of a special type, with the following features:

■ Keys and values are strings.
■ The table can be saved to a stream and restored from a stream with a single command.
■ Default values can be specified in a secondary table.

A typical use for a `Properties` object is to store user preferences in a program.

```
Properties preferences = new Properties();
preferences.put("Name", "Harry Hacker");
preferences.put("Color", "Purple");
preferences.put("Font", "18 pt Troglodyte Bold");
```

The `getProperty` (not `get`) operation gets a property, already cast as a string.

```
String font = preferences.get("Font");
```

This table can be written to a file:

```
FileOutputStream out = new FileOutputStream("myprog.ini");
preferences.save(out, "Preferences");
```

The file `myprog.ini` then contains the following lines:

```
#Preferences
#Thu Dec 3 11:30:14 1996
Name=Harry Hacker
Color=Purple
Font=18 pt Troglodyte Bold
```

Of course, the file can be read back in with the `load` command.

```
FileInputStream in = new FileInputStream("myprog.ini");
preferences.load(in);
```

You can build a table of default values and pass that table to the constructor of another property set. Whenever a key is not found in that property set, the default table is searched.

```
Properties defaults = new Properties();
defaults.put("Name", "Unknown");
defaults.put("Color", "Blue");
defaults.put("Font", "10 pt Courier");
Properties preferences = new Properties(default);
preferences.put("Name", "Harry Hacker");
. . .
String name = preferences.getProperty("Name");
   // returns Harry Hacker
String color = preferences.getProperty("Color");
   // returns Blue from the defaults
```

You can even have defaults to defaults, but that probably has no practical use.

## Enumerations

It is easy to find out what is stored in a vector—just traverse it from the beginning to the end.

```
for (i = 0; i < v.size(); i++)
   do something with v.elementAt(i);
```

However, to find what is in a hash table is not so straightforward. Of course, you can't try all possible keys. In C++, you would use an iterator to traverse the container. The Java equivalent is an `Enumeration`.

`Enumeration` is an abstract class with two operations, `hasMoreElements` and `nextElement`. The `hasMoreElements` operation is equivalent to the test `it != c.end()`, but it is more convenient because you can test just the enumeration object, without having to involve the container. Calling `nextElement` returns the current element and advances the position; it is equivalent to calling `*it++` in C++.

Every Java container defines a derived enumeration class that is suitable for traversing that particular data structure. The `elements` operation returns an enumeration object to iterate through the container.

```
Hashtable map = new Hashtable();
. . .
Enumeration enum = map.elements();
while (enum.hasMoreElements())
{  Object obj = enum.nextElement();
   do something with obj;
}
```

You can use the enumeration for generic programming. For example,

```
int count(Enumeration e, Object obj)
{  int c = 0;
   while (e.hasMoreElements())
      if (e.nextElement().equals(obj)) c++;
   return c;
}
. . .
Vector v = new Vector();
Hashtable h = new Hashtable();
Employee harry = new Employee("Harry Hacker");
. . .
int a = count(v.elements(), harry);
int b = count(h.elements(), harry);
```

If you define your own data structure in Java, you should support the `Enumeration` interface.

# Design Hints

This chapter described the design of the standard container libraries in C++ and Java. Here are some hints for designing your own class libraries.

## Naming Consistency

If a consistent naming scheme is important for a single class, it is even more so for a class library. If `add` adds an element to an array, then the operation to add an element to a `map` should also be `add`, not `put`.

Be consistent with capitalization. Users get extremely annoyed when they have to use capitals like `StringBuffer` for some classes, no capitals like `Hashtable` for others. In a nutshell, don't surprise the class users, and don't force them to look up details constantly.

Choose reasonable names. In one widely distributed class library, all containers have an operation `getItemsInContainer`. Contrary to what you may think, it does not simultaneously get all items in the container. Instead, it gets a *count* of the items. Surely a better name can be found for this operation—`count` comes to mind.

For very common names and operations, try to choose short but unabbreviated names. Your users will appreciate it. Use `get` instead of `elementAt`. Try `add` instead of `insert`. One library uses `Set_of_p` for a set of pointers. The "of" adds no information.

Choose good pairs of names for complementary operations: `get`/`set` works better than `get`/`insert`.

## Consistent Mechanisms

Use the same mechanisms to carry out related tasks in different classes. If the vector class can use an arbitrary comparison function to compare elements, the list class should not require a < operator. If a set can be inspected with an iterator, an iterator with the same interface should be available to inspect a map.

## Consistent Error Handling

A class library should present a consistent error model to the user. Recall the actions that an operation can perform when an error condition is detected:

- Ignore or work around the error
- Return a status code
- Place the object in an invalid state
- Throw an exception

Errors of the same severity should be handled in the same way by the various classes in the library. For example, if popping an empty stack simply returns a default value, removing an element from an empty queue should not throw an exception.

## Memory Allocation

The golden rule is this: If the library object allocates memory, the library object deletes it. If the library user allocates memory, the library user deletes it.

This is particularly true for containers. Users may insert the same pointer into multiple containers, and it would be a disaster if the container destructor always deleted all objects inside it. Of course, the container object needs to delete links or other auxiliary memory that it allocated.

Sometimes it makes sense for a container to delete its elements, but the behavior must be clearly advertised. For example, a dialog box object may contain a collection of polymorphic control objects:

```
ConnectionDialog::ConnectionDialog()
{  add(new EditControl(IDD_LABEL));
   add(new RadioButtonControl(IDD_TYPE));
   . . .
}
```

Then the dialog destructor may reasonably delete the control objects.

A popular graphical user interface framework features a rather bizarre convention to remind the programmer not to delete the objects. To add a button or other widget to a dialog box, you write code of the form

```
ConnectionDialog::ConnectionDialog()
{  new EditControl(this, IDD_LABEL);
   new RadioButtonControl(this, IDD_TYPE);
   . . .
}
```

Note that the return value of new is not used. The control element constructors call an operation of the surrounding dialog box (whose address was passed as this) that adds them to a list of child controls. Because you aren't capturing the return value of new, you aren't tempted to delete it.

## Favor the Library User over the Library Implementor

Library designers are often enamored with "elegant" or "extensible" constructs that make their own life, and that of their fellow library designers, easy while forgetting the needs of those who use the library for routine purposes.

STL is an example of this phenomenon. A user who simply wants to find an element in a container would be happier to write

```
p = staff.find(harry);
if (p.is_valid())
    (*p).raise_salary(5.5);
```

instead of

```
p = find(staff.begin(), staff.end(), harry);
if (p != staff.end())
    (*p).raise_salary(5.5);
```

STL cannot do that because of the dogma that iterators must generalize pointers into C arrays. This attitude penalizes those users who have no interest in C arrays.

It is splendid to have libraries that are extensible, but if a library is unusable, it does not matter how extensible it is. Most users simply want to use the library, not extend it, and it is the responsibility of the library designer to keep those users in mind.

# 18

# Multiple
# Inheritance

When deriving from a base class, we obtain two benefits: The derived class inherits the operations of its parent, and all virtual functions can be invoked polymorphically, on either base-class or derived-class objects.

If deriving from one class is beneficial, it seems reasonable that deriving from more than one class would be even better. We inherit even more operations, and polymorphism can be exploited for each parent class. The process of deriving from two or more base classes simultaneously is called *multiple inheritance*.

C++ permits multiple inheritance, and we will study its mechanisms in this chapter. As we will see, multiple inheritance is manageable in simple cases, but it can get very complex if data is inherited from multiple base classes. For that reason, Java does not support multiple base classes. However, Java allows you to inherit from multiple *interfaces*. A Java interface is an abstract class with no data, just virtual functions. We will analyze the Java approach and see why it is a good compromise, delivering most of the essential functionality of multiple inheritance, without the implementation complexities.

## Multiple Base Classes

In this section we will study the mechanics of multiple inheritance in C++. For simplicity, we use a somewhat contrived example. The `Text` class of Chapter 7 implements text that can be positioned anywhere on the screen. Let us implement this class by deriving from both `Shape` and `string`:

```
class Text : public Shape, public string
{
public:
   Text(Point, string);
   void move(int x, int y);
   void scale(Point p, double s);
   void plot(Graphics& g) const;
private:
   Point _start;
};
```

This seems like an excellent idea. As before, `Text` fits into the shape hierarchy. `Text` objects can be included in a list of shapes to be displayed or manipulated. Moreover, we inherit all the functionality of the `string` class.

Operations from both `Shape` and `string` can be applied to `Text` objects:

```
Text t(p, "Hello, World");
if (t == "Howdy") . . . // OK, uses string::operator==
t.move(x, y); // OK
```

From the point of view of object-oriented design, this seems a bit dubious. It is not clear that a text object *is* a string. The substitution principle would demand that a text object can always be used in place of a string object. However, not all inherited operations make sense for texts. For example, what is the meaning of concatenating two texts with different base points? We will discuss this concern in greater detail later in this chapter.

In fact, we have resisted the temptation to derive `Text` from `Point` and `string`.

```
class Text : public Point, public string // DON'T
```

At first glance, this would seem to work very well. The `scale` and `move` operations for `Point` can be inherited without change to transform the base point of the text. But a text object *isn't* a point, and it is not a good idea to pretend otherwise just to save recoding two operations. It would be difficult to

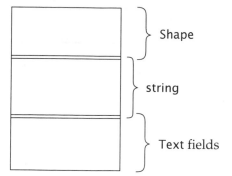

**FIGURE 18.1**   The layout of a text object.

envision a situation in which we could meaningfully exploit polymorphism, applying a virtual function to an object that might either be a point or a text.

An object of type `Text` is made up of three parts, as shown in Figure 18.1: the inherited parts from both base classes and those fields that were added in the `Text` class.

`Text` objects can be converted automatically into either `Shape` or `string` objects. Suppose a function exists to test whether a string is correctly spelled.

```
bool spell_check(const string& s);
```

It can be invoked to check the string portion of a `text` object:

```
Text t(...);
if (spell_check(t)) ... // OK
```

Multiple inheritance is useful to have the same object simultaneously used in multiple ways. For example, the same text object can be contained both in a list of (pointers to) shapes for redisplay and a list of (pointers to) strings for spell checking:

```
list<Shape*> shape_list; // for display
list<string> string_list; // for spell checking
Text* t = new Text(...);
shape_list.push_back(t); // OK
string_list.push_back(*t); // OK
```

When multiple inheritance is involved, the inheritance graph is no longer a tree (see Figure 18.2). In our example, `Text` has two base classes. The inheritance graph is a directed acyclic graph (DAG). There can be no cycles because no class can be its own direct or indirect parent class.

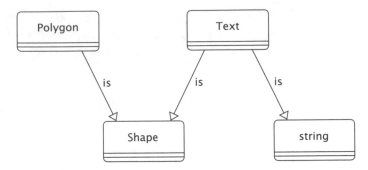

**FIGURE 18.2**   Multiple inheritance for Text.

A class can have any number of base classes, but duplicates are not allowed. For example,

```
class Car : public Tire, public Tire,
   public Tire, public Tire // ERROR
```

is illegal.

## Repeated Base Classes

Although it is not possible to derive directly from the same base class more than once, it is easy to produce scenarios in which a class has a common base class as an ancestor along more than one inheritance path.

Consider a TrafficSign class that is both a text and a polygon.

```
class TrafficSign : public Text, public Polygon
{
public:
   TrafficSign(Point c, int nvert, string t);
   . . .
};

TrafficSign sign(p, 8, "sTOP");
sign[0] = 'S';
x = sign.circumference();
```

This is not necessarily a reasonable way of defining a traffic sign class, but it does show the phenomenon of repeated base classes, illustrated in Figure 18.3. A TrafficSign object contains two shape subobjects, shown in Figure 18.4.

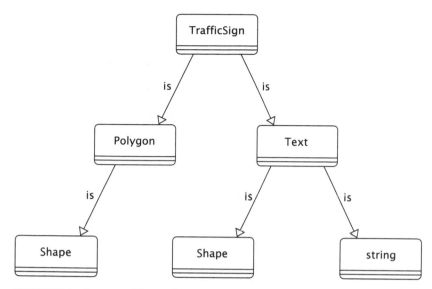

**FIGURE 18.3**  Repeated base classes.

Because Shape is a class without data, this does not seem like a big problem. To make the matter more interesting, let us add a data field to Shape to specify a color:

```
class Shape
{  . . .
```

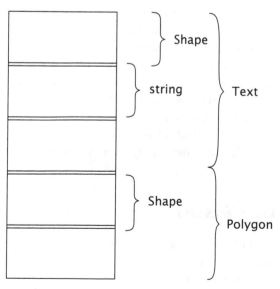

**FIGURE 18.4**  The layout of a traffic sign object.

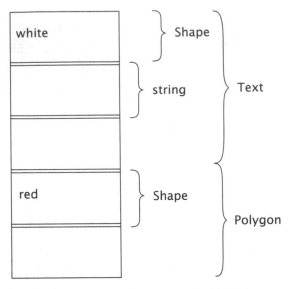

**FIGURE 18.5** Color fields in the shape subobjects.

```
private:
  Color _color;
};
```

Then it is entirely possible that the two shape subobjects contain different color values, as shown in Figure 18.5.

We may indeed want to have different colors for the polygon and the text, in which case the two color fields are just what we need. But the use of inheritance now becomes highly questionable. If `TrafficSign` inherits (indirectly) from `Shape`, each traffic sign is a shape. A shape of what color? The call `sign.color()` is ambiguous and does not compile. (We will see later in this chapter how to make the call unambiguous.) Conceptually, the traffic light objects no longer conform to the `Shape` protocol, and inheritance is out of place.

This situation is typical. Repeated occurrences of the same base indirect class are usually incompatible with the "is-a" relationship.

## Shared Base Classes

Usually, it is not desirable to have repeated copies of a common indirect base class. Rather, all common bases should be merged into one.

Recall the `Person`/`Student`/`Employee`/`Professor` example from Chapter 7, shown in Figure 18.6.

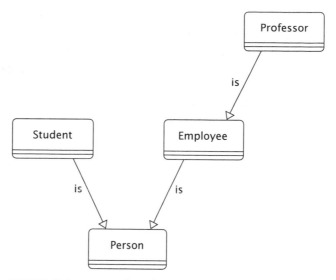

**FIGURE 18.6** Hierarchy of university students and employees.

Let us model a teaching assistant. Teaching assistants are both students and employees:

```
class TeachingAsst : public Student, public Employee
```

TeachingAsst derives twice from Person: once through Student and once through Employee, as shown in Figure 18.7.

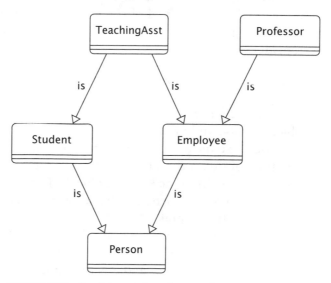

**FIGURE 18.7** Deriving a class for teaching assistants.

Each object of type `TeachingAsst` contains two `Person` subobjects, each with fields for name and address. This makes little sense. Certainly we would want that information to be identical. Replicating the same data in two `Person` subobjects wastes storage and imposes a burden on the programmer to ensure that it stays the same.

With a bit of foresight, it is possible to merge multiple instances of a common indirect base into one. The direct descendants of the common base must prepare for that merging by specifying the inheritance as `virtual`:

```
class Student : virtual public Person
class Employee : virtual public Person
```

The `TeachingAsst` class derives in the usual way from both parents:

```
class TeachingAsst : public Student, public Employee
```

Now all virtual bases are merged together.

The keyword `virtual` is not very descriptive. It has no direct connection with virtual functions. Virtual inheritance is similar to, but not quite the same as, regular inheritance. It affects the layout of the derived class, preparing the base class for merging in subsequent derivations. A better term might be "sharable". Specifically, a pointer is introduced in place of the base object, making it possible to locate the base object elsewhere in the class. Figure 18.8 illustrates the difference between regular and virtual inheritance.

Of course, the compiler must generate code to indirect through that pointer whenever a field of the virtual base class is accessed. The reason for making the virtual base movable becomes apparent when it occurs repeatedly.

```
class TeachingAsst : public Student, public Employee
```

The `TeachingAsst` class contains two pointers to the same `Person` subobject, as shown in Figure 18.9.

Because the access to a `Person` field is automatically translated to follow the pointer, it does not matter that the `Person` subobject is now some distance away from the `Student` object. (In our illustrations, we have placed the shared bases at the end of the derived objects. Naturally, the exact layout depends on the compiler.)

Shared common bases solve the base replication problem of multiple inheritance. The "is-a" nature of inheritance is preserved. A `TeachingAsst` is a `Person` in just one way, and it is the same person, whether first considered as a `Student` or first considered as an `Employee`.

class Student : public Person

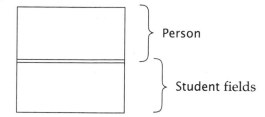

class Student : virtual public Person

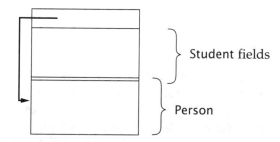

**FIGURE 18.8** The data layout with regular and virtual base classes.

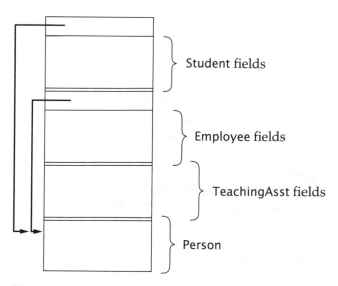

**FIGURE 18.9** A shared base class.

From a theoretical point of view, it would be desirable if sharing of common bases was the default. Some programming languages, such as Eiffel, take just that route. For performance reasons, C++ requires manual intervention. Adding a pointer for every base class, just on the suspicion that some class may later use multiple inheritance and require merging of common bases, is indeed inefficient.

Virtual base classes require foresight. The `TeachingAsst` class is the one creating the sharing problem because it introduces the duplicate `Person` objects, but it can do nothing to solve it. Instead, a previous generation must have anticipated the problem and made `Person` a virtual (sharable) base.

## Mixins

A common use of multiple inheritance is the addition of service protocols to class hierarchies. We have seen examples of such protocols in previous sections. The Microsoft Foundation Classes (MFC) expect that all classes derive from the base class `CObject`. A database library may expect that all classes derive from the base class `DBData`. Neither of these base classes has any data, but they each have virtual functions that define the *protocols* that the derived classes must implement.

If only one of these service protocols is desired, single inheritance is sufficient:

```
class Person : public CObject
```

Multiple inheritance is required if two or more protocols are added:

```
class Person : public CObject, public DBData
```

In this case, we do not use inheritance to express an "is-a" relationship between design level classes, but to add certain implementation mechanisms. The base classes `CObject` and `DBData` have no data fields. Their contribution is to specify an obligation for the derived class to redefine virtual functions.

Derivation from such service classes is often called *mixin* inheritance. (Rumor has it that the term "mixin" originates from the disgusting habit of some ice cream stores to mix pieces of cookies or candy into a scoop of ice cream, at the customer's request.) Mixin classes do not typically share common bases, and it is unlikely that the sharing problem described in the previous section will apply. But if multiple inheritance is anticipated at a higher level, then the mixin inheritance needs to be virtual:

```
class Person : virtual public CObject,
   virtual public DBData
class Robot : virtual public CObject,
   virtual public DBData
class Android : public Person, public Robot
```

## Construction

In the absence of virtual base classes, construction of multiple bases is straightforward. Simply construct all bases in the initializer list:

```
TrafficSign::TrafficSign(Point p, int nvert, string t)
:  Text(p, t),
   Polygon(nvert)
{  // make nvert calls to set_vertex
}
```

In general, the initializer list is a mixture of base and field constructions:

```
Text::Text(Point p, string t, Color c)
:  string(t),
   Shape(c),
   _start(p)
{}
```

Shared base classes raise a knotty problem. An object must be guaranteed to be constructed exactly once. This is in conflict with the normal construction sequence of derived classes. Consider the construction of a teaching assistant object. TeachingAsst invokes the constructors of its bases, Student and Employee. The Student constructor in turn constructs its base, Person, and the Employee constructor constructs its base, Person. Unless special steps are taken, the Person subobject is constructed twice. That might be harmless if the constructor merely zeroes out some fields, or it might be disastrous if the constructor acquires some resources twice that later will be released only once.

To avoid this problem, the normal construction sequence is suspended for virtual bases. Virtual bases are constructed separately from the rest of the object. The preferred method is to supply a default constructor for the virtual base and let the compiler invoke that. It is also possible to construct the virtual base separately from the most derived class:

```
TeachingAsst::TeachingAsst(string name, double salary)
:  Employee(salary),
   Person(name) // Person is an indirect virtual base
{}
```

That can be problematic. What is "most derived" today can be the base of further derivation tomorrow. A constructor that invokes the virtual base constructor cannot be invoked from the next derived class. This again shows that virtual base classes require a high level of planning and foresight.

## Pointer Conversion

Conversion of derived-class pointers to base-class pointers is an essential feature of polymorphism. In single inheritance, pointer conversion between derived and base classes is simple. The address of a derived class object is automatically the address of its base class because the base class is allocated before the derived-class fields. But if a class has more than one base class, this simple rule must fail for all but one of the base classes.

Consider the Text class derived from two base classes. Suppose that the memory layout is as shown in Figure 18.10. (There is no guarantee for that—the compiler is free to sort the base classes in any order.)

A pointer Text* p points automatically to the Shape portion but not the string portion. However, all code that interprets p as a string must have the pointer adjusted to the string subobject. For example, p == "Howdy" must pass the starting address of the string portion to operator==.

The compiler handles this automatically. When a pointer to a derived class is converted to a pointer to one of the base classes (either by an explicit cast or by a base-class operation), the appropriate offset is added to the address:

```
Text* p;
string* q = p; // adds an offset
```

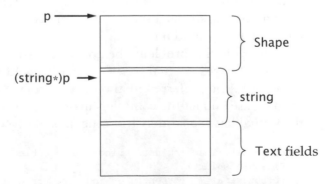

**FIGURE 18.10**   Pointer conversion to a base class.

Occasionally the opposite cast is required: A `string*` pointer is known to actually point to a `Text` object. When performing the cast, the address is adjusted again.

```
string* q;
Text* p = (Text*)q; // subtracts offset
string* s = dynamic_cast<string*>(p); // subtracts offset
```

These adjustments are transparent to the programmer.

C programmers are used to the idea that pointer conversions and casts are "do-nothing" operations. In the presence of multiple inheritance, this is no longer true. In particular, the time-honored strategy of converting pointers to `void*` and casting back can lead to disaster:

```
Text* p;
void* r = p;
string* q = (string*)r; // does not point to a string!
```

As you might suspect, pointer conversion becomes more complex when virtual base classes are involved. Casting to a virtual base is permitted, as shown in Figure 18.11, and the cast follows the indirection:

```
TeachingAsst* t;
Person* p = t; // follows indirection
```

The converse cast cannot be resolved at compile time. If a pointer points to a virtual base, there is no way of knowing where a derived class

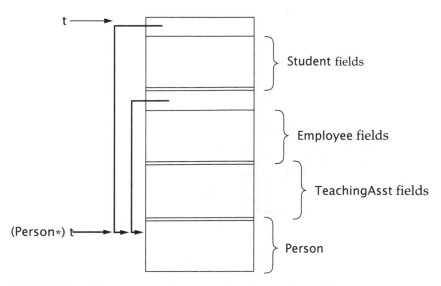

**FIGURE 18.11** Pointer conversion to a virtual base class.

containing it is located. Consider a `Person*` pointer p that we know actually points to a `Student`. The adjustment amount depends on the actual object into which p points. If p points into a plain `Student` object, the adjustment is smaller than if p points into a `TeachingAsst` object, as shown in Figure 18.12.

Because the adjustment cannot be determined at compile time, the static cast from a virtual base to a descendant is illegal:

```
Person* p; // we know it points to a student
Student* s;
s = (Student*) p; // ERROR
```

However, there must be some way of getting back. After all, if `Person` has a virtual function (say `print`) and `Student` redefines that virtual function, the call `p->print()` invokes `Student::print()` (or a descendant). The virtual function mechanism keeps a complete record of the necessary pointer adjustments. Provided the virtual base has at least one virtual function, we can use a dynamic cast to locate the derived-class pointer at run time:

```
s = dynamic_cast<Student*>(p); // OK
```

For that reason, it is a good idea to place at least one virtual function into a virtual base. A virtual destructor is a good choice.

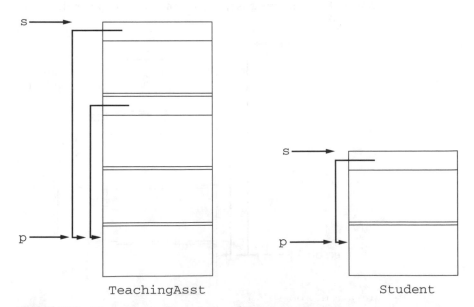

**FIGURE 18.12** Variation in the pointer adjustment amount.

## *Ambiguity Resolution*

### Repeated Feature Names

When inheriting from two base classes, it is possible to inherit operations with the same signature from each class. For example, the `TrafficSign` class inherits a plot function from both `Text` and `Polygon`. This is fine as long as you never call that function.

Suppose `TrafficSign` does not define its own `plot`. Then the call

```
TrafficSign s(...);
s.plot(g);
```

is rejected as ambiguous. You must specify which `plot` you mean:

```
s.Polygon::plot(g);
s.Text::plot(g);
```

### Merging Features

The `plot` function that `TrafficSign` inherits from both base classes should actually be implemented in the derived class:

```
void TrafficSign::plot(Graphics& g) const
{  Polygon::plot(g);
   Text::plot(g);
}
```

Because `plot` is virtual in both base classes, the new `plot` overrides both of their `plot` functions. The `TrafficSign::plot` function is selected if a `TrafficSign` object is accessed either through a `Text*` or a `Polygon*`. hence `TrafficSign::plot` merges the two virtual plot function hierarchies that are inherited from both ancestors.

### Renaming

It is conceivable that a class may derive from two base classes, with virtual functions of the same name and signature but completely different functionalities. It is difficult to come up with realistic examples for this scenario, so we will look at a contrived example instead.

Suppose a class `Story` has a virtual operation `int plot()` that returns a number indicating a description of the story plot (1 = murder, 2 = alien invasion, and so forth). Suppose class `Window` has a virtual operation `int plot()` that plots the contents of the window and returns some number related to the drawing (1 = window hidden, 2 = window iconized, and so forth). We derive `StoryWindow` from both `Story` and `Window` to display the story in a window. (We warned you that this is a contrived example!)

We need to define `StoryWindow::plot()` to display the story text in the window:

```
StoryWindow* sw;
sw->plot(); // plots window with story contents
```

Having done that, we still can find out the story plot:

```
sw->Story::plot();
```

But now we have destroyed the virtual function hierarchy of `Story::plot` in a strange way. If `s` is a pointer to a story, the call `s->plot()` either checks for the plot or renders a window because `s` may point to a plain story or to a `StoryWindow` object. We have merged the two inheritance hierarchies with the same function name even though they should not be merged.

Some object-oriented programming languages, such as Eiffel, let you solve such problems by renaming functions in a derived class. In fact, Eiffel forces you to rename any features that clash with others when you derive from multiple base classes. That neatly solves the problems discussed in this section, but it makes it more difficult to evolve the base classes. Adding a feature to a base class may break a derived class in existing code.

In C++, there is no explicit renaming feature, but renaming can be done by introducing intermediate classes, as shown in Figure 18.13.

```
class WindowRenamer : public Window
{
public:
   virtual void window_plot() const = 0;
   virtual void plot() const { window_plot(); }
};

class StoryWindow : public WindowRenamer, public Story
{
public:
   . . .
   virtual void window_plot() const; // plot text in window
};
```

Consider again the call `s->plot()` for a story pointer `s`. If `s` points to a plain story, then `Story::plot` is invoked. The same is true if `s` points to a `StoryWindow`. There is no problem because that class has not redefined `plot`. Conversely, let `w` point to a `Window` that is actually a `StoryWindow`. The

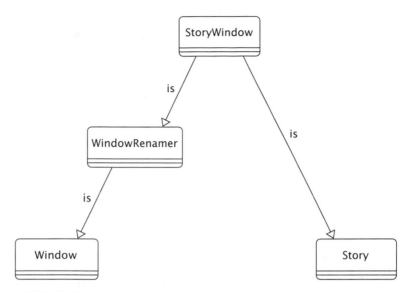

**FIGURE 18.13**   Adding an intermediate class to the story window hierarchy.

call `w->plot()` calls `WindowRenamer::plot()`, the closest function named `plot` on the path from the static type `Window` to the actual type `StoryWindow`. That function calls the renamed `StoryWindow::window_plot`.

This renaming is tedious and unintuitive. Fortunately, it is rarely, if ever, necessary. It is good to know that it can be done because it guarantees that there is a way of combining any number of base classes, no matter what name clashes among virtual functions may exist.

## Virtual Bases and Dominance

A feature of a virtual base class may be redefined along exactly one path without introducing an ambiguity. Suppose the class `Person` defines `id()` to return, say, the social security number, and suppose `Employee` redefines `id()` to return a different employee identification number, as shown in Figure 18.14. When `id()` is invoked on a `Student` object, it clearly refers to `Person::id()`. Hence, asking for the `id()` of a teaching assistant appears to be ambiguous:

```
TeachingAsst ta;
n = ta.id();
```

Is this the student identification number, `Person::id()`, or the employee number?

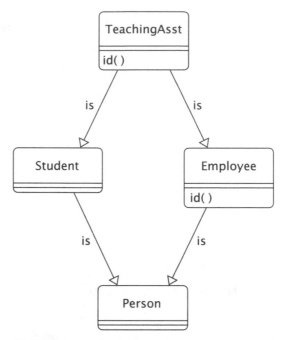

**FIGURE 18.14**  Dominance.

Suppose `id()` is a virtual function. Then we would expect that for every descendant of `Employee` the derived class version `Employee::id()` takes precedence over the base class version `Person::id()`. The social security number of the `Person` subobject of any `Employee` should never be the result of `id()`. Because `TeachingAsst` derives from `Employee`, it would be odd if the base class number could surface again in any way, even to create an ambiguity.

The dominance rule formalizes this reasoning. It states that a name in a virtual base class can be redefined along exactly one inheritance path without creating an ambiguity. This holds for any feature name—in particular, for both virtual and nonvirtual functions.

In our example, the call `ta.id()` is considered nonambiguous and refers to the redefinition `Employee::id()`. It does not matter whether `id` is a virtual function. Of course, if `Student` were also to redefine `id()`, an ambiguity would result.

The dominance rule applies only to virtual base classes. If `Person` were a nonvirtual base, then the call to `id()` would be ambiguous because there would be two distinct `Person` objects: a student object with its notion of identification number and an employee object with a different notion.

## Repeated Bases

Consider the `TrafficSign` class that derives from `Text` and `Polygon`. Suppose we want to place a `TrafficSign` object onto a display list of shapes. Because `TrafficSign` derives indirectly from `Shape` (even twice!), it should be possible to convert a `TrafficSign*` into a `Shape*`:

```
list<Shape*> figure;
figure.push_back(new TrafficSign(...)); // ERROR
```

But the compiler does not admit this conversion. Looking at the data layout, shown in Figure 18.15, reveals why. Because there are actually two copies of a `Shape` object in a `TrafficSign`, the compiler does not know to which one you want to point.

You can resolve the ambiguity by explicitly casting to one or the other direct base.

```
figure.push_back((Polygon*)new TrafficSign(...)); // OK
```

Because the direct bases of `TrafficSign` are distinct, casting to either selects a path to one of the repeated bases.

This ambiguity shows the conflict between repeated occurrences of a base class and the concept of inheritance as an "is-a" relationship.

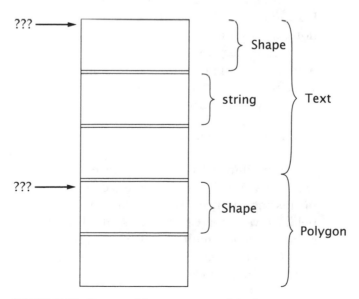

**FIGURE 18.15**  Repeated bases cause ambiguity.

# *Is Multiple Inheritance Useful?*

## Multiple Inheritance Increases Complexity

Everyone will agree that multiple inheritance is far more complex than single inheritance. Virtual base classes are a difficult programming construct. The rules for ambiguity resolution are arcane.

There is one case in which multiple inheritance is simple: when inheriting from disjoint base classes. Disjoint base classes have nothing in common. There are no common base classes further down the hierarchy; hence, there are no repeated or shared bases. There are no operations with a common signature; therefore, there are no name clashes, and no virtual functions are redefined along more than one path.

The most common case for this disjoint inheritance is the addition of mixins. When the protocol for a certain functionality, such as persistence, is expressed in a base class, and more than one functionality is desired for a particular class, then one simply derives from all these base classes. As long as there are no name conflicts, this is straightforward.

## Conceptually Correct Multiple Inheritance Is Rare

Inheritance models the "is-a" relationship. It turns out to be quite uncommon for one class to be a special case of two separate classes.

Consider the `Text` class. Multiple inheritance was not forced on us. Instead of inheriting from `Shape` and `string`, we could have used aggregation and used a data field of type `Shape` or `string` (or both). By deriving `Text` from `Shape`, we are able to place a `Text` object onto a list of `Shape*` pointers and apply `virtual` functions. That is a true benefit. By deriving `Text` from `string`, we were able to reuse the `operator==` function. We could have added an operation

```
bool Text::equals(string s).
```

Inheritance from `string` saved us from that effort. But note that `string` has no virtual functions, so we gain no advantage of polymorphism in this inheritance. Deriving `Text` from `Shape`, and adding a `string` data field, as we did in Chapter 7, is simple and does not give up much expressiveness. Hence, multiple inheritance is not necessary here.

Consider the `TrafficSign` class. Is a traffic sign a shape consisting of text and a polygon?

```
class TrafficSign : public Shape
{
```

```
    Text _notice;
    Polygon _border
};
```

A polygon with some text inside?

```
class TrafficSign : public Polygon { Text _notice; };
```

Text surrounded by a polygon?

```
class TrafficSign : public Text { Polygon _border; };
```

Both text and polygon?

```
class TrafficSign : public Text, public Polygon { };
```

All these seem reasonable. The "is-a" versus "has-a" test is inconclusive here. An advantage of using inheritance is the possibility of exploiting polymorphism. Do we envision a situation in which we have a container of objects, some of which are mere polygons, others traffic signs? A container of objects, some of which are plain text, the other traffic signs? Neither seems terribly likely. The only meaningful base class is Shape. To plot traffic signs, they may well be located in a display list of shapes. In this case, inheritance from both Text and Polygon is the worst solution. A polygon is no longer a shape unless Shape is a virtual base class of Text and Polygon.

Some authors believe that this pattern is universal and that multiple inheritance has not proven to be a useful feature in actual programming. At the time of this writing, there seem to be no known examples that are generally acknowledged as compelling evidence of the usefulness of multiple inheritance. See [Cargill], ch. 9, for more information on this topic.

The literature contains lots of silly examples (like our StoryWindow). Figure 18.16 shows a common one ([Stroustrup], p. 207).

On the face of it, it makes a lot of sense. A window with a border is a special case of a window; ditto a window with a menu; and windows that have both borders and menus are special cases of both. However, as a programming style, it must fail. Windows have other decorations, such as scrollbars, toolbars, and message panes. If we use inheritance, we end up with 32 classes and a bewildering collection of virtual base classes. It seems much better to model borders and menus as attributes. A window *has* a border (possibly of zero thickness), and it *has* a menu (possibly with no options).

We all use one library of classes that was built with multiple inheritance: iostream. Figure 18.17 shows a part of the class relationship graph.

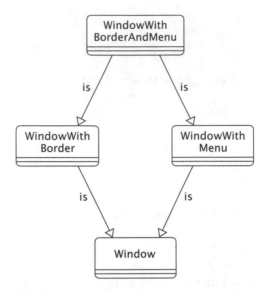

**FIGURE 18.16**   A hierarchy for windows with menus and borders.

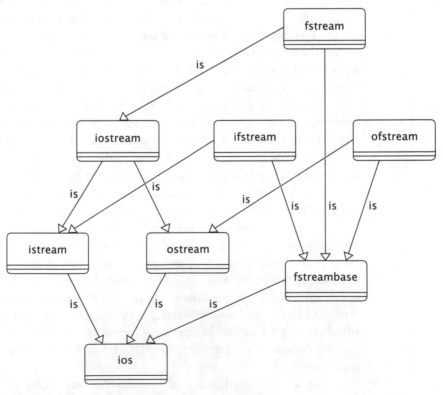

**FIGURE 18.17**   A portion of the `iostream` hierarchy.

Both `istream` and `ostream` derive from a class named `ios` that keeps track of format and error state. It is not intuitively clear what an `ios` is, so it is difficult to say what is more appropriate: does an `istream` have an `ios`, or is it an `ios`? The class `ios` has no virtual functions, and polymorphism is not an issue. It does make sense that an `iostream` is both an `istream` and an `ostream`. Because each of them has an `ios` subobject, the inheritance from `ios` must be virtual.

This splendid idea has been completely given up for the other stream classes. The file stream class for both input and output does not derive from `ifstream` and `ofstream`, and neither does `stringstream` derive from `istringstream` and `ostringstream`, undoubtedly because of the complexity of factoring out yet more common information into virtual base classes. Multiple inheritance can be avoided altogether, at the cost of repeating some code, by having `iostream` derive directly from `ios`. This does not have to be done, but it can be done easily. The fact that multiple inheritance is used in the `iostream` class library does not prove that it is a necessary design feature.

The point is not that multiple inheritance should be avoided at all cost, merely that the gain from using it must be weighed against the cost of the added complexity.

# Java Interfaces

## Implementing Interfaces

 As we saw from the discussion of multiple inheritance in C++, inheriting data from multiple base classes is very complex. Pointers must be adjusted, and in some cases common base classes must be merged. The designers of Java decided that the disadvantages of a complex data layout outweighed the advantages of multiple inheritance. Hence, in Java, a class can have only a single base class.

There are, however, occasions when it is desirable to take an object reference and cast it to one of several types. Consider a class `Animation` that implements an applet showing an animation. To be an applet, the class must inherit from `Applet` and implement operations such as `init`, `start`, and `paint`. To have the animation run in a thread, the class must derive from `Thread` and implement a `run` operation that keeps changing the image. Thus, `Animation` would need to derive both from `Applet` and from `Thread`, which is not possible in Java.

The sole purpose of deriving from `Thread` is to place the code that changes the picture into an operation with a known name, namely `run`, so that the thread mechanism can call that function.

If you just need to implement a function, or a set of functions, with fixed names, then you don't actually need a base class but can use an *interface* instead. An interface has no data, only abstract functions. For example, the Java standard library defines

```
interface Runnable
{  public void run();
}
```

Then the `Animation` class can derive from `Applet` and *implement* the `Runnable` interface:

```
class Animation extends Applet implements Runnable
{  public void init() { . . . }
   public void start() { . . . }
   public void paint(Graphics g) { . . . }
   public void run() { . . . }
   . . .
}
```

The key observation is that an `Animation` object can be cast both to its base class and its base interfaces:

```
Animation a;
Applet ap = a; // OK
Runnable r = a; // OK
```

We take advantage of the second cast to start a thread, using the constructor `Thread(Runnable r)`. That constructor makes a thread whose `start` operation calls `r.run()`. Here we pass `this` to the thread constructor, taking advantage of the fact than an `Animation` reference can be cast to a `Runnable` reference.

```
class Animation extends Applet implements Runnable
{  public void start()
   {  Thread t = new Thread(this);
      t.start(); // calls this.run()
   }
   public void run() { . . . }
   . . .
}
```

Another common interface is `Cloneable`. A class must implement the `Cloneable` interface to demonstrate its ability to clone itself.

```
class Date implements Cloneable
{ . . .
}
```

Actually, `Cloneable` is a very strange interface. It has neither data nor operations:

```
interface Cloneable
{
}
```

Its sole reason for existence is to tag classes that know about cloning. The `Object.clone` operation, which makes a bitwise copy of an object, first checks if the object has implemented `Cloneable`.

```
class Object
{  Object clone()
   {  if (!(this instanceof Cloneable))
        throw new CloneNotSupportedException();
      . . .
   }
   . . .
}
```

By implementing `Cloneable`, a class agrees that it understands the cloning process.

A class can implement as many interfaces as it likes.

```
class Animation extends Applet implements Runnable, Cloneable
```

By allowing an object to be cast to multiple interfaces while avoiding the complexity of having multiple base objects, Java has found an excellent balance betwcen expressiveness and simplicity.

## Callbacks

A key use for interfaces is to implement *callbacks*. Suppose we want to be notified whenever a button has been clicked. We don't want to go into the details of Java event handling—see [Cornell & Horstmann] for details. But the idea is that an object can register with the window containing the button, and when a button is clicked, it is notified of the event.

When the button click comes, we want to call

```
obj.clicked(button);
```

for every registered object `obj`. It is then necessary that `obj` is of a type that supports the `clicked` operation. We can enforce that by specifying a `Clickable` interface:

```
interface Clickable
{  public void clicked(Button b);
}
```

An object of a class that implements `Clickable` can register itself with the window. The window keeps a vector of registered objects. It calls the `clicked` operation on all of them when a button is clicked.

```
class ButtonPanel extends Panel
{  public void register(Clickable obj)
   {  _registered.addElement(obj);
   }

   public void action(Event evt, Object arg)
   {  if (evt.target instanceof Button)
      {  Button button = (Button)evt.target;
         for (int i = 0; i < _registered.size(); i++)
         {  Clickable obj = (Clickable)_registered.elementAt(i);
            obj.clicked(button);
         }
      }
   }
   . . .
   private Vector _registered;
}
```

Here is how a window can repaint itself whenever a button is clicked. The window needs to implement the `Clickable` interface and put the code for the button click action into the `clicked` operation.

```
class ResultWindow implements Clickable
{  public void clicked(Button b)
   {  if (b.getLabel() == "Compute")
      {  computeResult();
         repaint();
      }
   }
   . . .
}
```

That window must be registered with the `ButtonWindow`.

```
class ClickerApplet extends Applet
{  public void init()
   {  _rw.add(new Button("Compute"));
      _rw.register(rw);
   }
   . . .
```

```
      private ResultWindow _rw;
      private ButtonPanel _bp;
}
```

Now, whenever a button is clicked, the `_rw` object is notified through the `clicked` callback. It checks if the button with the label `"Compute"` is clicked and if so, computes the result and displays it.

The drawback of using interfaces for callbacks is that the *name* of the callback is fixed by the interface. In our example, the callback *must* be called `clicked`. Suppose we want to give an `Employee` object a raise every time a button is clicked; then we have a problem. The `Employee` class does not implement `Clickable` and does not have a `clicked` operation. Instead, we would need to design a whole new class

```
class ClickableEmployee extends Employee implements Clickable
```

That sounds like a lot of trouble just to get a button click notification. In contrast, in C++, we could pass a function pointer, or an object with an overloaded `()` operator, to the `ButtonPanel` and request to be called back through that function pointer or object. But Java does not have function pointers or overloaded operators.

In the next section, we will see how a new Java feature, *inner classes*, is designed to make it easier to implement callbacks.

## Inner Classes

We have seen in Chapter 10 that a Java class can define another class inside the class scope. However, that chapter did not show a compelling use for that feature. Inner classes were designed to make it easier to implement classes "on the fly", in particular for implementing callbacks. Inner classes are a new feature announced for Java 1.1. However, at the time of this writing, no actual implementation of this feature was available. There may be minor differences between the behavior described in this section and the behavior that Java 1.1 will implement.

We will continue with the `Clickable` interface developed in the preceding section. Let us first develop a simple example, a callback that keeps track of how many times a button has been clicked.

```
class ClickerApplet extends Applet
{ class Counter implements Clickable
   { public void clicked(Button b)
      { _clicks++;
```

516 ■ CHAPTER EIGHTEEN

```
            // accesses the _clicks field of the outer class!
      }
   }

   public void init()
   {  _clicks = 0;
      _bp = new ButtonPanel();
      _bp.add(new Button("Click me"));
      _bp.register(new Counter());
   }
   . . .
   private ButtonPanel _bp;
   private int _clicks;
}
```

The inner class is printed in boldface. The most remarkable aspect is
that the `clicked` operation of the inner class has access to the data fields of
its surrounding class! Actually, if there are multiple instances of the outer
class, it is not clear which of the instances the inner class accesses. The rule
is that an inner class can access the data fields *of the object that creates it.*

Using inner classes dramatically eases the work for defining callbacks.
Without the inner class feature, the `Counter` class would have been a top-
level class, and there would have to be some communication path between
the `Counter` and `ClickerApplet` classes. Here is a possible solution, with the
added overhead shown in bold:

```
class ClickerApplet extends Applet
{  public void init()
   {  _clicks = 0;
      _bp = new ButtonPanel();
      _bp.add(new Button("Click me"));
      _bp.register(new Counter(this));
   }

   public void incrementCounter() { _clicks++; }
   . . .
   private ButtonPanel _bp;
   private int _clicks;
}

class Counter implements Clickable
{  public Counter(ClickerApplet a) { _applet = a; }
   public void clicked(Button b)
   {  _applet.incrementCounter();
   }
   private ClickerApplet _applet;
}
```

Allowing inner classes to access the data fields of the objects that create them avoids this added communication overhead.

Furthermore, it is even possible to make inner classes *anonymous:*

```
class ClickerApplet extends Applet
{  public void init()
   {  _clicks = 0;
      _bp = new ButtonPanel();
      _bp.add(new Button("Click me"));
      Clickable c = new Clickable()
      {  public void clicked(Button b)
         {  _clicks++;
         }
      }
      _bp.register(c);
   }
   . . .
   private ButtonPanel _bp;
   private int _clicks;
}
```

The key code is

```
Clickable c = new Clickable()
{  public void clicked(Button b)
   {  _clicks++;
   }
}
```

This means "Make a new object of a class that implements `Clickable` and that increments the _clicks counter whenever its `clicked` operation is called. Don't bother to give that class a name—we only need a single object."

You can even dispense with the variable c:

```
_bp.register(new Clickable()
   {  public void clicked(Button b)
      {  _clicks++;
      }
   });
```

This is quite an amazing shorthand, which makes defining callbacks with a minimum of fuss possible. Admittedly, the code looks quite obscure, and only time will tell if this idiom becomes second nature to Java programmers.

## *Design Hints*

### Beware of the Complexities of Multiple Inheritance

Multiple inheritance is much more intricate than single inheritance. It is complex to program, and you might produce more errors in your code as a result. It is complex to implement, and your compiler writer might have had a less than perfect understanding of all the subtleties.

For those reasons, the advice to use inheritance for "is-a" design relationships only, not for convenience, holds even more strongly for multiple inheritance. In many cases, multiple inheritance is not terribly convenient.

### Avoid Repeated Base Classes

Suppose a class D inherits from two base classes B and C. The easy case is if B and C have nothing in common.

If the base classes themselves have a common base A, that base should be a shared base, and virtual inheritance will be required to derive B and C from A.

If it is a repeated base, it is likely that not all inheritance represents an "is-a" relationship. A D object cannot be an A object in two ways.

### Initialize Virtual Base Classes with the Default Constructor

There are two ways to initialize a virtual base: with a default constructor or explicitly from the "most derived" class. The notion of "most derived" is not stable. As soon as another class is derived, that one becomes the most derived class.

If you must initialize the virtual base explicitly from a derived-class constructor, also supply some other constructor for that derived class that doesn't initialize the virtual base. Otherwise, it is impossible to derive further classes from that class.

### Place a Virtual Destructor into Each Base Class

Destroying an object with multiple bases is complicated by the fact that the destruction may be invoked through a pointer to any one of the bases. For example, a TeachingAsst object can be held in, and deleted from, a list of

`Student*` or `Employee*` pointers. Either way, we don't just want the `Student` or `Employee` destructor called.

Place a virtual destructor (that is probably empty) into the `Person` base. That makes all derived destructors virtual. If there is more than one common base, place virtual destructors into all of them.

C H A P T E R

# 19

# Frameworks

## *Designing for Inheritance*

We have seen many cases in which inheritance relationships between classes were discovered in the design phase and then modeled in C++ with inheritance and virtual functions. In this chapter we will go beyond that point of view and discuss how to design classes that serve as the basis from which other, as yet undiscovered, classes may inherit.

## Protocol Specification

By specifying a set of virtual functions, a base class can impose a protocol on its derived classes, relieving the derived-class designer from the task of rediscovering the required functionality.

Consider a class `Window` to describe a window in a graphical user interface environment. The base class `Window` is supplied as a basis for derivation. The programmer of an actual application derives classes, such as `SpreadsheetWindow` and `GraphWindow`, from the class `Window`.

Suppose the contents of a window on the screen needs to be redrawn, perhaps because another window temporarily popped up before it and was removed or because the window was restored from its icon. Typically, graphical user interfaces do not cache pixels of obscured or minimized windows but rely on the ability of each window to repaint itself when notified in some way.

The details of the notification mechanism can be handled by the base class `Window`. That class specifies a pure virtual function

```
Window::paint()
```

whose task is to repaint the window. Each class that derives from `Window` must redefine `paint` to render its data in the form of spreadsheet cells, a graph, or some other representation.

Because `Window::paint` is a pure virtual function for which no definition is supplied, each derived class must override this function. Similarly, the base class will specify virtual functions for other actions; for example, reaction to keystrokes or mouse clicks. In this way, the base class enforces the services that a derived class must provide to fit into the windowing system.

Not all virtual functions need be pure. If a satisfactory default can be specified in the base class, the operation can be implemented at that level and overridden by only those derived classes for which the generic behavior is inappropriate. For example, to react to a timer event, `Window` may supply a virtual function whose action is to ignore the timer. Those classes that wish to take some action that depends on the system timer, such as animation, can redefine the virtual function. Most classes will be happy with the default.

Understanding the event flow in a graphical user interface environment requires expert knowledge. This knowledge can be mapped into the design of a base class or a set of base classes (the *framework*), which can be extended by a programmer who is an expert in the application domain but not in the user interface architecture. The base class specifies what services a derived class must provide to fit into the system. The application programmer overrides the virtual functions to display the application data or to handle user commands. These application-specific tasks cannot be undertaken by the basic `Window` class. Conversely, the application programmer is completely freed from user-interface issues, such as moving, sizing, and scrolling of windows.

## Operation Sequencing

A base class that supplies virtual functions for derivation may call these virtual functions in other operations. For example, `Window` may have an operation that takes care of scrolling. That operation changes the coordinate origin, moves existing pixels, and then invokes the virtual `paint` function to render the portion of the image that has been scrolled in. The base class has no idea *what* is being painted, but it knows *when* the painting is necessary.

In this way, the base class imposes an *order of execution* on the services that the derived classes supply.

The most compelling example of operation sequencing occurs in an application framework. An *application framework* consists of a set of classes that implement all services common to a certain type of application. To build an actual application, the programmer derives from some of the framework classes and adds operations that are specific to the application that the programmer is building.

However, the programmer has little or no influence as to the order in which these operations are called. The program starts with `main` (or its equivalent, such as `WinMain`), but that function is somewhere in the framework. Execution starts, and eventually some objects of the programmer-defined classes are constructed. Then the framework calls their operations in the order that it deems appropriate.

The programmer who builds an application on top of an application framework handles isolated events, such as painting, menu commands, mouse clicks, timer events, and so on. Whenever a particular event is handled, control immediately returns to the code in the framework.

It is the role of the framework to determine which function to call, and its designers have expert knowledge to call the correct functions in the correct order. It is the job of the application programmer to redefine those functions to fulfill the application-specific tasks.

## `Applet` *as a Simple Framework*

 Recall that Java applets are Java programs that run inside a Web browser (see Figure 19.1).

To design an applet, you must write a class `MyApplet` that derives from `Applet`. You must override some or all of the following functions:

- `init`: Called exactly once, when the applet is first loaded. Purpose: Initialize data structures, add user interface elements.
- `start`: Called when the applet is first loaded and every time the user reenters the Web page containing the applet. Purpose: Start or restart threads that perform animation or other tasks.

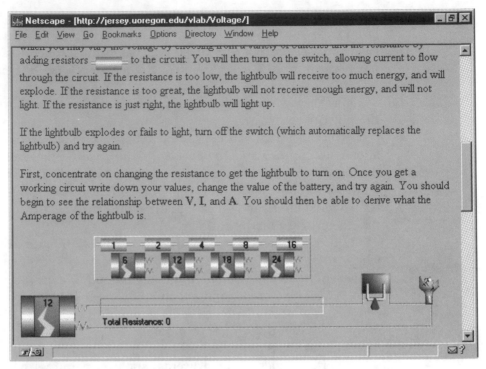

**FIGURE 19.1**  An applet.

- ■ stop: Called when the user leaves the applet and when the browser terminates. Purpose: Stop threads from updating the applet to conserve computing resources while the applet is not being viewed.
- ■ destroy: Called when the browser terminates. Purpose: Relinquish any resources that were acquired during init or other processing.
- ■ paint: Called when the applet window needs repainting. Purpose: Redraw the window contents to reflect the current state of the applet data structures.
- ■ action: Called when a so-called *action event* occurs. Action events are button clicks and the selection of a check box, choice list, or menu item. Purpose: To find out which action event occurred and to handle it.
- ■ mouseDown, mouseDrag, mouseUp: Called when a mouse event occurs. Purpose: To handle mouse events.

In this book, we will not discuss in detail how to write applets. For a discussion on the Java user interface and threads and their applications for building applets, see [Cornell & Horstmann].

The java.applet package is a simple application framework: It contains base classes to make applets, and the user adds classes and overrides operations to make an actual applet. Note that the main program is not supplied by the programmer of a specific applet and that the sequencing of the operations that the programmer supplies is under the control of the framework.

Here is a sample applet that reacts to mouse clicks. When you click with the mouse, a new point is added to the screen. In addition, the *regression line,* that is, the straight line with the best fit through the cloud of points, is computed and plotted (see Figure 19.2).

To implement this applet, we derive a class CloudApplet from Applet and override two operations: mouseDown and paint. The paint operation draws all points and the regression line. The mouseDown operation adds the mouse position to the vector of points and calls repaint. That causes the framework to call paint.

Here is the complete code of the applet. Note how the code defines only the reactions to two isolated events and that the framework calls these event handlers as it sees fit.

```
import java.applet.*;
import java.awt.*;
import java.util.*;
public class CloudApplet extends Applet
```

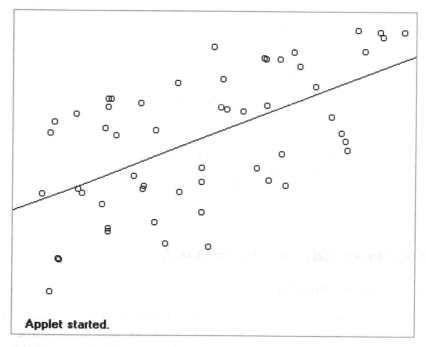

Applet started.

**FIGURE 19.2**  The cloud applet.

```
{  public boolean mouseDown(Event evt, int x, int y)
   {  _points.addElement(new Point(x, y));
      repaint();
      return true;
   }
   public void paint(Graphics g)
   {  for (int i = 0; i < _points.size(); i++)
      {  Point p = (Point)_points.elementAt(i);
         g.drawOval(p.x - 2, p.y - 2, 5, 5);
      }
      if (regression())
      {  int xright = size().width;
         g.drawLine(0, (int)b, xright, (int) (m * xright + b));
      }
   }
   private boolean regression()
   {  double sx = 0;
      double sxx = 0;
      double sy = 0;
      double sxy = 0;
      int n = _points.size();
      if (n < 2) return false;
      for (int i = 0; i < n; i++)
      {  Point p = (Point)_points.elementAt(i);
         int x = p.x;
         int y = p.y;
         sx += x;
         sy += y;
         sxx += x * x;
         sxy += x * y;
      }
      double den = sxx - sx * sx / n;
      if (den == 0) return false;
      m = (sxy - sx * sy / n) / den;
      b = (sy - m * sx) / n;
      return true;
   }
   private Vector _points = new Vector();
   private double m;
   private double b;
}
```

# A Diagram Editor Framework

## The Problem Domain

In this section we will develop a simple application framework in which the programmer has to add a number of classes to complete an application. The problem domain that we address is the *interactive editing of diagrams*. A *dia-*

*gram* is made up of *nodes* and *edges* that have certain shapes. Consider a class diagram. The nodes are rectangles, and the edges are either arrows or lines with diamonds or circles. A different example is an electronic circuit diagram, where vertices are transistors, diodes, resistors, and capacitors. Connections are simply wires. There are numerous other examples, such as chemical formulas, flowcharts, organization charts, and logic circuits.

Traditionally, a programmer who wanted to implement, say, a class diagram editor starts from scratch and creates an application that can edit just class diagrams. If the programmer is lucky, code for a similar program, say a flowchart editor, is available for inspection; however, it may well be difficult to separate the code that is common to all diagrams from the flowchart-specific tasks, and much of the code may need to be recreated for the class diagram editor.

In contrast, a framework encapsulates those aspects that are common to all diagrams and provides a way for specific diagram types to express their special demands.

## The User Interface

Many of the tasks, such as selecting, moving, and connecting elements, are similar for all editors. Let us be specific and describe the user interface that our very primitive editor will have. The screen is divided into two parts, shown in Figure 19.3.

On the left is a collection of buttons, one for each node type and one for each edge type. We will see later how a specific instance of the application supplies the icons for the buttons. Exactly one of the node buttons and one of the edge buttons are active at any time.

At the bottom of the display is a selector for the edit mode. There are three modes: insert, erase, and move. In insert mode, new nodes or edges are inserted. In erase mode, clicking on an existing node or edge erases it. In move mode, clicking and dragging a node moves it to another location.

On the right is the diagram drawing area. The mouse is used for drawing. The mouse events consist of clicking (pushing down the physical button on the mouse and then releasing it) on a node, an edge, a button, or empty space, and dragging (pushing down the mouse button, moving the mouse to another location, and then releasing the mouse button). The mouse actions depend on the edit mode:

- When clicking on an empty space in insert mode, a new node is inserted. Its type is that of the currently selected node in the icon bar.
- When clicking inside an existing node in insert mode and dragging the cursor inside another existing node, then a new edge is inserted. Its type is that of the currently selected edge in the icon bar.

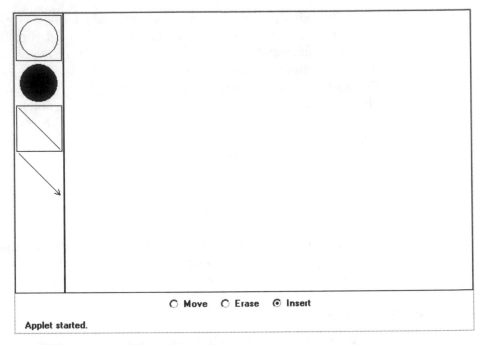

**FIGURE 19.3** Graph editor screen.

- When clicking inside an existing node in erase mode, that node and all edges that meet it are erased.
- When clicking anywhere on an edge in erase mode, that edge is erased.
- When clicking inside an existing node in move mode, the node can be dragged to a new location. All edges are updated as well.

This graph editor framework is written in Java.

Of course, programs written with this framework are so primitive as to be barely usable. There is no provision to supply text labels for edges and nodes. There is no scrolling to handle larger diagrams. There is no cut and paste. The graphs created by the program user cannot be saved or restored. These features could be handled by an extended version of this framework. This example is kept as simple as possible to show the main concept: the separation of framework code and application-specific code.

## Division of Responsibility

When designing a framework, we must divide responsibilities between the framework and specific instances of the framework. For example, it is clear that the code to render a transistor-shaped node is not part of the general framework—only of the electric circuit instance.

Rendering the shapes of nodes and edges cannot be part of the framework—it depends on the actual shapes in a particular application, and it must be deferred to the application programmer. The same holds for *hit testing:* finding out whether a node or edge is hit by a mouse click. This can be tricky for odd shapes and cannot be the responsibility of the framework.

Drawing the shapes of the node and edge icons is an instance-level task, but rendering the button column and managing the mouse clicks is the job of the framework. This brings up a very interesting problem. The framework must have some idea of the node and edge classes in the application so that it can tell each type of node or edge to render its icon in a button. The application must give the framework a list of all type names that it needs.

```
String[] get_types()
{  String[] types =
   { "Transistor", "Capacitor", "Resistor", "Wire" };
   return types;
}
```

The framework must turn each of these strings into an object. These objects are used to draw the icons. When a user inserts a new node or edge, the currently active icon object is cloned. Here is what the framework does to turn type names into node and edge objects:

```
String[] typenames = get_types();
   // get type names from derived class
for (i = 0; i < typenames.length; i++)
{  Class cls = Class.forName(typenames[i]);
      // get the Class object for the type name
   Object obj = Class.newInstance(cls);
      // make an object of that class
   if (obj instanceof Node)
     add to node icon vector
   else if (obj instanceof Edge)
     add to edge icon vector
}
```

To render the button icons, the framework traverses the collection of node and edge class objects and invokes `plot_icon` on each of them.

## Framework Classes

The framework defines base classes `Node` and `Edge` with the following interface:

```
abstract class Node implements Cloneable
{  public abstract void plot(Graphics g);
   public abstract Rectangle enclosing_rect();
   public abstract boolean is_inside(Point p);
   public abstract Point boundary_point(Point exterior);
   public Object clone()
   {  try
      { return super.clone();
      } catch(CloneNotSupportedException e)
      { return null;
      }
   }
   public void move(Point p) { _center = p; }
   public Point center() { return _center; }

   private Point _center;
}

abstract class Edge implements Cloneable
{  public abstract void plot(Graphics g, Point a, Point b);
   public abstract boolean is_on(Point p, Point a, Point b);
   public Object clone()
   {  try
      { return super.clone();
      } catch(CloneNotSupportedException e)
      { return null;
      }
   }
   public void plot(Graphics g) {. . .}
   public boolean is_on(Point p) {. . .}
   public Node from() { return _from; }
   public Node to() { return _to; }
   public void connect(Node f, Node t) { _from = f; _to = t; }

   private Node _from;
   private Node _to;
};
```

These are abstract classes, and the programmer using this framework must derive node and edge types from these bases and override the virtual functions:

```
class Transistor extends Node
class Wire extends Edge
```

The graph editor uses the following classes:

■ GraphEditor, derived from Applet. Its job is to hold the state of the user interface, namely the current editing mode and node and edge types.

- IconCanvas, derived from Canvas. In Java, a canvas is a rectangular area on which graphics can be drawn. It draws the icons for the node and edge types and handles the mouse clicks to select the current types.
- GraphCanvas, also derived from Canvas. It holds the nodes and edges that the user entered, and it handles the mouse clicks and drags for the editing.

Interestingly enough, the abstract classes for nodes and edges suffice to implement these classes completely. The mechanics of mouse movement, rubber bands (outlines that show the positions of objects as the user drags them with the mouse), and screen update are completely solved at this level and are of no concern to the programmer using the framework. Because all drawing and mouse operations are taken care of in the framework classes, the programmer building a graphical editor on top of the framework can simply focus on implementing the node and edge types.

The programmer must perform one important task: It must inform the framework of the names of the node and edge types that are actually used, by overriding the get_types function of the GraphEditor class.

```
class CircuitEditor extends GraphEditor
{  public String[] get_types()
   {  String[] types =
      {  "Transistor", "Capacitor", "Resistor", "Wire" };
      return types;
   }
}
```

The classes for a circuit editor are summarized in Figure 19.4.

Let us summarize the responsibilities of the programmer creating a specific diagram editor:

- For each node and edge type, derive a class from Node or Edge and supply all required operations, such as plot and hit testing.
- Supply the names of all classes.

Note that the programmer who turns the framework into an application supplies only the behavior of the classes that the application manipulates, none of the user interface or control flow. This is characteristic of using a framework.

## Implementing Node and Edge Classes

Let us write a sample application using this framework. We will edit diagrams with two node types, a circle and a dot (see Figure 19.5). They can be joined by lines and arrows.

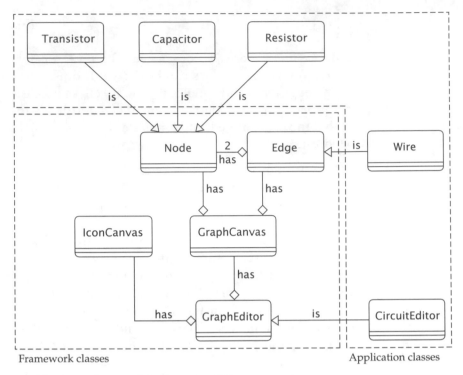

**FIGURE 19.4**   Classes of the circuit editor.

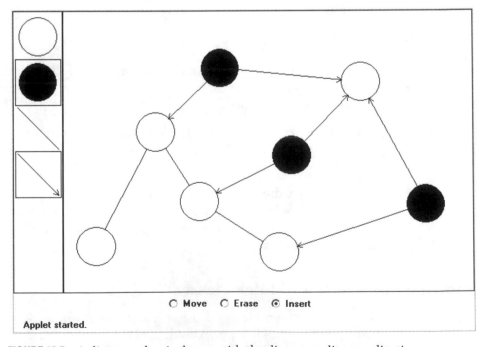

**FIGURE 19.5**   A diagram that is drawn with the diagram editor application.

Let us look at the code for circles and lines only; the dots and arrows are similar.

Every node type must override four operations:

- The `plot` operation draws the node.
- The `is_inside` operation tests whether a point, namely the mouse pointer, falls into the inside of the node shape.
- The `enclosing_rect` operation returns a rectangle that encloses the node. When a node is dragged to a new location, only the enclosing rectangle is displayed during the mouse movement. Mouse movement must give rapid feedback to the user, and a complex shape may not redraw fast enough. Therefore, each node must compute the rectangle enclosing it.
- The `boundary_point` operation is supplied because edges need it. Edges typically join not the centers of node shapes but points on the shape boundaries. Each node shape must be able to compute boundary points in any direction.

Here are the implementations of these four operations for the `Circle-Node` class.

```
class CircleNode extends Node
{  public void plot(Graphics g)
   {  g.drawOval(center() .x() - RADIUS, center.y() - RADIUS,
         2 * RADIUS, 2 * RADIUS);
   }

   public boolean is_inside(Point p)
   {  return new Ellipse(center(), RADIUS, RADIUS).is_inside(p);
   }

   public Rectangle enclosing_rect()
   {  Point a = (Point)center().clone();
      a.move(-RADIUS, -RADIUS);
      Point b = (Point)center().clone();
      b.move(RADIUS, RADIUS);
      return new Rectangle(a, b);
   }

   public Point boundary_point(Point exterior)
   {  Point r = (Point)center().clone();
      double a = r.angle(exterior);
      r.move((int) (RADIUS * Math.cos(a)), (int) (RADIUS *
         Math.sin(a)));
      return r;
   }

   private static int RADIUS = 25;
}
```

Every class that extends Edge must provide two services.

■ The plot operation plots the edge. The parameters to plot are the graphics object and the two boundary points of the node shapes that need to be joined. These are precomputed by the plot operation in the Edge base class.

```
class Edge
{  . . .
   public void plot(Graphics g)
   {  Point a = _from.center();
      Point b = _to.center();
      Point a1 = a.boundary_point(b);
      Point b1 = b.boundary_point(a);
      plot(g, a1, b1);
   }
   . . .
}
```

Having the boundary points precomputed makes it easier for the programmer to implement the plot operation in the derived class.

■ The is_on operation checks whether the mouse pointer is close to the edge. It too receives the points where the edge is attached to the nodes.

Here is the implementation of the LineEdge class.

```
class LineEdge extends Edge
{  public void plot(Graphics g, Point a, Point b)
   {  new Segment(a, b).plot(g);
   }
   public boolean is_on(Point p, Point a, Point b)
   {  return new Segment(a, b).distance(p) < 3;
   }
}
```

In this fashion, any number of node and edge types can be implemented. The effort that is required is minimal. Only those operations that are absolutely necessary, such as plotting and hit testing, must be coded.

After implementing four classes, CircleNode, DotNode, LineEdge, and ArrowEdge, the final obligation is to derive a class from GraphEditor and to override the get_types operation.

```
class DiagramEditor extends GraphEditor
{  public String[] get_types()
   {  String[] types = { "CircleNode", "DotNode",
         "LineEdge", "ArrowEdge" };
      return types;
   }
}
```

## Generic Framework Code

In the last section we saw how to customize the framework to a specific editor application. In this section we will investigate how the framework code is able to function without knowing anything about the types of nodes and edges.

The framework code is too long to analyze here in its entirety, and some technical details, particularly of the mouse tracking, are not terribly interesting. Let us consider two: moving an existing node and adding a new node.

First let us look at adding a new node. When the editor is in insert mode and the mouse is clicked outside an existing node, then a new node of the current type is added. This is where the clone operation comes in. We have a pointer to one object of the desired node type. Of course, we cannot simply insert that pointer into the diagram. If we did, all nodes of the diagram would end up identical. Instead we invoke clone to get an exact duplicate, move it to the desired position, and add it to the diagram:

```
class GraphCanvas extends Canvas
{  public boolean mouseDown(Event evt, int x, int y)
   {  int mode = ((GraphEditor)getParent()).mode();
      Point mousePos = new Point(x, y);
      Node n = search_node(mousePos);
      if (mode == INSERT && n == null)
      {  Node t = ((GraphEditor)getParent()).current_node();
         Node i = t.clone();
         i.move(mousePos);
         _nodes.addElement(i);
         repaint();
      }
      else . . .
   }

   public Node search_node(Point p)
   {  for (int i = 0; i < _nodes.size(); i++)
      {  Node n = (Node)_nodes.elementAt(i);
         if (n.is_inside(p)) return n;
      }
      return null;
   }
   . . .
   private Vector _nodes = new Vector();
   . . .
}
```

Note how the code is completely independent of the actual node type in a particular application. The search_node operation uses the virtual

536 ■ CHAPTER NINETEEN

is_inside operation to test if the mouse pointer falls inside one of the existing nodes. If so, then an edge must be inserted. If not, we are ready to insert a new node. This is done simply by cloning the active node from the icon canvas.

Next, let us next consider a more involved action, moving a node. When the mouse is clicked, we must first find whether the current mode is "Move" and whether the mouse hit a node. If so, we remember the node for subsequent mouse move operations. We also plot the rectangle that encloses the node because we anticipate that the node will be dragged elsewhere. We draw the rectangles in XOR mode. That makes it easy to erase them by simply drawing them a second time.

```
class GraphCanvas extends Canvas
{  public boolean mouseDown(Event evt, int x, int y)
   {  int mode = ((GraphEditor)getParent()).mode();
      Point mousePos = new Point(x, y);
      Node n = search_node(mousePos);
      . . .
      else if (mode == MOVE && n != null)
      {  _current_point = mousePos;
         _current_node = n;
         _rubberband_rect = _current_node.enclosing_rect();
         Graphics g = getGraphics();
         g.setXORMode(getBackground());
         _rubberband_rect.plot(g);
         g.dispose();
      }
      else . . .
   }
   . . .
}
```

When the mouse moves, we erase and redraw the enclosing rectangle to track the node position.

```
class GraphCanvas extends Canvas
{  public boolean mouseDrag(Event evt, int x, int y)
   {  if (_rubberband_rect != null)
      {  Graphics g = getGraphics();
         g.setXORMode(getBackground());
         _rubberband_rect.plot(g);
         int dx = x - _current_point.x();
         int dy = y - _current_point.y();
         _rubberband_rect.move(dx, dy);
         _rubberband_rect.plot(g);
         g.dispose();
         _current_point.move(dx, dy);
      }
```

```
          else . . .
       }
       . . .
}
```

When the mouse button goes up, we are ready to move the node to the final mouse position and to redisplay the entire screen. The new display shows the updated position of the node and its edges.

```
class GraphCanvas extends Canvas
{  public boolean mouseUp(Event evt, int x, int y)
   {  if (_rubberband_rect != null)
      {  Graphics g = getGraphics();
         g.setXORMode(getBackground());
         _rubberband_rect.plot(g);
         g.dispose();
         _rubberband_rect = null;
         _current_node.move(new Point(x, y));
         repaint();
      }
      . . .
   }
}
```

These scenarios are representative of the ability of the framework code to operate without an exact knowledge of the node and edge types.

## *Graphical User Interfaces*

Writing an application in a graphical user interface is much more complex than reading commands from standard input and writing them to standard output. The programmer is no longer in control over the order of user input. The program user can click on buttons and windows in any order, close or size windows, pick menu commands, or enter keystrokes. The program must be able to perform the appropriate reaction to any events as they occur.

Furthermore, users have recently come to expect a great deal of comfort and convenience from their applications. A successful program must sport multiple windows, a toolbar with an array of buttons, and a status line, as well as fancy dialog boxes. Yet window management systems, in their effort to be user interface-neutral, give little or no support for these features.

Application frameworks are an effective tool for giving guidance to programmers. The framework defines the basics, such as the mechanics that are required to manage multiple windows, menus, and toolbar buttons for standard commands (File Open, Edit, Paste). Just as importantly, the framework supplies base classes that direct the programmer to a program structure that is compatible with the event flow of the graphical user interface.

We will discuss a number of features implemented in the Microsoft Foundation Classes (MFC) for programming in the Microsoft Windows environment. A complete discussion of MFC would greatly exceed the scope of this book. We will focus on one particular aspect, the *document/view* architecture.

## Documents and Views

Many modern Windows applications can show the same information in multiple ways in different windows. One window might display data in a table; another window might display the same data in a graph.

When the user edits the table, the graph needs to be updated. When the user edits the graph by adding or dragging data points, the table needs to be updated. This updating seems fiendishly complex and error-prone. Have you ever opened two windows into the same word processor document, edited one of them, and wondered how the word processor manages to update both windows simultaneously? A very elegant division of responsibilities, the so-called *document/view* architecture, makes it manageable. We distinguish between the underlying data, in the computer memory or a file, and the visual representations of that data on the screen.

The underlying data are called a *document*, even though they are not usually a document in the sense used in word processing. Instead, they can describe data points for statistical analysis, schedule information, or any other kind of data. The visual representation of the document is called a *view*. A view might be a table, a graph, or a calendar.

Somewhat unfortunately, in Microsoft Windows, an application that can open multiple windows, such as the one shown in Figure 19.6, is called a multiple document interface (MDI) application. Of course, the windows are views, not documents, and the application should really be called a multiple view application!

One set of data may be viewed in multiple ways. A schedule can be viewed as a table and as a calendar. One document can also have multiple views of the same type. That is handy if one view cannot contain the whole document. For example, you might view a large data set by opening two tables, one to view the beginning and one to view the end.

The document has no associated window and intrinsic visual representation, and no user interface is associated with it. It is accessible to the

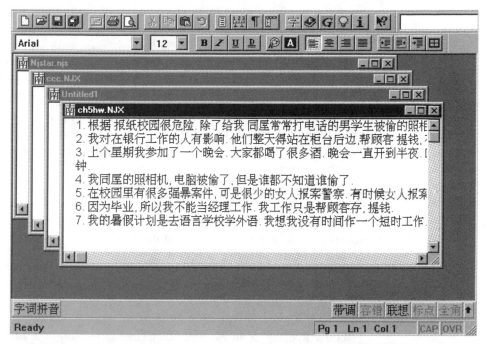

**FIGURE 19.6** An MDI application.

user only through its views. Views have windows and receive commands and events. A table window receives keystrokes. A graph window receives mouse clicks. If the keystroke or mouse click signifies a request for data change, the view notifies the document. The document changes its data and forces the refresh of all its views. In the most basic case, the document simply marks the surfaces of all of its view windows as invalid. Then the windowing system will ask each of the views to repaint itself. Each view then asks the document for the necessary data values and repaints itself from scratch. In particular, the view that received the user input is repainted in exactly the same way as all other views. This explains how multiple views into the same section of a word processor document can get updated simultaneously without any particular programming effort.

Of course, for optimal response, an application cannot redraw all windows at every keystroke or mouse click. There are several strategies for optimization. The document figures out the approximate difference between the old and the new information and tells each view to redraw only the information that has changed, by passing a "hint" to each view. In addition, the view that receives the user command can opt to redraw itself more efficiently than the other views. These strategies are usually sufficient to guarantee good performance. In our sample application, we will not carry out this optimization, though.

In the following sections, we will study a sample MFC application that uses the *document/view* model. This program is similar to the applet that we saw earlier in this chapter. The user can click with the mouse into a window to add data points, and the straight line that is the best fit to the cloud of points is recomputed and drawn with every new data point. However, this sample application has two kinds of views: A graphical view is used for entering data points and for showing the regression line. A text view is used to list the coordinates of all data points, followed by the equation of the regression line. Figure 19.7 shows the MFC application. Note that there are two text views and two graph views, all viewing the same data. When the user clicks with the mouse on either of the graph views, then all four views are automatically updated. For simplicity, the text views are read-only.

The MFC framework supplies two base classes:

```
CDocument
Cview
```

There are also a number of specialized view classes such as `CEditView` and `CTreeView` that derive from `CView`. We will use `CEditView` to display text in our sample application.

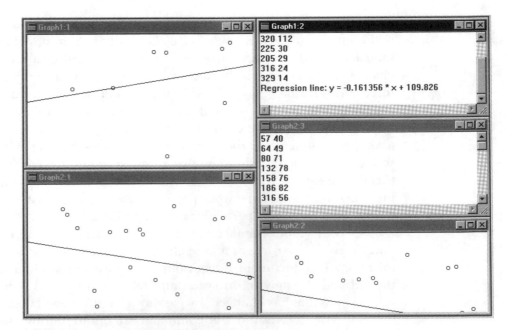

**FIGURE 19.7**  Sample MFC application.

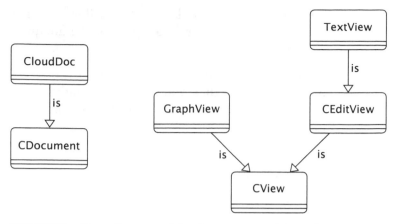

**FIGURE 19.8** Class diagram of the document and view classes.

To implement the sample application, we derive the following classes, as illustrated in Figure 19.8:

```
class CloudDoc : public CDocument
class GraphView : public CView
class TextView : public CEditView
```

## Window Classes

In addition to the document and view classes, every MFC application needs to add a number of other classes.

- A class deriving from CWinApp. Its most important activity is to register the documents and views that the application needs to manipulate. In our example, we will derive CloudApp from CWinApp.
- A class CMainFrame deriving from CMDIFrameWnd.
- If specialized behavior for the view windows is desired, one or more classes derived from CMDIChildWnd.

These classes do not do any display; they merely handle user interface chores. For example, we derive CMainFrame to supply a better functionality for the Window|New command than provided by the MFC default. To specify window attributes for the window in which a view lives, you must supply a separate child window class. In our case, we will be able to live with the default CMDIChildWnd for our views.

Thus, a view is associated with three classes:

- The view class that specifies how to paint the view and how to react to events

- The child window class that describes the surrounding child window
- The document class that specifies the document from which the view gets its data

You need to inform MFC which document, child window, and view classes belong together. You do that by building objects of type `CMultiDoc-Template` and adding the tempates to the application object. (Really, these should be called view templates, not document templates.)

```
CMultiDocTemplate* pDocTemplate
    = new CMultiDocTemplate(IDR_GRAPHVIEWTYPE,
        RUNTIME_CLASS(CloudDoc),
        RUNTIME_CLASS(CMDIChildWnd),
        RUNTIME_CLASS(GraphView));
AddDocTemplate(pDocTemplate);


pDocTemplate
    = new CMultiDocTemplate(IDR_TEXTVIEWTYPE,
        RUNTIME_CLASS(CloudDoc),
        RUNTIME_CLASS(CMDIChildWnd),
        RUNTIME_CLASS(TextView));
AddDocTemplate(pDocTemplate);
```

This code is placed in the `InitInstance` operation of the `CloudApp` class.

The `RUNTIME_CLASS` macro is an MFC construct that is similar to the `typeid` operator of ANSI C++, except that the resulting class descriptor has more capabilities. It is more comparable to the functionality of the `Class` class in Java. The implementation of this macro and the underlying infrastructure are complex, and we will not delve into the details here.

The `IDR_GRAPHVIEWTYPE` and `IDR_TEXTVIEWTYPE` resource identifiers must be defined in the resource editor. You must add a string resource that describes the file names and extensions and window titles to be used with each view, and you can add icons that are used for each view. For details, see the MFC documentation.

Figure 19.9 shows a class diagram of all classes used for our sample application.

## The Document Class

The `CloudDoc` class is a simple, nonvisual class. It just stores the points that the user enters. The view classes can query that information so that they can render their different views. They can update the information by adding data points. (For simplicity, we are omitting the macros that MFC requires for run-time type identification and message maps.)

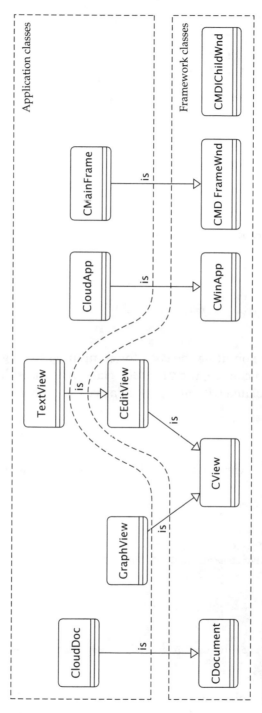

**FIGURE 19.9**  The classes used for the sample MFC application.

```
class CloudDoc : public CDocument
{
public:
    void add_point(CPoint p);
    CPoint get_point(int n) const;
    int size() const;
    bool regression(double& m, double& b);
private:
    vector<CPoint> _points;
};

void CloudDoc::add_point(CPoint p)
{   _points.push_back(p);
}

CPoint CloudDoc::get_point(int n) const
{   return _points[n];
}

int CloudDoc::size() const
{   return _points.size();
}
```

We are omitting the code for computing the regression line.

As you can see, the `CloudDoc` class just stores the data set and by itself is not associated with any particular visual representation.

## The View Classes

We need two view classes, to display graphs and text.

```
class GraphView : public CView
{
public:
    void OnDraw(CDC* pDC);
    void OnLButtonDown(UINT nFlags, CPoint point);
};

class TextView : public CEditView
{
public:
    void OnUpdate(CView* pSender, LPARAM lHint, Object* pHint);
};
```

The graph view reacts to mouse clicks. It adds the mouse position to the data set and calls `UpdateAllViews`. That function causes all views (including the one handling the mouse click) to repaint themselves.

```
void GraphView::OnLButtonDown(UINT flags, CPOint point)
{ CloudDoc* pDoc = dynamic_cast<CloudDoc*>(GetDocument());
  pDoc->add_point(point);
  pDoc->UpdateAllViews(NULL);
  CView::OnLButtonDown(nFlags, point);
}
```

The paint procedure asks the document for the position of all dots and the parameters of the regression line and plots them.

```
void GraphView::OnDraw(CDC* pDC)
{ CloudDoc* pDoc = dynamic_cast<CloudDoc*>(GetDocument());
  for (int i = 0; i < pDoc->size(); i++)
  {  CPoint p = pDoc->getPoint(i);
     plot the point
  }
  double m, b;
  if (pDoc->regression(m, b))
    draw the regression line
}
```

The `TextView` class inherits from `CEditView`, a view class that already includes an edit control to display and edit text. (We won't let the user edit the text, but supply the view for text display only.) The only function that needs to be overridden is `OnUpdate`. Whenever the graph view calls `UpdateAllViews`, the framework calls `OnUpdate`. By default, that just calls `OnPaint`, but here we want to change the text in the edit control.

This procedure produces a long string with all the point coordinates, followed by the equation of the regression line. It uses a string stream (see Chapter 13) to put together the string and then sets the text of the edit control to that string.

```
void TextView::OnUpdate(CView* pSender, LPARAM lHint,
   Object* pHint)
{ CloudDoc* pDoc = dynamic_cast<CloudDoc*>(GetDocument());
  stringstream sstr;
  for (int i = 0; i < pDoc->size(); i++)
  {  CPoint p = pDoc->getPoint(i);
     sstr << p.x << " " << p.y << "\r\n";
  }
  double m, b;
  if (pDoc->regression(m, b))
    sstr << "y = " << m << " * x + " << b << "\r\n";
  set text in edit control
}
```

Here is a summary of the additions that we needed to provide on top of the MFC framework to implement the cloud application:

- Derive a class `CloudDoc` from `CDocument` to store the data points
- Derive two classes `GraphView` and `TextView`, to display the data points and to gather new data points through mouse clicks
- Derive `CloudApp` from `CWinApp` and add two document templates
- Add two document template strings to the string table in the resource file
- Derive a class `CMainFrame` from `CMDIFrame` and override the `Window|New` handler to do what Microsoft should have implemented, namely present a list of views for the current document type (this requires some MFC wizardry—see the source code for details)

Except for the last step (which really should have been a part of standard MFC), these tasks are quite straightforward. With less than 50 lines of code, we were able to build an application that automatically keeps multiple views of the same data updated. This is quite a tribute to the power of programming with frameworks.

# Design Hints

## Using a Framework

When you use a framework, you take existing classes and build more classes, or even an entire application, on the top. The framework contains expert knowledge on the interaction of system components. Having that expertise already embodied in code is the reason for using the framework.

You will need to find out how to fit in the application-specific aspects. There are several essential questions:

- What classes are provided as bases for derivation?
- How many classes can I derive from these bases?
- What virtual functions must I redefine?
- What virtual functions can I redefine, and what do they do by default?
- Are there special initialization requirements?

In the diagram editor, there are two base classes: `Node` and `Edge`. Both can serve as the base for multiple derived classes. A number of abstract operations, such as `is_inside` and `plot`, must be redefined. In addition, for proper initialization, all node and edge types must be registered.

## Framework Design Challenges

In framework design, keep in mind who your customers are. Your customers are programmers. They build an application on top of the framework. Their customers are the users of the product.

Designing a single class is an order of magnitude harder than designing a single function because you must anticipate what other programmers will do with it. Similarly, designing a framework is much harder than designing a class library or a single application because you must anticipate what other programmers want to achieve.

The encapsulation of the framework implementation leaves little room for error. If a framework does not provide a hook for integrating an essential task, the framework itself needs to be redesigned or discarded. It is notoriously difficult to predict the complexities of real-world problems. A good rule of thumb for validating the design of a framework is to use it to build at least three different applications.

# R E F E R E N C E S

[Aho, Hopcroft, and Ullmann] Alfred V. Aho, John E. Hopcroft, and Jeffrey D. Ullmann, *The Design and Analysis of Computer Algorithms*, Addison-Wesley, 1974.

[Bar-David] Tsvi Bar-David, *Object-Oriented Design for C++*, Prentice Hall, 1993.

[Beck] Kent Beck and Ward Cunningham, A Laboratory for Teaching Object-Oriented Thinking, *Proc. OOPSLA 1989, Sigplan Notices*, vol. 14, no. 10 (1989), pp. 1–6.

[Bentley 1986] Jon Bentley, *Programming Pearls*, Addison-Wesley, 1986.

[Booch] Grady Booch, *Object-Oriented Analysis and Design*, 2nd ed., Benjamin-Cummings, 1994.

[Budd] Timothy Budd, *An Introduction to Object-Oriented Programming*, Addison-Wesley, 1991.

[Cargill] Tom Cargill, *C++ Programming Style*, Addison-Wesley, 1992.

[Cleaveland] J. Craig Cleaveland, *All Introduction to Data Types*, Addison-Wesley, 1986.

[Coad] Peter Coad and Edward Yourdon, *Object-Oriented Analysis*, 2nd ed., Prentice Hall, 1991.

[Coplien] James O. Coplien, *Advanced C++ Programming Styles and Idioms*, Addison-Wesley, 1992.

[Cornell] Gary Cornell and Cay Horstmann, *Core Java*, 2nd ed., SunSoft Press, 1997.

[Ellis and Stroustrup] Margaret Ellis and Bjarne Stroustrup, *The Annotated C++ Reference Manual*, Addison-Wesley, 1990.

[Goldberg and Robson] A. Goldberg and D. Robson, *Smalltalk 80—The Language and Its Implementation*, Addison-Wesley, 1983.

[Horowitz] Ellis Horowitz and Sartaj Sahni, *Fundamentals of Data Structures in Pascal*, Computer Science Press, 1984.

[Kernighan and Ritchie] Brian Kernighan and Dennis Ritchie, *The C Programming Language*, 2nd ed., Prentice Hall, 1988.

[Koenig] Andrew Koenig, *C Traps and Pitfalls*, Addison-Wesley, 1988.

[Martin] James Martin and James O. Ocell, *Object-Oriented Analysis and Design*, Prentice Hall, 1992.

[Meyer] Bertrand Meyer, *Object-Oriented Software Construction*, Prentice Hall, 1988.

[Murray 1989] Robert B. Murray, Building Well-Behaved Type Relationships in C++, *Proc. Usenix C++ Conf.*, Denver, CO, 1988, pp. 19–30.

[Petzold] Charles Petzold, *Programming Windows 95*, Microsoft Press, 1996.

[Press] William H. Press, Saul A. Teukolsky, William T. Vetterling, and Brian P. Flannery, *Numerical Recipes in C*, 2nd ed., Cambridge University Press, 1992.

[Plum and Saks] Thomas Plum and Dan Saks, *C++ Programming Guidelines*, Plum Hall, 1991.

[Riel] Arthur J. Riel, *Object-Oriented Design Heuristics*, Addison-Wesley, 1996.

[Rumbaugh] James Rumbaugh, Michael Blaha, William Premerlani, Frederick Eddy, and William Lorensen, *Object Modeling and Design*, Prentice Hall, 1991.

[Stroustrup] Bjarne Stroustrup, *The C++ Programming Language*, 2nd ed., Addison-Wesley, 1991.

[Tufte] Edward R. Tufte, *Envisioning Information*, Graphics Press, Cheshire, CT, 1990.

[Wiener and Pinson] Richard S. Wiener and Lewis J. Pinson, *An Introduction to Object-Oriented Programming and C++*, Addison-Wesley, 1988.

# I  N  D  E  X